Disputing New France

Companies, Law, and Sovereignty in the French Atlantic, 1598–1663

Helen Dewar

McGill-Queen's University Press
Montreal & Kingston • London • Chicago

ISBN 978-0-2280-0820-0 (cloth)
ISBN 978-0-2280-0821-7 (paper)
ISBN 978-0-2280-0939-9 (ePDF)
ISBN 978-0-2280-0940-5 (ePUB)

Legal deposit first quarter 2022
Bibliothèque nationale du Québec

Printed in Canada on acid-free paper that is 100% ancient forest free (100% post-consumer recycled), processed chlorine free

This book has been published with the help of a grant from the Canadian Federation for the Humanities and Social Sciences, through the Awards to Scholarly Publications Program, using funds provided by the Social Sciences and Humanities Research Council of Canada.

Funded by the Government of Canada | Financé par le gouvernement du Canada | Canada

Canada Council for the Arts | Conseil des arts du Canada

We acknowledge the support of the Canada Council for the Arts.

Nous remercions le Conseil des arts du Canada de son soutien.

Library and Archives Canada Cataloguing in Publication

Title: Disputing New France : companies, law, and sovereignty in the French Atlantic, 1598–1663 / Helen Dewar.

Names: Dewar, Helen, author.

Series: McGill-Queen's French Atlantic worlds series ; 7.

Description: Series statement: McGill-Queen's French Atlantic worlds series ; 7 | Includes bibliographical references and index.

Identifiers: Canadiana (print) 20210301627 | Canadiana (ebook) 20210301716 | ISBN 9780228008217 (paper) | ISBN 9780228008200 (cloth) | ISBN 9780228009399 (ePDF) | ISBN 9780228009405 (ePUB)

Subjects: LCSH: French – North America – History – 17th century. | LCSH: France – Colonies – Administration – History – 17th century. | LCSH: France – Colonies – America – History – 17th century. | LCSH: Commercial law – France – History – 17th century. | LCSH: Canada – History – To 1763 (New France)

Classification: LCC E29.F8 D49 2022 | DDC 971.01 – dc23

This book was designed and typeset by Peggy & Co. Design in 11/14 Adobe Garamond Pro.

Contents

Figures vii

Acknowledgments ix

Introduction: A Transatlantic Enterprise 3

1 Royal Commissions and the Culture of Privilege 22

2 Disputing New France 61

3 The Maritime and Territorial Landscapes of New France 91

4 A Crisis of Sovereignty?
Commerce, Catholicism, and Subjecthood 123

5 The Consolidation of Maritime Authority
and the Compagnie de la Nouvelle-France 158

6 Corporate Governance, Delegation, and Usurpation 197

Epilogue: The Struggle to Shape French Imperial Expansion 236

Notes 245

Bibliography 303

Index 331

Figures

0.1 Decree of the Parlement of Rouen, 25 June 1633. Courtesy of the Archives départementales de Seine-Maritime, 1B981, Parlement de Rouen, 25 June 1633. 17

1.1 Principal French ports involved in the privileged commercial and colonizing enterprises in New France, 1603–63. Map by Andrée Héroux. 28

1.2 Parlement of Brittany. Author's photo, 2015. 35

1.3 Samuel de Champlain, eastern portion of "Carte de la Nouvelle-France," *Les voyages du Sieur de Champlain*, 1632. Courtesy of the John Carter Brown Library at Brown University, Providence, Rhode Island. 41

3.1 French posts, forts, and habitations in Acadia and the Saint Lawrence Valley, including the privileged trading zone, 1603–20. Map by Andrée Héroux. 98

3.2 Vincenzo Coronelli, "Partie orientale du Canada ou de la Nouvelle France," 1689. Courtesy of the John Carter Brown Library at Brown University, Providence, Rhode Island. 99

3.3 Samuel de Champlain, "Abitation de Quebecq," *Les voyages du Sieur de Champlain*, 1613. Courtesy of the John Carter Brown Library at Brown University, Providence, Rhode Island. 114

5.1 Entrance to the inner harbour of La Rochelle, flanked by the Tour Saint-Nicolas and the Tour de la Chaîne. Author's photo, 2008. 174

6.1 Seigneurial concessions accorded to associates of subsidiary companies and other title-holders in Acadia, 1632–36. Map by Andrée Héroux. 207

6.2 Principal French settlements in Acadia and the Saint Lawrence Valley, 1628–63. Map by Andrée Héroux. 212

Acknowledgments

This project has been in the making in various forms for thirteen years. It is a pleasure to have the opportunity to thank all of the people who have played a role in its development and completion.

It was Jack Crowley at Dalhousie University and Ian K. Steele and Nancy Rhoden at the University of Western Ontario who showed me the possibilities of Atlantic history. Jack has continued to be an enthusiastic and stimulating interlocutor over the years. I owe my greatest debt of gratitude to Allan Greer, who encouraged me to turn to the French Atlantic. Allan's careful and dedicated doctoral supervision helped me see the significance of my findings. His scholarly rigour, engagement, and curiosity are a constant source of inspiration to me. I am also grateful to Paul Cheney, Paul Cohen, Ken Mills, and Nicholas Terpstra, whose insightful comments helped me to begin to turn my dissertation into a book. As a post-doctoral fellow at McGill University, I was immensely fortunate to have Catherine Desbarats as a supervisor. Her deep erudition, wide reading, and creative thinking challenged me to become a better historian and writer. Kate and Allan have had the greatest impact on my intellectual development and continue to be valued mentors, colleagues, and good friends.

Many of my most rewarding and valuable exchanges have occurred at workshops and conferences. These include the Journée d'études sur les compagnies à charte et l'État, XVIIe siècle, at the Université du Littoral, Côte d'Opale; the seminar L'absolutisme dans l'Atlantique français at the Université de Nantes; the weekly seminar of the Centre d'études nord-américaines at the École des Hautes Études en Sciences Sociales; the *William and Mary Quarterly* – Early Modern Studies Institute Workshop on Early American Legal Histories; the Emerging Histories of the Early Modern French Atlantic conference at the Omohundro Institute for

Early American History and Culture; the Forum on European Expansion and Global Interaction at Leiden University; the Alternative States workshop at Duke University; the Symposium on Comparative Early Modern Legal History: Law and the French Atlantic at the Newberry Library; and the Harvard Atlantic Seminar on European Justice in the Americas. I would particularly like to thank Lauren Benton, Céline Carayon, Alexandre Dubé, Gilles Havard, Amalia Kessler, Daniel Lee, James Muldoon, William Pettigrew, John G. Reid, Richard Ross, Éric Roulet, Brett Rushforth, Tristan Stein, Philip Stern, Fredrika J. Teute, Christopher Tomlins, and Cécile Vidal for stimulating comments and conversations that helped to deepen my reflections.

The members of the Groupe d'histoire de l'Atlantique français of Montreal deserve special mention. The group's timely foundation at the start of my doctoral career provided a stimulating and energizing atmosphere in which to begin and develop this project. It has since been a constant presence and source of scholarly exchange, financial support, mentoring, and sociability over the years. Several chapters in this book have benefited from the insightful comments and criticisms of its members at different stages. Special thanks go to the core group of organizers, whom I now have the pleasure of working closely with in Montreal: Catherine Desbarats, Nicholas Dew, Carolyn Fick, Allan Greer, Ollivier Hubert, Jean-Pierre Le Glaunec, and Thomas Wien.

Several friends and colleagues have read various versions of chapters and provided valuable comments that have made this a better book. They include Will Brown, Jess Clark, Catherine Desbarats, Allan Greer, Gilles Havard, Gregory Kennedy, Jeffers Lennox, and Nadine Zimmerli. A warm thanks also to Deborah Barton for the Zoom work sessions that kept me going on revisions in the context of the global COVID-19 pandemic. I am especially indebted to my good friend, Chris Parsons, with whom I began my doctoral studies and who has remained an inspiration, a wonderful interlocutor, and an enthusiastic cheerleader, especially during the final stages of this project. His support and critical insights have been indispensable.

I have benefited from the support of, and stimulating exchanges with, friends and colleagues at various institutions over the years. The Department of History at the University of Toronto provided an intellectually enriching and convivial environment in which to begin this project. Particular thanks go to Camille Bégin, Philip Girard, Vanessa McCarthy,

Denis McKim, Jim Phillips, Jen Polk, Candace Sobers, and Natalie Zemon Davis, as well as the members of the Premodern and Policy and Politics discussion groups and Toronto-area France seminar. I am especially grateful to Adrienne Hood and Eric Jennings, who were valuable mentors during a later post-doctoral year in Toronto. A post-doctoral fellowship at McGill University allowed me to broaden the historiographical framework of the project. I was lucky enough to join an interesting and congenial group of post-docs, including Jess Clark, Leslie Tomory, Sarah Waurechen, and Anna Winterbottom. Special thanks to Jess, who made the post-doc experience much more enjoyable than it otherwise would have been. Nicholas Dew, Elsbeth Heaman, Jason Opal, and Daviken Studnicki-Gizbert gave generously of their time by giving advice on the publishing process, talking over challenges, and reading my book proposal. I'd also like to thank the fellows at the John Carter Brown Library during May–June 2013, whose dedication to scholarship as well as good sense of fun made my fellowship there a rewarding experience. During a post-doctoral fellowship at Boston College, I benefited from the warm welcome of members of the History Department, especially Kevin Kenny, Virginia Reinberg, Sarah Ross, and Owen Stanwood, as well as from the support of my fellow post-docs, Hannah Farber and Burleigh Hendrickson. Over the past five years at the Université de Montréal, several colleagues, some of whom are now very good friends, have provided much-appreciated counsel, intellectual discussion, and good cheer, including Deborah Barton, Susan Dalton, Michael Huberman, Ollivier Hubert, David Meren, Laurence Monnais, and Thomas Wien.

Numerous institutions have provided generous support for the research and writing of this book. The initial stages of the project benefited greatly from an Ontario Graduate Scholarship and several scholarships from the University of Toronto. The Social Sciences and Humanities Research Council has financed several stages through a Canada Graduate Scholarship, a Postdoctoral Fellowship and an Insight Development Grant. Research travel was made possible through awards from the Cromwell Foundation, the Harvard Atlantic Center, and the Institut français d'Amérique. The stimulating environment of the John Carter Brown Library helped me to move the project from dissertation to book during a two-month fellowship.

I would like to thank the archivists and staff of Library and Archives Canada, the Archives nationales de France, the Bibliothèque nationale de France, the Archives départementales d'Ille-et-Vilaine, the Archives départementales de la Charente-Maritime, the Archives départementales de Seine-Maritime, the Archives municipales de Saint-Malo, and the Thomas Fisher Rare Book Library at the University of Toronto. Special thanks to Lorraine Gadoury of Library and Archives Canada, who helped orient me in the early stages of this project, to Pauline Arsenault of the Archives départementales de la Charente-Maritime for her guidance and enthusiasm, and to Philippe Hamon of the Université de Rennes for sharing his extensive knowledge of the records of the Parlement of Brittany. I am also indebted to Marie-Ève Ménard of the Bibliothèque des lettres et sciences humaines at the Université de Montréal for her help in obtaining books and articles, especially in the context of the pandemic, which created challenges for the revisions stage.

I am grateful to the staff of McGill-Queen's University Press for shepherding the book through the publication process. I particularly appreciate Kyla Madden's belief in, and enthusiasm for, the project from the early stages of manuscript preparation. Thanks also to the anonymous reviewers, Ryan Perks for his careful copy-editing, Peter Feldstein for the verification of translations, Andrée Héroux for the accompanying maps, and Ariane Chasle and Caroline Gendron for valuable editorial assistance.

Portions of this book were previously published as articles or book chapters: "Government by Trading Company? The Corporate Legal Status of the Company of New France and Colonial Governance," *Nuevo mundo mundos nuevos*, "Gouverner de manière impériale: Expériences françaises et ibériques aux Amériques (XVIe–XIXe siècle)," June 2018; "Une rupture avec le passé? La Compagnie de la Nouvelle-France et les grandes compagnies de commerce transatlantique," in *Les premières compagnies dans l'Atlantique, 1600–1650: Structures et modes de fonctionnement*, edited by Eric Roulet (Shaker Verlag, 2017); "Litigating Empire: The Role of French Courts in Establishing Colonial Sovereignties," in *Legal Pluralism and Empires, 1500–1850*, edited by Lauren Benton and Richard J. Ross (New York University Press, 2013); "Souveraineté dans les colonies, souveraineté en métropole: Le rôle de la Nouvelle-France dans la consolidation de l'autorité maritime en France, 1620–1628," in "La Nouvelle-France et l'Atlantique," special issue, *Revue d'histoire de l'Amérique française* 64, nos. 3–4 (2011). I thank these journals and presses for permission to reprint parts of this material.

The development and completion of this project would not have been possible without the unfailing support of friends and family. I am particularly grateful to my long-standing and dear friend, Andrea Wilson, who has never wavered in her belief in me amid all the ups and downs. My sister, Megan, her partner, Chris, and my nieces, Madeline and Imogen, have been sources of much-needed breaks and fun. My parents, Marged and Ken Dewar, instilled in me an intellectual curiosity that prompted me to choose the academic path. Without their constant love and support, this book would never have come into being.

Disputing New France

INTRODUCTION

A Transatlantic Enterprise

In the spring of 1620, the couple dozen French inhabitants of the small Quebec habitation on the shores of the Saint Lawrence River greeted the first ship to arrive from France after the long winter. On board were the representatives of the new viceroy of New France, Henri de Montmorency, admiral of France. In honour of the occasion, a Récollet father performed Holy Mass and called upon all to serve the king and his viceroy and to obey the latter's lieutenant, Samuel de Champlain. The viceroy's commissioner, Guers, then read aloud Montmorency's letters patent and Champlain's commission. Champlain describes the conclusion of the ceremony as follows: "'This having been done, everybody cried, 'Long Live the King!'; the cannon was fired in sign of joy, and thus I took possession of the settlement and the country in the name of His Grace the Viceroy. The said Guers drew up an account of the proceedings for use when and where required."[1] Describing a typical ceremony of possession, this passage gives the impression that the establishment of sovereignty, authority, and law in the spaces of New France was orderly, natural, and uncomplicated. Yet the last sentence hints at a more complex reality; the subtext of anticipated contestations of claimed authority and sovereignty adds a note of uncertainty to an otherwise straightforward event.

This book reinterprets the history of the first half-century of French colonization in North America by considering empire and sovereignty as processes that were actively constructed, contested, defended, and reaffirmed. The Crown had not always intervened in the overseas activities of French subjects. When Montmorency became viceroy, royal letters patent granting some combination of exclusive privileges to the fur trade and regal powers to a nobleman in return for colonizing obligations had been the "norm" for little more than twenty years. For much of the sixteenth century, the Crown did not regulate transatlantic travel. From the early 1500s, thousands of fishermen from Basque, Breton, and Norman ports crossed the Atlantic each year for the Banks of Newfoundland and the coasts of present-day Labrador, Quebec, and Nova Scotia to engage in fishing, whaling, and later, fur trading. They came to regard this activity, conditional on little more than the acquisition of a *congé*, or licence, from the Admiralty, as part of their customary rights. The granting of royal commissions – fitfully over the sixteenth century, beginning with Jacques Cartier's voyage in 1534, and more consistently from 1598 – thus took place in the context of existing practices. Seen from this perspective, these documents were not blueprints of colonization, as scholars have often portrayed them, but sets of claims to authority and privileges that came up against those of others.

The study of the beginnings of a French imperial presence in North America demands an Atlantic approach. Far from an exclusively North American phenomenon, colonization was considered a domestic issue, not only by the fishermen-traders whose customary voyages were threatened but also by powerful provincial and local corporate bodies, like the Estates of Brittany or the Parlement of Paris, which saw it as a royal attack on their political, commercial, and maritime autonomy. The king may have granted a royal commission to Montmorency as viceroy, but the powers and privileges of such a title meant little if provincial justices, customs officers, and local Admiralty officials refused to recognize it. Rather than suggesting that metropolitan actors determined the evolution of commercial and colonizing enterprises in New France, these points underscore the imperative of examining the interconnections between the processes of state formation in France and empire building across the Atlantic. *Disputing New France* realizes this objective by exploring French efforts to articulate sovereign claims to North America through proprietorships and companies, beginning in 1598 with the first royal commission to grant exclusive trading privileges in exchange for colonization and ending with the Compagnie de la Nouvelle-France's cession of the colony to the king in 1663. Studying the nature and evolution of these tools takes us into discussions over the revitalization of French navigation and maritime commerce, metropolitan struggles over maritime authority, and international experimentations with the company form. It lays bare the political, legal, and social structures that both limited the actions of subjects and provided them with opportunities. Above all, it exposes the negotiation and contestation that animated both processes.

Putting empire and state formation within the same frame makes visible the multiple visions of New France that coexisted and competed with each other. The prominence given to royal representatives in passages like the one cited above has led to a narrow understanding of "agents of empire," confined to colonial and imperial officials like Champlain or later intendants, governors, and chief ministers.[2] Yet they did not have a monopoly on views of the direction New France should take or on claims to jurisdiction and sovereign representation. *Disputing New France* broadens the cast of characters to include all those involved directly or indirectly in New France – ranging from independent traders and fishermen to associates and agents of privileged trading companies to missionaries and metropolitan corporate bodies.[3] For example, protests against royal regulation of transatlantic activity in general, and exclusive trading privileges in particular, forced both king and title-holders to make adjustments, which had a direct impact on the forms of power and authority that developed in New France. Commercial authority and jurisdiction (legal authority) were intimately intertwined, determining, on the one hand, the geographical extent of effective control, and, on the other, the shape of governmental bodies. In a period in which the terms of the imperial project were being worked out, diverse actors, whether on the ground in New France or in France, shaped the developing repertoire of tools of governance, capital formation, and privilege granting.

The need to record the ceremony of possession "for use when and where required" points to where we must look to understand the transatlantic dynamics of empire building in New France. Law is fundamental to the act of colonization. It is embodied in the royal commissions, company charters, and other regulations governing travel across the Atlantic and access to resources in North America by French subjects. On an international level, European powers drew on Roman law, natural law, and the law of nations to justify conquest, colonization, and (dis)possession. For the French king, the pre-eminent mark of sovereignty, and his most important duty, was to render justice, thereby protecting the respective rights and privileges of his subjects.[4] The creation of judicial mechanisms was an important feature of colonial spaces like the fledgling settlement of Quebec and, therefore, a powerful "expression of sovereignty."[5] Law was not, however, the sole preserve of the king and his delegated representatives. A set of languages, procedures, and institutions, it was eminently portable. French subjects who crossed the Atlantic, whether company associates, interlopers, fishermen, or viceregal representatives, carried legal knowledge and instruments with them. While Champlain claimed judicial authority in New France through his lieutenant's commission, others came armed with their own legal documents, including their own commissions, judicial sentences, and royal decrees, which they used to advance and legitimize their actions and interests. Despite their embryonic nature, trading posts and settlements were "full of law."[6]

To acknowledge law as foundational to French colonizing ventures to North America brings new significance to the disputes that erupted among French subjects in the trading posts and along the waterways of New France. These conflicts, long neglected by historians, consistently had second acts in the courts of France.[7] Most commonly precipitated through the seizure of a ship and its crew and cargo and pitting the privileged trading company against rival traders (and their patrons), the ensuing lawsuits proved to be about much more profound matters than the confiscation of property. Some were conflicts over who would control the fur trade in New France among French ports engaged in fierce competition over status and resources. Others, expanding to include several third parties such as a missionary representative of the colony's inhabitants, were at their heart conflicts over the direction and governance of New France. Cumulatively, they reveal that metropolitan courts of justice played a central role in the historical construction of authority in North America.

Claimants' recourse to the multiple and overlapping jurisdictions of France similarly exposes the fluid and contested nature of legal, political, and commercial authority in the kingdom itself. Apart from the fishermen-traders who harnessed the influence and connections of local and provincial bodies, the colonization of North America played into rivalries among legal jurisdictions, disputes among great nobles and regents, and the conflict between Huguenots and the Crown. When the Crown was in a vulnerable position – a frequent occurrence in this period, which followed a half-century of divisive civil war and included two regencies – the power of corporate bodies and highly placed individuals increased; at such moments, opponents of the colonial enterprise in New France made inroads against it. At the same time, New France became implicated in initiatives to strengthen royal authority during the comparatively stable periods when an adult king was on the throne.

Looking at state and empire formation from the western side of the Atlantic brings into focus the role of the sea. With the growing commercial activity associated with European expansion, the sea became a strategically important and contested space among rival powers. It also became a route to authority in the metropole, a point missed if we only study the state from France. This context sheds light on what might seem like surprising interest on the part of the admiral of France in the fledgling habitation on the shores of the Saint Lawrence River. Having spent the previous eight years consolidating his authority as admiral in the kingdom's ports, Montmorency became attracted to New France as a maritime space. Commercial and governmental control of the colony was a means to supervise one of the major French Atlantic trade routes used by French subjects. In the contest for control over maritime space, and the bodies and goods moving through it, the developing entity of the chartered company played a leading role. From experienced sea captains to high-ranking officials in the Admiralty and the royal government, contemporaries considered the chartered company – which innovatively combined the corporate form with joint-stock capital – a vehicle that promised to enhance French standing, wealth, and personal power.[8] It is through the Compagnie de la Nouvelle-France (1627–63), the first and longest-lasting such enterprise in the Atlantic, among other such companies, that disparate but constitutive elements of state and empire formation come to the fore and interact: maritime security, control over maritime trade and colonial projects, confessional struggle, and law.

Empire, State Formation, Companies, and Law

This book brings together several major, but habitually separate, historiographical fields: early modern state formation; "European expansion" overseas; the legal history of empire; and the development of large-scale capitalist organizations. It draws on the substantial literature on state formation that has thoroughly challenged the idea that early modern European states were powerful enough to readily impose policies on, and regulate the behaviour of, subject populations.[9] Instead, sovereigns exercised and expanded their authority not primarily through the creation of bureaucratic forms of government but through the co-option of elites by means of offices and juridical, fiscal, and economic privileges.[10] In addition, the importance of the delegation of powers to the functioning of early modern states has led scholars to go beyond the sovereign and his ministers to include the entire "network of agents exercising political power," right down to the lowest office-holder.[11] Monarchs were not the only ones to see advantage in an expanding state presence; subjects were able to harness institutions, languages, and procedures associated with the state to advance their own familial and professional interests and ambitions.[12]

Subjects' capacity to negotiate has also been at the heart of revisionist views of absolutism in early modern France. Rejecting older interpretations in which seventeenth-century monarchs – notably Louis XIV – were assumed to disempower provincial nobles and institute sweeping programs of administrative reform, revisionist historians locate the impetus for increasing governmental reach in subjects' own initiatives and in existing institutions and practices. Other scholars have tempered this notion of "limited absolutism," arguing that if the monarch could not simply impose his will on subjects, his power was nevertheless very real.[13] This book builds on recent work that considers these subjects through law and the justice system. Turning their attention to local courts, which were among the most frequently used of state institutions, French historians have demonstrated that local magistrates enjoyed considerable autonomy and authority in a period of state centralization.[14] These studies also confirm assertions in other contexts that official institutions such as courts of justice coexisted and were interdependent with patronage networks based on kinship and marriage alliances.[15] As the term "state formation" implies, this literature has reconceptualized the state as a process that was subject to negotiation and contestation.

Disputing New France joins scholars of empire who emphasize the interdependence of the processes of state formation and sovereignty in the imperial realm.[16] Elizabeth Mancke argues that the extension of sovereign authority overseas came about as the result of subjects' commercial and colonizing activities, which forced states to confront complex questions such as how far their control over (and protection of) subjects reached beyond the realm. In *A Search for Sovereignty*, Lauren Benton explores the "disorderly combination of rituals" subjects performed and the variety of legal tools they used overseas to present themselves as both official and unofficial representatives of the monarch.[17] Other historians have begun to examine the variety of imperial agendas – whether those of colonists, colonial or imperial officials, or merchants – that coexisted and competed with each other within a single empire.[18] These works are part of a substantial (and growing) literature that puts claims-making at the centre of sovereignty construction. Complex and uncertain, sovereignty was not uniform across an empire but "shared out, layered, overlapping."[19]

The predominantly Anglo-American literature on law's central role in European imperial and colonizing projects provides methodological inspiration for this study. Like Benton, other scholars have considered the ways in which subjects and rulers used legal instruments to extend jurisdiction across the Atlantic. Examining charters, letters patent, and other legal documents, Christopher Tomlins portrays colonization as a legal construct. Law had a variety of modes, "as technology, discourse, modality of rule and expression of sovereignty," and thus gave shape not only to each colonizing venture but also to the system of governance developed in American colonies. For his part, Ken Macmillan rethinks the role of the English Crown in its "colonial peripheries" over the first half of the seventeenth century, arguing that this role gave rise to an "Atlantic imperial constitution" encompassing documents like letters patent as well as unwritten guarantees of customary rights.[20] All of these works consider law as foundational to the relationship forged between sovereigns and their subjects who ventured overseas.

Attention to the role of subjects and law in the formation of empires has encouraged historians over the past fifteen years to investigate how those to whom the state delegated powers and privileges fit into this process. *Disputing New France* addresses this question in the case of New France. In what is to date the only collection on proprietorships in the Atlantic, L.H. Roper and Bertrand Van Ruymbeke question whether company or individual proprietors, upon whom "imperial development" depended, served the objectives of the monarch, given that their own interests may have been quite distinct from a king's or minister's intentions.[21] Much recent scholarship concerns the relationship between states and chartered companies.[22] Considering these enterprises as deeply implicated in rather than aloof from social and political phenomena, some scholars examine how the practices and policies of chartered companies confronted or converged with the interests of other constituencies to shape imperialism.[23] Others explore their capacity as governmental institutions. Focusing primarily on the Netherlands, Julia Adams examines the "institutional nexus fusing a set of elite patriarchal families with a merchant capitalist class and a locally grounded patrimonial state," thereby preserving certain traditions while fostering innovations such as chartered companies – which, in turn, shaped state formation.[24] Similarly situating companies in dialogue with other corporations and the developing English state, Philip Stern asserts that all these organizations were themselves political communities, in the case of chartered companies exercising jurisdiction over territory and trade routes and possessing their own internal regulations. In this sense, the early modern state was one body politic among many, all of which competed for jurisdiction. Building on Stern's analysis of the English East India Company, Andrew Phillips and J.C. Sharman emphasize the hybrid nature of this form by extending the term "company-state" to all such chartered companies.[25] Collectively, this burgeoning literature shows that companies and proprietors could be both a means to extend, and a challenge to, sovereignty. As such, they played key roles in shaping empires and states.

Fifteen years ago, Catherine Desbarats called on historians of New France to engage with the theoretical literature on the state.[26] One might add empire, sovereignty, and law to this list. For much of the twentieth century, scholars did not problematize these terms. One early exception is Louise Dechêne's meticulous study of the regulation of grain supply and distribution in New France. By studying administrative practice – in this case the local grain redistribution networks involving merchants, inhabitants, and priests – Dechêne concludes that the role of government in driving the economy has been exaggerated, due in part to an overreliance on government sources on the part of historians. Central to Dechêne's approach is her attention to the entanglement of "the social and the political."[27] Much more recently, Allan Greer has historicized property in early modern North America, reminding us that it was "a set of multiple claims – communal, familial, aristocratic, and state." Adopting the term "property formation," he underscores the unstable, dynamic nature of this process, paying attention to the social, political, and environmental contexts in which it took place.[28]

This book follows in the same spirit as Dechêne and Greer by breaking down abstractions, in this case, law and sovereignty. To do so, it begins with what French subjects themselves thought they were doing in North America, and the material foundations of the actual forms of power and authority that developed. It also takes a quintessentially economic institution often treated as fixed and singular, the company, and resituates it in legal, political, and social, as well as commercial, contexts to reveal the particular role it played in empire formation in New France.

Disputing New France complements the rich and multi-faceted literature on French-Indigenous relations and Indigenous sovereignty that, over the past few decades, has transformed our understanding of the nature of

"New France" and French colonialism. Far from a uniform space under French imperial control, "New France" consisted of mutually constructed spaces born of French-Indigenous interactions. As Gilles Havard has demonstrated, the *pays d'en haut* was a culturally and geographically unique region, characterized by various forms of acculturation and *métissage*. More recently, Jean-François Lozier has reconsidered the Saint Lawrence Valley mission settlements from an Indigenous perspective. Rather than missionary-driven, these settlements were a joint initiative directed by, and serving particular (and often temporary) purposes for, their Algonquian residents.[29] If intercultural negotiation and collaboration shaped French colonization, Indigenous autonomy lasted much longer than previously recognized.[30] Recent studies have shown that French power and authority in the seventeenth century was largely limited to a handful of fortified settlements, while imperial control was more future aspiration than current reality. The centrality of the French-Indigenous alliance to French colonization was such that sovereignty would be extended through Indigenous spaces rather than by eliminating them.[31] As this literature has shown that French colonization was anything but inexorable, it is necessary to look more closely at the transatlantic dynamics and the multiple agendas among the French that helped shape it.

Applying the approaches outlined above produces a different portrait of New France than that contained in the traditional narrative. Here, the state is weak; representatives of the king and viceroy are routinely outnumbered by associates and agents of the privileged trading company. The powers and privileges granted in commissions contend with other claims, whether backed by documents or force. Far from uncomplicated, sovereignty and authority are constructed fragment by fragment, in a series of acts occurring at specific moments and involving multiple parties – taking a ship under protection against unlawful threat of force, pulling up a settlement's drawbridge upon arrival of a ship, fighting over powers and trading rights before an Admiralty court, and so forth. The boundaries of the story of New France told in this book extend beyond the shores of the Saint Lawrence River to penetrate French courts of justice and assemblies of provincial estates as well as *communautés d'habitants* in Atlantic ports. Lest this sound like a customary tale of the opposition between centre and periphery, metropole and colony, *Disputing New France* instead shows the unexpected ways in which sovereignty assertion abroad and the developing state at home were mutually influential and constitutive.

If the literature on sovereignty, state and empire formation, and law renders New France less familiar, the resulting portrait in turn unsettles our sense of Atlantic European empires. New France does not fit easily into traditional imperial categories, with the Protestant, enterprising, capitalist, and modern British and Dutch Empires driven by merchants at one end, and the Catholic, statist, mercantilist, and feudal French, Spanish, and Portuguese Empires directed by royal officials at the other. While few specialists would subscribe to such a rigid dichotomy today, Spain frequently stands in for its fellow Catholic powers and relatively few comparative studies seriously consider France.[32] Yet the French Empire straddles these categories, making it – and early seventeenth-century New France in particular – especially rich for working through some of the questions raised by this literature. France and its "Most Christian Majesty" aspired, like Spain, to universal monarchy, with the propagation of Christianity its particular destiny.[33] This Catholic ideology not only undergirded the Crown but also, together with the Catholic Reformation, shaped French expansion overseas. However, the kingdom, if officially Catholic, was also northwestern European and its subjects ventured out into the Atlantic and Indian Oceans at the same time as the Dutch and English, not their Iberian co-religionists. The three countries, partly as a result of the contemporaneous nature of their overseas expansion, deployed a similar repertoire of tools for expansion and governance – namely, proprietorships, chartered companies, and, more rarely, royal government. Over the course of the first sixty years of New France's history, all three of these modes of rule were used, making it a particularly fruitful site in which to investigate each.[34] Moreover, the lines between them were fluid, with elements of each coexisting at particular times.

By examining the different constellations of power, authority, and privilege in New France, this book broadens our understanding of what a company was in the early modern period. The history of chartered companies is dominated by the Dutch and English East India Companies. In many respects, this focus is understandable: they were pioneers of the chartered company form, long-lasting and financially successful. As a result, other countries used them as models and historians have come to see them as archetypes.[35] In comparison with their Dutch and English counterparts, French chartered companies always come up short. An older French literature characterizes them as weak or clumsy imitations, especially hampered by the numerous royal office-holders among their membership.[36] Recent comparative studies qualify them as failures, whether based on purely commercial performance or on how well they balanced state and commercial imperatives.[37] Such assessments are not completely satisfying. If French chartered companies were not profitable – something this study does not dispute – then why did an enterprise like the Compagnie de la Nouvelle-France (CNF) last for thirty-five years? Why was the form repeatedly used? Both the duration of certain chartered companies and their continued creation suggests that they served a purpose that contemporaries deemed worthwhile, even if it is not one that we would expect. This study shifts the focus to examine the transatlantic legal, political, commercial, and social contexts in which the CNF, the first French chartered company in the Atlantic, emerged and evolved. It also considers all types of trading company active in New France in the first half of the seventeenth century. This approach reveals an evolution between 1603 and 1627 in the company form, from proprietors in small partnerships in which all merchant-associates were active to associations with a distinction between managers and investors. Whereas the colonies of Virginia and Massachusetts Bay began under a plantation company, the French already had more than two decades of colonizing experience in New France before the CNF emerged in 1627. The latter's configuration was shaped by this longer colonial and associational history.

The history of the CNF also belongs to the longer transatlantic story of the consolidation of maritime authority under the Crown or its office-holders. One of the most striking differences between Dutch, English, and French enterprises was the role of local institutions: whereas Dutch and English municipal governments tended to support overseas enterprises, communautés d'habitants in France were often openly against them because commercial operations moved to Paris, thereby diminishing rather than strengthening their power and wealth.[38] Chartered companies for New France and elsewhere, whether proposed by individuals or at the behest of the Crown, were thus centralizing instruments. At the same time, this centralization was not inexorable; concessions, repeals, and adjustments were made. The range of companies operating in New France perhaps did not compete with the state, as was the case in England,[39] nor were they a means to shape governance and overseas interests for the benefit of elite dynastic interests, as in the Netherlands,[40] but they were a focus of the struggle and negotiation between competing corporate interests and between the provinces and the Crown that lay at the heart of both empire and state formation.

The particularities of the interactions between state and empire formation in the French case become visible when viewed through a legal lens. Unlike in the developing English Empire, where common law courts had no jurisdiction overseas and plantation companies soon established their own courts, French courts heard all disputes relating to powers and privileges in New France during the first half of the seventeenth century. While Montmorency and his fellow viceroys had the power to establish courts of justice, a power passed on to Champlain as lieutenant, the first court system was not founded until 1651 under the CNF, more than twenty years after its establishment. Before that, Champlain or successive governors had the power to judge both civil and criminal matters without appeal.[41] Title-holders, including privileged companies under a proprietor, enjoyed the privilege of being heard before a particular metropolitan jurisdiction, such as a provincial Admiralty court or the royal council. The effect of this arrangement was to tie colonial activities closely to domestic affairs and link the developing forms of colonial power and authority to the centralizing state in France. The role of legal instruments and institutions in the French colonization of North America explains in part the particular cast of colony-metropole relations that developed.

French Courts of Justice and Authority in New France

Disputing New France is the first study to systematically mine the rich cache of civil suits that arose over powers and privileges in New France among company associates, independent traders, and viceroys and their representatives during the first half of the seventeenth century. At most, previous studies of early New France have referred only briefly to these sources. Part of this neglect stems from the prominent role of traders in the lawsuits, actors whom scholars have not traditionally considered as playing a legitimate or important role in the development of the colony.[42] As this book demonstrates, however, this litigation helped shape the developing repertoire of tools of privilege granting, governance, and capital formation and was also connected to metropolitan jurisdictional struggles.

As sources, the more than two dozen lawsuits studied here are both invaluable and challenging. They are invaluable because they multiply the perspectives available on a period for which the majority of extant sources are accounts by missionaries and royal representatives, most notably Champlain's *Voyages*, Gabriel Sagard's *Histoire du Canada*, and, from

1632, the Jesuit *Relations de la Nouvelle France*. In the absence of other records from most of the key parties involved – especially privileged and independent traders – these lawsuits illuminate how litigants presented their positions, the underlying structures of authority on which their actions and justifications rested, and the connections between metropolitan and colonial affairs. Following the naming of the parties concerned, each record lists the supporting documents in the case, ranging from previous acts or judgments to royal commissions and notarial records. This list helps to expand the source base by locating documents that are otherwise difficult to find, particularly notarial acts. When the sources are no longer extant, the court record provides at least minimal information on their tenor. These lawsuits also present a number of challenges. Difficult to read and understand, they require extensive knowledge of the labyrinthine early modern French legal system. The records are also patchy and widely dispersed. With each case involving a variety of jurisdictions, the relevant documents are stored in different departmental and national archives. The majority of them register an act, accord one party's request, or summon both parties to appear before the court with more information. The resolution of a case is not always known, whether because of missing records or a settlement out of court. Before analyzing these lawsuits, then, it is first necessary to reconstruct the events leading to them and their evolution over time.

While some lawsuits began with verbal or physical confrontations in New France, others concerned compensation for prematurely revoked privileges, disputes among associates over profits and losses, or the respective obligations and prerogatives of a viceroy and a privileged company. Their diversity aside, these suits share several characteristics. They involve a variety of jurisdictions, including local and regional Admiralty courts, provincial *parlements* (the highest provincial sovereign courts), and royal councils (the Conseil d'État du roi and the Conseil privé). As was typical of privileged individuals and corporate bodies in early modern France, successive privileged trading companies to New France had the right to have all suits heard before one particular jurisdiction, usually the Admiralty of Rouen or, in the CNF's case, the royal council. This provision did not, however, prevent adversaries from seeking redress before other courts, resulting in contradictory decrees. It was not uncommon for suits to precipitate others between the same parties or to become entwined with parallel suits. For example, particularly contentious litigation between the privileged

Compagnie de Rouen et Saint-Malo and merchants from La Rochelle over the latter's entry into the association in the 1610s merged with another dispute concerning the seizure of one of the company's ships (see figure 0.1).[43] Lawsuits between two parties frequently expanded to include one or more interveners, ranging from a deputy of the French inhabitants of Quebec to a representative of the admiral of France. Contrary to modern expectations, resolution was not necessarily the litigants' primary goal. The aim was, instead, to continue the conflict by channelling it into the courts, to wear down an opponent and deplete their material and financial resources. Indeed, parties at times deliberately prolonged these disputes by summoning an adversary before another court or failing to show up for a hearing. Such strategies, and litigation more generally, were widespread in early modern France and Europe.[44] What sets these lawsuits apart, however, is the unique window they offer onto the interconnections between the developing state and sovereign ambitions in North America.

My attention to the dialectical relationship between state formation in France and empire formation in North America makes other archival collections newly relevant to the history of New France. I examine French memoranda on navigation and commerce as well as proposals for other chartered companies in France, two types of sources that cluster particularly around the mid-1620s when Louis XIII and Chief Minister Richelieu turned their attention to maritime affairs. When put together with familiar records such as those of the CNF, they illuminate the place of New France within these larger developments. Deliberations and resolutions of municipal and provincial corporate bodies, such as the communauté d'habitants of Saint-Malo, the Estates of Brittany, and provincial parlements, reveal their perceptions of transatlantic colonizing and commercial enterprises and their strategies to protect the autonomy and interests of their communities. Using municipal, genealogical, and notarial records, I determine the local standing and connections of the merchants of Saint-Malo, Rouen, and La Rochelle who were most involved in New France. These sources, together with the civil suits, are combined with familiar texts, including royal commissions and decrees, notarial acts, and travel and missionary accounts, to newly situate New France within the larger context of French and international developments, of which New France was an integral part.

In its analysis of these various sources, this book draws on methodologies associated with recent approaches to state formation and sovereignty.

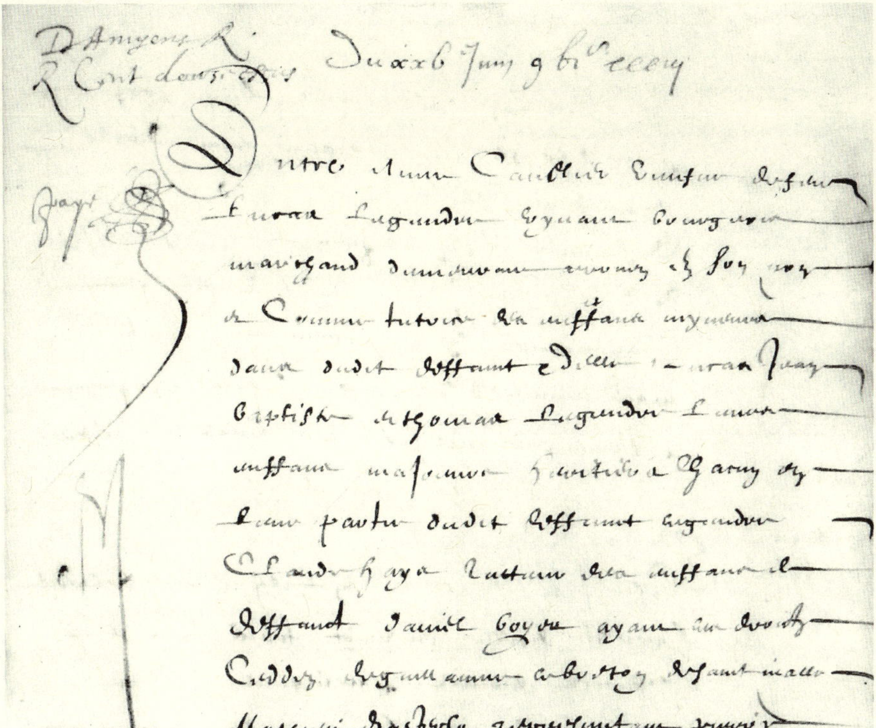

Figure 0.1 Decree of the Parlement of Rouen, 25 June 1633. An example of a lawsuit over powers and privileges in New France. This is the first page of the final sentence in what was a twenty-year dispute between Rochelais traders Samuel Georges, Jean Macain, and consorts, and the associates of the Compagnie de Rouen et Saint-Malo over the two men's entrance into the company.

Adopting Lauren Benton's idea of "legal posturing," by which individuals consciously "reenacted legal rituals as they remembered them and imperfectly reconstructed legal practices and arguments," I analyze subjects' use of legal instruments and institutions through their actions in New France, the language in court records, and their judicial strategies.[45] Under what circumstances and with what objectives did subjects choose conflict or negotiation? My reading of sources, more broadly, is guided by Michael Braddick's "transactional view of the relationship between state, community, locality and centre."[46] How did the actors directly or indirectly involved in New France – ranging from independent traders to company associates, from missionaries to viceroys, and from royal officials to *parlementaires* – shape the developing repertoire of tools of governance, capital formation, and privilege granting? In what ways did underlying political, legal, and social structures enable and limit individual and corporate action? How did interactions among these (sometimes) competing actors affect the material forms of power, authority, and sovereignty in New France? Such questions illuminate the legal, political, and personal relationships that shaped the processes of state and empire formation.

Modes of Governance, Privilege Granting, and Capital Formation

Adopting an Atlantic perspective, *Disputing New France* traces the developing repertoire of tools of governance, capital formation, and privilege granting in New France to illuminate the interdependent processes of empire and state formation. This is not a unidirectional story of the metropole transmitting practices to a colony. Instead, this book advances a sort of cis-Atlantic history, to borrow David Armitage's typology, in its exploration of the interconnections and continuities between these processes that unfolded in both France and New France.[47] While this is primarily a North Atlantic story, I expand the frame as needed to follow the circulation of legal and governmental practices and instruments of colonization and commerce, sometimes leading to the French Antilles for comparison or to the Indian Ocean, in this way following trade routes that were connected in the minds of contemporaries to those of the Atlantic. The Atlantic was also a meaningful space for the principal actors in this story. Claims to power, privileges, and rights on one side of the Atlantic had an impact on, and became interwoven with, claims on the other side. I use the term "French Atlantic" as a shorthand for this space in which French actors and practices circulated. In short, the Atlantic provides a useful geographical and explanatory framework for the subjects examined here.[48]

Organized chronologically and moving back and forth between France and New France, successive chapters investigate a particular aspect of the processes of empire and state formation. Chapter 1 sets up the French context of North American commissions and introduces the legal, political, and commercial arrangements that would be the basis of the enterprise for the following half century. Using the proprietorship of Pierre Dugua, Sieur de Mons, and his eponymous company (active from 1603 to 1612) in particular, it explores the domestic stakes of overseas expansion. By investigating the role of privileges and corporate bodies, which were at the foundation of French politics and society, in securing loyalty to the Crown at a particularly delicate moment politically and socially, it advances a new explanation for the changing configurations of de Mons's authority and trading rights over the decade.

French subjects who travelled overseas drew on a range of tools, including law and legal instruments, personal authority, and force, to advance their own interests and maintain their relationship with king and patron in France. Opening with the assassination of Henri IV and the beginning of a regency, chapter 2 considers a series of disputes that erupted over powers and privileges in New France in the 1610s to explore the calculations behind subjects' pursuit of conflict or negotiation. The jockeying occurred simultaneously on a number of levels: among outside traders and title-holders, among claimants to the viceroyalty of New France, between the company with trading privileges and the viceroy's lieutenant, and within the company itself. Through this lens we see the connection between contests for authority on both sides of the Atlantic. Common to all was the strategy of drawing metropolitan authorities into overseas spaces. While this intervention took a variety of forms, metropolitan courts of justice were a key forum for working out – and containing – struggles over authority, privileges, and sovereign representation in New France.

Waterways, whether oceanic or riverine, were the principal means by which parties accessed the resources at the heart of many of these disputes. Chapter 3 interrogates the relationship between maritime and territorial jurisdictions by focusing on the 1620s, a time when the two were explicitly connected. When Admiral Montmorency became viceroy at the opening of the decade, it marked the first time that control over maritime traffic in

France was linked to control over territory overseas. For different groups, New France itself was a maritime space: a means to supervise trade routes and the movement of subjects and goods or a seasonal fishing and trading destination. Jurisdiction was defined by aquatic features and spread through travel along water routes. Through an exploration of spaces of different scale and nature, the chapter re-centres mobility and circulation (of subjects, of goods) as key components of the construction of sovereignty and authority on both sides of the Atlantic.

If the 1620s saw the incorporation of New France into a metropolitan institution, it was also a moment of converging interests between two corporate bodies in France, the church and the monarchy. Chapter 4 locates the moment when religion became a central issue in the colonization of the Saint Lawrence Valley. The arrival of new groups in the 1620s – a second privileged trading company, Récollet and then Jesuit missionaries – escalated the struggle among parties to take the reins of the colony. With a new sense of urgency, each suggested that the very sovereignty of the king in North America was at stake and they sought to position themselves as the legitimate representatives of the Crown. This "crisis of sovereignty" turned the heretofore minor evangelizing mission into a hot political issue and marked a turning point in the construction of authority in French North America. By examining the effects on the actions and rhetoric of the various parties in the colony, the chapter argues that the new focus denoted a shift in the balance of power among royal, religious, and commercial interests, and, more fundamentally, in the target of sovereignty to people.

Chapter 5 retells the story of the establishment of the CNF, the first and longest-lasting French chartered company in the Atlantic, by connecting it to the wider French and global contexts of the "age of companies." Beginning with the terms of the company's charter of 1627, it considers the CNF and other companies like it as instruments of power at both the international and the domestic level. While they were vehicles to increase French commercial and maritime standing in competition with – and emulation of – the country's European rivals, they also played a role in internal power struggles, at the heart of which was sea power. Pitting admiral against chief minister, provincial estates against the royal council, and Huguenots against the king's forces, seemingly separate political, commercial, and confessional matters were in fact intimately intertwined, an entanglement that becomes visible through the CNF. This enterprise was not an exact copy of Dutch and English models but instead combined some of the principal elements of this innovative form with traditional French methods of gathering financial and organizational resources to pursue particular French political, commercial, colonizing, and maritime objectives.

The CNF constituted not only a new tool of capital formation but also a new mode of governance for the Crown. The sixth and final chapter explores the strategies used by company associates to execute their extensive mandate and their evolving relationship with the king and his representatives, other corporate bodies, and fellow title-holders in New France over the company's roughly thirty-year tenure. Employing a variety of types of delegation, associates granted trading privileges, land concessions, and authority to individuals and corporate groups in various combinations from the Saint Lawrence Valley to Acadia. These delegations were voluntary, but the 1640s saw the establishment of a regency government on the eastern side of the Atlantic followed by the introduction of new corporate bodies in the Saint Lawrence Valley, both of which resulted in the usurpation of the company's authority. If this marginalization was temporary, the ongoing experimentations in structures of commerce and governance during the CNF's tenure reflected a half-century search for viable ways to fulfill an extensive mandate and render the venture financially sustainable.

The epilogue takes the story through to the CNF's cession of the colony to the king in 1663, comparing the circumstances in the French Atlantic to those at the time of its creation, before proposing a conception of empire quite different from that found in existing histories. Ultimately, *Disputing New France* demonstrates that the fledgling colony and the realm of France constituted interconnected spaces in which layers of legal, political, and personal relationships, and of sovereignty, privileges, and authority, were constructed, challenged, and remade.

1

Royal Commissions and the Culture of Privilege

We have resolved for the perfection of ... so holy and worthy an enterprise, instead of the late Sieur de Roberval, to give the charge of this conquest to some brave and experienced person ... with the same powers, authority, prerogatives and pre-eminence that were accorded to the said late Sieur de Roberval by the letters patent of the late King François I ... For the good and complete faith that we have in the person of our beloved and loyal Troilus de Mesgouetz, Knight of our Order, Counsellor in our State Council ... Sieur de la Roche, Marquis de Coteanmoreal ... we have ... hereby made, make, create, order, establish by these present letters signed by our hand, our Lieutenant general of the said country of Canadas, Hochelaga, Newfoundland, Labrador, rivers of the great Bay of Norumbega and adjoining lands.

Royal commission to the Marquis de La Roche, 1598[1]

In early January 1598, Henri IV granted the above commission to Troilus de La Roche de Mesgouez, Marquis de La Roche-Mesgouez, chevalier, royal counsellor, and governor of Fougères in Brittany, who had fought on his side against the Catholic League during the Wars of Religion. The closing years of the sixteenth century were an auspicious time for France domestically and internationally following a half century of bloody and divisive civil war between Catholics and Protestants. A few months after the commission to La Roche, Henri IV, who had earlier converted to Catholicism to legitimize his reign, promulgated the Edict of Nantes, which guaranteed civil and certain religious rights to Protestants, and entered a peace treaty with Catholic Spain, thereby robbing the hardline Catholic Leaguers of important external support. If the restoration of order and stability in France was henceforth the priority, these measures also laid the groundwork for France to pursue its overseas imperial ambitions. As the reference to Jean-François de La Rocque de Roberval in the above passage attests, Henri IV and his contemporaries drew inspiration from the first period of royal encouragement of and investment in overseas enterprise. François I had challenged the pretentions of Spain and Portugal to exclusive rights to travel to, conquer, and occupy territories beyond Europe by issuing his own commissions to corsairs to attack Spanish and Portuguese settlements and ships and to such explorers as Giovanni de Verrazano, Jacques Cartier, and the Sieur de Roberval to explore parts of North America. Modelling himself explicitly on the late king, Henri IV shared the latter's expansionist ambitions and drive to limit Spanish power and standing in Europe and the Americas alike.

While the nine royal commissions granted for travel to Canada over the sixteenth century to 1603 (only six of which led to actual voyages) varied considerably in their objectives, powers, privileges, geographical scope, and duration, there remained two constant elements.[2] First, all title-holders had the right to profits gained from the voyage in order to cover expenses, which stemmed from such activities as transporting colonists, building forts and habitations, and organizing exploratory ventures. In Roberval's case, for example, he could keep "a third to provide, if we think fit, for a portion of the costs and outlay that he might incur for the continuation of the said voyage in the next five years, as well as to compensate him in some way for his labours and expenses." The other two-thirds were to go to those who accompanied him on the voyage and to the Crown to be put into other expeditions, an arrangement largely echoed in La Roche's 1598 letters patent.[3] Pierre Chauvin's commission, granted a year later, had somewhat different and more explicit terms. Having requested exclusive trading privileges from the start, the Huguenot military and naval captain's enjoyment of the latter (and thus any profits) was conditional on transporting fifty settlers annually.

The second common element among these commissions was the restrictions imposed on those who could travel to the area covered in the grant. Subjects needed to be associated with the title-holder or to have his express permission to go to the region under his command. With two exceptions, this restriction was directly related to commerce.[4] La Roche could be accompanied by "all gentlemen, merchants and others of our subjects who wish to go or send [and] pay men on the said voyages, and equip and outfit ships [*nefz*] at their expense. Which we expressly prohibit them from doing, nor to traffic there without the seal and consent of our said lieutenant."[5] As La Roche's commission demonstrates, exclusive privileges accorded to title-holders were typically expressed in negative terms, as a ban on others. Contemporary definitions of privilege linked it to the term *priver*, meaning to deprive or exclude someone from something. The *Thresor de la langue francoyse* of 1606 defined privilege as a "particular law, *for or against* someone."[6] Privilege was, therefore, fundamentally relational. It conferred power and status that others did not have.[7]

The relational cast to privilege added a third constant to the granting of royal commissions to Canada in the sixteenth and early seventeenth centuries – namely, protest on the part of those excluded. Protesters articulated their objections in terms that highlighted the loss that accompanied any privilege. In 1588, Henri IV's predecessor, Henri III, accorded Cartier's nephew, Jacques Noel, and his business partner Étienne Chaton de La Jannaye, exclusive privileges to all commerce in "the said country of Canada, Coujugon and other adjacent territories" for a period of twelve years.[8] Two months later, the communauté d'habitants of Saint-Malo in Brittany – which was, not incidentally, Cartier's hometown – appeared before the provincial Estates to request its support in overturning the commission on the grounds that the privileges "deprive and take away the negotiation of ordinary commerce which is traditionally permitted to everyone in the said country as to foreign nations [*autres*]."[9] Portraying travel to and trade in North America as heretofore open to all, the Malouins (as those from Saint-Malo are called) presented the exclusive rights granted to Noel and La Jannaye as an unorthodox departure from custom. In contrast to attempts to thwart Cartier's own voyages fifty years earlier, the Estates' deputy at court successfully lobbied the king to revoke the duo's commission four months later.[10]

While Malouin traders consistently called for the revocation of privileges following the granting of each commission, traders from the Norman port of Rouen adopted a different approach. Sometime after Chauvin received exclusive permission to trade in return for transporting settlers to New France in 1599, representatives from Rouen requested to join the enterprise. Henri IV accordingly struck a commission to investigate the current trade. Based on its findings, he decided at the end of 1602 to extend the privileges to Rouennais (and Malouin) traders "so as not to thwart you in the ordinary trade that you have long had with the said countries." Each port could thus send out one ship "jointly or separately" on condition that they contribute one-third to the enterprise's colonizing expenses.[11] Although the community of Saint-Malo objected vociferously to this condition, a handful of the port's traders joined together to organize a voyage according to the king's terms, as did the Rouennais traders.

If the two protests and the king's response underscore the relative newness of the Crown's intervention in the overseas fishery and fur trade, they show more broadly that so-called exclusive privileges were not absolute: they could be rescinded, expanded to other groups, or upheld. The royal commissions granted from Cartier's first voyage in 1534 to the last voyage under Chauvin's commission in 1603 raised fundamental questions for the fishermen and traders directly involved, members of provincial and municipal bodies like the Breton Estates and the community of Saint-Malo, and the king and his ministers: What should be the terms governing voyages to North America? And who would decide? From the point of view of a fisherman active from the 1510s on the Banks off Newfoundland and his descendants, royal commissions constituted a serious infringement on what they considered to be well-established customary rights. From the perspective of title-holders like La Roche, their commissions may have come from the king, but the execution of these commissions depended on a host of other corporate groups, provincial and local, that may well have been more favourable to the fisherman.

This chapter traces the development of a repertoire by which the Crown came to regulate colonial enterprises in North America, focusing particularly on the proprietorship of Pierre Dugua, Sieur de Mons from 1603 to 1612. Close analysis of de Mons's commissions illuminates several important themes of this book: the elastic and contested nature of commercial privilege; the transatlantic jockeying it precipitated among rival interests; the tensions between royal and local/provincial power; the intertwining and colliding of political and economic concerns; and the symbolic value of titles and privileges. By investigating how the centrality of privileges and corporate structures in the exercise of authority in France affected the configuration of the enterprise, the chapter demonstrates that overseas expansion was a domestic issue.

Trade for Colonization

The royal commissions for North America granted during Henri IV's reign, three in total, turned out to mark the beginning of sustained royal regulation of transatlantic colonial and commercial activity. These regulations came to take a variety of forms. While the king drew on the terms of earlier letters patent, the third and last one he issued became a template for commissions granted over the following decades. In November 1603, Pierre Dugua, Sieur de Mons, a Protestant nobleman from Saintonge on

France's central Atlantic coast and gentleman in ordinary of the king's chamber, submitted a proposal for the "discovery and settlement of the coasts and territories of La Cadie" (comprised of the present-day Maritime provinces of Canada and the northeastern portion of the state of Maine).[12] To this end, he promised to take a hundred people per voyage, with an emphasis put on artisans skilled in the building trades. A participant in Chauvin's earlier voyages, de Mons was already armed with an extensive commission as vice admiral and lieutenant general "in all seas, coasts, islands, roadsteads, and shores found in and about the said province and district of La Cadie" and as far inland as he could penetrate.[13] His powers included the recruitment of captains, sailors, and artisans, the outfitting of ships, the establishment of forts and ports, the appointment of captains, lieutenants, and guards of the coasts, and the commissioning of officers to judge and enforce laws. The admiral of France, Charles de Montmorency, had promised to contribute one-third of the expense. As the latter's representative in New France, de Mons wished to complement his maritime jurisdiction with regal powers from the king, including the power to declare war, enter alliances, confer privileges, and grant lands and titles. In recognition of the considerable powers and responsibilities he proposed, the nobleman requested the title of "viceroy and captain general both on sea and on land" as well as privileges in the fur trade for ten years "to provide for the expenses that need to be made with all the necessary risks, hazards and advances at the start of the enterprise," a request that highlights the substantial start-up costs of such an undertaking before any hope of a return.[14]

Two days later, Henri IV appointed his faithful supporter "lieutenant general in the countries, territories, coasts, and confines of La Cadie … to establish, extend, and make to be known our name, might, and authority." As with the sixteenth-century commissions, de Mons's combined religious and dynastic goals. The king presented his new lieutenant general with four main objectives: the conversion of the Indigenous inhabitants to Christianity; the extension of France's dominion and reputation; the occupation, habitation, and cultivation of land; and the exploration and discovery of the wider region from the fortieth to the forty-sixth parallel. To achieve them, Henri IV granted the regal powers requested and instructed de Mons to build forts, habitations, ports, and garrisons, cultivate and settle the land, and "do generally whatsoever may make for the conquest, peopling, inhabiting, and preservation of the said land of La Cadie."[15]

The letters patent did not include either privileges or colonizing obligations. Instead, these appeared separately, the first in the form of a ban on trade to others: "We make express prohibition for all masters, ship captains, sailors, and others our subjects of whatever status, quality, or condition … to outfit any vessels, and in these to go or to send others for the traffic and trade of furs and other things with the Natives, or to frequent, negotiate, or communicate with them, during the said period of ten years." While the wording recalls that of the ban in La Roche's commission, it is here more detailed, both in the activities forbidden and in the list of particular bays, rivers, and coasts where it is in effect, including the Baie de Chaleur, the "river of Canada," and the island of Cape Breton.[16] Any who disobeyed the ban would be subject to a fine of 30,000 livres. The same day on which the king issued this decree, de Mons requested that the number of settlers he was obliged to take to Acadia be reduced from the original hundred. He avowed that he was having difficulty recruiting merchants to the enterprise because, according to them, "all expenses that would need to be made in the accomplishment of this condition [i.e., colonization] would greatly exceed the profit that he could make from the permission to traffic in furs." The king accordingly reduced the number to sixty and offered a guarantee: if Acadia turned out to be unsuitable for habitation, de Mons could bring back the settlers and be relieved of his obligations. If this occurred, however, open trade would resume.[17]

The distinctive nature of de Mons's commission lay in its combination of the powers, privileges, and responsibilities accorded Roberval and Chauvin in their respective letters patent. He received both the proprietary powers of government and justice of the former and the trading rights of the latter to cover the costs of settlement.[18] Considering the original number of settlers and the geographical extent of the lieutenant general's jurisdiction, de Mons's commission was more ambitious than previous patents. Its particular terms demonstrate an attempt on the king's part to balance a variety of interests: de Mons's, the king's own, and those of fishermen and merchants involved in the fur trade. For de Mons, who along with the three previous commission-holders had led companies of soldiers on Henri IV's behalf during the Wars of Religion, the commission was partly a recognition of his service and followed the tradition of granting titles and privileges to loyal liegemen.[19] The commission offered the prospect, from Henri IV's perspective, of expanding his dominion, advancing France's anti-Spanish objectives, and consolidating support among Catholics. If royal intervention in transatlantic trading and fishing was unwelcome

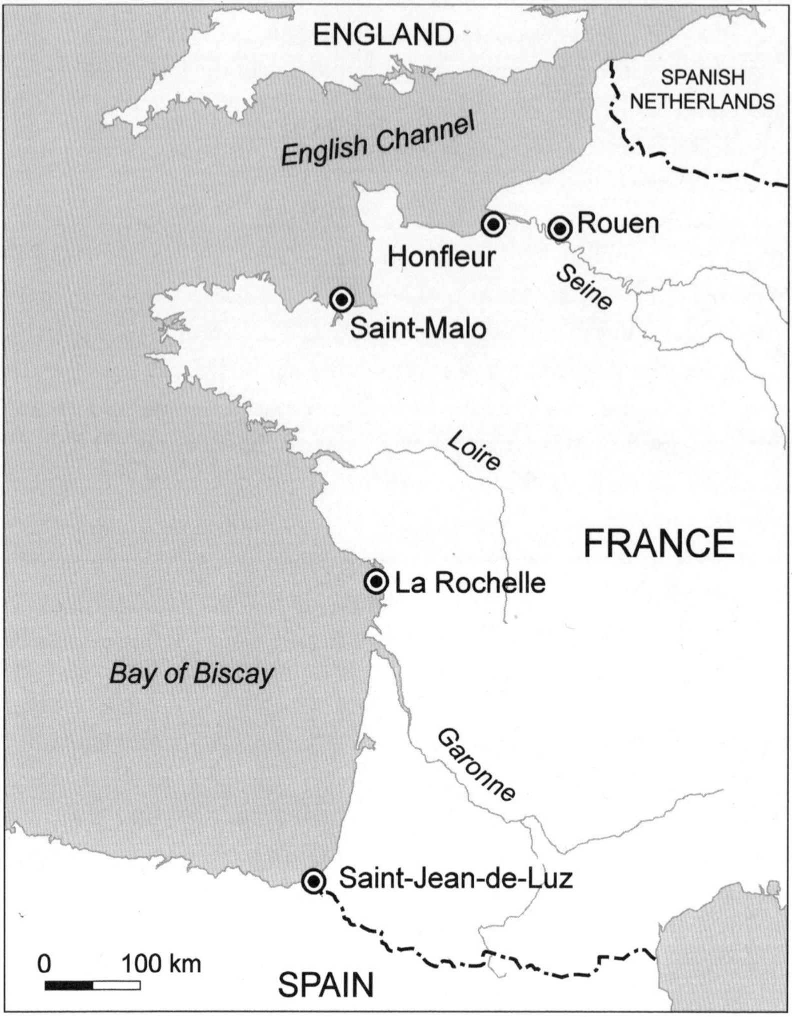

Figure 1.1 Principal French ports involved in the privileged commercial and colonizing enterprises in New France, 1603–63.

among fishermen and traders in Breton and Norman ports, the letters patent nevertheless reveal the king's strategy toward their demands for freedom of trade. The condition for trading privileges was colonization. By this logic, if no settlements were established, restrictions on trade lost their justification. This close and uneasy relationship between colonizing obligations and trading privileges persisted in the New France enterprise throughout the first three decades of the seventeenth century.

De Mons's previous experience in Chauvin's venture involving traders from Honfleur, Rouen, and Saint-Malo likely influenced his decision to create a multi-port association. Given the scale of the enterprise and the previous protests over privileges, the recruitment of merchants from several ports lent legitimacy to his commission. With some overlap in membership from the earlier undertaking, de Mons associated with traders in his home port of Rouen, Saint-Malo, and La Rochelle over the winter of 1604 (see figure 1.1). These were the most active ports in the North Atlantic fishery and the fur trade, as well as fierce rivals. Enjoying certain commercial privileges and relative political autonomy, all three benefited from their status as free ports, which exempted them from duties on imports and exports and was an important element in their prosperity. Rouen and La Rochelle had permission to engage in the spice trade, which opened up an expansive commercial space, both in Europe and internationally. They participated in extensive trade networks encompassing North and South America, Africa, England, the Netherlands, Portugal, and Spain. On a domestic level, the three ports were well-connected to their respective interiors, serving as important centres of distribution and sources of capital for mercantile activity. A substantial portion of their populations were involved in commerce and played an influential role in the general assembly of the communauté d'habitants and municipal government. In the case of Saint-Malo, the smallest of the three with the fewest institutions, its elite was almost exclusively mercantile.[20]

While Rouen, La Rochelle, and Saint-Malo all guarded their privileges closely, both against other ports and against royal encroachment, the latter two in particular had a history of opposition to external authority. La Rochelle's independent spirit was visible in the city's architecture, the entrance to its inner harbour well-fortified with towers and the city hall itself a château fort. During the Wars of Religion, the inhabitants of Saint-Malo had thrown their support behind the Catholic League against the future Henri IV, killing the "royalist" governor and forming a sort of republic under the League for four years.[21] The fierce rivalry among these ports was likely owed in part to their religious differences. Saint-Malo's staunch Catholicism contrasted with La Rochelle's status as a Protestant stronghold; Rouen, whose most prominent merchants were predominantly Protestant, was both the object of a Protestant siege and a subject of the Catholic League during the confessional conflict. If the mercantile activities of all three were severely disrupted during the Wars of Religion, when many merchants left the towns, the long-term effects varied. In Rouen, for example, a smaller merchant community returned to fewer opportunities and more restricted capital.[22] Broadly speaking, over the course of the late sixteenth and seventeenth centuries, the ports' influence in Newfoundland, Acadia, and Quebec relative to one another shifted from Saint-Malo to Rouen and La Rochelle.[23]

Given the trio's importance, it was crucial to an enterprise's success – especially one as ambitious and contentious as de Mons's – to engage merchants in all of them, a practice that would continue for the next two decades. De Mons therefore associated with some of the most prominent participants in the international fur trade, including Corneille de Bellois of Rouen and Samuel Georges and Jean Macain of La Rochelle. The latter two were brothers-in-law and among the seventy-six peers on the town council, positions that were highly sought after among the port's wealthy, influential, and tightly knit elite families. Frequent business partners, the pair had invested in voyages to New France since at least 1599, when they provided a loan to and purchased furs in advance from a Basque vessel, and they may have also participated in Chauvin's voyages. Typical of merchants of the time, Bellois, Georges, and Macain were simultaneously lenders, traders, ship owners, and suppliers.[24] The Malouin associates were, like de Mons, noblemen, some of whom had joined in the previous enterprise under Chauvin while others had protested against it.[25] These and other associates belonged to the upper echelon of merchants in their respective ports, those with the wealth, knowledge, and fortitude to engage in long-distance commerce within Europe and overseas.[26] In this sense, participation in transatlantic enterprises was a mark of success.

Although de Mons had already made written contracts, or *actes sous seing privé*, with merchants in each port, the scale of the undertaking encouraged him to have these formalized before a notary, which would give them legal force.[27] On 10 February 1604, de Mons, Georges, and Macain signed an agreement before a notary by which the Rochelais (or those from La Rochelle) entered the association for a one-sixth share of expenses and profits, the latter including fish, furs, minerals, "and all that to him [de Mons] granted by his said commission and articles." That same day, the lieutenant general also gave them power of attorney to enter notarized contracts with those merchants of Saint-Malo and the Basque whaling port of Saint-Jean-de-Luz with whom he already had a private arrangement.[28] The end result was a partnership among the four ports, in which Rouen and Saint-Malo each had a one-third share, while La Rochelle and Saint-Jean-de-Luz combined for the last third. De Mons detailed how the organization would be regulated in a series of articles. Each port was to outfit one to two ships per year, according to its share in the enterprise. The associates were to keep their own accounts; at the end of each season, the company's receiver general, Corneille de Bellois, was to pool the individual accounts and divide up profits and losses. De Mons contributed 10,000 livres to help cover the expenses of sending two ships to New France. He and his Rouennais associates were to pool an additional 8,000 livres for a total of 18,000 livres, which would constitute a one-third part in the association. Saint-Malo undertook to provision and man another two ships with its 18,000 livres. The cost, however, of both ports' commitments exceeded their shares. As a result, Georges, Macain, and their Saint-Jean-de-Luz partners gave 10,000 livres to their Rouennais counterparts and 900 livres to the Malouins. Their remaining 7,100 livres were invested in a whaling ship from Saint-Jean-de-Luz. The total capital of the association amounted to 54,000 livres. At the end of the first voyage, 10,000 livres were to be reinvested in the enterprise.[29]

As these arrangements indicate, the Compagnie de Mons was a complex organization, lying somewhere between a loose association among ports and a partnership in which capital was pooled and used. The division of responsibilities by port meant that the company was, in one sense, an umbrella organization bringing together three smaller partnerships. As was common at the time, several members of the three associations were related, particularly notable being the intermarriage among the Malouin participants.[30] Each port was responsible for collecting the sums due from its members and undertaking preparations for the next voyage. Indeed, when an agreement was drawn up on 19 February 1604 between Georges, in de Mons's name, and Pierre Ribertière, Etienne Goret, François Martin, Luc Sere, and Jehan Sarcel, all of Saint-Malo, for a one-third share in the undertaking, the Malouins had already bought a vessel and begun outfitting it for the coming season's voyage.[31] Profits were also apportioned by port among associates. Upon arrival back in France, a vessel's merchandise, mainly furs, was traded on behalf of the associates of that port. De Mons, acting for himself and his Rouennais associates, entered a contract – the same day as the establishment of articles – with Georges and Macain by which the Rochelais merchants would buy one-third of their furs in each of the next two years for a fixed price depending on the quality and type of fur.[32] It was only after merchandise was sold that the company's accounts were pooled. In this sense, it resembled a regulated company in England, in which merchants traded on their own account but the larger association offered them protection.[33]

The division among ports was not, however, absolute. La Rochelle and Saint-Jean-de-Luz, for example, did contribute directly to the efforts of Rouen and Saint-Malo. The active participation of all members and the sharing of expenses and profits at season's end recalled a traditional *société générale* or *société en participation*, a partnership, the most common association during this period. All members were merchants or traders who engaged for a specific length of time and were considered *solidairement responsable*, or liable for all of the company's affairs. Organized around the people who were part of it, a *société génerale* needed to dissolve and re-form following a change in composition.[34] While the typical partnership was short-term, de Mons's company resembled other longer-term associations that engaged internationally in a particular type of commerce.[35] The flexibility within the association's structure accommodated the ports with fewer resources to outfit ships as well as the fierce inter-port rivalries, which encouraged associations involving traders of only one town.

The balance of power within the Compagnie de Mons shifted considerably a year after its constitution. In the fall of 1605, the Saint-Jean-de-Luz partners withdrew. The final article of the company had outlined the terms by which any of the ports or individual members could renounce their shares. They were only allowed to do so after the second voyage and before 15 November of that year to allow the remaining partners time to reorganize before the following spring's voyage. The withdrawal of Saint-Jean-de-Luz was not a complete surprise. Indeed, provision had already been made on 10 February 1604 for those traders' departure after two years; Georges and Macain had received permission to take the Basques' part in the company. The company accordingly divided its shares anew, this time into fifths. Georges and Macain and the Malouins increased their parts to two-fifths each, while de Mons and his Rouennais partners reduced theirs to one-fifth.[36] Although La Rochelle and Saint-Malo had equal weight, there were several more contributors in the latter group. In this respect, the main outcome of the reorganization was the increased influence of Georges and Macain. That said, de Mons's reduced share in the enterprise belied his continued control over his trading privileges as lieutenant general, producing a somewhat odd dynamic with his partners that would, at times, be a source of tension among them.

Domestic Corporate Interests and New France

The execution of the powers, privileges, and obligations contained in de Mons's extensive commission and the ability of the newly formed company to trade without challenge in Acadia were only possible with the support of intermediary bodies. *Corps*, or corporations, were one of the foundations of the social and political order in France and served as intermediaries between the king and his subjects. Membership in a corporation accorded a subject civil status. For example, Samuel Georges, like many of his contemporaries, was a member of several corporations at once, notably La Rochelle's city council, the communauté d'habitants, and the bourgeois population of the city. Each of these gave the Rochelais merchant a right to certain privileges. Constituted by the king, corporations depended on him for their continued existence. They served both symbolic and practical purposes. Arranged hierarchically, corporations ordered society based on status. They also provided a range of services, whether fiscal, magisterial, professional, or governmental. While guilds ensured quality of production within a trade and regulated promotion from apprentice to journeyman to master, provincial sovereign courts rendered justice and registered royal laws. Limited in the number of agents it could send out to provinces and municipalities, the Crown relied on such bodies as communautés d'habitants and town councils to govern. Corporations were also an important source of royal revenue, particularly in the form of loans and other fees.[37]

The basis of relations between the king and corporations rested on the contractual nature of power.[38] In feudal terms, the king offered protection in return for the loyalty and obedience of his subjects. Corporations received certain privileges and exemptions. When France incorporated a new region, as was the case with the duchy of Brittany in 1532, the king typically confirmed the region's ancient privileges, customs, liberties, and institutions to win the allegiance of his new subjects. One of the most important Breton institutions was the Estates, which represented the three orders of the province (clergy, nobility, and commoners) and had the power to negotiate taxation with the king. There were seven *pays d'états* or provinces with a representative body in the late sixteenth century, a number that declined sharply in the following century. As long as the king continued to receive money from the Breton body, he allowed the institution to continue, as it ensured the all-important loyalty of the provincial elites. The latter, for their part, used the Estates and other institutions, such as the Parlement, to defend their rights, power, and autonomy. While particularly visible in *pays d'états*, the "dialectic" between king and local and provincial corporate bodies in Brittany was a feature of French governance in all regions.[39]

The fragmented nature of authority in the kingdom had direct consequences for de Mons's enterprise. For provinces such as Brittany and Normandy, the two jurisdictions with the most traders operating in North America, exclusive trading privileges to New France were considered a direct threat to provincial autonomy, and both pursued various strategies of delay and obstruction in response. By law, letters patent from the king had to be registered in the kingdom's sovereign courts to take full effect. Provincial parlements, notoriously protective of their jurisdiction, took this prerogative very seriously, often submitting remonstrances (a refusal to register due to particular concerns) to the king. When de Mons received his commission in November 1603, he encountered significant delays before these bodies. The Parlement of Rouen delivered remonstrances in 1604 based on de Mons's Protestantism and the proposed trading privileges, before registering the commission sometime after a response from the Palais de Justice the following January.[40] Later that month, perhaps at the urging of de Mons's secretary, Henri IV issued a *lettre de jussion* (a royal letter ordering a sovereign court to register an ordinance) to the Parlement of Paris in which he ordered it to "read, register, keep, and observe" the commission.[41] In mid-March, the sovereign court obeyed, following on the heels of the Parlement of Bordeaux.

Well-organized lobbying by the traders of Saint-Malo made the Parlement of Brittany (shown in figure 1.2) the most recalcitrant. In January 1605, the court had chosen a counsellor to "hear the Inhabitants of Saint-Malo on their opposition."[42] Dominated by the port's most prominent merchants, the communauté d'habitants of Saint-Malo was the most vocal opponent to exclusive trading privileges to New France during the first half century of French activity there. It exercised powers comparable to an Admiralty, from supervising ship traffic and the port's organization to ensuring the maintenance and security of facilities. As the delay in registration of de Mons's commission attests, the community mounted a highly organized effort to mobilize provincial bodies to support its interests, ranging from electing deputies to appear before both the Parlement and the Estates on specific issues to directing the latter's commercial policy. In late March 1605, the community instructed its deputy at the sovereign court to continue to lobby the magistrates against registration.[43] The king sent a

Figure 1.2 Parlement of Brittany (Rennes). The Parlement of Brittany, along with the provincial Estates, defended the autonomy of the province and the customary rights of the fishermen-traders of Saint-Malo and other ports against all privileges and commissions granted, and regulations imposed, by the Crown.

lettre de jussion the following month. Although the Parlement ratified the commission in June, the accompanying caveat showed the effectiveness of the Malouins' actions: "without endorsement of the ban made in the said letters of 29 January [from the king], and that the traffic continues as in the past."[44] The registration was, in short, all but meaningless.

The outcome before the Breton Parlement underscores the limits to Henri IV's ability to support his loyal servant's enterprise. The long delay in recognizing the letters patent – and their partial registration – severely weakened their force. Neither de Mons nor his associates could expect redress in the event of infraction in any of these jurisdictions in 1604. Although the king issued commissions and edicts intended to apply throughout the kingdom, in practice their application varied. Henri IV could have forced the obstinate Parlement to register the commission in its entirety by convoking a *lit de justice*, a session of parlement over which the king presided to push through edicts that the court had refused and at which magistrates served merely as counsellors rather than judges. Both the *lit de justice* and the *lettre de jussion* were extraordinary expressions of the king's will, and as such, to be used sparingly.[45] Although the king was in a more stable and powerful position by the early 1600s than at the start of his reign, he did not wish to risk alienating the influential magistrates in these bodies unless it was absolutely necessary to assert his integrity as king. De Mons's commission for the colonization and exploitation of New France was not worth the conflict that such heavy-handedness would ignite. The firm reprimand of a *lettre de jussion* or, in the case of the Parlement of Rouen, the gentle reminder that the commission involved and mattered personally to the king, was as far as he was willing to go.[46] Henri IV's strategy throughout his reign was to negotiate, accommodate, and work with the parlements and other provincial and municipal institutions as much as possible in order to coax rather than force their loyalty.[47] If the protection of the interests and privileges of subjects in such Atlantic ports as Saint-Malo and Rouen motivated their provincial parlements in their criticism of de Mons's commission, it was also important to the king's own exercise of power.

Brittany's position at the forefront of opposition to royal commissions granting powers and privileges overseas was fuelled in part by a long-standing struggle over who controlled maritime affairs in the province. Throughout the sixteenth century, the Crown tried to incorporate the Breton Admiralty into the Admiralty of France without much success. Despite repeated royal declarations reaffirming the latter's authority in the northwestern province, efforts to establish a central Admiralty court in the capital city of Rennes foundered and provincial royal courts continued to mete out maritime justice. Breton governors claimed to have inherited Admiralty rights from the dukes of Brittany, a claim with some legitimacy as kings throughout the sixteenth century and into the seventeenth sporadically granted governors such rights in their commissions. For their part, provincial bodies consistently supported the governor of Brittany. The Estates opposed time and again the powers accorded the admiral of France in the province on the grounds that they violated the ancient rights of the duchy, which François I had promised to protect at the time of incorporation.[48]

One of the most protracted and public conflicts of the period erupted between Admiral Joyeuse and the Duc de Mercoeur in the 1580s. Although the two men reached an agreement concerning the division of Admiralty powers in 1585, it did not last. The arguments brought forth against Admiral Joyeuse before the Breton Parlement and Estates are instructive. At the same time as the sovereign court accepted the agreement between governor and admiral, it registered the opposition of Mercoeur's supporters, who asserted that the admiral would only give licences for travel to "a certain number of sailors, who would make the law for merchants."[49] The Estates argued that the admiral of France's authority would "pervert the authority of Messieurs your [the king's] Lieutenants general, the order and regulation of your justice, both ordinary and sovereign, of the said country, and would alter the freedom of commerce and the peace of the whole province, counter and with prejudice to the ancient exemptions, rights and liberties of your said country."[50]

All three objections to Joyeuse's letters patent – concerning commerce, justice, and the duchy's ancient rights – amounted to a protest against outside infringement on the province's privileges and jurisdiction. If the Estates' defence of the duchy's rights was perhaps the most predictable objection, one frequently wielded against royal legislation, it effectively recalled the king's obligations to the province. A chief concern raised before both provincial bodies about the admiral of France's powers was their effect on subjects' liberty of commerce. Similar to the community of Saint-Malo's objections to commissions to North America, opponents suggested that this constituted a break with custom and amounted to an unfair advantage for a few. Finally, Admiralty courts would diminish the authority of the king's own courts in the province. Although this is shrewdly portrayed as primarily the king's loss, provincial elites did not welcome the introduction of new courts outside of their control and with which they would have to compete for power, privileges, and jurisdiction. In the event, Mercoeur emerged victorious from this battle, obtaining a royal declaration that confirmed the governor's Admiralty powers in 1588. Royal efforts nevertheless continued to consolidate the admiral of France's authority in the province under Henri IV, with the Estates registering opposition to royal orders in 1600 and 1606.[51]

The strong echo of these arguments in the well-organized, vociferous response to de Mons's commission was part of an ongoing effort to fend off royal encroachment in the province begun a century earlier. De Mons's commission, as we have seen, threatened to restrict the activities of seasonal traders who had been fishing and fur trading annually over the previous decades. Royal regulation of this traffic confirmed provincial suspicions of the Crown's intention to take a more interventionist approach to maritime affairs. Perhaps more seriously still from the point of view of the Parlement and Estates, the lieutenant general's letters patent took disputes arising from de Mons's powers and privileges out of the province's control, reserving them to the Admiralty of Rouen and the royal council in Paris. In the context of the return of a more aggressive monarchical power and greater royal support for colonizing ventures since the Wars of Religion, these arguments took on new force and new stakes at the opening of the seventeenth century.

Outside of Brittany, even if the parlements eventually bowed to the king's will, local officials did their part to obstruct de Mons's enterprise. In the fall of 1604, following the return of the Compagnie de Mons's ships, the associates saw their merchandise confiscated by guards on two separate occasions in different provinces. In Normandy, "the so-called horse-mounted guard of taxes and tolls," François Buffé, seized a cargo of twenty-two bales of beaver skins belonging to de Mons and his associates at Condé-sur-Noireau.[52] He demanded the duty levied on merchandise from foreign countries. Yet the principle established by the king in 1603 was that, as a region under the French Crown's protection, New France should be treated as a province and its products therefore subjected to the same duty as between provinces.[53] The Crown upheld this designation in 1605, first by granting de Mons's request for the return of his furs and then by issuing a declaration to the Admiralty and customs officers of Normandy restating New France's status within the kingdom. It read in part, "we gave clearly to understand [in the letters patent of 1603] that the said countries were by us taken under our control, and that we held and proclaimed them as dependencies of our kingdom and Crown of France … We have declared and by these presents do declare, that all merchandise … brought by the said Monsieur de Mons and his partners from the said places into our kingdom … shall not pay other or any larger sums than the entrance dues, and those which are ordinarily paid upon merchandise passing from one of our provinces, of which it is the produce, into another."[54] Despite these royal orders, Buffé remained unmoved. It took another decree from the royal council at the end of March before the customs officer restored the furs to the association.[55]

By contrast, the second incident, which occurred several weeks before Buffé's seizure, took much less time to resolve, although its details are somewhat obscure. It appears that master furriers, acting in their capacity as *gardes jurés* of the fur trade in Paris, seized beaver and otter skins belonging to the Compagnie de Mons from a third-party residence. In response, Jean Ralluau, de Mons's secretary, went to Paris to obtain the restitution of the merchandise. The royal court at the Châtelet de Paris ordered that the guards proceed with the inspection of the skins, despite Ralluau's appeal. The sole extant document about the incident, a notarial act releasing the furs to Ralluau, records the meeting between Ralluau and the master furriers in their chambers. In exchange for his assurance that he had no intention of selling them, the guards inspected the furs and released them into the hands of the third party to be returned to Ralluau. While the latter paid the inspection fees to the guards, he protested them, along with the costs of his stay in Paris, other expenses, damages, and interest.[56]

These two seizures highlight the number of political and judicial jurisdictions and corporate interests involved in the execution of a royal decree or commission. To start with, furs were subject to each province's authority, complicating business for de Mons's multi-port association.[57] If confusion over the status of furs from Acadia might be expected during the company's first season, Buffé's willful disregard of two royal orders points to a deliberate obstruction of the enterprise. Just what motivated him remains unclear. He may have hoped to receive a cut of the money obtained from the foreign duties before handing over the equivalent of the domestic duties to the farmer general, or he may have been encouraged or bribed by interested Norman traders who wished to cause de Mons trouble. More obvious are the negative effects of the seizure on the privileged company. Considering the length of time it took to resolve the dispute, the furs would no longer have been in prime condition, making it doubtful that de Mons and his associates received much, if any, profit from them. Added to this loss was the time and money spent going to court. Apart from the material consequences for the company, the incident underscores the weakness of royal decrees in the face of officials determined to ignore them. It also reveals that, despite de Mons's close ties to Henri IV, the former was not so important as to have these problems resolved for him by the Crown.

Whereas the Norman affair was a question of ignoring royal instructions, the Paris seizure concerned corporate regulation. The guild of furriers oversaw all aspects of the city's fur industry, including the importation and distribution of furs, their treatment and sale, the fabrication of fur goods, as well as the training and accreditation of its members. Four elected guards, all master furriers, performed these duties. De Mons's company having failed to present their furs to the guild for inspection, the guards considered the merchandise to have been imported illegally. The associates may well have tried to avoid paying the duties demanded by the guild and to escape the latter's control over any sale or distribution. At the same time, the furriers took this opportunity to assert their power as a corporation and claim their jurisdiction against what could be considered a rival privilege-holder. It is perhaps notable that neither party decided to pursue further court action; the furriers had made their point and Ralluau, though threatening to pursue the furriers for expenses, acquiesced to the inspection and attendant fees. Regardless of the legality of each party's actions, the Compagnie de Mons found itself in conflict with the furriers on their own turf. Members of the Six-Corps des marchands de Paris, which grouped together the most prominent guilds and enjoyed certain exemptions, the furriers could readily draw upon support in both the municipal government and at court, where many of their clients lived.[58] The incidents in Paris and Normandy, along with the responses of the parlements, demonstrate that the execution of the king's orders fell on local and provincial officials who had their own corporate and personal interests and loyalties to defend. They also point to a more general pattern by which corporate bodies and individuals aimed to delay and inconvenience opponents rather than obtain a definitive victory.

The Policing of Privileges and Redress in France

When de Mons and his associates set out in the spring of 1604 on their first voyage under his commission, they probably expected fishermen and traders used to making the seasonal voyage to test their privileges. They would certainly have had no doubt of the powerful provincial and local bodies behind them. In the waterways and along the long, indented coastlines of Acadia (see figure 1.3), enforcement of the company's privileged trading zone was left up to the associates. The impracticability of regularly policing the coasts without any support from the Crown in the form of ships and men meant that catching interlopers was often a matter of chance.[59] While the Admiralty kept track of the comings and goings in the Atlantic ports and required all ships to have a licence, it was possible to deceive Admiralty officials or take advantage of licences.[60] More seriously, the continuation of the open fishery off what is now Newfoundland and Nova Scotia complicated the already-considerable task of patrolling the harbours inside the exclusive trading area. The presence of thousands of fishermen raised the likelihood that some interlopers might pass unnoticed, especially considering that many had established trading

Figure 1.3 Samuel de Champlain, eastern portion of the "Carte de la Nouvelle-France," *Les voyages du Sieur de Champlain*, 1632.

relationships with the Mi'kmaq and other Indigenous groups, who had come to expect a demand for furs – and the availability of desired European goods – at certain locations during the spring and summer months.[61] Certainly, Basques and Bretons claimed only to be fishing when intercepted by de Mons and his associates in Acadia. All told, at least eight vessels contravened the company's trading privileges in 1604, with the masters of four of these vessels – all from Saint-Jean-de-Luz – brought before de Mons.[62] By 1607, there were perhaps as many as eighty interlopers each season in the Saint Lawrence alone. As Champlain noted several times in his accounts, it was not easy to catch these ships, as they were often small, light, fast, and well-armed.[63] In short, it came down to a competition of force, speed, and aggression between company and interloper each time. François Gravé Du Pont, de Mons's stalwart company agent, was known to be a particularly aggressive trader and patroller of the coasts; ships from La Rochelle were especially adept at evading capture. If de Mons was determined to catch violators, the latter were just as determined to trade – sometimes openly – in defiance.[64]

Despite the protection afforded de Mons in his commission, his exclusive privileges were not upheld when he and his associates did manage to bring interlopers before the courts. In 1604, a company ship, the *Don de Dieu*, captained by Timothée Le Barbier, encountered a French ship, *La Levrette*, trading for furs near the LaHave River. Le Barbier and his men seized and escorted the ship, its captain, Jean Rossignol, and crew back to France at the end of the season to stand trial. When Rossignol and *La Levrette* returned to France with the company's ships, the owners of the seized ship went before the Admiralty of Rouen to effect its release along with its merchandise. The judge sent the parties to the royal council as per de Mons's commission, where the Sieur de Vic was put in charge of the case. As Vic's other affairs postponed the suit, de Mons and his associates and the ship's owners reached a compromise in April 1608. Rossignol dropped his suit requesting the release of his ship and merchandise. In return, the company allowed him and his partners to recover their ship and paid them 900 livres for the furs they had seized and sold. The associates, "moved by mercy and compassion," presented the 900 livres as a *don gratuit*, or free gift, "without creating a precedent [*sans tirer à conséquences*]," a clause designed to prevent the weakening of their position with regard to other interlopers. Both sides made a decision to cut their losses: Rossignol had at first denied any contravention of de Mons's privileges, claiming that he had gone to Florida as per his licence from the Admiralty; the company had initially treated *La Levrette* and its cargo as their own, as stipulated in de Mons's commission from the king.[65]

When cases did reach resolution before the royal council, the ban on trade was no more likely to be upheld than in private settlements. In January 1606, de Mons requested redress from the royal council for contravention of his privileges in 1605 by a ship captained by one Le Sueur: "that a certain ship ... be declared acquired and confiscated in the hands of him [de Mons] and his associates together with the merchandise on it if it is in kind if not the fair value, and in addition [the owners] condemned to the fine of thirty thousand livres for having violated the said bans and with all expenses, damages, and interest."[66] De Mons identified the owner of the ship as Hector Nourry, a merchant in Paris, under whom Michel Aulbin, a Rouennais merchant, had sent the ship to Acadia to trade. In response, Nourry claimed to have no part in the vessel and received permission from the council to summon Aulbin and Le Sueur before it to refute these charges against him. (It appears that Aulbin was the front man in the arrangement, acting "in the name of" Nourry.)[67] Like Rossignol before him, Le Sueur had received a licence from the Admiralty for a different destination, this time Cap de Nord, Peru. In a ruling at the end of June 1606, the council declared the parties "dismissed [*hors de cours et de procès*]," thereby rejecting de Mons's position, save his right to publish the edict banning trade in New France.[68] There is no indication that de Mons pursued Aulbin and Le Sueur any further.

The tendency of the royal council not to uphold the trading ban in Acadia suggests that it recognized that exclusive trading privileges to North America were unenforceable and politically unworkable. The Le Sueur and Rossignol cases both involved licences from the Admiralty for destinations at some distance from New France. While some captains may have been great deceivers, others took advantage of clientele connections within the institution. In Rossignol's case, he could count on powerful members of the Norman nobility in his quest to evade punishment. The other part owner of *La Levrette*, Antoine Bonnet, was the *maître d'hôtel* of the governor of Le Havre, Georges de Brancas, Marquis de Villars, who had been both a lieutenant general of the province and admiral of France.[69] Rather than a simple failure to enforce the terms of a commission, the royal council's unwillingness to impose the 30,000-livres fine – or even a quarter of that amount – may well have been a deliberate strategy to circumvent what appeared to be fixed and unambiguous privileges in order to accommodate both the material and political interests of the provincial constituencies upon which the king depended.[70] At the same time, the council's decision conveyed to other French traders that illegal activity could well be worth the risk: not only was it rather easy to evade capture, but it was also unlikely that the punishment would be great if they did end up before the courts. The multiple jurisdictions and institutions within which an interloper might seek support, together with the virtual impossibility of effectively patrolling the coastlines of Acadia, played a role in rendering exclusive trading privileges a near fiction.

The lack of enforcement of the protections contained in de Mons's commission raises the question of the attractiveness and value of privileges to the title-holder. Privileges conferred power and status. Guaranteed by law, they had both a symbolic dimension, by reinforcing social status, and a material one, in the form of tax exemptions or control of a particular industry, for example. Privileges thus helped order society hierarchically and redistribute resources. The ones that most readily come to mind are fiscal and political privileges connected to high status, such as exemptions from the *taille* granted the nobility and clergy. Closely associated with rent-seeking, such privileges were considered unproductive and exploitative, as they did not expand the economy and the fiscal burden fell on the Third Estate.[71]

Why did the king continue to grant exemptions and privileges to such bodies as provincial estates when he was perennially short of funds? Privileges had their uses and could even be productive: they secured loyalty and political co-operation, were a source of loans and other revenue, and developed the economy.[72] Economic privileges could stimulate the development of particular sectors or industries through the granting of a royal monopoly for a limited period – indeed, de Mons's commission had such a goal, among others. The ban on trade promulgated in December 1603 instructed him to establish the king's authority in Acadia so that "our subjects can henceforth be received, frequent and live there, [and] trade with the Natives."[73] By referring to a future context in which the privileges would no longer be necessary, the passage reveals the intent behind certain economic privileges: they were to be temporary. In this respect, de Mons's privileges were comparable to others conferred in France.

While the Crown undertook to protect the privileges it granted, it also considered them something that subjects had to pay for, often several times over. There is no record of the amount de Mons or his predecessors under Henri IV may have paid for the exclusive trading privileges to Acadia/New France. It is just possible that there was no payment and that they all received them in recognition of their military service during the Wars of Religion.[74] In return for the privileges and title of lieutenant general, de Mons assumed certain knowable costs, including the annual transportation of goods, provisions, and colonists, the salaries of sailors, agents like Gravé Du Pont, and his second-in-command, Champlain, the rental or purchase of ships, and some anticipated legal costs. As the interloping cases of 1604–06 demonstrate, the cost of privileges included substantial unknown expenses, notably the buying out of interlopers and competitors. Henri IV may have considered these extra costs just payment for privileges granted, but for de Mons, they decreased their material and symbolic value. The lieutenant general and his associates suffered significant financial losses due to the settlements and de Mons's title and authority diminished because of the evident absence of Crown protection.

Why did de Mons and Champlain continue their enterprise in the following years, and despite even greater obstacles, as we will see below? For an enterprise that was theoretically to last ten years, these were early days during which de Mons and his associates were finding their footing. Along with the lieutenant general, Champlain soon emerged as a leader of what was a multi-faceted venture, one not limited to commerce. He, like his superior, was a loyal servant to the king and had received considerable favour from Henri IV. Since 1601, he had collected a royal pension and, in addition to his roles as map-maker and explorer, furnished reports to the king about his expeditions in North America, outlining discoveries made and future possibilities. Both Champlain and de Mons shared Henri IV's ambition to create a firm French foothold in North America, establish a prosperous and populous settlement, and cultivate the surrounding area. Further, the extensive nature of de Mons's powers and obligations outlined in the commission encouraged a long-term view. If the value of the trading privileges had diminished in 1606, de Mons and his associates nevertheless still considered their benefits – perhaps most notably prestige, glory, and proximity to the king – to outweigh the (unexpectedly high) transaction costs.

Measuring the Value of Competing Privileges

The period 1606 to 1609 saw a number of shifts in the regulation of French activity in North America that reveal the several factors contributing to the nature and durability of privileges. In 1607, Henri IV revoked de Mons's privileges after only four years. A year later, he renewed them for one year, before opening commerce in Acadia to all subjects in 1609. Several catalysts, both domestic and international, prompted these changes in approach. The early seventeenth century saw growing Dutch interest in North America, particularly in the fur trade of the Saint Lawrence. In 1606, a company established in Amsterdam prepared a ship, the *Lion Blanc*, for a trading and pirating voyage. The ship attacked two of de Mons's ships, the *Jonas* and the *Grégoire*, that summer, stealing their merchandise, cannons, and munitions.[75] This aggression prompted Henri IV to send a request through his ambassador to the States General of the Netherlands to "forbid those of your country and under your obedience from trafficking any longer in the river of the said Canada." Although the Dutch government did intervene in the dispute over the goods seized by the *Lion Blanc*, it refused to limit its merchants' movements or their "commercial liberty" in North America.[76] De Mons and his associates recovered the value of the seized cannons and munitions, but it is doubtful that they recouped their losses, given the number and length of suits launched as a result of the dispute.[77]

Domestic calls for "commercial liberty" had, for their part, not only continued but grown more vociferous in response to the Compagnie de Mons's own actions. Petitions to the king came from several quarters. Basque and Breton fishermen resented the aggressive patrolling of coasts by company associates and captains of ships engaged on their behalf.[78] Outside traders pointed to the declining numbers of settlers sent over in an effort to undermine de Mons's position. Supported by influential furriers, Parisian hatters complained of the higher prices they had to pay for furs. Together, these "clamours" culminated in the revocation of de Mons's privileges in July 1607.[79] The reason cited was "the permission accorded the Sieur de Mont [*sic*] to withhold beaver skins by which means merchants are forced to buy them from him." De Mons's was not the only commission revoked on this occasion. While they covered a wide variety of areas, ranging from the sale of "unclaimed and uncultivated lands" to "the levy of monies made by communities without a commission from His Majesty," they all focused on fiscal and economic matters that had prompted complaints from subjects who protested that they were "extremely burdened" by these impositions.[80]

Undeterred by this most recent setback – arguably the most serious to date – de Mons lobbied at court for an extension. The return of Jean de Biencourt de Poutrincourt, lieutenant of the habitation in 1606–07, and the rest of the settlers in the fall of 1607 with samples of grain grown in Acadia seemed to have the desired effect on the king. At the beginning of January 1608, "on the advice that has been given to us by those who have come from new France, of the goodness and fertility of the land of the said country," Henri IV renewed de Mons's privileges in order to "continue the habitation that had been previously begun in the said country, so that our subjects can go there to traffic freely."[81] This commission was, in effect, a continuation of that of 1603, with the same goals and justification.

If the king had hoped to silence critics with a renewal for one year only, this strategy proved a dismal failure. Indeed, according to Champlain, "the cry began louder than before that the Council must be appealed to" against the year-long privileges. Protest came from the same constituencies as in 1607, particularly from Basque, Breton, and Norman fishermen and merchants, many of whom were well represented at court. Beginning in the fall of 1608, various communities, including Saint-Malo and the Basque ports of Bayonne, Saint-Jean-de-Luz, Ciboure, and Urrugne, submitted petitions to the king in favour of liberty of commerce in New France. Some argued that this was "a national matter, an advantage to be shared by the people at large."[82] Others, like the Malouins, focused on local conditions, lamenting that trade "has been completely destroyed in the said city" as a result of de Mons's privileges. Like the Malouins' request to the king, de Mons's response predicted the dire consequences if his opposing request was not met: "he had incurred great expenses, losses, and adverse effects, which would cause his ruin if the said privilege were diminished, because in the first years he did nothing but spend and make commitments without any profit." De Mons accordingly asked for the continuation of his exclusive privileges "unless the said inhabitants of Sainct-Malo [*sic*] should be better disposed to reimburse him for the said above expense.[83]

In the event, Henri IV chose to implement the latter option. From 1609 onward, trade with New France was open to all French subjects; in return, "this community [of inhabitants of Saint-Malo] [will] pay to monsieur Dumont for a portion of the expenses he made in Canada, the sum of six or ten thousand livres." The community of Saint-Malo brusquely riposted that "this community will not submit itself to pay the said six or ten thousand livres … but if any individuals of this community who traffic to Canada want to submit themselves to pay … if they choose to [they] will do so without the general body of this community entering into the said obligation."[84] Lacking the power to force the community to comply, the royal council devised another method by which de Mons would receive payment. This time, the king ordered "the said inhabitants of Saint-Malo, Bayonne, villages and parishes above mentioned, and other subjects of His said Majesty trafficking to the said places" to pay de Mons 6,000 livres, which was to be divided among them by the Admiralties of Saint-Malo and Bayonne according to each ship's tonnage.[85]

The evolving terms of French commerce in North America were in part shaped by geopolitical changes in Europe during this period. While Henri IV was willing to protest Dutch aggression against the Compagnie de Mons's ships in 1606, he stopped short of pressing the issue of Dutch navigation in the Saint Lawrence River. The French king needed Dutch support in his ongoing campaign to decrease Spanish power on the Continent and overseas. Having declared their independence from Spain in 1581, the seven United Provinces of the Netherlands were still at war with their former Catholic rulers in the first decade of the seventeenth century. For France's own interests, Henri IV was anxious for the nascent republic not to capitulate until better terms were available. This diplomatic situation may have also contributed to his decision to revoke de Mons's privileges a year later.[86] By the beginning of 1608, however, international circumstances had changed considerably. In November 1607, the Netherlands entered treaty negotiations with Spain, which ultimately led to the Twelve Years' Truce two years later. Henri IV was now no longer reluctant to risk provoking the Dutch overseas. To the contrary, the activities of France's rivals in the Americas made the need for continued French presence all the more urgent. The English had established Jamestown in 1607 and, more troubling still, had built Fort George on the Kennebec River (in present-day Maine), a move that infringed on de Mons's own commission. One year later, the Dutch founded a company of the Indies, whose jurisdiction also overlapped with that of the lieutenant general.[87] If this latter initiative did not in fact come into being until after the Twelve Years' Truce, the competition in these years from both countries strengthened Henri IV's determination to develop a strong and lasting French settlement in North America.

Alongside international concerns, domestic economic interests carried considerable weight within Henri IV's government. The hatters' protest was all the more powerful with the support of the furriers. As a member of the Six-Corps, the latter were an important guild to have on one's side in any cause; they possessed substantial resources, several of their members held posts in the municipal government, and some had royal titles such as *valet de chambre du roi*.[88] Their seizure of the Compagnie de Mons's furs three years earlier further suggests that they had their own reasons for supporting the hatters' petition. Intermediaries between external suppliers of furs and members of the city's fur-related trades, they controlled imports and exports. The most powerful and successful master furriers were wholesalers, who spent little of their time actually treating furs. For example,

Mathieu Duisterlo, one of the signatories and a long-time fur merchant from Cologne who had established himself in Paris at the beginning of the century, procured high-quality furs from northern and eastern Europe through his international connections.[89] De Mons's commission risked undermining the furriers' role as gatekeepers of the Parisian fur industry. It is worth noting that Duisterlo would himself become a member of the privileged trading company to New France in the following decade.[90]

At court, the furriers and hatters found a sympathetic ear in the superintendent of finances, Maximilien de Béthune, Duc de Sully. Indeed, both de Mons and Champlain later held him responsible for the loss of privileges, the latter going so far as to imply that he had accepted bribes in return.[91] Sully had spent the previous decade introducing measures to revitalize royal finances and the economy in the wake of the Wars of Religion, including the creation of the *paulette*, an annual tax on offices that in return became hereditary. A Protestant in favour of attacking Spain's colonies, Sully was against the French investing in their own colonial enterprises.[92] He considered France's interests to be best served by prioritizing domestic and continental matters. While he and the king differed on this point, the number of positions Sully occupied, ranging from master of artillery to superintendent of public works and minister of transport, attests to his influence on Henri IV's policies.[93] Sully's approach, then, as superintendent of finances converged with the interests of the hatters and furriers. Known for eliminating opportunities for personal gain within the fiscal and economic system, he may also have been moved by the implication that de Mons had deliberately withheld furs to increase prices. This charge went beyond the usual complaint that the privileges deprived others of a customary commerce to suggest that they were iniquitous, a quality that came to be associated with "monopoly" when the term emerged later in the century.[94]

The king's reaction to the pressures brought to bear internationally and domestically and the response of various subjects to the resulting shifts in the regulation of French traffic to North America shed light on contemporary approaches to privilege and liberty.[95] On first reading, the community of Saint-Malo's plea for freedom of traffic and refusal of the king's offer in 1609 may appear contradictory. On the one hand, exclusive trading privileges in North America would do nothing less than ruin the port's commerce, while on the other, that commerce was not important enough to rescue at the king's price.[96] If the rhetoric of imminent catastrophe was not exclusive to Saint-Malo's mercantile community, its refusal to pay de Mons compensation in return for opening up transatlantic trade is revealing. This decision, together with the Malouins' rejection of the extension of Chauvin's privileges to them in exchange for contributing to colonization six years earlier, demonstrates that the community was against any privileges or liberties that imposed a condition. Saint-Malo was not categorically against privileges; indeed, it enjoyed many, including its status as a free port. Like other ports, it supported free trade when it caused the revocation of others' privileges and opposed it when privileges benefited them.[97] This elastic approach to privileges is also visible in a request made by the communauté d'habitants of Saint-Jean-de-Luz, which had received permission from François I in 1539 to travel and trade to the area that became New France. Having obtained confirmation of its privileges at the accession of each new monarch to the throne until Henri IV's reign, the port's community appeared before the royal council in the 1620s to request permission to travel to New France without a passport from the privileged trading company, a successor of the Compagnie de Mons. The community was, in short, asking for an exemption from the company's privileges. While the royal council ultimately refused this request, both examples show that communities and other holders of privileges and liberties played an active role in shaping their parameters.[98] They saw neither privilege nor liberty as absolute concepts. Instead, these were always subject to negotiation, something contemporaries understood very well.

In confirming privilege or granting liberty, the king had to weigh the relative value and importance of competing privileges and corporate groups. This situation reveals the dissonance between the king's princely role as arbiter of the competing claims of his subjects and the horse-trading he engaged in to win the much-needed loyalty of various constituencies. As we have seen, the exclusive privileges accorded de Mons had the ultimate objective of expanding commercial opportunities for all French subjects. His commission also served a geopolitical purpose by challenging Spanish hegemony, countering English and Dutch claims in North America, expanding French dominion, and spreading Christianity. In 1607 and 1609, these were, however, still incomplete and aspirational goals.

Vocal opposition from Breton, Basque, and Norman fishermen and traders, Parisian furriers and hatters, provincial parlements, and the Estates of Brittany raised the question of whether these privileges came at too high a price, politically and fiscally. De Mons's lieutenant generalship and company were not a great source of royal revenue, nor, given the financial burdens of the enterprise, were they likely to become significant lenders to the king in the near future. Politically, champions of colonizing ventures were in the minority; in the royal council, these were limited to Henri IV and Pierre Jeannin, the president of the Parlement of Paris. By contrast, powerful and well-connected corporate groups such as the guild of furriers, the Breton Estates and Parlement, and the community of Saint-Malo constituted indispensable sources of both political and financial support to the Crown. In the early seventeenth century, the Parlement of Brittany expanded in size and worked closely with the Estates to defend the interests and privileges of the province. The Estates, for its part, consolidated its position as a crucial furnisher of funds to the king through the levy of a wine tax. In return, the king directed the bulk of the revenue to the provincial and local elite.[99] As a staunchly Catholic town, Saint-Malo was a constituency Henri IV needed to win over to strengthen his legitimacy as king in post–Wars of Religion France. The symbolic and monetary value of these corporate groups' support eclipsed the actual and potential worth of de Mons's exclusive trading privileges. The value of privileges was thus in constant flux, judged according to the benefits – either financial or political – they had recently brought the king.

The domestic and overseas contexts in which exclusive privileges were granted in North America rendered them distinct from those in France. Specific to a locale or a region, economic privileges in the kingdom were spatially delineated. The ubiquity of guilds and seigneuries in town and countryside created a patchwork of legal rights throughout the country, a situation that contributed to the fragmentation of the economy. Under these circumstances, one way to stimulate development was to grant further privileges or liberties. Manufacturers, for example, might be encouraged to innovate through permission to bypass guild regulations, or merchants might receive the privilege to engage in a particular commerce.[100] De Mons's privileges in Acadia were also spatially delimited – from the fortieth to forty-sixth parallel. On both sides of the Atlantic, these privileges or exemptions were open to negotiation and contestation. In these respects, de Mons's commission reflects the application of traditional methods of the culture of privilege to a new trade in a new space.

The effects of such contestation and negotiation on the transatlantic enterprise were, however, more exaggerated than in France because de Mons's privileges involved a particularly large, geographically dispersed, and varied set of interests and constituencies. Subjects were banned from travelling to the privileged zone to trade without de Mons's permission, but the open fishery created a form of exception to such restrictions on travel. Both of these elements escalated costs beyond those incurred in the exercise of privileges in France, notably those of policing, building infrastructure, and legal action. Domestically, de Mons's privileges affected occupations and interests in several regions, ranging from Saint-Jean-de-Luz to Saint-Malo to Paris. Transcending a particular region, they fit uncomfortably within the kingdom's fragmented economic structure.

If the 1608 renewal of privileges and the 1609 declaration of open trade show an attempt to balance a variety of interests – the king's, de Mons's, and those of independent traders, fishermen, and artisans – the loser each time was the title-holder. Despite the loss of his privileges in 1609, de Mons remained lieutenant general of Acadia; in the eyes of the king, then, trading privileges and the lieutenant generalship were not inextricably linked. De Mons theoretically retained considerable powers. In practical terms, however, the commission meant little without exclusive trade. Not only did de Mons and his associates no longer have a source of funds theoretically free from outside competition, they also lacked any incentive to fulfill their heavy obligations and had little foundation on which to rest the authority conferred in the 1603 commission. Indeed, de Mons would lose his two remaining associates, the Rouennais merchants Pierre Caulier and Lucas Legendre, in 1611 because of the absence of "a commission that can stop everyone from going to our new discoveries to trade with the inhabitants of the country."[101] In the absence of any formal institutional structure, de Mons's governmental role from 1604 to 1608 depended to a large extent on his ability to exercise his trading privileges and resulting powers – notably, patrolling the coasts, seizing interloping ships, and prosecuting their owners and captains before French courts. The frequent reconfiguration of the regulations governing activity in New France from 1606 to 1609 further damaged an authority already weakened by the lack of royal enforcement of the fine stipulated in de Mons's commission.

De Mons's response to the royal decisions of 1608–09 demonstrates that he, no more than the community of Saint-Malo or the king himself, considered privileges to be absolute. At the end of the 1608 season, de Mons attempted to have his commission renewed once more.[102] He presumably hoped that the foundation of Quebec that summer, a site more easily defensible than the shores of Acadia and close to high-quality fur sources, would convince the king. As we have seen, the king opted instead to open trade to all subjects in return for compensation to de Mons from the community of Saint-Malo. At the same time that de Mons lobbied to receive this payment, he suggested alternative forms of compensation that show an attempt to compromise with the traders who demanded unrestricted traffic. His subsequent proposals divided the area accorded in his lieutenant general's commission into privileged and open trading zones. Sometime before the king's second decree ordering all traders who had travelled to New France in 1609 to pay de Mons, the latter submitted a second request in which he proposed that trade along the coast of Acadia, in the Baie Sainte-Claire, and in the entrance to the Saint Lawrence River be free while he would enjoy exclusive trade in the region from Tadoussac to the Quebec habitation for ten years. Three years later, he suggested more circumscribed privileges, applying to Quebec and "up the Saint Lawrence River, to which places no vessels go," for a duration of three years. His final proposal – submitted sometime between October 1612 and the same month a year later – focused once more on Tadoussac, again for three years.[103]

De Mons employed here the principle of commerce in return for discovery: he requested "the trade of new discoveries, that we have made, where no one has before traded." In fact, this principle had earlier been accepted by the Crown, appearing in royal commissions such as Noel and La Jannaye's in 1588.[104] The lieutenant general may also have been drawing on the precedent, set by Chauvin's commission, of granting exclusive privileges only in the Saint Lawrence River. Although de Mons was unsuccessful in this bid, his successor as lieutenant general – following the former's resignation in 1612 – received exclusive trading privileges in the circumscribed zone requested by de Mons, suggesting a receptivity on the part of the Crown to such logic. Indeed, these proposals represent an effort to give the king the space to accord de Mons compensatory privileges while simultaneously lowering the political cost of exclusive privileges for the Crown.

De Mons: Sole Holder of Exclusive Privileges?

Even if de Mons had obtained consistent royal support for his trading privileges, they were never exclusive in practice. The Compagnie de Mons's associates numbered about nine, but the enterprise's operations depended on many more individuals.[105] For example, the preparations for and financing of each voyage required outside help from *avitailleurs*, or outfitters, shipowners, captains, other merchants, and lenders. Both Rouennais vessels in 1604 were owned by several outside individuals, each with one or more shares. The precise terms of recompense in these cases are unknown, but it was common for owners to receive a share of the return cargo.[106] In 1607, the captain of the *Jonas* received forty-two livres for outfitting. The Rochelais merchant who had lent him the money was to receive in return half of the profits at season's end, while the ship's captain was himself to receive a share of the returns as payment.[107] Besides renting ships and hiring crews, de Mons and his associates contracted loans, such as one of three hundred livres at a rate of 25 per cent that Gravé Du Pont received to outfit the Rouennais ship under his command in 1604. The terms of the loan were "at the peril and fortune of the sea and other accidents that can happen on the said ship." Typical of the period, these loans, called *prêts à la grosse aventure*, stipulated that the lender could make no claim to the principal or the interest if the vessel were shipwrecked or attacked by pirates.[108] Like the Compagnie de Mons itself, this sort of loan helped to further spread the risks of overseas enterprise.

Apart from contracting with a variety of individuals in preparation for each season's voyage, de Mons delegated a part of his privileges to others on a temporary basis. In July 1606, he issued a licence to two pilots, Benzamin and du Bois, "to trade and negotiate with the said Natives from the fortieth degree to the forty-second and a half of latitude."[109] Nothing is known about these men, but they were probably in de Mons's service as pilots. The following year, Champlain, Ralluau, François Edenon, Pierre de Champdon, and others acquired "permission … from the said Sieur de Mons" to engage in the fur trade for the season. Upon arrival in France, Georges and Ribertière, the Malouins' representative, seized the furs and merchandise belonging to Champlain and his partners. The parties ended up before a notary to settle the matter.[110]

The dispute over de Mons's delegation of privileges to a third party underscores the complex relationship between his position as lieutenant general of Acadia and as active participant in the company bearing his name. In the history of New France enterprises, de Mons was in the unique position of having both of these roles, and his actions demonstrate that he maintained a distinction between them. Considering himself the principal privilege-holder, he had not subdelegated his trading privileges to the company in their entirety. He claimed the prerogative throughout his tenure to share his privileges as he wished. Needless to say, his associates did not share his perspective. If Georges appears to have been playing a game of deception by tricking Ralluau into thinking he had Champlain's authority for the seizure, Ribertière's actions suggest that the other associates were unhappy with de Mons's sharing of the privileges and wanted to create difficulties, if not for him, then for those to whom he had accorded trading rights. De Mons was, after all, a fairly equal partner in the enterprise, holding less than one-fifth of the shares before 1606 and one-fifth thereafter, following a change in membership.[111] He held, then, roughly the equivalent number as Georges and Macain. Even if de Mons only favoured those in his employ, delegation increased competition for furs and diluted the associates' profits. It was, however, advantageous to him as lieutenant general. Similar to the powers of policing and seizure, the power to dispense favours in the form of privileges for a season was a means to exercise and consolidate his authority. De Mons's approach to privileges resembled, to a degree, that of the king: privileges were rights that could be extended to others. The elasticity of privileges could in fact benefit the title-holder when he had control over their configuration.

The relationships that de Mons's new 1608 association formed, not only with independent traders and suppliers but also with his former associates, underscore the various degrees of engagement in the enterprise by non-members. That year saw the establishment of a small partnership involving de Mons and fellow Rouennais Pierre Caulier and Lucas Legendre; the lieutenant general also retained his loyal lieutenant of Saint-Malo, Gravé Du Pont. Both Caulier and Legendre were from well-established Protestant commercial families who had left Rouen while it was under the control of the Catholic League but had returned at the end of the sixteenth century. Caulier's family was engaged in the fishery as well as international trading networks. Legendre, his brother-in-law, had experience in the fur trade and had, in fact, partnered with Gravé Du Pont in an illegal trading expedition to Tadoussac in 1607. According to the extant sources, neither Caulier nor Legendre appear to have been members of the Compagnie de Mons.[112] De Mons's decision to limit his association to these merchants was probably a result of the short duration of the privileges. With the partners together in one port, they could more easily meet, and de Mons could keep closer track of their affairs. Given the small size of their association, they needed the help of other merchants and ships. After all, their own ships were transporting colonists in addition to merchandise for the fur trade, which meant that any returns from the latter would likely be used to meet expenses. They relied on other ships to transport a portion of the merchandise needed in exchange for a sum or the extension of their privileges. At least twenty vessels sailed to the Saint Lawrence or Acadia that year, some or all of which may have had an arrangement with de Mons and his consorts.[113] In drawing on the resources of the mercantile and maritime communities in one or more French ports, the association's voyages functioned much like the far more numerous annual fishing expeditions.

If the Malouin and Rochelais traders of the former Compagnie de Mons chose not to associate with the lieutenant general this time around, they did enter contracts for discrete business transactions with him and his partners, both of which ended in dispute.[114] Less than a week after the king granted the renewal of de Mons's privileges, Georges and Macain protested against it before the Admiralty of La Rochelle; rejecting their plea, the judge registered the commission. Having already planned to send a ship from the southern French port of Saint Vincent under Georges's relative, Pierre Georges, the savvy merchants accepted a proposition from de Mons, Caulier, and Legendre by which they would send their Basque vessel to Tadoussac with "merchandise … to trade with the said Natives"; upon arrival, the merchandise would be turned over to Gravé Du Pont. Caulier received a *lettre de change*, or bill of exchange, for 5,680 livres 15 sols from Georges in June for the value of the merchandise. In August, he paid the Rochelais merchant 2,400 livres. In the meantime, however, problems had arisen in New France over the merchandise and de Mons's privileges.[115] When the Basque vessel arrived at Tadoussac, Captain Pierre Georges and Master Martin Dareche refused to give the merchandise to Gravé Du Pont. Further, the heavily armed ship openly flouted de Mons's privileges: "they ceased not from forcibly carrying on barter." When Gravé Du Pont warned them of the consequences, the interlopers fired on his ship, killing one crew member and wounding several others, including Gravé Du Pont himself, before seizing the vessel's cannons and munitions.[116]

Back in France, the dispute over the contract became intertwined with charges of illegal trading and depredations to the association's ships. Georges summoned Caulier to pay the outstanding sum for the merchandise, threatening to call him before the judges and consuls of Rouen if he did not. That same day in October, de Mons and his associates successfully requested a writ by which Georges was required to appear before the Admiralty of Rouen to answer charges of interloping. The parties appeared before multiple jurisdictions until 1611, when the royal council sent the dispute to the *maîtres des requêtes* (members of the king's household who held court at the Palais de Justice) in Paris. A ruling of 2 June 1612 "absolve[d] the said de Mont [*sic*] and consorts" of responsibility to pay for the merchandise and required Georges and Macain to pay damages for the losses that the association had suffered that season. While the judges gave Macain and Georges the option of entering retroactively into the 1608 association for the same share as they had had in the first company, a private agreement made between the parties in September 1613 suggests that they chose to pay the damages. By the time of the ruling, the association had already been dissolved for about a year.[117]

The Basques' open challenge to his privileges and the protracted dispute in court may have influenced de Mons's response to difficulties with his former Malouin associates that same year. As with the Rochelais, he and his associates entered a contract with Ribertière, Goret, Sere, Martin, and Sarcel, by which the latter outfitted two ships to Canso and Gaspé for fishing and "the fur trade and traffic." De Mons, Caulier, and Legendre were to receive one-quarter of the profits in return. In mid-October, however, de Mons issued a procuration to "have summoned before the said Sieurs of the Admiralty of France at the seat of the Table de marbre du pallais at Rouen [the Malouins] … for the contravention by them made of the ban." De Mons subsequently launched several suits against Ribertière and his associates. It was not until the end of December that the two parties reached an agreement before a notary, in which the lieutenant general recognized their having traded with his "good pleasure, authority, and honourable permission." De Mons received his quarter share in one vessel's cargo and sold his share in the second to the Malouins for 1,050 livres.[118]

The disputes of 1608 demonstrate the range of strategies employed for maximizing revenue in the context of the royal regulation of traffic to New France. At different points during the year, Georges and Macain were variously protesters against de Mons's privileges, a contracting party with the association, and openly illegal traders. As former associates of de Mons, they had themselves been privilege-holders and, as such, party to various arrangements within the company, including contracting to buy furs from the Rouennais associates in advance. Their status as partners had not stopped disputes arising over the sharing of returns from voyages in the past. In the fall of 1607, as the company wrapped up its business following the last season of trading, de Mons launched suits against both the Rochelais and the Malouins because he had not received his portion of the furs traded, the remaining merchandise, and other assets brought back from the habitation. While there may have been some confusion around the arrangements for the 1607 voyage, given the company's somewhat uncertain status that year, it is just as likely that the Rochelais and Malouins were attempting to increase their own returns and hoping that de Mons would not notice.[119]

These various relationships between de Mons and his sometime partners underscore that there was not a simple line between inclusion and exclusion or privilege and liberty – rather, there were several configurations within each. In 1608, for example, the Malouins benefited from de Mons's privileges as outside traders. They may also have taken advantage of that permission to trade on their own account. Indeed, one of the most effective ways to contravene privileges was to play a direct role in their exploitation.[120] The Basques' openly illegal trading and violent reaction to challenge, for their part, foregrounded the disadvantageous position of de Mons and his associates in these contractual agreements. Dependent on both outside parties for the success of their own enterprise, they nevertheless exercised no control over them. As we have seen, it was relatively easy for other French ships to trade for furs if they were determined to do so. This was perhaps never truer than in 1608, when de Mons's association shifted its attention to the Saint Lawrence and established the habitation at Quebec. Although the new site provided better defence against foreigners and interlopers and access to richer furs, it also left the large expanse of Acadia with little surveillance.[121] If some traders took their chances on their own, the Rochelais and Malouins played on the fluidity of the lines between inclusion and exclusion by associating with de Mons and his partners.

Whether to protest, seek redress from interlopers, call fellow associates to account, or dispute a contract, courts of justice lay at the heart of the strategies of Georges and Macain, on the one hand, and de Mons, on the other. Over the course of their 1608 dispute, the Rochelais sought support from a variety of jurisdictions, including the Admiralty of La Rochelle, the consuls of Rouen, and the royal council, among others. For de Mons, the best defence seemed to be a good offence. Anticipating the presence of illegal traders, he had already appointed Legendre as his *procureur* the previous winter to pursue interlopers in court.[122] Although the Malouins may have been trading on their own account, de Mons may also have decided to pursue them aggressively, after failing to receive his share of the profits. Previous experience had, however, amply demonstrated to de

Mons that recourse to the French justice system itself carried considerable risk. In this case, his adversaries were as well acquainted with the intricacies of legal procedure as he was himself, which in practice meant long suits involving a number of jurisdictions. That de Mons had to pursue these two cases simultaneously probably encouraged him to settle with the Malouins out of court.[123] By all accounts, the suit against Georges and Macain appears to have been the most contentious. The drain on the company's resources to fight such disputes was just as damaging, if not more so, than the illegal trading itself. While estimates vary as to how much de Mons, Caulier, and Legendre made from the fur trade in 1608, given the illegal trading and the ensuing suits, it seems unlikely that they recovered their costs.[124]

Recourse to courts of justice was but one strategy in the jockeying that royal commissions granting trade and authority in New France precipitated among rival interests. It is tempting to see such jockeying – as many historians have – as evidence of the Crown's failure to uphold privileges granted, to enforce a fine, or to honour the terms of a commission. Yet this is to misunderstand the logics at work here. The evolution in the terms of de Mons's commission both on paper and in practice over the first decade of the seventeenth century demonstrates that privileges were a starting point for negotiation rather than a definite set of rules to govern French trading and colonizing activities in North America. Contemporaries *expected* them to be unstable. A large and diverse number of constituencies drew on existing metropolitan forms of privilege in order to make claims to what was a relatively new trade in a new space. Backed by the Breton Estates and Parlement, the communauté d'habitants of Saint-Malo portrayed the seasonal voyages undertaken by its fishermen and traders as a customary right. Henri IV, for his part, granted exclusive fur trading privileges to de Mons as a temporary measure, one which, like other commercial privileges, was intended to help develop a nascent trade. If New France was a distant and new space for the French, overseas expansion was nevertheless a domestic and dynastic issue. Corporate bodies as diverse as furriers, provincial customs officers, commercial ports, and parlements, the king and his officers, and independent and privileged traders collaborated and collided to shape the parameters of privilege intended to incentivize and regulate colonizing and commercial ventures to New France. The inability of any one constituency to maintain claims for long led to a constant reworking, highlighting the elasticity of privilege. Following the loss of his privileges in 1609, de Mons's various proposals for an exclusive circumscribed trading zone attest to the balancing of interests that was at the core of the culture of privilege. The search for a politically and commercially workable configuration of privileges and powers would continue in the following decade, shaped at once by the previous experiences of all involved and a transformed political climate.

2

Disputing New France

The early 1610s were fraught with uncertainty in the French Atlantic. On 14 May 1610, Catholic zealot and unemployed schoolteacher François Ravaillac fatally stabbed King Henri IV while the lightly armed royal coach was stopped in traffic on a busy Paris thoroughfare. That such an attempt was made did not in itself elicit surprise; it followed at least twenty-three other plots against the king's life over the previous two decades. But its success brought into reality the fear that had hung over France since Henri had ascended the throne in 1589. Would the country descend back into the civil war that had engulfed it for most of the second half of the sixteenth century? Religious conciliator and convert to Catholicism, the slain king left behind a sickly eight-year-old boy, Louis, to succeed him. Until he reached the age of majority, Louis's mother, the devout Catholic Marie de Médicis, would rule in his stead as queen regent. This situation had, in the eyes of contemporaries, alarming parallels with the minority of another boy king, Charles IX, a half century earlier, a reign that had begun during the Wars of Religion: an Italian regent, a restless prince of the blood in the wings.[1] History did not in fact repeat itself in 1610. But the stability and order achieved over the previous decade had been badly shaken and, with an uncompromising Catholic at the head of government, the fate of the uneasy entente between Protestants and Catholics was once more in question.

De Mons and Champlain watched the unfolding events anxiously. As they were both long-time supporters of the king, the dreadful news no doubt came as a blow.[2] De Mons, the first to receive it, had likely just returned to the royal court from Rouen, having secured loans and conferred with his partners about the coming season's trade. If he had been left on his own to resolve the matter of compensation for his lost trading privileges in 1609, de Mons nevertheless owed both of his current positions – as gentleman in ordinary of the king's chamber and lieutenant general of Acadia – to Henri IV. As a Protestant, de Mons was likely to see his prospects diminish under the staunchly Catholic queen regent. Across the Atlantic, at the small wooden habitation of Quebec, Champlain's mind was no doubt occupied with the repairs to be done over the summer months when a ship arrived from France bringing word of the king's assassination. He had, as de Mons's indefatigable lieutenant, chosen the site of the current habitation two years before and served as its commander. With news of the king's death, Champlain prepared to return to France to confer with the lieutenant general. For both men, the loss of a principal patron meant that not only their personal fortunes but those of their enterprise more generally faced an uncertain future.

Even without the threat of full-on civil war, regencies were by definition unstable periods. Changes at the very top of the social and political hierarchy precipitated reversals in the political fortunes of those at court and in provincial circles, as different projects and people gained favour. Much as he had feared, de Mons lost his position of gentleman of the king's chamber shortly after Henri IV's death; Champlain, for his part, had his royal pension rescinded. Both losses severely curtailed their access to the royal inner circle. At the same time, the very precariousness of a child king on the throne encouraged manoeuvring and outright challenge on the part of the nobility. With the Crown preoccupied with placating restless princes and great nobles, a regency represented more broadly a moment of negotiation, of which provincial and local corporate bodies and individual subjects were quick to take advantage.

This chapter takes a series of disputes over powers and privileges in New France in the 1610s – some a direct result of the regency, others only tangentially related – to explore the ways in which French subjects used conflict to advance their own interests. The strategies subjects adopted to engender, continue, and resolve disputes and to build support through institutional and personal channels reveal the role of conflict in the making of the state at home and the construction of sovereignty overseas.

Law and legal institutions pervaded daily life in early modern France. At a basic level, law provided a structure and set of rules through statutes and courts of justice. These latter were among "the most highly developed governmental institutions," the main forum through which subjects came into contact with the French state.[3] A civil suit unfolded in a series of stages. Once a plaintiff appeared before a local or intermediate court, the judge requested the appearance of procureurs by each party, followed by a presentation of supporting documents on both sides. While the judge could render his decision immediately, he more commonly named a *rapporteur* to examine the dossier, interrogate witnesses, and report back to the court. Each time new documents were presented to the court by either party, a bailiff advised the opposing party. The defendant could challenge any part of the plaintiff's claim. After the court made its decision, either party could appeal; if the suit were deemed "badly judged," it would go to a superior court; if considered "well-judged," the parties were ordered to return to the original sentencing court.[4]

If law and the courts constituted a powerful structure of authority that constrained action, they also provided a language and a set of procedures and concepts that subjects could use strategically in the service of their own interests. In a social and political structure based on privilege and composed of multiple and overlapping jurisdictions, individuals and corporate groups articulated their claims to resources, power, and jurisdiction in legal terms. They also made use simultaneously or successively of infra-judicial mechanisms, such as mediation or arbitration. Law, then, was a dynamic social and cultural process, one shaped by the interaction between structures and individual actions.[5]

In the case of disputes over power and privileges in New France, recourse to courts of justice was one strategy among others, often pursued simultaneously. Common to all was that of drawing metropolitan authorities into overseas spaces. If some corporate bodies, notably the Breton Estates and provincial parlements, considered transatlantic activity a domestic issue, as we saw in chapter 1, what emerges from an analysis of the disputes in the 1610s is the ways in which those involved in New France – whether independent traders, associates of the privileged trading company, or representatives of the lieutenant general/viceroy – skilfully tailored their actions and rhetoric to mobilize other powerful groups who lacked direct connections to, interests in, or in some cases even knowledge of, the colonizing and commercial enterprise in New France, in their favour. With parties choosing particular avenues to pursue disputes, contests for authority on both sides of the Atlantic became intertwined.

Champlain, Lieutenant: Equal or Superior to His Trading Associates?

For de Mons and Champlain, a new king and regent required new avenues at court. In this sense, the regency represented an opportunity to strengthen the foundations of their colonizing and trading enterprise to New France. Indeed, the previous decade had already revealed the need for a new strategy to combat the vocal and influential domestic opposition to exclusive privileges in the colony. Fishermen and traders in Atlantic ports had, after all, succeeded in getting the company's exclusive fur trading rights overturned in 1609. With diminished returns from the fur trade in light of the resulting increase in competition, de Mons and Champlain had found it nearly impossible to fund the settlement at Quebec over the ensuing four years. De Mons's weakened position at court prompted him to resign his lieutenant generalship and retreat into the background, all the while remaining an investor and supporter of the enterprise. In his stead, Champlain became the chief negotiator and lobbyist in the corridors of power in Paris, in addition to his role as head of the habitation at Quebec.

Using what remained of his and de Mons's network at court, Champlain approached Pierre Jeannin, the president of the Parlement of Paris, and the Sieur Boileau, counsellor and chaplain to the king, with a plan to put the enterprise under a highly placed protector, a member of the Bourbon royal family, who could effectively stifle any attempts to strip the company of its rights. Through Boileau, Champlain reached out to the Comte de Soissons, a prince of the blood, cousin to Louis XIII, and governor of Normandy and Dauphiné. Evincing interest in the overseas enterprise, Soissons agreed to the appointment and received a commission as lieutenant general of New France from the king in October 1612. About a month later, however, he suddenly died, leaving the enterprise again on uncertain terms. Champlain and his advisers at court then chose Soissons's nephew, Henri de Bourbon, Prince de Condé, governor and lieutenant general of Guyenne, cousin to Louis XIII, and now second in line to the throne. Both Champlain and de Mons had connections to the prince's household, the former through his young wife Hélène Boullé, who was the sister-in-law of Condé's secretary, and the latter through his parents-in-law.[6] The two men hoped that Condé would provide the legitimacy and connections they required to continue the enterprise.

Condé did not come without considerable risk. Twenty-four years old, he had already shown himself to be headstrong and rebellious. Having left court abruptly in the latter years of Henri IV's reign over the king's all-too-obvious affection for the young prince's wife, Condé sought refuge in Hapsburg territories, raising questions about his loyalty and intentions. If he returned to court in a submissive posture following Henri IV's death and the establishment of the regency, Condé soon sought to assert his right to a political role in the regency government as first prince of the blood. He, like other princes – including his uncle, the Comte de Soissons – objected to the queen regent's policies, particularly her plan to create closer ties with Spain by marrying her son and daughter to members of the Spanish royal family. Indeed, six months before his acceptance of the lieutenant generalship of New France, Condé had, along with Soissons, left court in protest of the marriage celebrations. Acutely aware of the queen regent's need for his support as well as that of the other princes and great nobles, Condé demanded an increasingly higher price, obtaining, for example, a *place forte* in exchange for recognizing the marriages.[7] While Champlain and de Mons may have been attracted to Condé's position as first prince of the blood, Condé's actions thus far suggested that further disputes with the queen regent and her government were likely.

Condé's commission as lieutenant general marked a turning point in the management of colonizing and trading activities in New France.[8] Although his powers and privileges resembled those of de Mons, ranging from the power to negotiate alliances with Indigenous Peoples to appointing captains and officers of justice, Condé's exercise of authority was of a fundamentally different character. Both men held the title of lieutenant general, but de Mons alone had exercised significant elements of his authority directly. First and foremost, de Mons had participated in voyages to New France since 1598. As lieutenant general of New France, he commanded the habitation at Sainte-Croix through the winter of 1604–05 and led an exploratory voyage to the south of Acadia along the northeastern coast of the present-day United States. Based in France from the end of 1605 onward, he continued to manage and promote his New France affairs. He lobbied at court, recruited artisans and labourers for the habitation, outfitted vessels, negotiated with his partners, and engaged in suits against those who violated his trading privileges.[9] In his absence, de Mons appointed a lieutenant or deputy in New France to build and command the habitation over the winter, conduct trade, explore the country, and patrol the coast for interlopers. These appointments were made each year and were restricted in their judicial and administrative powers, although the need to maintain order in the colony meant that they also carried considerable discretion.[10]

In contrast to de Mons, the Prince de Condé chose to delegate his authority in New France to others, thereby becoming the honorary head of the enterprise. Condé had no particular connection to New France; rather, what was important was his position at court and his connections. When opposition to the enterprise arose in France, he was to help Champlain and the trading associates obtain a hearing. His role was thus intended to be largely symbolic. Condé delegated separately his powers and privileges. Appointing Champlain his lieutenant in November 1612, Condé transferred to him all of the governmental responsibilities of his lieutenant generalship. As with the commission from de Mons, Champlain was instructed to develop the habitation at Quebec, build forts for the safety of the inhabitants, and explore the surrounding country. His lieutenancy in 1612, however, extended far beyond this to include "commission[ing] officers for administration of justice and maintenance of police authority, regulations and ordinances, to negotiate and contract, with the same purpose, peace, alliance and federation, friendly relations, correspondence and intercourse with the said peoples and their princes … to keep and carefully preserve the treaties and alliances that he shall contract with them, provided that they on their part satisfy the terms of these. And in their default to make open war upon them."[11] He was also to seize the ships and merchandise of those caught trading illegally, send them to France for prosecution, encourage the conversion of Indigenous people to Catholicism, and take all other action necessary "as if all were expressly and in detail specified and declared." Given the extent of his authority, it is perhaps not surprising that Champlain was mistakenly considered by contemporaries – and later by scholars – to be governor.[12] Champlain's commission became the template that later viceroys would come to follow. His execution of it established the broad pattern of governance for the next fifteen years, by which the title-holder remained permanently in France and his lieutenant straddled the Atlantic to varying degrees, depending on what the circumstances demanded.

Condé divided his executive authority from the rewards attached to it in his commission by delegating his trading privileges to merchants in return for a fixed sum. The negotiation of these agreements was left to Champlain: "we have allowed and do allow the said Sieur de Champlain to associate and take with him such persons and for such amounts of money as he shall think proper for the furtherance of our undertaking." Despite the impression here of a complete delegation, Condé did not leave the choice of merchants entirely to Champlain. He granted licences to other traders in Atlantic ports on more than one occasion. When Condé (via his lieutenant) granted exclusive privileges to Champlain's assembled company of merchants in early 1613, the other privileged traders reacted, predictably, with confusion and protest. For his part, Champlain preferred the creation of one large association involving merchants in several ports.[13] To this end, he sought the participation of established traders in Rouen, La Rochelle, and Saint-Malo, the trio of ports active in the Atlantic trade and that had, not coincidentally, come together in the Compagnie de Mons nine years earlier. With these networks already established, it was no surprise that several former associates entered the new association, which became known as the Compagnie de Rouen et Saint-Malo (CRSM).[14]

The precise nature of Champlain's relationship with the company became a source of tension during the negotiations, which dragged on for nine months and produced three successive agreements. It is not difficult to see why. Champlain had, after all, recruited these merchants on the part of Condé, but he also held his own extensive commission, which could conceivably put his interests in conflict with those of the company. Company members were particularly preoccupied by the question of whether the lieutenant was subordinate, equal, or superior to them. In broad strokes, the agreements saw the associates obtain exclusive privileges to trade in the Saint Lawrence River for an eleven-year period beginning in 1614. In keeping with the ban on trade to all other subjects, they and their agents alone were eligible for passports from Condé for travel to New France. In exchange, the company agreed to provide transportation for Champlain and his men and to pay the lieutenant's salary (*gages et appointements*). Successive drafts of the contract show that the parties struggled to settle on an amount and a justification for Champlain's salary. Ranging from 600 livres to the final figure of 1,200 livres annually, his salary was, in the lieutenant's eyes, designed to help realize the colonizing objectives of the enterprise. The associates, however, viewed it more narrowly in terms of their own trading interests. In the final agreement, Champlain was to "stand by His Greatness [Condé] in France, for the good of the said company and to prevent any surprises that might harm its interests."[15] This mandate to protect the company's privileges in the face of opposition put Champlain and his influence explicitly in its service. The parties' preoccupation with defining the relationship between Champlain and company members was particularly visible in the first draft of the agreement, which declared, "That which will be resolved and decided upon by the said merchant deputies for the government of the company, the said associates, including the said Sieur de Champlain, will be held to well and faithfully execute, neither allowing some to prevail over others nor claim any superiority, *not even the said Sieur de Champlain by virtue of his commission Monseigneur the prince addressed to him.*"[16] Despite his position, Champlain was to be considered equal to the associates and explicitly bound, like them, to implement the decisions made concerning the company's affairs. In the end, the final treaty did not single out Champlain and his role as lieutenant, stating simply that all associates were to be equal.

If Champlain managed to keep his own authority unfettered by his association with the company, the negotiations nevertheless highlight the complex relationship between the two delegated authorities. The lieutenant and the company occupied separate jurisdictions, the one governmental, the other commercial. Yet they intersected in ways that appear, from our modern standpoint, to be contradictory or even to represent a conflict of interest. Such tangled and ill-defined lines of authority were, however, part of the fabric of early modern government. A source of creative tension, they provided the suppleness necessary to respond to changing circumstances and could prove advantageous to a monarch if he or she were in a position to play one authority off another to advance royal interests. At the same time, that very flexibility meant there was frequent ambiguity about "who should obey whom in what circumstances."[17] When legitimacy of authority came into question, such as during regency rule, that tension could erupt into a dispute over claims. Subsequent crises of authority in New France prompted both Champlain and the company to exploit the porous nature of jurisdictional boundaries at the other party's expense. Condé's separate delegation of authority and privileges, then, introduced two new parties with claims in New France, in addition to his own – and to the many independent traders with their own claims based on custom – each with distinct but overlapping responsibilities and sometimes competing visions of the fledgling French overseas possession.

Saint-Malo Objects

After four years of unrestricted traffic in the Saint Lawrence River, the announcement of newly established exclusive privileges in the fur-rich region met with a swift and fierce response from traders in Atlantic ports of France. The strongest and most anticipated opposition came from the Breton port of Saint-Malo, which had led the attack with such success in 1609. In 1613, the Malouins resumed their campaign for freedom of trade, drawing on a discourse of rights based on custom. The opening volley came in early January 1613 with the publication of a factum, or legal brief, against Champlain, whom the Malouins held responsible for the ban on trade contained in Condé's letters patent. The publication of factums was a common strategy among litigants in the period. While they awaited the judgment of the courts, litigants submitted their case to a sort of popular tribunal – that of the wider public. Available from booksellers and peddlers, posted in public spaces and read aloud, factums brought people into the world of law and the courts, inviting them to become arbiters of "social entitlements."[18] In the case of the Malouin traders, their factum appealed to the broader public of Saint-Malo, with the particular goal of mobilizing the port's influential communauté d'habitants. Winning the support and resources of this body would strengthen the second prong of the traders' campaign, the presentation of their case before select provincial parlements.

Developing two lines of argument, the factum first brought Champlain's credibility and motives into question. Neither a discoverer of new lands in North America, as he claimed, nor a contributor to the expenses of trade, Champlain was described as a mere "painter" who came along as a passenger on voyages to New France.[19] Ignoring the evidence of past failures to colonize, the lieutenant, charged the factum, was someone who drained the resources of others, ranging from the king to company associates, to satisfy his own ambitions: "the said Sieur Champlain will do all in his power to have invested and exhausted the monarch's treasury to win, at someone else's expense, some vain glory for having gone 800 leagues into a desert."[20] The enterprise, then, was to the benefit of only one man and detrimental to the majority of French subjects, and indeed the king himself.

Grounding their case in custom, history, and lineage, the Malouins' second argument put traders and explorers from their port at the centre of discoveries in New France. They pointed out that the region had been a destination for fishing and exploration by Normans, Bretons, English, and Portuguese since 1504. It was Jacques Cartier, the proud son of Saint-Malo, who had been the first to travel up the Saint Lawrence beyond the site of Quebec. In subsequent years, other Bretons, Normans, and fellow Malouins, including long-time trader and CRSM agent François Gravé

Du Pont, had followed to trade with the Indigenous inhabitants. In short, the factum contended, it had primarily been the people of Saint-Malo – and not Champlain or his associates – "who had made the discovery of the said country of Canada and adjacent countries," and it was the resulting fish and fur traffic that provided "occupation for men and ships in most of the towns of the kingdom."[21] According to this line of reasoning, discovery and long-term use conferred customary rights on Malouin traders; it was they who should, by right, be enjoying the fruits of the trade.

Lending its considerable weight to the traders' campaign in the wake of the factum, the communauté d'habitants of Saint-Malo leveraged the desire of sovereign court justices to promote the interests of their province and assert their prerogatives in the face of royal will. To this end, it appeared before the Parlement of Rouen some weeks after the factum's publication. Like de Mons's commission before it, Condé's had to be registered in provincial sovereign courts to take full effect. The choice of the Norman body was strategic. Having objected to de Mons's letters patent nine years earlier, this body seemed well disposed to the Malouins' point of view. The community accordingly sent a deputy, Josselin Crosnier, to convey its protest against the letters and the exclusive trading privileges therein. Among the documents Crosnier presented before the court was the royal decree of 6 October 1609, by which the Malouins had obtained freedom of traffic. Receiving the community's protest, the sovereign court only registered Condé's letters patent after considerable delay and royal pressure. In a decree of 4 March 1613, the court recognized the privileges and powers of the Prince de Condé "without prejudice to the execution of the decree of the Privy Council in favour of the bourgeois and inhabitants of Saint-Malo of 6 October 1609 and of the liberty of navigation, trade, and commerce except in the lands and rivers that empty into the Saint Laurence River above the said place of Mantenne [Matane, on the Gaspé Peninsula]."[22] In other words, they tried to uphold the freedom of traffic granted in 1609 as far as they could, in support of the majority of traders excluded from the trading privileges, an approach previously adopted by the Breton Parlement in the face of de Mons's commission. The Malouins had succeeded in setting the stage for future trouble.

The communauté d'habitants of Saint-Malo's subsequent campaign expanded the issue into one that threatened the very rights and jurisdiction of the entire province of Brittany. At the end of 1614, it turned to the Estates of Brittany for support. The Estates were at the time drawing up their *cahier de doléances*, or list of grievances, in preparation for the meeting of the Estates General slated for later that fall and the following winter. In a cunning move, interested merchants slipped an entreaty into this document exhorting the deputies to "submit that Canada had been discovered by Jacques Cartier, native of Saint-Malo, and to protest the Letters that grant exclusive commerce in the area and places where it [commerce] is favourable."[23] (In an ironic twist, the Estates General was being called at the behest of Condé, the very man who would lose the annual duty from the privileged company if such an entreaty won general approval.[24]) Unlikely to have their case taken up by the Estates if potential benefits were to accrue only to themselves, the Malouins asked for freedom of trade in New France for all of Brittany. In the event, the prospect of a challenge to Condé's (and the CRSM's) rights from the powerful provincial body reached Champlain, who responded as follows: "Having gotten wind of this … [I] spoke to Monseigneur the Prince [Condé] and explained to him the interest he had in so justly preventing the adoption of this clause, and that if it was his pleasure to do me the honour of getting me a hearing, [I] would make plain that Brittany had no interest in that except the people of St Malo." Through the prince's intervention, Champlain was able to have the clause removed.[25] This episode reveals, more than anything, the determination and willingness of the corporate community of Saint-Malo to exploit all possible avenues and connections to overturn trade conditions that it deemed contrary to its traders' long-held rights. In giving a voice to opponents of trading privileges, local and provincial bodies competed with the traders grouped together in the CRSM and their patron for legitimacy and influence in France.

While Saint-Malo's communauté d'habitants called each time for the restoration of "liberty of commerce," what it had in mind was far removed from the modern notion of free trade. Liberty of trade itself constituted a "vested right or privilege," one that would grant special treatment rather than ensure the absence of regulations, as we tend to understand the term today.[26] The distinction here is best seen in the changing parameters of the Malouins' calls for freedom of traffic. In the factum, they claimed that *their* traders and explorers alone had discovered New France and its fur trading regions. Although the period of free trade from 1609 to 1612 appeared to put merchants of all ports on an equal footing, Saint-Malo had continued to distinguish itself from other ports through its long association with North America and its customary rights. Before the Estates of Brittany, the Malouins extended their call for freedom of traffic with New France to *all Breton ports*, in the hopes of gaining more supporters to their cause.

Far from the blanket removal of all restrictions across France, this "liberty of trade" would be a designation granted to select ports permitting traffic to a particular region and was thus comparable to the designation of a free port. Had the king, therefore, reopened trade to all in 1613, the Breton port would not have stopped pushing for favour and advantage at the expense of its rivals.

The community of Saint-Malo, and corporate groups more generally, pushed at once for liberty – the freedom to make their own rules – and protection – the upholding of privileges. These impulses appear contradictory to modern eyes but were at the heart of contemporary understandings of the relationship between the king and his subjects. Seen in this light, the community of Saint-Malo was not asking the king to stay out of New France commerce but rather to regulate it in its favour. Royal intervention could be useful.[27] The case presented by Saint-Malo proved to be a highly effective argument in a society in which privilege defined relations among individuals and with the king, via corporations. The challenge this presented to the CRSM, Champlain, and Condé was that their exclusive privileges were frequently at risk of being undermined, a situation that could have serious consequences if they were not in a position to confront competing claims together.

Who Was the Legitimate Viceroy of New France?

Few in the New France enterprise could have predicted that their protector, the Prince de Condé, would be imprisoned and accused of treason by summer's end in 1616. It is no small irony that the very man charged with giving the enterprise legitimacy and stability should be responsible for plunging it into the greatest uncertainty. The prince's imprisonment was the culmination of two years of moves and countermoves on the part of the regency government, on the one hand, and the great nobility, on the other. Princely revolt, a routine occurrence during regencies, was seen as a legitimate route to negotiation rather than an unpardonable offence. Following a set of informal conventions, it could in fact lead to an improvement in position for the prince(s) in question.[28] Isolated at court since his uncle's death in 1612, Condé had become increasingly discontent with the queen regent's refusal to admit him into the inner chambers of government, which were tightly controlled by her Italian first minister, Concino Concini. With the encouragement of other disaffected nobles, and despite royal attempts to mollify him, the prince assembled his forces and waged an open rebellion in 1615. A peace treaty ended hostilities the following spring, granting Condé a seat on the regency council and the authority to sign all decrees alongside the chancellor. His revolt would have been a success had he stopped there, but the prince contravened the traditions governing such agitation by continuing to foment resistance to the regent, especially in the Huguenot stronghold of La Rochelle. Other great nobles continued to plot against the government and, specifically, Concini. Their patience exhausted, the regent and her first minister ordered Condé's arrest in September 1616. The apprehension of the first prince of the blood was no small matter and was met with fierce criticism, including by former supporters of the queen regent. Sending royal forces to the provinces, the government succeeded in negotiating an end to this latest revolt of the princes.[29]

Condé's incarceration had a direct impact on governance in New France. He was stripped of all privileges and titles, including viceroy of the colony. Eager to reward a faithful servant, the queen regent appointed Pons de Lauzière, Marquis de Thémines, marshal of France, and captain of the Queen's Guard – the very man who had arrested the prince – to the viceroyalty for as long as the prince remained incarcerated. Declaring all previous commissions "void and of no effect," Thémines's letters patent transferred to him all of the powers granted Condé in 1613. In a bid to reassure those who might wish to associate with the new viceroy but were discouraged by the uncertainty of the situation, they made clear that "we [the king in his council] … have validated and do henceforward validate any treaties that may be made with any persons whatsoever by our said cousin the Marquis de Themines … These treaties shall have force and effect for as long as the said power lasts."[30] This last clause, combined with the notable absence of any mention of the existing agreement between Condé, Champlain, and the CRSM, threatened the latter with the loss of its rights less than halfway through its eleven-year contract. The associates consequently entered a new agreement with Thémines in November, by which they committed to pay him 4,500 livres annually; Champlain was named the new viceroy's lieutenant the following January.[31]

Despite the appearance of resolution that the company's agreement with Thémines afforded, the association was soon caught in the middle of a dispute between past and present viceroys. Condé, never one to go quietly, refused to relinquish his title and the attendant annual duty paid to him by the association since 1614. From prison, he ordered his intendant, Nicolas Vignier, to "ma[k]e seizure of what was owed to my Lord the Prince," requiring the company, in effect, to pay twice. Unsure to whom they owed their rights, the associates appeared before the royal council, along with Thémines, Condé's representative, and the intendant of the Admiralty of France, the Sieur de Villemenon, who was present to defend the admiral's jurisdiction. After a lengthy suit that involved the Parlement of Paris as well as the council, the associates were eventually ordered to pay Thémines.[32] Condé nevertheless continued to demand his rights as viceroy throughout the ensuing three years of his imprisonment.

The dispute among Condé, Thémines, and the company tied the political situations of France and New France together in unexpected ways. A dramatic example of what was a fairly common occurrence during periods of regency rule, Condé's rebellion and subsequent imprisonment precipitated a change in viceroy in New France. The connections might have ended there had the prince not chosen to insist on his viceregal rights as a way to continue his resistance to the queen regent's government. A conflict, in other words, could branch out into other disputes ostensibly concerning completely separate matters – in this case, the trading activities and administration of a colony an ocean away, where none of the principal protagonists had ever set foot. In the grand scheme of things, perhaps, the viceroyalty and the attendant annual payment of 3,000 livres did not merit the effort and expense of a legal suit.[33] But they offered an opportunity to make things difficult, if not directly for the regent, then for one of her clients, Thémines. Litigation also allowed Condé to retain some means to negotiate now that other avenues, like use of force, were no longer open. The responses of independent traders, the company, and Champlain to Condé's arrest reinforces this picture of calculated conflict.

A Second Round for Freedom of Trade

In the face of a weakened Crown and distracted privilege-holders in New France, Malouin traders drew on the institutional power of the provincial Estates and their town's communauté d'habitants to pursue their case for freedom of trade throughout the viceregal conflict. Although some had decided to enter the company, others continued to voice their opposition in the courts of France.[34] In the fall of 1616, the Estates of Brittany accepted a remonstrance from the community of Saint-Malo, which they then brought before the royal council. Using the same justifications as in previous representations, the grievance asked the king to "revoke the said commissions granted … as prejudicial to the common good of the country, and in consequence to declare the said traffic of Canada open and free to all of your subjects without distinction."[35] The following March, in direct contradiction of earlier assurances that the Crown would support any contract with Viceroy Thémines, the king acceded to the Bretons' request and suspended the CRSM's trading privileges.[36]

Coming as it did on the heels of the surprise arrest of Condé and Thémines's appointment as viceroy, the request only came to Champlain's attention after a decision had been made in the Bretons' favour. Frustrated that the royal council had not bothered to hear both parties involved before taking action, Champlain presented his own request for a hearing before the body, and "immediately wrote to our partners at Rouen that they must come quickly, which they did, for the matter touched them closely."[37] Accordingly, company representatives Thomas Porée and Daniel Boyer appeared before the council in May to ask for the restoration of their privileges and the ban on all other traders. One month later, the procureur syndic of the Breton Estates received notification of this action with orders to appear before the council and "consent to or challenge the ends and conclusions of the said Porée and his associates." Having instructed their syndic and deputies in Paris "to defend with all their power [the position of freedom of trade]," the Estates pursued the case for the duration of the viceregal dispute and into 1619.[38]

Although the council eventually reaffirmed the CRSM's exclusive trading privileges, the Estates of Brittany and the community of Saint-Malo seized the opportunity presented by the political confusion at court to disrupt the New France enterprise.[39] For both bodies, the extension of the Crown's reach overseas into the well-established North American trade infringed on their province's closely guarded autonomy. Due to their institutional power, the local and provincial Breton bodies were in a strong position to push for the restoration of liberty of trade to New France when the Crown was in an even moderately weak state. The merchant-dominated community of Saint-Malo, for one, controlled the Estates' approach to commercial affairs. The latter thus sent deputies to Paris every year during the suit expressly to advocate for its side in the event of any challenges.[40] As we saw in chapter 1, the Estates, for its part, had recently strengthened its position vis-à-vis the king through the annual levies it made on his behalf. If the Estates regarded this relationship as a contract between equals, while Louis XIII and his predecessors saw it as grounded in their own generosity, royal dependence on the negotiated taxes and other exceptional sums, together with the province's frontier position, nevertheless meant that both the king and his council generally paid attention to lobbying by the Estates.[41]

By November 1616, the political instability at court occasioned by Condé's revolt had given middling authorities like the Estates of Brittany more manoeuvrability. Unrest had in fact intensified with the increase of the queen regent's and her minister Concini's control over the government. While the Estates and the CRSM continued their dispute before the royal council the following year, Louis XIII, desiring to assert his full authority as king now that he was of age, had Concini killed in April 1617 and subsequently exiled the queen regent to a royal chateau in Blois, in the Loire Valley. This veritable coup d'état put the king in charge, but it also encouraged the regent's supporters to plot her restoration to power, culminating in a revolt in 1619–20.[42] With such upheaval at the centres of political power, the savvy and well-connected traders of Saint-Malo exploited the upswing in the Estates' influence to push against the already vulnerable CRSM and Champlain.

If independent traders knew when to strike out at the New France enterprise, they must also have known that any success before a distracted royal council would prove fleeting. Why bother, then, going to the trouble of sending a deputy of the Estates before the royal council or slipping a free trade clause into the list of grievances? Like Condé's refusal to meekly give up his viceroy's rights, the Breton Estates' dogged pursuit of freedom of traffic created, at the very least, obstacles for the company and Champlain. It required time, energy, and money for Boyer and Porée to travel to Paris to appear before the council, resources they could have used to outfit ships, recruit artisans and crew, and buy merchandise. The Malouins' lobbying also created a paper trail, which they could draw on in future disputes. In the eyes of the traders and their provincial advocates, the temporary nature of their success was almost immaterial. They had managed to inconvenience the associates and damage the credibility of the enterprise. Above all, the Malouins had taken a stand in defence of their customary rights and the autonomy of their province. The moves and countermoves of the Malouin traders and Breton authorities, on the one side, and the CRSM and Champlain, on the other, point to a logic of power in which positions, never secure, required constant affirmation.

Delegated Authorities Play for Power

While Malouin traders exploited royal weakness and viceregal uncertainty, Champlain and the CRSM both sought leverage against the other in the power vacuum left by Condé's arrest and Thémines's contested appointment. The Crown may have considered authority in New France to be under one lieutenant general and viceroy, but the exercise of that authority rested to a large degree on the dynamic between lieutenant and company. As lieutenant, Champlain relied on the company for the timely transportation of provisions to the habitation each spring, for his own maintenance and expenses, and for the conduct of the fur trade, which, aside from providing revenue, formed part of his diplomatic approach toward the Wendats and Algonquins. The company in turn depended on Champlain's extensive connections at court to counter attempts to overturn their trading privileges and to keep New France on the Crown's agenda. As we have seen, it was Champlain who more than once learned of a challenge to the enterprise's commission, alerted the other parties, and made the first move to counter it. Charged initially with finding associates for the enterprise, the lieutenant subsequently served as the intermediary between the CRSM and Condé. The company no doubt benefited from Champlain's growing reputation and the legitimacy and support his writings lent to the project. As would become evident in 1617, however, their intersecting jurisdictions precipitated jockeying when lines of authority were called into question at court and in the colony.

To assert their respective positions at the other's expense, both parties appealed to the authority of various metropolitan jurisdictions, in the process revealing skilful manipulation of the tools at hand. In the spring of 1617, shortly before the annual voyage, one of the deputies of the associates, Daniel Boyer, took advantage of the uncertainty over the viceroyalty to test the limits of the company's authority relative to Champlain's. He informed Champlain that the Parlement had exonerated the company from paying either viceroy and that he "could no longer claim the honour of functioning as Lieutenant of my lord the Prince." Although the other associates subsequently denied that Boyer had acted under their instruction, Champlain was vehement in his rebuttal: "All this was no concern of mine; for, as I had served, they could not deprive me either of the appointment or much less of the salary to which they had voluntarily bound themselves when I made them partners."[43] His response distinguished between his appointment, which was not connected to – let alone determined by – the associates, and the contract of association he had made with the latter, which fixed his salary. Having asserted his own position, Champlain then departed for New France as planned. This brief episode demonstrates the common practice among title-holders of resting their actions on a sentence issued by one court or another, all the while going far beyond it. A party's brandishing of one decree often precipitated a contest over contrasting decrees from different jurisdictions. Although Champlain did seek support from the king and royal council in this case, his own play for power came in the form of a new enterprise.

Champlain's appeal to two bodies with different interests highlights the ways in which parties skilfully tailored their rhetoric to particular audiences. New France was to many in the metropole a space to be filled. (While some accorded Indigenous Peoples particular roles in their vision, no one recognized their rights and claims to control.) The proposed vision for this space depended upon the particular constituency. Champlain's proposal of 1618, presented first to the Chamber of Commerce in Paris and then to the king and royal council, outlined a plan for the colonization and development of New France over a period of fifteen years.[44] In his presentations, the lieutenant evoked two different imagined "New Frances." Before the Chamber of Commerce, he outlined what might be called a "prospective inventory," both a plan for development and a prediction of what resources could in time be had with "the establishment of a great and permanent trade in New France."[45] He listed the types of fish available, the variety of woods and their uses, suitable crops, minerals from silver to lead, different types of furs and hides, and prospects for the cultivation of hemp and the introduction of cattle.[46] Each of these commodities was followed by the estimated profit France could expect to accrue annually. Concluding with the possibility of a passage to China by way of the Saint Lawrence, Champlain opined that, while he "has been toiling at this quest for sixteen years … the scant assistance he has received" has thus far prevented him from succeeding "as he will do when assisted." Champlain hoped that the emphasis on the potential economic and commercial value of the colony would win him the backing of these Parisian businessmen, thus strengthening his case before the king and royal council. Success came in the form of a letter from the Chamber of Commerce to the king on 9 February 1618 urging the latter to "grant means and funds to the said Champlain" for the execution of the enterprise.[47]

Champlain's address before the king and royal council appealed to a different vision of New France through the invocation of sovereignty and potential threats to it. Where his earlier presentation had highlighted the abundance of commodities available in New France, this one focused on the colony's role in the extension of God's and His Majesty's dominions and France's geopolitical standing.[48] He began with his discoveries and interactions with Indigenous inhabitants over the previous sixteen years, the efforts at evangelization, the reports of an interior sea that would likely lead to China, and the goods available there. Not only would all this be forfeited "should this said country be given up and the settlement abandoned, for want of bestowing upon it the needed attention," but also, more seriously, "the English or Flemings, envious of our prosperity, would seize upon it, thereby enjoying the fruits of our labours," as they had already done in Acadia and at Saint-Sauveur, a settlement across the Bay of Fundy south of the Sainte-Croix River.[49] France's standing in North America vis-à-vis its rivals thus depended on adequate funding for existing and future habitations. Champlain therefore requested "the means of strengthening and extending his design."[50]

Having been engaged in New France affairs for over fifteen years, Champlain had come to the conclusion – as had many of his contemporaries – that material support from the Crown was crucial for overseas colonizing ventures.[51] The administration and government of New France, according to this view, could not continue to rely on the commercial activities of a company if the existing posts were to develop into populous, well-established colonies. Planning to use the profits from the various commodities that would come from New France, Champlain hoped as well for "other moneys it may please His Majesty to have paid over for the carrying out and execution of the said undertaking." Such funds, Champlain assured his audience, would not come at the expense of the profits from the fur trade currently enjoyed by the CRSM, nor would the enterprise as a whole affect the company's obligations or Champlain's position as lieutenant. In fact, he recommended that under the plan "the said merchants should be preferred above all others in the matter of the trade of the said country."[52] There would, then, be more than one privileged, Crown-sanctioned venture underway in the same region. Champlain accomplished a clever sleight of hand here: while ostensibly leaving the rights and privileges of the company intact, the new enterprise would in practice narrow the company's jurisdiction to commerce, thereby making it subordinate to the lieutenant, placing both colonization and administrative authority under him.

Champlain's simultaneous appeals to sovereign interests and to the economic preoccupations of the Paris Chamber of Commerce illuminate more generally the ways in which parties overseas at once depended upon metropolitan patrons and institutions and steered the latter's engagement in expansionist enterprises. Like all claimants, Champlain depended upon the continued favour of the king and viceroy. Central to the assertion of claims overseas was a subject's ability to identify themselves with the preoccupations of their sovereign and demonstrate that their actions advanced those interests.[53] Champlain's emphasis on his past accomplishments was part of his self-fashioning as the king's representative in New France. At the same time, the lieutenant also sought to expand his metropolitan support by bringing in the Parisian businessmen. It is here that we can best see how title-holders used the available resources and jurisdictions to advance their own interests. Heretofore unengaged in the New France enterprise, the Chamber of Commerce was transformed into an interested party by Champlain's construction of an imagined New France that appealed to their commercial orientation. This is not to say that Champlain did not believe in his proposal and hope for the colonization and material development of New France. It does, however, highlight the dialectical relationship between claimants overseas and authorities at home. At the same time that they depended on patronage, title-holders drew metropolitan authorities and institutions into overseas spaces.

The royal council's response to the manoeuvring by lieutenant and company underscores the king's role as arbiter of jurisdictional disputes among rivals for power. In a letter addressed to the company associates dated 12 March 1618, the king called on them to support Champlain in the colonization and development of New France: "Information having been given to us that heretofore there has been bad management in the establishment of families and workmen that have been taken to the settlement at Quebec and other places in New France, We write you this letter … to make known to you that it is our pleasure that you assist … the Sieur de Champlain with the things requisite and necessary for executing the commands he has received from us, to choose tried and faithful men for employment in exploring, inhabiting, clearing, cultivating, and planting the land, and to carry on all work he shall judge necessary for establishing the colonies we wish to found in the said country, in the interest of our service and for the advantage of our subjects."[54] Neither a full endorsement of the enterprise proposed by the lieutenant nor an outright rejection of it, the king's letter affirmed the goal of a large permanent settlement while declining Champlain's primary request for a source of funds independent from the company with trading privileges.[55] Still, the king called on the company to co-operate in this endeavour. The letter concluded, however, with an important caveat underscoring the limits to the lieutenant's jurisdiction: to be sure, the king ordered the merchant associates to do all in their power to aid Champlain in his colonizing activities, "yet without allowing the said exploration and colonization *to disturb or hinder your factors, clerks and agents in the matter of the fur-trade in any manner and fashion whatsoever*, during the period which we have allowed you."[56] This attempt to walk a fine line between the two commissions, affirming both parties' positions, left open to interpretation the extent to which colonizing activities would interfere with the conduct of trade. The following year, a royal decree in response to another company challenge to Champlain's command over the Quebec habitation was even more explicit in its equivocation, simultaneously forbidding both parties to "trouble or hinder" the other in their activities.[57]

Overlapping jurisdictions were a common phenomenon in France and throughout Europe, so there was nothing unusual in the letter's and the decree's ambivalence. Indeed, as historian Michael Breen argues, royal attempts to resolve such disputes aimed "not to define boundaries" but to restore equilibrium among the parties so that "the system [could continue] functioning."[58] This strategy allowed the Crown, when it was strong, to play parties off against each other to advance its own objectives; in a period of political instability, however, it fuelled plays for power. By not imposing any conditions on either party in their interactions with each other, both the letter and the decree left the parties to continue their jockeying for position.

The manner in which both Champlain and the company asserted and sought confirmation of their prerogatives highlights the importance of strong personal networks and the support of influential metropolitan corporate groups. Champlain, for his part, fostered connections at court, both directly, through face-to-face meetings, and through his travel accounts. As his proposal demonstrated, he was adept at tailoring his rhetoric to a particular audience and garnering the support of a wide variety of interests – skills that were reflected in his service to several viceroys.[59] The company associates, by contrast, do not appear to have built their own lobby at court; instead, they relied on Champlain. As a result, when they came into conflict with him, they lacked the connections and profile to circulate their own case at court. The two parties' legal positions were also substantially different. Champlain's was relatively straightforward; representing the person of the viceroy, he assumed in law his superior's rights and responsibilities. By comparison, the company's legal identity was undefined. The absence of a written body of commercial law, the CRSM's status as an association among individuals without the security of an incorporated company, and the short history of such privileged overseas ventures in France together put it in a weaker position than Champlain before the courts.[60] In this respect, the king's and the royal council's tendency to confirm both Champlain's lieutenancy and the company's privileges without defining the jurisdictions in relation to one another provided the CRSM with an opening in which to assert its power over Champlain and the New France enterprise. On a larger scale, the strategies of company, lieutenant, and royal council point to the negotiation and contestation that lay at the centre of relations of authority in France.

The Battleground of the Courts

While those with a stake in New France engaged various metropolitan bodies in their cause, they made the most of the labyrinthine French legal system. Courts provided a key forum in which to test the limits of one's power. At the same time as the manoeuvrings among independent traders, viceroys, company, and lieutenant, the CRSM associates were embroiled in a lawsuit with a group of traders from La Rochelle over the latter's entry into the company. The evolution of this dispute was distinct from the others involving the CRSM. To begin with, the matter wended its way through the courts over a period of more than twenty years and expanded into other lawsuits. Both developments indicate that different intentions and stakes were involved here. Whereas in the struggle between the company and Champlain, the parties appeared before the royal council with the goal of re-establishing harmonious relations (even if they had different views of how to achieve this), here, company associates and Rochelais traders went to court to pursue conflict rather than to seek a resolution.

If all had gone according to plan, the Rochelais would have been at the heart of the trading company. Indeed, among the first traders Champlain contacted in January 1613 were Samuel Georges and Jean Macain, de Mons's former partners from the Atlantic port. By early February 1613, Champlain, the Rochelais, and a group of traders from Rouen had made an agreement for the following season's voyage by which expenses and profits would be split one to three between the two ports, with the Rouennais providing two-thirds of the ships and receiving two-thirds of the returns, and the Rochelais contributing and receiving a third. After Malouin traders joined the discussions over the summer, the prospective company became a three-way partnership. When the time came to sign the contract in November 1613, however, the Rochelais failed to show up, and the enterprise became known as the Compagnie de Rouen et Saint-Malo.[61]

Far more than a misunderstanding among the parties about the date and time of the meeting, the Rochelais' failure to appear at the vital moment reveals the complex tension between alliance and competition that characterized relations among merchants of the three ports. If they had wanted to resolve the issue, the parties could easily have arranged for the Rochelais to sign the contract in the following weeks. Instead, both sides made declarations on the subject – on the one hand, to summon the Rochelais to enter if they so desired; on the other, to announce their intention to become associates – but took no concrete action.[62] Champlain deemed the Rochelais too slow: "They were so long about the affair that, as they did not put in an appearance in time, they were dropped." In a notarial act of 1618, the Rochelais claimed that they were refused entry.[63] There is the sense of a game being played here. The parties involved were well-established participants in New France commercial and colonizing enterprises. Georges and Macain had previously joined forces with some of the Malouin and Rouennais traders in the new company. Associates in the Compagnie de Mons, they had gone to court against de Mons over the division of merchandise in 1608, a dispute that had not prevented fruitful partnerships among the three traders in subsequent years. But these men were first and foremost traders of Rouen, La Rochelle, and Saint-Malo. Wealthy, prominent, and experienced international merchants in their respective ports, they had an aggressive and ambitious approach to business and a preference for working independently. Each port's privileges, ranging from tax exemptions to the right to trade in particular regions, fostered an atmosphere of competition over status and material resources.[64] The prospect of control over the fur trade in New France meant that the stakes were high, a factor that determined whether the traders would decide to co-operate with or obstruct the actions of former partners.

From 1614 to 1622, the Rochelais continued to trade in New France in open defiance of the CRSM's privileges, testing the company's authority overseas and the strength of its connections in France. The Innu, who themselves objected to the exclusive privileges, since they implied control of the Saint Lawrence River itself, traded every year near Tadoussac with fishermen-traders from the Atlantic port, with whom they had a long relationship.[65] Having sent notification of Condé's letters patent to La Rochelle's mayor and Admiralty judge as well as to Georges and associates in January 1614, the CRSM clearly expected protest from that quarter, if not outright illegal trading.[66] The associates may have received word that the Rochelais had managed to obtain a licence from Condé to trade in New France for the coming season, despite their failure to join the company. Whether the Rochelais acquired this permission "by a trick," as Champlain believed, or whether Condé had freely given it in exchange for a sum, the very visibility of the Rochelais' illegal activity dared the company to seize their vessels or challenge them in court.[67] Like the back and forth over the Rochelais' entry into the company, this baiting has a game-like quality, as though each party was trying to get the other to blink first.

The Rochelais' behaviour suggests that they were sufficiently confident and secure in their connections and backing in France to handle any retaliatory measures on the part of the company. Their confidence points to the variety of sources of privileges and legitimacy in seventeenth-century France. For starters, they could rely on the support of Admiralty officials on both sides of the Atlantic. They enjoyed a special relationship with both the admiral of France, Henri de Montmorency, and his vice admiral, Charles de Biencourt.[68] Just as Georges, Macain, and their consorts considered the association's privileges to impinge on their own rights, so Montmorency viewed Condé's prerogative to give out passports to New France as a threat to his own. As admiral, Montmorency theoretically had jurisdiction over all ships arriving in or departing from French ports; in practice, however, his authority was limited and subject to contestation. A competing title-holder like Condé, his brother-in-law, and later Thémines, compromised his oversight of the awarding of licences at a time when he was looking to consolidate his authority at home and abroad.[69] For privilege-holders and interlopers alike, ties to the Admiralty could facilitate everything from the granting of passports to the prosecution of suits before the institution's courts. Condé may not have granted the Rochelais passage to New France after 1614, but they had connections to equally powerful patrons, in whose professional interests it was to challenge the viceroy's jurisdiction.

Well-connected or not, the Rochelais found themselves the object of a seizure on the part of the CRSM, precipitating a lengthy and convoluted court battle. In the summer of 1614, representatives of the CRSM, finding the interlopers in the Saint Lawrence River, confiscated their vessel and merchandise. Protesting first before the Admiralty of La Rochelle and then before the royal council that fall, Samuel Georges and associates obtained permission to summon the company's associates to account for the seizure.[70] The case soon expanded beyond the specific triggering incident to encompass the Rochelais' status vis-à-vis the association more generally. In October 1617, an arbitrated settlement by the Sieurs Renard and Amelot, both royal counsellors and *maîtres des requêtes*, aimed to reach a compromise between the two parties' positions. It ordered, on the one hand, that "the said merchants of Rouen and Saint-Malo shall be bound to receive into the company created by the contracts and articles [of 15 November 1613] the said merchants of La Rochelle, whom they are bound to accept within five months"; the associates were also to return merchandise belonging to Georges et al. that they had seized at Quebec, worth 8,000 livres. On the other hand, the Rochelais ship, *Le Soleil*, and its merchandise and provisions, seized by the company in 1614 and 1615, were to be "acquired and confiscated to their profit."[71]

Although both parties had agreed to abide by the arbitrators' decision on pain of 10,000 livres, they each submitted an appeal in December. Georges and associates protested against the confiscation of *Le Soleil* and its cargo; Boyer and associates requested that they be released from admitting the Rochelais into the association.[72] The same month, the former party declared that they "intend to enter into the said company of Canada for the cargo beginning in 1618 and [for the] remaining years … and to contribute one-third in the future and protestation in the case of refusal against all expenses."[73] The results were twofold: both parties claimed that the other owed 10,000 livres for having appealed the arbitrators' decision; and the case henceforth split into two issues – the admission of the Rochelais into the CRSM, on the one hand, and the Rochelais' continued contravention of the trading ban, on the other – sometimes heard together, sometimes separately in the courts.[74]

In the final years of the suits, the cases turned decidedly against the CRSM. A decree of 14 August 1632 ordered the latter to pay Georges and associates a third of all monies it had received from 1618 to 1622, including not only profits from trade but also compensation awarded the company in 1622 against its successor.[75] The other half of the ruling, on the Rochelais' contravention of trading privileges, did not offset the loss to the CRSM associates. It awarded the latter 1,000 livres in interest from Samuel Georges and consorts for their having gone to Canada in 1615 without waiting for permission from the royal council and for legal costs from March 1631 onward.[76] An appeal launched the following year (1633) by the CRSM before the Parlement of Rouen resulted in the dismissal of the majority of grievances on both sides. The sovereign court "condemned and does condemn the said defendants [the Rouennais and Malouin associates] [to pay] jointly and severally toward the said plaintiffs [Georges and associates] the sum of 6,000 livres in interest" as a result of the arbitrated settlement of October 1617, plus legal costs, which, given the length and complexity of the case, must have been at least as much; Georges et al. were still required to pay the interest from the August 1632 sentence as well as the expenses of the present ruling. In the end, both parties were found at fault and subject to an indemnity in one of the two suits, although the company arguably suffered the most.[77]

Given the somewhat anti-climactic outcome of the suits, why did the parties persist for so long? By the time the Parlement of Rouen reached its decision, the CRSM had long since ceased to be active, the merchandise in question had either spoiled or been sold, and some of the parties had died. The detrimental effects of protracted lawsuits on commercial affairs were well-known and encouraged merchants to seek an end to their disputes as quickly as possible. The frequent practice of including an arbitration clause in contracts attests to this concern.[78] Even with the help of a lawyer (*avocat*) or procureur, lengthy suits took a great deal of time, energy, and money that could otherwise have gone into the business itself. The Rochelais, Rouennais, and Malouins were following a completely different logic here. In fact, their behaviour resembled much more that of nobles, who sought out royal justice in various contests over status.[79] For the CRSM and the Rochelais, what was at stake – control over the fur trade of New France and inter-port standing in France – was far more important than the costs of the legal proceedings and the penalties incurred. The rewards, like the risks, were high and the competition between the three ports ran deep.

Over the course of the litigation, the two sides made decisions that deliberately prolonged rather than shortened the dispute. The Rochelais and the company appealed the arbitrators' settlement, despite their avowals to let it stand. At times, they refused to appear when called, such as when Georges had Mathieu Duisterlo, the company's representative and a Parisian furrier, summoned before the Châtelet de Paris. At others, they came before a court to record their displeasure with a previous act in their opponent's favour. Thus, Georges blocked an act obtained by the CRSM that would have acknowledged the evidence presented by each, thereby requiring both sides to present their documents anew, once again increasing legal costs.[80] Inaction as much as action proved an effective tactic. While requests and sentences abound in the years 1614–18, the matter largely disappeared from the courts during the 1620s. Only a decree in the middle of the decade ordered the company to have their appeal judged within the month. It was not until 1630 that the parties picked up the case again.[81] Of course, long-drawn-out lawsuits were not uncommon in early modern France, and lawyers and procureurs were certainly known to deliberately prolong cases for their own profit.[82] But, taken together with the Rochelais' no-show in 1613 and their openly defiant trade in the Saint Lawrence, the evolution of the suit over time points not just to a lack of interest in seeking a resolution but an outright determination to delay one.

The antagonism between the CRSM and the Rochelais traders was not limited to the dispute over participation in the trade of the Saint Lawrence River but fuelled other incidents as well. In the spring of 1614, a ship sailing in the name of Charles de Biencourt, vice admiral of New France, seized two CRSM ships trading along the fur-rich shores of the Saint John River, an area of supposedly open trade. While Biencourt's agent and the ship's captain had confiscated the goods, the CRSM summoned Georges and Macain to appear before the royal council that fall "to be condemned to return all that they have robbed them of, their men, ships and goods, interest, damages and expenses."[83] Georges's and Macain's involvement here demands some explanation. The Rochelais pair had entered a business arrangement with Biencourt and his father in the fall of 1613, by which they provided sizable loans, outfitted ships to Acadia, and contracted with ships' masters on behalf of the father and son. In exchange, they received first choice of furs on the ships' return to France and, eventually, a more active role in Biencourt's affairs as he became heavily indebted to them.[84] As receivers of furs each fall from Acadia, Georges and Macain were ostensibly called before the court in 1614 by the CRSM associates to return the 642 furs taken from their ship.

Developing in parallel, the two suits show that the courts became a second battleground, a forum for the *continuation* rather than the resolution of disputes that began on the ground with the seizure of a ship.[85] While it is not clear which of the two seizures came first – whether in the Saint Lawrence or the Saint John Rivers – nor, indeed, which party initiated litigation, the suits became intertwined and mutually reinforcing in the courts. This intertwining is most clearly seen with respect to those whom the CRSM pursued over the Saint John River seizure. Arguably, the key figures were those who had seized the ship, the captain and Biencourt's agent; yet the Rouennais and Malouins spent the bulk of their energy and resources pursuing Georges and Macain. The higher the number of suits pursued simultaneously, the greater one's chances of wearing down one's adversary, of costing him money, and forcing him to negotiate in one's favour.

The parties' skilful manipulation of the multiple and overlapping jurisdictions in France highlights the ways in which the legal system served to contain conflicts, not only among those who came before it, but also among the courts themselves. Both the CRSM and the Rochelais perceived that they would obtain the best results in their home provinces. Samuel Georges and his associates made frequent appeals to the Admiralty of La Rochelle, where they expected – and usually received – a favourable hearing, as well as to the royal councils. The Rouennais and Malouins appeared most often before the Admiralty of Rouen. A request by one party in one jurisdiction was frequently met with a counter-request in another, resulting in contradictory sentences.[86] One of many disputes over jurisdiction occurred in 1614–15, when the CRSM requested an order for Georges and associates to appear before the Admiralty of Rouen and the latter responded with a like order for the company associates to appear before the royal council. In January 1615, the council ordered both parties before the Admiralty. As a privileged company under the viceroy, the CRSM appeared to enjoy an advantage over its adversaries: its cases were to be heard before a specified jurisdiction, a privilege granted corporations and individuals of a certain status.[87] First reserved to the royal council by Condé's letters patent of November 1612, the king soon transferred all suits to the courts of Normandy: "lawsuits and disputes that arise among our subjects of Normandy, as regards the trade and voyages of Canada, will be treated in the first instance before our judges of the Admiralty of Rouen and on appeal before you [the Parlement of Rouen]."[88] While this order did lend legitimacy to the Rouennais' and Malouins' actions before the Admiralty of Rouen, it did not stop the Rochelais from appearing before local courts or the royal councils.

The advantage to the company was heavily dependent upon the co-operation of other competing jurisdictions; if unrecognized or ignored, a royal decree had no force. Revealing the strength of regional jealousies and suspicion, Samuel Georges made a request in January 1618 for the proceedings between the two parties to take place either before the Admiralty of La Rochelle, the royal council, or another judge appointed by the king "outside the province of Normandy."[89] With such strong rivalries among Rochelais and Norman traders, each court was biased. Competing and overlapping jurisdictions encouraged such strategies as seeking sentences in one's home province, "shopping around" for a sympathetic jurisdiction, or prolonging a suit in the hopes of a favourable sentence.[90] Happy to pronounce upon a case if it privileged their power over another's, courts employed their own tactics, from taking their time sending particular documents to another court to ruling on a case expressly reserved to the royal council.[91] Legal authority in France was, then, as much at stake in these lawsuits as was power in New France.

During the 1610s – and in the case of the CRSM and the Rochelais, over the following two decades – those with a stake in New France used conflict in a variety of ways to advance their own claims and to challenge those of others. Contests of authority on both sides of the Atlantic were closely intertwined and mutually influential. Condé's refusal to give up his claim to viceregal rights was part of his resistance to the queen regent's government; the ensuing legal dispute offered an opening for others involved in New France – including Champlain, the CRSM, and independent traders – to increase their own power.

Regardless of a party's position, each sought to bring metropolitan authorities into overseas spaces. The question of which authorities and how best to approach them depended on the calculations behind each party's pursuit of conflict. Taking advantage of political instability to gain more leverage, Champlain and the CRSM sought out the arbitration of the king, who "resolved" the conflict in a manner typical of jurisdictional spats: by ordering both parties to respect the prerogatives of the other, all the while leaving these undefined. If material resources and standing were equally at stake for the Malouin and Rochelais traders who challenged the CRSM, the Malouins were content to make their point by inconveniencing their opponents. The conflict between the Rochelais and the company had an extra intensity, due to the degree of inter-port rivalry and competition over control of the fur trade between Rouen and La Rochelle. Both parties channelled the intensity of their rivalry into the justice system, allowing the conflict to play out with minimal damage. Indeed, the fact that the two lawsuits between the CRSM and the Rochelais ended in a virtual draw after twenty years at court did not seem all that important. What *was* important was the parties' respective decisions not to capitulate. The relationship between claimants in New France and metropolitan bodies was not unidirectional. While justices granted a party a hearing or pronounced upon a case to assert their own jurisdiction against another's, other office-holders made direct claims to the fledgling colony as part of their own strategies for consolidating institutional and personal authority.

3

The Maritime and Territorial Landscapes of New France

In the fall of 1619, in a well-appointed notary's office in Paris, representatives of the Prince de Condé, newly released from prison, and the admiral of France, Henri II de Montmorency, Condé's brother-in-law, signed a piece of paper by which the viceroyalty of New France passed from one to the other at the cost of 30,000 livres. Connected by marriage, these great nobles were shuffling assets – here the title of viceroy – the better to position both families. But Admiral Montmorency was also removing a rival in the granting of licences to French subjects for travel overseas. Indeed, over the previous six years, Viceroy Condé had given licences on numerous occasions, not only to the privileged trading company to New France, but also to independent traders from Atlantic ports. When Montmorency purchased the viceroyalty from the prince, he was probably unaware of the colony's actual situation: a small habitation with little infrastructure and a handful of settlers, in a territory under the control of Indigenous Peoples. What attracted the admiral, instead, was New France's status as a maritime space.

European expansion into the Indian and Atlantic Oceans over the late fifteenth and sixteenth centuries had begun to raise questions about the nature of sovereignty on a number of levels. With the sea becoming increasingly important economically and politically to a nation's standing in Europe, questions of sovereignty were especially maritime.[1] Could a state or an individual claim legitimate ownership of the sea? Was it possible to own a particular maritime trade route? The series of papal bulls in the 1490s granting Spain and Portugal access to "undiscovered" lands made the issue of immediate concern, particularly to the two countries' European competitors. Contrary to popular understanding, Pope Alexander VI did not grant possession (*dominium*) of the world's lands and oceans to the

Iberians (nor did he have the temporal authority to do so). Rather, he gave permission to the Portuguese and Spanish to explore and claim lands to the east and west, respectively. The role of the ocean in this division was as a "connecting space," over which both powers claimed exclusive jurisdictional rights but not territorial possession.[2] Since the 1520s, the French Crown had challenged Iberian claims to control navigation in the Atlantic. The establishment of "lines of amity" in 1559, by which the area west of the Azores remained a militarized space, gave France a partial victory, freeing it from the obligation to crack down on its corsairs in this area.[3]

Arguably the most famous and influential intervention in this debate over the legitimacy of claims to oceanic space was by Dutch jurist Hugo Grotius in *Mare Liberum*, or *The Free Sea*. Published in 1609 at the behest of the Dutch East India Company, the pamphlet appeared in the context of negotiations between Spain and the newly independent United Provinces and, more particularly, Dutch attempts to preserve its access to trade with Asia.[4] Drawing on both Roman and natural law, Grotius argued that the sea could not be possessed, owing to its great extent and to the fact that its principal resources, including fish, could never be used up. If the sea did not constitute private property, neither was it a commons, the property of all. According to the Dutch jurist, states could still claim jurisdiction in order to regulate and manage the ocean's resources. The limit to this jurisdiction was the obligation to maintain common-use rights to fishing and navigation, both open to all by natural law. In other words, for Grotius, the key question was one of access.[5] Given the implications of *The Free Sea* for maritime European countries, responses came from several quarters, ranging from the Catholic Church, which banned the pamphlet, to English and Portuguese jurists. English jurists argued for a distinction between territorial waters (subject to *dominium*) and the high seas (open to unrestricted navigation), while the Portuguese saw the sea as common property susceptible to division into zones of private-use rights, allowing states exclusive use of specific trade routes.[6] Although Grotius's work has had the most lasting impact and is at the foundation of modern international law, the prevailing behaviour of European states at the time did not correspond to it. Instead, they continued throughout the seventeenth and into the eighteenth centuries to lay claim to exclusive jurisdiction over particular regions of the sea.[7]

Waterways were key corridors for spreading jurisdiction. In France, a licence granted by the admiral dictated where a ship could travel and what resources its crew could access. The ship – whether headed to the Banks of Newfoundland or to New France for fishing or trading – in turn carried jurisdiction with it. Each voyage reaffirmed French control over the maritime route, while exploration upriver into the interior of North America held the promise of extending sovereign claims to territory. This chapter explores the relationship between aquatic and terrestrial spaces, and more specifically, between maritime and territorial jurisdiction. What kind of space was constructed between France and New France? What kind of space did New France become, and for whom? Drawing on the notion of spaces of power – that is, "systems of social power, whether political, military, religious, etc. that we can describe functionally and spatially"[8] – the chapter examines three different types and scales of space: oceanic, terrestrial, and riverine. Beginning with the initiatives Montmorency took to realize his maritime vision of New France, it then turns to the relationship between different forms of power along the waterways and within and without French trading posts on the ground. The compatibility or opposition between these various forms at specific moments shaped the possibilities for, and obstacles to, sovereignty and authority in New France.

New France Becomes Attached to the Admiralty of France

The debate over the nature of ocean space sparked by Dutch-Spanish negotiations was closely watched throughout maritime Europe. There is little doubt that these pressing international maritime questions shaped Henri II de Montmorency's approach to his roles as admiral and viceroy of New France. Certainly, the sea was as strategically important and contested a space domestically as internationally. The Montmorencys had long recognized its significance and become one of the most powerful noble families by acquiring the highest maritime military offices. In 1538, Anne de Montmorency, who had married the sister of the admiral of Provence, became *connétable*, or constable, of France, the first officer of the Crown and commander of the king's army. Coupled with his position as *grand maître de France*, the head of the king's household, the *Connétablie* made Anne one of the most powerful men in the kingdom, and he used this power to propel the Montmorencys to the top of the peerage. In 1552, the year after he became Duc de Montmorency, Anne had Gaspard de Coligny, his nephew, appointed admiral of France. Coligny was a strong proponent of maritime and colonial enterprises, including Vice Admiral of Brittany

Nicholas Durand de Villegaignon's expedition to Brazil in the 1550s, as well as privateering activities against Spain's American colonies. Although the Montmorencys lost their hold on maritime offices for a generation during the Wars of Religion, they returned to favour with the accession of Henri IV to the throne in 1589. Having fought on the king's behalf, Henri I de Montmorency, son of Anne, was named constable, his brother Charles, colonel-general of the Swiss Guards and admiral of France, while both became members of l'Ordre du Saint-Esprit, the highest order of knighthood in France. It was into these favourable conditions that Henri II de Montmorency, son of Henri I and godson of King Henri IV, was born and raised. Favoured by Henri IV and Marie de Médicis, Henri II succeeded his uncle Charles to the Admiralty of France in 1612 and, two years later, became Duc de Montmorency and governor of Languedoc upon the death of his father. Henri II, like his predecessors, showed a keen awareness of the importance of maritime issues both for France's standing in Europe and for the Montmorency power base inside the kingdom. In particular, he saw the Admiralty as an institution that could help France compete directly with England and the Netherlands by developing the kingdom's naval forces and encouraging overseas colonizing and commercial enterprises.[9]

When Henri II de Montmorency became admiral (eight years before becoming viceroy of New France), he was following in a line of admirals who had made fitful progress in extending the Admiralty's – and, by extension, the Crown's – jurisdiction to the peripheries of France. The authority of the admiral of France had long been extensive in theory and restricted in practice, due to the competing claims of seigneurs, governors, and other regional admirals.[10] Since 1582, the admiral of France had claimed control over ports, fortifications, ships, munitions, and maritime justice in Picardy, Normandy, Poitou, Saintonge, Guyenne, and Brittany, claims backed up by royal declarations in his favour. Provence, Languedoc, and several seigneuries, including Sables d'Olonne and Saint-Valéry, remained officially outside his jurisdiction. In practice, however, the admiral's authority was only secured in Picardy and Normandy (and even there it was subject to challenge on occasion). In provinces like Brittany and Guyenne, on the Atlantic coast, governors kept a tight hold on Admiralty rights, justifying their claims with reference to traditional practices predating their attachment to the kingdom.[11]

Resistance to the admiral's authority was particularly strong in the province of Brittany and the port of La Rochelle, in the province of Aunis.

As we saw in chapter 1, Breton governors regularly tangled with successive admirals of France from the 1580s to the mid-1620s over control of commerce and the administration of maritime justice. The Breton Parlement and Estates were staunch supporters of governors' claims, protesting the admiral of France's prerogatives and only registering his letters with strong caveats. Any agreements on dividing maritime authority between the two positions were short-lived. Indeed, Montmorency's tenure was no exception. His dispute with Governor Vendôme continued throughout his time as viceroy of New France.[12] In the case of La Rochelle, the Atlantic port and Huguenot stronghold created its own Admiralty whenever it was in conflict with the Crown, a frequent occurrence in the 1610s and 20s. La Rochelle was especially well positioned to command effective naval and commercial control of the Atlantic coast, with its well-armed ships and well-connected international merchants involved in overseas trade. This situation meant that the admiral's impact in a given province or port depended on the strength of his personal power, which was wielded in part through his collection of his share of prizes and *droits d'ancrage et du guet*.[13]

With the king's encouragement, Montmorency, like his Uncle Charles before him, used a combination of administrative and personal authority to strengthen his jurisdiction. To counter the claims of governors and regional admirals, he issued a decree asserting his prerogative as the sole legitimate provider of licences, called upon all captains to diligently register them, attempted to strengthen the local Admiralty courts, and sent personal agents to ports to collect the duties owed him from these proceedings.[14] In 1622, he received direct support from the Crown when the king increased the authority of the Admiralty courts, the admiral himself, and the royal council; four years later, the king named a secretary for each of the navies in the Ponant and Levant. Montmorency increased his personal authority by buying out rival claimants.[15] In 1613, for example, he purchased the office of admiral of Guyenne from Henri de Châtillon, Comte de Coligny, the grandson of Gaspard de Coligny. This move expanded his and the Crown's jurisdiction to the southwest, a region with an important Protestant population. Montmorency henceforth became "admiral of France, Brittany, and Guyenne." This title underscores the fragmented nature of the Admiralty's authority in France; it was his status as Coligny's successor, and not his capacity as admiral of France, that gave Montmorency legitimate power in the latter province.[16] These initiatives together formed the foundations of a developing, multi-faceted maritime policy.[17]

It is in this context that the purchase of the viceroyalty of New France should be seen. Like the acquisition of the Admiralty of Guyenne, it served a dual purpose: dynastically, it realigned strategic interests among allied houses; institutionally, it strengthened the admiral's authority. Upon his release from prison in 1619, the rebellious Condé had a change of heart and subsequently spent the 1620s leading royal armies on the king's behalf against Protestant dissidents.[18] The viceregal commission was perhaps no longer of personal interest to him and fit better with his brother-in-law's position of admiral; the two jurisdictions did, after all, overlap. On the advice of the intendant of the Admiralty, the Sieur de Villemenon, Montmorency thus added the viceroyalty to his personal and institutional domain. Authority over the colony, like that over any port in France, extended Montmorency's surveillance over commercial and naval traffic. As importantly, it allowed the admiral to develop his maritime vision. Connecting directly to the questions raised by European expansion, becoming viceroy of New France was a way of claiming jurisdiction over present and any future maritime commercial routes taken by French subjects. As one of the highest-ranking military officers in the realm, and now viceroy, Montmorency became a key figure in the extension of the king's sovereignty to the peripheries of France and across the Atlantic to New France.

The Maritime Landscape of Commercial Power

Montmorency was not alone in conceiving of New France as essentially maritime. Maps prominently featured rivers as corridors for increasing knowledge (of new lands and peoples) and, from there, sovereignty. For their part, royal commissions to viceroys, and later governors, generally delineated jurisdictions based on "watermarks." They emphasized coasts, harbours, and islands, rather than lands and countries.[19] In the case of early seventeenth-century letters patent, political and commercial jurisdictions were articulated differently. Following his purchase of the viceregal title from Condé in 1619, Montmorency received another set of papers, this time from the king.[20] Although they are no longer extant, the letters patent appear to have been the same as Condé's, conferring governmental authority over the Saint Lawrence Valley and Acadia and exclusive trading privileges from Matane to Quebec and beyond. In Condé's commission, the description of the viceroy's/lieutenant general's jurisdiction is land-based. The preamble refers to the "countries, lands and confines of New France," while the king calls on Condé to "represent our person throughout this country of New France."[21] This description of the viceroy's political jurisdiction is one bounded in space, with a sense (albeit vague) of limits.

The articulation of commercial spaces of power is, by contrast, aquatic. In Condé's commission, waterways are designated as particular types of commercial zones. For example, the king extended Condé's trading area below Quebec in 1613: "our cousin and those who will have power from him to trade and traffic with the Natives of the said country and to establish there our authority and the habitations of our subjects, from the place of Quebec and above it, alone shall have the same power, for their greater security, to trade *from the said river of Matane up to the said Quebec and in all the ports, harbours, roadsteads and rivers being between those of Matane and Quebec on either shore* and to build such forts and strongholds as they may find the most useful."[22] The Saint Lawrence River and its tributaries thus constituted a privileged fur trading area, enjoyed by the viceroy and the company to whom he subsequently delegated these privileges. The non-privileged trading space below Matane is similarly described according to maritime features: "reserving nevertheless to all our said subjects the liberty to trade *the length of the other coasts, ports and harbours* of the said New France, except as stated above the said place of Quebec and above as far as one can extend."[23] In other words, the shores of Acadia are open to all subjects to trade and fish (see figure 3.1). Since the first grants of exclusive privileges in the late sixteenth century, the Crown had kept the fishery open to all subjects, a policy that had roots in Roman legal codes. Those resources considered eligible for restricted use were those on land.[24] The long practice of Bretons, Normans, and Basques of combining fishing and whaling voyages with fur trading on the shores of what would become Nova Scotia, Quebec, and Labrador might explain the use of watermarks to delineate privileged and open fur trading zones.

At the most basic level, New France constitutes a maritime space because exploitation of its resources was seasonal. Thousands of ships annually carried fishermen, private fur traders, and members or agents of the privileged trading company across the Atlantic in the spring and returned them to their home ports each fall. Only a skeleton crew remained at Quebec and Port-Royal through the winter to protect both commercial

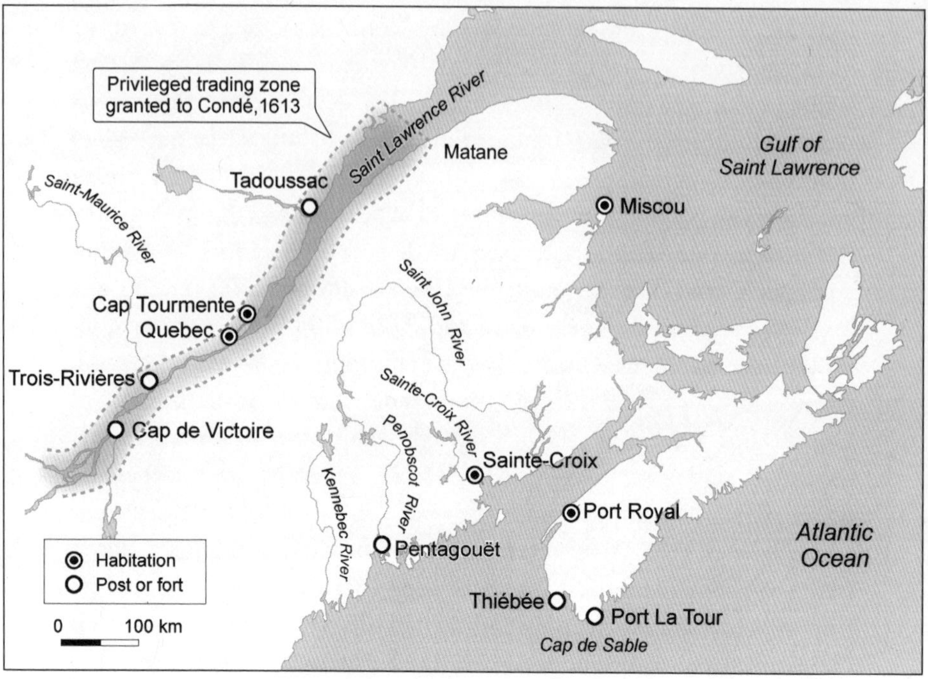

Figure 3.1 French posts, forts, and habitations in Acadia and the Saint Lawrence Valley, including the privileged trading zone, 1603–20.

and sovereign claims. In a certain sense, the privileged and open trading zones were themselves seasonal, emerging with the first ship's arrival from France and dissolving for all practical purposes once the winter set in.

The use of aquatic features to differentiate between various commercial zones underscores different degrees of access.[25] Only certain subjects – those tied to the privileged trading company – could travel up the Saint Lawrence for particular purposes – in this case, for fur trading. The royal commissions to Condé and later Montmorency thus regulated access to and the use of resources and the waterways leading to them. Following the common practice of dividing the Atlantic Ocean into many seas, contemporary maps frequently name the waters off the coast of today's Nova Scotia the "Sea of Canada or New France" (see figure 3.2). Such naming implied sovereign claims to jurisdiction, if not actual possession.[26] Not limited to coastal waters (territorial seas), this jurisdiction traced a line across the ocean, as claims to control the movement of people and goods to New France implied a certain claim to jurisdiction over the ocean itself.[27]

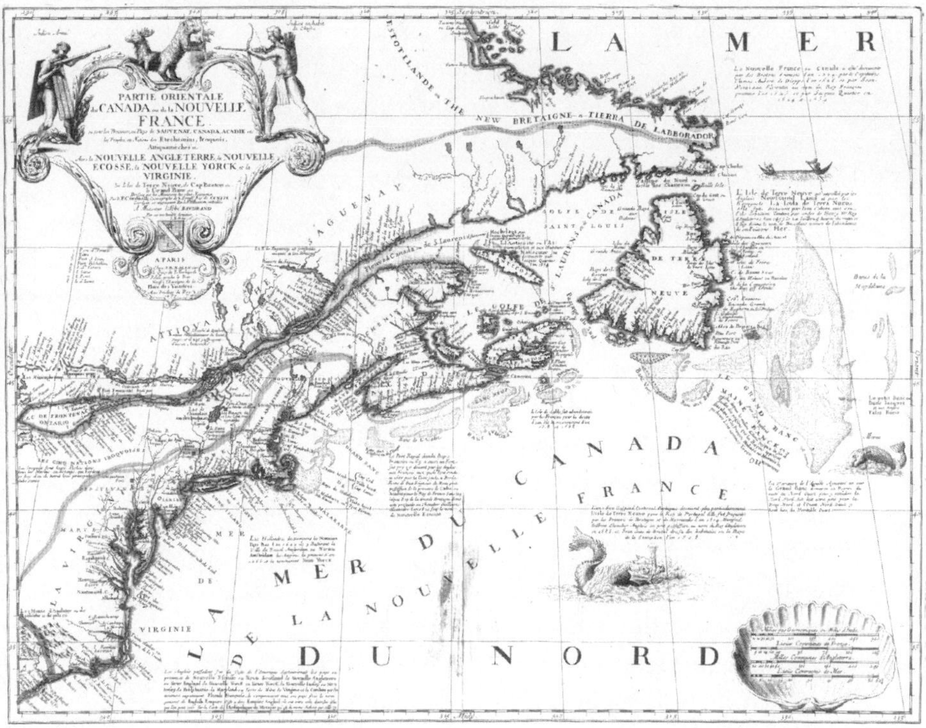

Figure 3.2 Vincenzo Coronelli, "Partie orientale du Canada ou de la Nouvelle France," 1689

Territorial Jurisdiction and Maritime Power

The growing traffic across the Atlantic in the 1610s strengthened New France's status as a maritime space. Given his supervision, in theory, of all traffic entering and leaving France, the admiral of France had always had some claim to jurisdiction over travel to New France. When de Mons received his commission as lieutenant general of Acadia from Henri IV in 1603, for example, he had already been granted "commissions and powers" from Charles de Montmorency, then admiral of France, concerning "the affaires and the charge of the Admiraltie, in the exploit, expedition, and executing of the things above said [i.e., the lieutenant general's commission]."[28] Subsequent appointments of vice admirals of New France reaffirmed the legitimacy of the admiral's transatlantic authority. Montmorency's acquisition of the viceroyalty in 1620 precipitated, however, a significant shift in practice in that the colony became directly connected to the metropolitan institution and person responsible for maritime affairs. In other words, Montmorency's viceroyalty marked the first time that control over maritime traffic in France was linked to control over territory overseas.

The close relationship between the two positions is evident in the three-pronged strategy Montmorency deployed to assert his newfound authority as viceroy. On a governmental level, he established a combination of personal agents and administrative positions, similar to those that helped to execute his authority as admiral. While Montmorency followed the established pattern in New France by (re)naming Samuel de Champlain lieutenant with almost identical powers to those delegated by Condé, the commander of Quebec was no longer the sole representative of the viceroy. Instead, Montmorency appointed an intendant of New France, the first in the colony's history. Jean-Jacques Dolu, royal counsellor and *grand audiencier* of France, was charged with overseeing "things concerning the affairs of New France," a wonderfully vague mandate. Among his broad responsibilities (some of which comprised Champlain's former duties) were making treaties with merchants for provisions and merchandise and deciding the fate of the CRSM.[29] Champlain greeted Dolu's appointment with enthusiasm, hoping it would "put our Company into a better condition of prosperity than it had been." This new position changed the way the lieutenant carried out his own. No longer straddling the Atlantic, Champlain commanded the habitation during five consecutive winters under Montmorency, a responsibility he had not undertaken for the previous seven years due to colonial business in France.[30] The admiral also named two commissioners, Baptiste Guers and Captain Du May, who travelled to New France in 1620 to report on its condition. Both made subsequent voyages to the same ends and acted as messengers, delivering letters to Champlain from the king, Montmorency, Dolu, the company associates, and the intendant of the Admiralty, the Sieur de Villemenon. The latter was not accorded a particular position relative to New France but served at times as Montmorency's liaison to the new company granted trading privileges in 1620.[31] The full extent of Dolu's, Guers's, and Du May's duties is not known, but it is possible – and even likely – that, like the intendant of the Admiralty and clerks in French ports, they also asserted and protected Montmorency's rights as viceroy.[32] Drawing on the administrative and maritime expertise of the Admiralty, Montmorency thus used much the same strategy in his new position: he bought out the claims of rivals (and relatives) following the common practice of venality, or the sale of government offices, created new positions in which he installed clients, and asserted his rights to duties and other privileges owed him.

Following these appointments, a two-act drama ensued that made visible the twin forces of law and force behind Montmorency's authority as viceroy. Both were partly pre-emptive strikes, reflecting the competing French claims to maritime commercial rights and navigation on both sides of the Atlantic. The first act was a typical ceremony of possession, undertaken to claim the territory for the viceroy (in the name of the king) and to inform those who had wintered there of the change in government. Armed with their commissions from Montmorency, Champlain, Guers, and Du May sailed to New France in the spring of 1620. Upon their arrival at Quebec, the colony's couple dozen inhabitants gathered around to hear the news from France. A Récollet father performed Holy Mass and called upon all to serve the king and his viceroy and to obey the latter's lieutenant. Guers then read aloud Montmorency's letters patent and Champlain's commission. Champlain describes the conclusion of the ceremony as follows: "This having been done, everybody cried, 'Long Live the King!'; the cannon was fired in a sign of joy, and thus I took possession of the settlement and the country in the name of His Grace the Viceroy. The said Guers drew up an account of the proceedings for use when and where required."[33]

As Champlain's description demonstrates, the ceremony was directed toward fellow French rather than Indigenous Peoples or European rivals. Its main component, the reading of the commissions, intended to inform and serve as a warning "so that no one might plead ignorance of them," as did countless other similar announcements of royal decrees in French cities and ports.[34] It also aimed to convey, through the gun salute, the grandeur of Montmorency's authority. Like comparable acts of possession performed by other Europeans, this one was provisional, to be followed by "effective occupation" through the construction of a fort at Quebec and other habitations elsewhere in the region.[35] Lastly, the viceroy's representatives were careful to make a record of the ceremony, in anticipation of future challenges. The previous decades of trading and colonizing enterprises to New France had, after all, shown that contest was certain and that claims needed to be constantly asserted and defended as a result. The ceremony highlighted more than anything else that the viceroy's jurisdiction was personal, attached to the particular person in the position, rather than territorial. Taking "possession of the settlement and the country" anew,

Champlain and Montmorency's other agents re-inscribed the space with the viceroy's (and his lieutenant's) authority.

This dignified, symbolic act at Quebec had its aggressive corollary in France that fall when Montmorency marshalled the full weight of the Admiralty. On the wharf in the Norman port of Honfleur, the intendant of the Admiralty of Normandy and the *procureur du roi* seized a rich cargo of furs from the CRSM's ships, which had just returned from their journey across the Atlantic. They also forbade the crew from making further voyages to New France. The seizure, as with many aggressive displays of personal authority, proved to be just the beginning of a vigorous contest over rights. After the associates protested the action before the royal council, the parties reached a compromise out of court by which Dolu agreed to release the goods on condition that the CRSM reimburse the Admiralty of Normandy for the costs of the seizure and storage of the merchandise. More consequentially, the company associates further agreed to "desist ... from any pretention that these associates may have and claim to continue in the future the said voyages and trade to the said country of New France, under the pretence of powers granted to them by treaties made previously by the said associates with the preceding governors of the said lands for the king, without licence, confirmation or consent from the said Seigneur de Montmorency viceroy," while reserving the right to demand payment for any merchandise belonging to them still in New France.[36] Regretting the commitment they had made, they later withdrew their consent. Before the courts once more, the ensuing dispute focused on whether the trading privileges to the colony remained in the hands of the CRSM, as per its eleven-year contract with Condé, or whether the revocation of all previous commissions allowed Montmorency to enter into new agreements with other parties. It expanded to involve several third parties, including the new company to which Montmorency had given trading privileges, and was not resolved for more than two years.[37]

These events demonstrate that, for Montmorency, the Admiralty and the viceroyalty went hand in hand. He could, after all, have simply given notice of the change in personnel to the company. But his decision to make a show of force underscores his intention to draw on the full legal apparatus of the Admiralty in the viceroyalty's favour. By forbidding the CRSM from sailing to New France, he asserted his prerogative to limit access to the Saint Lawrence River, along with the right to choose with whom to associate for the trade of the colony. In actual fact, the blanket ban on "voyages and trade to the said country of New France" goes somewhat beyond the powers conferred in his royal commission. As we have seen, all subjects were theoretically permitted to travel to the open trading zone of Acadia. It was, nevertheless, a warning shot to the former privileged company: the admiral and his agents were watching and would not hesitate to use force when necessary.

More than a straightforward dispute over the prerogatives of each party, the lawsuit between Montmorency and the CRSM reflected Montmorency's bid to incorporate the colony, and specifically the company with trading privileges, into the existing structure of the Admiralty's authority. The viceroyalty, in turn, consolidated Montmorency's authority as admiral. Montmorency was not attracted to New France as a settlement or a territory with particular resources. Control of the colony allowed him, instead, to affirm his exclusive supervision of one of the main Atlantic trade routes used by French subjects.[38] In other words, territorial possession was ancillary. It was valuable only insofar as it served this goal. Both positions secured Montmorency's hold on what was the most sought-after resource by European powers: movement, of both subjects and goods.[39]

The Company as a Route to Maritime Control

On a practical level, the seizure of the CRSM's trading ships cleared the way for Montmorency to establish a new trading company, one whose composition, organization, and terms he could control. The resulting company reflected international experimentations with a new tool of capital formation: the chartered company. Indeed, this innovative form became the preferred means among northwestern European powers to secure control of maritime trade routes and navigation in the seventeenth century.[40] The growing sea power and commercial might of the Netherlands and England led their European rivals – not least France, which was more than fifteen times the size of the former and twice as big as the latter – to search for its source so they could emulate them. Like many of his contemporaries, Montmorency considered those countries' overseas trading enterprises, the most famous and lucrative of which were their respective East India Companies, as the secret to their success. Founding similar companies would therefore offer France the means to challenge them.[41]

The principal innovation of the Dutch and English East India Companies was their combination of joint-stock capital and the corporation. While both of these instruments had existed prior to these enterprises, they had never been brought together for commercial purposes.[42] Pooled capital facilitated long-distance enterprises, like overseas trade and colonization, by spreading the risks and the burden of having substantial sums locked up in infrastructure (particularly ships, posts, and forts) among many investors.[43] Incorporation gave the company its own legal personality distinct from its individual members, allowing the company itself to sue and be sued and to own property. A charter from the Crown, or the States General in the Netherlands, afforded the company protection, in theory, from foreigners and competitors. The charter contained the company's powers, privileges, and obligations.[44] Companies on this model were typically delegated a portion of the ruler's sovereignty. It is for this reason that they are frequently referred to as hybrid entities, combining what we consider to be exclusive features of a company as well as of a state.[45] For example, the Dutch East India Company (Vereenigde Oostindische Compagnie, or VOC), like its companion enterprise the Dutch West India Company, had the power to declare war, enter treaties, and keep an army and navy.[46] Such extensive regal powers, along with considerable privileges – usually exclusive trade and often land concessions as well – made company officials "indistinguishable from public officers" and demanded that the company be for the public good as much as for private profit, like other corporations. The most visible manifestations of this in the case of the English East India Company (EIC) were the loans, credit, and customs duties accorded the king.[47] While governments passed off the heavy responsibilities of naval protection for commercial fleets, colonization, and government, they also sought to benefit directly or indirectly from an enterprise's activities.

The chartered company's independent legal status allowed it to exist indefinitely, a characteristic closely related to two emerging concepts, transferable shares and continuous capital. Subscribers purchased one or more shares. In theory, they were not responsible for more than their share. This feature had in part to do with the enterprise's governance structure. Given the size of such ventures – they often consisted of fifty to several hundred people – it was not practicable to expect all to have a hand in the management of business. Instead, the joint-stock company drew a distinction between investors and managers. In both the VOC and the EIC, daily operations were in the hands of a board of directors – the Heren XVII in the VOC, the Court of Directors in the EIC. The EIC also held annual general assemblies in which important decisions were made and in which each member had a vote.[48] The capital was in theory permanent, lasting for the life of the company. By contrast, most associations of the period in all countries were based on single voyages, at the end of which members divided up the assets. The concepts of continuous capital and limited liability took time to develop in practice.[49]

Companies modelled on Dutch and English commercial and colonizing enterprises constituted an ambitious departure in France, where the vast majority of associations were small partnerships among friends and relatives organized on an annual basis. In early modern France, there were two broad categories under which most associations fit. The first and most common was the *société de personnes*, which was organized around the people who took part. If a partner withdrew, the association itself dissolved.[50] One type of *société de personnes* was the *société générale* (also called the *société en nom collectif*), or partnership, which consisted of a handful of members, usually merchants, who were all active in the association's affairs. The association formed for a limited time, often one season, at the end of which members divided the profits and losses among themselves. Each associate, actively involved, was liable for the affairs of the company. Both the Compagnie de Mons and the CRSM were organized along these lines. A second type of member-centred company, the *société en commandite*, differed from the first in that not all members were engaged in the association's affairs to the same degree. Active partners contributed labour and handled the logistical side; "silent partners," or *commanditaires*, provided capital only.[51] As a result, the former were fully liable for the affairs of the company, while the latter were in theory only responsible for their individual shares. In practice, the line between the two types of associates, in terms of both engagement and liability, was not so definite.[52]

The second broad category of association was only beginning to develop in France over the course of the seventeenth and eighteenth centuries. Called the *société de capitaux*, it was organized around the pooled funds rather than the individual investors. Its principal features were the transferable share and separate management. In contrast to the partnership, a capital-centred company continued to exist when a member left and sold his or her share. A board of directors handled the day-to-day business of the company. Modelled on the VOC and EIC, it resembled them in its powers and prerogatives, management, size, and duration. It was no coincidence that the first *sociétés de capitaux* operated in the domain of maritime commerce and navigation, a high-risk arena in which stability was greatly prized.[53] Unlike other types of association but like other corporations, these companies were seen as serving the public interest, particularly through their responsibility for government on land and sea conferred by charter. It was only in the second half of the eighteenth century that private commercial enterprises based on capital became widespread in France, more than half a century later than in England.[54] Although it is possible to identify such different types of association, these categories prove to be largely artificial constructs when applied to on-the-ground arrangements among merchants and businessmen. Contemporaries did not take especial care to define an association and often used a mixture of elements from capital-centred and people-centred organizations.[55] While Montmorency and others looked to English and Dutch companies, they did not transplant them wholesale to France, but rather incorporated various elements into existing French forms of association.

Montmorency's interest in New France and the corporate form was shaped in part by his previous role in the beginnings of French trade in the Indian Ocean, which he considered a crucial element in France's ability to compete with Dutch and English maritime commercial power. When he became viceroy in 1620, he was already the patron of the Compagnie des Indes orientales (CIO), itself modelled on its Dutch and English counterparts. The company, which initially formed in 1604 under a Flemish naval captain and a French royal counsellor and treasurer, was granted exclusive privileges in the East Indian trade for fifteen years. Like its foreign models, the company was open to public subscription, offering shares at a minimum of 3,000 livres. It received material support, privileges, and significant powers from the king in the form of artillery, munitions, and vessels, a year's exemption from Admiralty rights, and the use of the Breton port of Brest. Despite these favourable terms, the company remained inactive over the next decade. Two Rouennais merchants, one by the name of Ézéchiel de Caën, consequently proposed their own enterprise to the region. "Recognizing that it would be hazardous if there were several companies and societies for the same undertaking," the king united the two companies under the protection and jurisdiction of Henri de Montmorency, a fairly common solution to rival claims during this period.[56] The admiral's stewardship saw annual trading voyages by the company's ships, henceforth known as "the fleet of Montmorency," the transfer of its headquarters to Paris, and an expansion in membership, before the association dissolved in 1620.[57] The CIO was the first French company created in the image of the still relatively new VOC and EIC.

While the trading company to New France under Montmorency did not have a royal charter or extensive regal powers and its mandate included colonization as well as commerce, the two enterprises shared the same context and goal. A part of the innovation and experimentation necessary to meet the challenges of European overseas expansion, they served to put two of the major maritime commercial routes more firmly under royal control, via the admiral. Montmorency did not see New France or Atlantic trade routes in isolation; rather, they were part of a transoceanic network, at the centre of which was the East Indian trade. Here, we see that the Atlantic had its own characteristics – all companies operating in this space had colonization as one of their objectives – and was, at the same time, connected to other maritime spaces.

A New Form of Trading Company in New France

The new trading company to New France under Montmorency reflected simultaneously previous company practices in the colony and new forms of capital-centred enterprise in its organization and responsibilities. In November 1620, the intendant of New France, Dolu, entered an agreement on the viceroy's behalf with the Protestant Guillaume de Caën, a captain in the king's navy, and his Catholic uncle Ézéchiel, the same Rouennais merchant active in the CIO, for the establishment of the Compagnie de Montmorency. Similar to the terms that the CRSM had previously enjoyed, the de Caëns and their associates received exclusive trading privileges for eleven years along with the power to seize interloping vessels. In exchange, they undertook to transport and provide for several different groups of people in the colony, ranging from ecclesiastics and families wishing to settle to men in Champlain's employ and a viceroy's representative. Where the CRSM had paid only Champlain's salary of 1,200 livres, the new associates would also pay 600 livres to "any Secretary of the said Seigneur vice-Roy that he wishes, for all troubles [*peines*], salaries, and fees of expeditions that it will be necessary for him to take for the said Seigneur vice-Roy" in exchange for the annual passport. Thus would Guers have been reimbursed on subsequent voyages to New France as messenger. This clause underscores the greater number of agents, and hence greater supervision of the enterprise, under Montmorency as viceroy. In addition, the company was required to build "a house and place of habitation with twelve *toises* frontage on the street," every three years, at a location chosen by the lieutenant.[58]

On balance, the Compagnie de Montmorency's access to the privileged trading area became less exclusive, while its obligations became more onerous than those of its predecessors. The provision to pay the salaries of the viceroy's representatives who travelled to New France put a price on access to the oceanic and riverine routes leading to the commerce promised by the exclusive privileges. In monetary terms, the viceroy charged a premium of 1,800 livres over and above the 3,000 livres due annually in exchange for trading rights. This element highlights the essential maritime dimension of the viceroy's jurisdiction. Both access and privileges were layered depending on status, whether one was a company associate or agent, a seasonal fisherman or a settler. Indeed, although the associates received exclusive trading privileges for eleven years, a subsequent provision permitted subjects who fished along the Newfoundland Banks and coasts of New France "to receive by gift and exchange with the Natives up to twelve Beaver pelts per vessel, which they will be bound to deliver to the said Company for 3 livres each."[59] Subjects without ties to the company were, therefore, no longer completely excluded from the privileged trading zone. This amendment opened the door more fully to illegal trading and increased the burden of policing for the company. The greater number of exceptions attached to exclusive access under Montmorency fits into a longer-standing pattern of increasingly circumscribed trading privileges in space within the colony.

If the Compagnie de Montmorency's obligations and privileges emerged from the long-standing preoccupations of the New France enterprise, management resembled the CIO and the Dutch and English companies on which the latter drew. The company had an *économie mixte*, or a combination of noble, bourgeois, and merchant associates, although there was no explicit assurance against derogation (the loss of privileges associated with nobility due to participation in commerce) in the company's articles, in contrast to the CIO's. A list of the company's associates in 1622 showed four merchant bourgeois, four office-holders – three of whom were financiers – and one naval captain.[60] This mixed membership, in which not all associates were active partners, marked a significant departure from previous trading companies to New France. For the previous two decades, associations like the CRSM had consisted of traders, all of whom were engaged in the association's business. The Compagnie de Montmorency, by contrast, functioned more like a *société en commandite* than a partnership. Some associates appear to have limited their participation to paying their share, while others, such as the de Caëns, managed the association's affairs.

What signalled most forcefully the company's ties to the broader development of the commercial corporation was the agreement's invocation of the public good: "the assemblies of the said Company will be held in Paris in the house of either the Sieur de Villemenon, intendant of the Admiralty, or of the said Sieur Dolu, intendant of the affairs of the said country, who will attend for the *public interest*, and the office of my said Seigneur the vice-Roy." The justification for the considerable privileges and exemptions enjoyed by not just chartered companies but all corporations at the time was that they also served a social function. In the case of the Compagnie de Montmorency, the enterprise would serve both the king (by extending his dominion through colonization) and subjects (through the expansion of commerce).[61]

The Compagnie de Montmorency was a means not only to claim French control of the North Atlantic trade route, but also to strengthen authority at home, both personally and institutionally. When seeking suitable heads for the new trading company, Montmorency chose two men who were already in his service in other capacities. Ézéchiel, in particular, was one of the administrators of the CIO, and thus was, if not an actual client of the admiral, someone who had credibility and experience in a similar undertaking. Montmorency also intended to have the affairs of the Compagnie de Montmorency closely supervised by his agents. By hosting the company's assemblies, the intendants would safeguard the viceroy's and admiral's interests and remind the associates of his ultimate authority.[62]

More significantly, the new location for the assemblies changed the relationship between metropolitan commercial and political spaces of power. Just like the CIO, the headquarters of the New France company was effectively transferred to Montmorency's base in Paris. Companies like the CRSM were traditionally based in the ports where members resided and ships were outfitted. Commercial power thus rested with those ports. With the company's business henceforth rooted in Paris, Montmorency intended to make political and commercial power coterminous.[63] In other words, this measure helped to wrest maritime control from autonomous and enterprising ports and peripheral provinces of France, in a manner complementary to the installation of more agents of the admiral in these same ports. Overseas colonizing and commercial ventures, then, played a direct role in the consolidation of maritime authority in France itself.

Sharing Jurisdiction on Land

If the Compagnie de Montmorency emerged partly out of international and domestic competition over maritime control, its articles of establishment redefined the role of privileged traders within the colony itself. As was the case with the CRSM, the act sought first to distinguish between the authority of the company, on the one hand, and that of the viceroy's lieutenant, on the other. These separate jurisdictions were articulated functionally and spatially, with a focus on the people who fell under each authority. Beginning with Champlain, the articles affirmed his superiority on land: "The Sieur de Champlain Lieutenant of my said Seigneur the vice-Roy will have precedence on land, will command at the habitation of Quebec … and generally throughout the land in the said country of new France, over French and others who will come there to live." His authority was rooted in the habitation and moved outward, primarily through the comings and goings of all those subject to it within the settlement, whether French or "others." For its part, the company exercised jurisdiction over commercial space, specifically the company storehouse, to which its agents alone had the key and which was at their "complete disposal."[64] It also had powers of policing within the privileged trading area of the Saint Lawrence River.

Like its authority in space, the company's authority over people was restricted. While the head of the company's ships "will command the members of his crew just as well on land as if he were at sea," authority over people living in the habitation and their labour was split between company and lieutenant. Champlain had the command of ten men maintained by the associates to perform tasks "for the good, service & utility of the habitation." The chief clerk would direct the work of the rest of the men in the colony according to "that which they [the associates] will find useful and necessary for the good and utility of their Company, without the said Lieutenant[,] under the pretext of the command that he has, being able to divert them in anything whatsoever."[65] In the event of outside attack, however, all would come under Champlain's authority. As with the CRSM's contract, this one established separate commercial and governmental jurisdictions in keeping with the two delegated parties' responsibilities and retained the flexibility enjoyed by each. By underscoring Champlain's superior authority on land, it drew a further distinction between maritime and territorial jurisdiction, largely leaving open the question of authority at sea.

Champlain and the company associates may have occupied different jurisdictions, but the latter were also integrated into the government of New France. For the first time in the colony's history, the company clerk collaborated with Champlain in managing the habitation's provisions, rendering justice, and commanding the settlement. The storehouse holding foodstuffs, munitions, and other necessities for overwinterers and residents was managed jointly: "the said Lieutenant together with the said Clerk shall each have a key, to be dispensed and used by the common understanding of the ordinance of the said Lieutenant." In the event of a shortage, the clerk would provide goods from the company's storehouse to supply the habitation. If disputes arose between the two parties over this responsibility, each was to appoint an arbitrator. This collaboration extended to the judgment of infractions and crimes committed by French men (or women) in New France. As the lieutenant of successive viceroys, Champlain had long had the power to establish a judicial administration in conformity with the laws and ordinances of France. Article 15 of the Compagnie de Montmorency's agreement sought to partially institutionalize this power. It stated that "to render his judgment more solemn," Champlain was to convene a tribunal of six principal inhabitants, including the clerk and any ships' commanders present at the time.[66] The participation of the clerk in judicial procedures had its administrative corollary in his appointment as Champlain's replacement as commander of the habitation whenever the latter was away in France, on exploratory voyages, or engaged in military campaigns with Indigenous allies. This provision contrasted with earlier practice by which Champlain appointed a man of his own choosing to assume control in his absence.[67] Finally, in the event of the lieutenant's death, the de Caëns and their associates could voice any objections they might have to the viceroy's chosen replacement "and [which would] be taken into consideration by my said Seigneur [Montmorency], so that he could better exercise his function of Lieutenant to the satisfaction of the said de Caens and of their Company."[68]

This collaboration between company and lieutenant created a shared space of judicial and governmental authority under particular circumstances. Thus, Émery de Caën, Guillaume's cousin and chief clerk of the company, became commander of the Quebec habitation in 1624–25 upon Champlain's return to France. Guillaume de Caën, for his part, was involved in judicial decision-making on at least one occasion. In 1622, the murder of a Frenchman by an Indigenous man (of unspecified nation) threatened the diplomatic and commercial relations between the French and their commercial partners. While Champlain was reluctant to cede any ground, de Caën persuaded him to pardon the offender, which was the king's and viceroy's preferred course.[69]

Although antagonism between company and lieutenant flared up from time to time, particularly over the funding and building of the habitation's fort, the Compagnie de Montmorency's articles made the jurisdictions of the associates and Champlain more intertwined and mutually dependent. This was a move in the opposite direction from the actions and proposals of the two parties under Condé. Although the articles established Champlain as the supreme authority in New France – one of the objectives of his 1618 proposal to the Parisian Chamber of Commerce and royal council – they expanded rather than shrank the parameters of the company's activities. It was, in part, a question of numbers: the majority of the small French population was in the employ of the company. In this sense, the integration of the Compagnie de Montmorency into the colony's government constituted a tacit acknowledgment of the company's de facto power in the habitation and along the watery corridors of trade and diplomacy that flowed from it. Champlain's ability to exercise authority in the name of the viceroy required, then, shared political and judicial authority to be recognized as legitimate.

The Trade Dispute of 1621: Deploying Law and Force

The designated spaces of power of company and lieutenant proved to be fragile and easily dissolved in practice. It was not until the spring of 1621 that news arrived in New France of the establishment of the new company under the de Caëns. In May, a ship carrying the viceroy's commissioners brought a letter to Champlain from their superior explaining that "for several reasons I have thought it right to exclude the old shareholders from Rouen and Saint Malo in the trade to New France from returning to that country." Other letters followed from Dolu with instructions to Champlain to seize the goods of the CRSM, and Guillaume de Caën, who signalled his imminent arrival with two armed ships and "some good declarations in his favour." Without a decree from the king authorizing a seizure and outnumbered by the employees of the CRSM, Champlain opted to allow the latter to continue trading until the arrival of de Caën, "who had all proper authority, bearing with him a decree in his favour."[70] After all, the suit before the royal council between the CRSM and Montmorency, which had expanded to include the new company, had not yet fully settled the matter in either enterprise's favour.[71] This situation set the stage for assertions of and contestations over political and commercial authority within the habitation and at trading posts along the Saint Lawrence over the course of the summer. Using law, force, or a combination of the two, rival traders and the viceroy's representatives alike sought to strengthen their claims to privileges and power and reinforce their relationship to their sovereign.

At the beginning of June, a CRSM vessel carrying company agent François Gravé, Sieur Du Pont, and three clerks was sighted in the river. Uncertain of their intentions, Champlain took the precaution of arming a group of men in the half-completed fort at Quebec, before joining the rest of the residents inside the habitation (shown in figure 3.3). "In this way we could hold our own in negotiation, and meantime continue to work at the fort to strengthen its defences." Two men met the company's clerks at the river to discover the nature of their business.[72] Gravé Du Pont's ship had set sail with no more than the company's approbation, having left before the council made its decision and in spite of the Admiralty's refusal to grant it a licence. With none of the customary papers, the CRSM's associates and agents "had determined to fall back on simple obedience to the King." While Champlain rebuked them for their actions, the clerks in turn questioned his authority to put a man in charge of the fort "without instructions from the King."[73] This manoeuvring continued until the arrival of de Caën with a decree from the royal council, which allowed both companies to trade for the 1621 season while deliberations continued over whether the two should be merged or a new company formed. Despite the decree's injunction against "causing the other any hindrance or violence on pain of death," de Caën announced his intention to seize Gravé Du Pont's vessel, which he planned to use to pursue interlopers in the river. This proposed aggression prompted various representations from Gravé Du Pont, the CRSM, de Caën, and his men over the course of the following month.[74] While Champlain exhorted de Caën "not to slacken in the service of his Majesty nor in the observance of his decrees," the latter referred to "his appointment, and … the special commands received from the King and my said Lord [Montmorency]," to justify his position. With no sign of a resolution, Champlain "[took] the Sieur du Pont's vessel under my protection, wishing to preserve it in order to uphold the King's authority and the honour of my said Lord, before all his crew: afterwards he

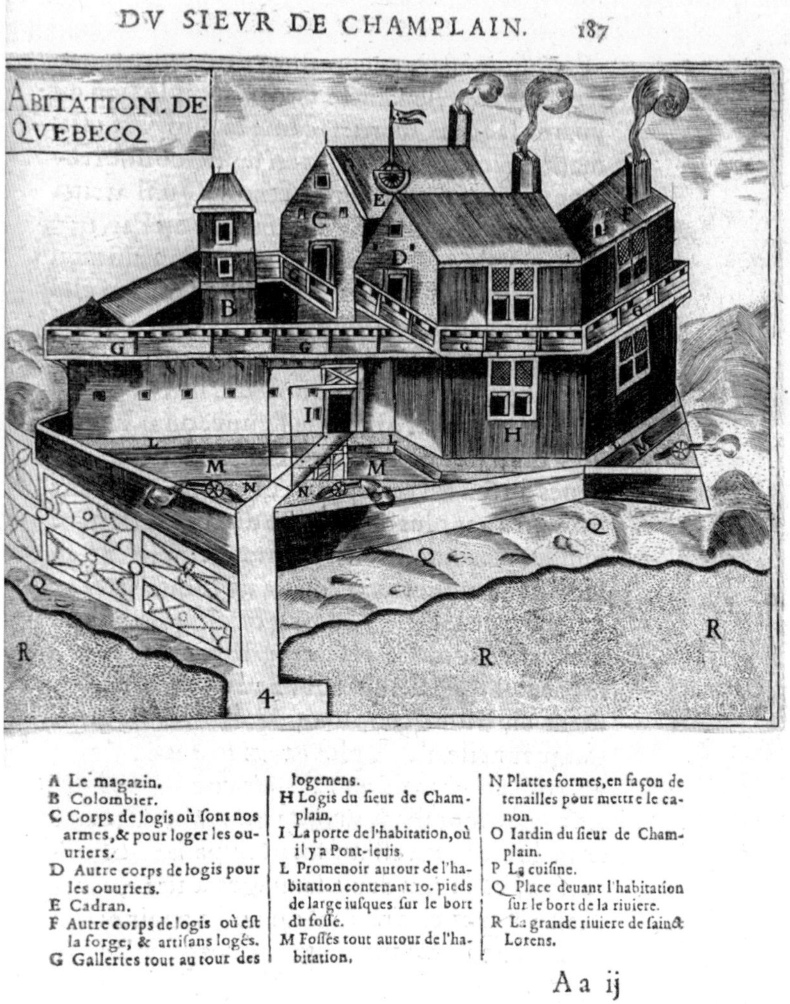

Figure 3.3 Samuel de Champlain, "Abitation de Quebecq," *Les voyages du Sieur de Champlain*, 1613.

[de Caën] could do as he liked, as he had force on his side; but in order to preserve the form of legality, I had to take up that position." The lieutenant then left the site and de Caën seized the vessel, refusing to recognize "any jurisdiction in that locality."[75] In the event, de Caën returned the ship to Gravé Du Pont, declaring it insufficiently armed. One suspects that the show was far more important than the outcome.[76]

The events of 1621 presented Champlain with an opportunity to construct sovereignty within the spaces of New France. In his version of events, he juxtaposed his lawfulness with de Caën's lawlessness. When Champlain took Gravé Du Pont's ship under his protection, he infused the post of Tadoussac with law and the king's imperium. His subsequent withdrawal, before de Caën's seizure, suggests he could also strip a space of legitimate authority, rendering it lawless. Together with manning the fort, these actions reminded witnesses of Champlain's own position as the sole legitimate legal authority in the king's name.[77] He employed the languages of law, sovereignty, and fidelity to Montmorency, opposing them to de Caën's use of force. Indeed, he told de Caën to seek redress for any grievance in the courts of France.[78] But the lieutenant's lawfulness also had to be backed by force to be effective. Thus, negotiations took place with the newly arrived CRSM agents within sight of the colony's fledgling defence works. For Champlain, the fort, once completed, would symbolize the triumph of imperial authority over unruly traders: "the whole reason of that [i.e., past and present companies' refusal to support the construction of a fort] was their fear lest, if there were a fort, they should be mastered and brought under the law." This passage, in which the lieutenant's frustration is palpable, points to the very real limits of royal authority in the colony.[79] Imperial power was demonstrably weak compared to the commercial power of the company and its agents. Like the Admiralty official in Honfleur a year earlier, Champlain had orders to seize the CRSM's goods and merchandise. Woefully outnumbered by employees of the company, however, he lacked the material power to uphold his theoretical authority. The lieutenant himself readily admitted as much, observing that "we could only hold our ground by force." Yet Champlain did not have a monopoly on either force or law in New France.[80]

All parties took advantage of the considerable room for manoeuvre within the confines of the law. Each pledged to recognize the legitimacy of royal decrees, but could, at the same time, produce decrees or other legal documents that contradicted or conflicted with those of other parties. The CRSM, for one, invoked royal sovereignty to defend its having sailed without any authorization and in turn challenged Champlain to produce a royal decree to justify his actions. Since it was in his own best interests, de Caën chose to see his contract from Montmorency as paramount, rather than the subsequent royal decree authorizing both companies to trade that season. Indeed, when he was presented with the decree on board ship in Dieppe just before his departure, he defiantly declared it "null and void."[81] De Caën had himself been expecting, and had earlier promised Champlain in his letter, a decree giving him permission to seize the CRSM's ships and goods. He thus exploited the latitude provided by two pieces of paper (contract and decree), two authorities (viceroy and king), and two conflicting orders.[82] That any royal decree trumped a contract from one of the king's officers was a mere technicality in a remote colony with a small French population and weak imperial authority. All parties engaged in "legal posturing," by which subjects sought to gain advantage on the ground, position themselves for continued patronage and rewards, and defend any contested actions before French courts.[83]

If law was an instrument that provided subjects with a framework within which to affirm and defend their privileges, force had its own uses. Up to a point, de Caën's seizure of the CRSM's ship resembled the same action in Honfleur on Montmorency's orders one year earlier. Both seizures signalled their arrival in a new position, served as a warning to any who dared to challenge or contravene their authority, and presented an opportunity to assert the newfound rights and powers conferred on them. The difference was, of course, that de Caën pursued the seizure even after he had failed to get royal approbation for it. His aggressive and defiant action sent a message not only to the CRSM and its agents but also to Champlain and the few men he could count on in the colony. While the lieutenant's departure from Tadoussac may have symbolically removed imperial authority from the site, de Caën's refusal to recognize any legal authority above himself was a direct challenge to political jurisdiction in the colony and, therefore, to Champlain himself. In colonial and maritime spaces, might frequently made right.

Contested Spaces

The events of 1621 exposed the bounded nature of sovereign space in New France. Imperial authority, such as it was, was strongest within the habitation and fort at Quebec. As a result, parties attached special significance to who was allowed in and who was excluded. Upon their arrival, Gravé Du Pont and the CRSM clerks found the settlement's drawbridge raised and its inhabitants armed and ready for confrontation. Gravé Du Pont and associates reacted, in the words of Champlain, with "great vexation at seeing themselves received in so extraordinary a fashion and one so different from what they had been accustomed to."[84] Besides their own dramatic reception, they objected particularly to Champlain's having admitted du May and his men into the fort and habitation without a royal decree authorizing him to do so. Indeed, Champlain had given du May command of the men in the fort, a motley group including four men from the Récollets and the same number from the CRSM. Part of the agents' objection was tactical: they, like many of their fellow subjects, invoked sovereign authority and law when it advanced their own cause. The CRSM risked losing the remaining years of its contract to the Compagnie de Montmorency. Representing the new viceroy and company, du May was suspect, at best, and illegitimate, at worst, in the eyes of the CRSM agents. Tactics aside, freedom of movement into and out of the habitation was fundamental to the company's own legitimacy. As the exclusive holder of commercial jurisdiction, company agents spread, affirmed, and defended French sovereignty through their activities. The fact that the agents were barred entry to the habitation – the main space of imperial power – and were greeted with arms threw their loyalty into question.

Authority in remote places, whether backed by royal decree or not, was precarious. Distance from sovereign power and possible reinforcement heightened the sense of danger. In 1624, another incident involving entry into the habitation and the legitimacy of parties underscored this pervasive threat. A vessel arrived in June of that year laden with provisions. Although the pilot claimed to have come on the orders of de Caën, who had been delayed, he carried no letter from the company head for Champlain. The lieutenant's reaction is telling: "I was greatly surprised that he [de Caën] had not sent me a word of his coming to the country, a matter of considerable consequence; for those who are in command of a fleet, or have other important affairs in hand, should never permit their vessels to leave *without some notification to the governor or lieutenant of a remote place such as this*, in order to testify that reliance may be placed upon the persons sent, and that *they may have free entry into the settlement or fort*, as persons belonging to the Company."[85] Champlain's description encapsulates the significance of admission to the fort and habitation. These were the only spaces that the sixty-odd French inhabitants had any hope of defending. The remoteness of the location only magnified the threat posed by people showing up without papers to confirm their trustworthiness.

Both this and the 1621 episode have an undercurrent of violence to them. They are full of dangers: from the CRSM agents' showing up without a licence from the Admiralty; from de Caën's determination to seize the CRSM's vessel in defiance of the royal decree; and from potential malefactors who arrived without word from de Caën. They also provide several opportunities to build and strengthen imperial authority: through the arming of inhabitants inside the fort and habitation upon the arrival of the CRSM agents; through Champlain's taking Gravé Du Pont's ship under his protection; and through the rebuke of the pilot for coming without proper papers. In a sense, then, these episodes highlight the symbiotic relationship between dangers posed to authority and the opportunity to construct sovereign spaces.

The preoccupation with entry into the fort and habitation underscores the fragility of imperial authority beyond these walls. As holders of the viceroy's powers and privileges, Champlain and the agents of the privileged trading companies claimed political and commercial jurisdiction over the Saint Lawrence River. Such claims were affirmed through frequent travel between Tadoussac, Quebec, Trois Rivières, and Gaspé each season. During May and June of 1621, for example, CRSM clerks travelled to Trois Rivières to trade; Champlain sent a boat to Tadoussac to await de Caën's arrival; Gravé Du Pont took a pinnace from Tadoussac to Quebec and on to Trois Rivières, ready for trading; Commissioner Guers along with Father Georges Le Baillif went on Champlain's instructions to Tadoussac to negotiate with de Caën; and Champlain sent a canoe to Gravé Du Pont at Trois Rivières to request that a pinnace be brought to Quebec, which the former then took to Tadoussac to dissuade de Caën from seizing Gravé Du Pont's vessel.[86] At the same time, however, the frequent presence of illegal French traders, their Indigenous trading partners, and European rivals undermined that control. Rochelais and Innu traders continued to trade in open defiance of royal restrictions on access. In his accounts, Champlain reports sightings throughout the first half of the 1620s. The Rochelais usually escaped any patrols by the trading company due to their small, fast, and well-armed ships.[87] (Champlain did not recognize what the Innu's actions represented: a deliberate protest against French pretentions.) In 1622, reports of a Spanish vessel engaged in whaling and spying near Tadoussac met with no response for "lack of sailors and men capable of a bold stroke."[88] Company and lieutenant alike lacked the material power to uphold their theoretical commercial and political jurisdiction, making the Saint Lawrence a corridor of contested control among the French and with Indigenous Peoples and European rivals.[89]

Beyond the Saint Lawrence River, French mobility was limited and imperial power dissolved completely. French traders, missionaries, and viceregal representatives found themselves in "vast native spaces of political, economic, cultural, and military power."[90] Rivers, streams, and lakes formed the spine of Wendat, Innu, and Algonquin homelands. Facilitating seasonal migrations, these waterways were integral to Indigenous approaches to the use and management of resources.[91] In contrast to frequent European characterizations of Indigenous migration as purposeless and undirected, mobility was "seasonally expected and politically negotiated." Access to and regulation of resources was closely tied to kinship networks and alliances.[92] The Innu, who had granted permission to the French to establish a post on their territory at Tadoussac in 1600, controlled who could trade directly with the French, thereby protecting their role as intermediaries in trade networks that extended as far north as James Bay and as far west as southern Ontario.[93] The principal chief at Tadoussac in 1603, Anadabijou, granted permission to the Kichesipirinis, an Anishinaabe group in the Ottawa Valley, to trade directly with the French, having secured their help in a raid against the Mohawk. Five years later, a Petite Nation chief, Iroquet, who was to participate in a planned 1609 war party against the Haudenosaunee, or Iroquois Confederacy, for which the French had given their support, invited his Wendat trading partner, Ochasteguin, to join them. The latter thus became the first Wendat to enter into direct relations with the French. As this constituted a new trade route for the Wendats, Ochasteguin and his family could control who would have access to it. In order to prevent bad feelings within their tribe and throughout the confederacy as a whole, they extended the trade to both groupings. The Kichesipirinis, for their part, required the Wendats to pay a toll in order to pass through their territory along the Ottawa River.[94] These examples underscore the intimate connections among kin relations, mobility along interior river routes, and knowledge of and access to lands and resources.

The French had to conform to this complex system of alliance and regulation. Exploration of interior lands and waterways depended on Indigenous guidance, which was not always forthcoming. In 1613, Champlain wished to set out toward Algonquin-Anishinabeg territory with the goal of encouraging bands to come downriver to trade and of reaching the "northern sea" by way of the Ottawa River. Having requested three canoes and three guides from a group of Algonquins, he obtained "with much difficulty" two canoes and one guide "by means of presents." Champlain and his men were discouraged at several points along their journey by parties of Algonquins they met along the route, who "declar[ed] that the way was bad."[95] Reaching Lower Allumette Lake, Champlain met with the chiefs of the region at the camp of Kichesipirini Chief Tessouat. Once again, the explorer asked for canoes and guides, to which the chiefs only reluctantly agreed, "on account of the toils I should undergo" and the unfriendliness of the peoples on Lake Nipissing. They subsequently withdrew this offer of support, however, forcing Champlain to cut short his expedition. Two years later, the Wendats succeeded in convincing the Algonquins to permit Champlain to travel through their territory to Wendake, where he met the chiefs and spent the winter. Both the Algonquins and the Wendats prevented him, however, from venturing further west to visit the Neutrals. As these two expeditions demonstrate, the two groups were not keen on having the French establish trade and diplomatic relations with nations to the north and west for whom the former were intermediaries. Both the Algonquins and the Wendats asserted cultural and political power to control with whom the French established relations, as well as their knowledge of interior waterways, lands, and peoples.[96]

For the French, access to and exploration of the rivers leading into the interior were a means to expand imperial space. The objective of extending sovereignty over Indigenous Peoples and lands, on the one hand, and the real limits to French power and authority, on the other, is illustrated by an agreement that Champlain reached with Innu Chief Anadabijou's son, Miristou, in 1622. Miristou and thirty followers had spent much of the year in the area around the Quebec habitation in order to develop ties with the French. Champlain agreed to convince members of Miristou's band to elect him as chief. In return, Miristou and his followers promised to settle and cultivate the land near Quebec. While the effect of the exchange for Miristou was a rise in status among his fellow band members – becoming Mahigan Aticq Ouche as chief – Champlain aimed to increase imperial power within Indigenous spaces.[97] He hoped that his intervention in this election of a chief would establish a precedent by which "we should begin to assume a certain control over them." The Indigenous settlement near Quebec would bring its inhabitants into "perfect friendship" and present an opportunity for conversion and assimilation.[98] Unsurprisingly, in Champlain's account, it is the French who wield political and cultural authority. For all the imperial bravado, however, the main goal of these overtures was to be "assured that, if we take them anywhere with us to make discoveries, they will not abandon us on the way … Without their help it would be impossible for us to make discoveries … nor could we make use of natives of other tribes, for … the moment anything vexed them, they would leave us in the middle of an expedition."[99] This passage exposes the fear, vulnerability, and powerlessness of Champlain and the other French inhabitants beyond the limits of the fortified habitation and trading posts. While explorers, missionaries, and other agents of empire carried jurisdiction with them along riverine corridors, their dependence on Indigenous allies for guidance diluted such claims. Mobility, then, at once promised to spread various forms of power and laid bare the weakness of imperial spaces.

On a macro level, the movement of French subjects across the ocean, along the coastal waterways, and into and out of trading posts in the spaces of New France spread imperial jurisdiction. In this sense, all were agents of empire, including interlopers. While the fort at Quebec, a potent symbol of imperial power, was fixed in space and thus limited in reach, the circulation of people allowed for various forms of power to move outward. It is on this level that the intertwining of maritime and territorial space and jurisdiction is most visible. Controlling space was about regulating access, whether by granting licences for transatlantic travel, raising the drawbridge to the Quebec habitation, policing the privileged trading zone, or guarding knowledge of inland routes. On a micro level, in specific sites, subjects' activities could have a destabilizing effect on sovereign claims. Parties' manoeuvring during the summer of 1621 exposed the multiple agendas among the French. It also put into sharp relief the power differential between political and commercial interests, a reality already tacitly acknowledged in the partial integration of the company into the colony's government. If contests among French traders provided Champlain opportunities for the construction of sovereignty and authority, these moments had little lasting effect, as de Caën's seizure of Gravé Du Pont's vessel demonstrates. Indeed, besides the habitation, control of "New France" was beyond reach of the French. Indigenous Peoples controlled navigation along interior waterways and access to land and resources.

In this context, Montmorency's maritime vision of New France looks like a classic example of imperial ambitions coming up against hard reality on the ground. Yet, his New France was an imagined one, one that allowed him to extend control over present and future trade routes and the circulation of subjects and goods. It was part of an expansive maritime policy that aimed to strengthen French standing in Europe and consolidate maritime authority in France itself. Through the Compagnie de Montmorency, he wrested commercial and maritime power from fiercely independent ports in the name of the king, underscoring the role of New France in the story of the centralizing state. While the viceroy's approach reflected domestic preoccupations, other parties took advantage of the localized contests on the ground to lobby for their own vision of the colony's future.

4

A Crisis of Sovereignty?

Commerce, Catholicism, and Subjecthood

Following the eventful summer of trading and competition between the Compagnie de Montmorency and the Compagnie de Rouen et Saint-Malo, "all principal French inhabitants of Canada" held an assembly on 18 August 1621. In attendance were Champlain, Baptiste Guers, the viceroy's commissioner, the Récollets Denis Jamet, Georges Le Baillif, and Joseph Le Caron, Louis Hébert, *procureur du roi*, Gilbert Courseron, the provost's lieutenant, Nicolas, law clerk of the assembly and Jurisdiction of Quebec, and four other residents.[1] Brought together in what is considered to have been the colony's first such gathering by a desire "to remedy and bring some order to these disorders," the participants wished "to inform through the most appropriate means on the ruin and desolation of the whole of this country, and to find the means to conserve the Catholic, Apostolic and Roman Religion absolute, the authority of the King inviolable and the obedience due to the said Seigneur Viceroy."[2] At the assembly's conclusion, they deputed Father Georges Le Baillif to travel to France to present their *cahier de doléances*, or list of grievances, to the viceroy and the king and to intervene on the inhabitants' behalf in the trade dispute among the companies and Montmorency currently before the courts. Five years later, one of the participants, the Récollet Le Caron, published the pamphlet *Au roy sur la Nouvelle France*, in which he called on the king to "have order put, where disorder reigns, under the mantle of your authority." The current situation, he argued, was contrary to "the intention of the king and his Council to have planted there the Catholic, Apostolic and Roman Religion."[3]

The reader of these appeals cannot help but feel the sense of unease, danger, and urgency that lies at their heart. They suggest that nothing less than the very sovereignty of the king was at stake. Painting a menacing portrait of a colony on the brink, they juxtapose this disorder with the order that would come with help from the king. Hardly the first such pleas by those involved in New France, they are nonetheless distinct from previous ones not only in their foreboding but also in the prominent place they accord Catholicism in the re-establishment of order. Indeed, Le Caron and the assembly draw an explicit relationship between order, royal authority, and the spread of Catholicism.

While parties regularly invoked the order/disorder dichotomy in seeking their sovereign's support during the period, the juxtaposition would have had particular resonance for French authorities, for whom the violence and upheaval of the sixteenth-century Wars of Religion were only beginning to fade from view.[4] Indeed, the quest for order and stability characterized early seventeenth-century French society and politics writ large. In order to make any progress toward this goal, it was necessary to find a solution to the thorny problem of the two confessions. Confessional unity had long been inextricably tied to social peace. The challenge facing France in the last two decades of the sixteenth century was "how to realign the dictates of piety and justice" so as to restore harmony.[5] Successive rulers adopted different strategies to achieve this. When Henri IV ascended the throne in 1589, peace did not appear imminent. A Protestant, his kingship seemed to present Catholics with the difficult choice between loyalty to their king or to their faith. His conversion to Catholicism shortly thereafter, however, reaffirmed Catholicism as the country's official religion and thus settled the question for many. If Henri's conversion reassured Catholics, the Edict of Nantes outlined certain political and religious privileges for Huguenots. Members of the "reformed religion" could practise freely on the land of Protestant seigneurs and in any town where services had been held in the previous two years, with the exception of certain cities, including Paris. They could also build houses of worship in these places and maintain their own cemeteries. Politically, Protestants could hold public office, had a right to be heard before the law, and, as a guarantee of these rights, were allowed to keep several *places de sûreté* to be maintained at the king's expense. Alongside these privileges were certain restrictions, including a prohibition on working on any Catholic holidays and the obligation to pay the *dîme*, a tax to support the clergy. In short, the edict granted Protestants full civil rights and restricted freedom of worship.[6] Henri IV's measures thus sought to restore stability through confessional coexistence.

As Henri's death at the hands of a Catholic zealot attests, this attempt to create legal and religious space for both Catholics and Protestants failed to win over everyone (above all, Catholic hardliners). The arrival of Marie de Médicis to the throne as queen regent in 1610, and with her a more stridently Catholic perspective at court, contributed to growing support in France, in general, and in royal circles, in particular, for a closer relationship to Rome over the following decade. For her part, the queen regent helped arrange dynastic marriages for her son and daughter with members of the royal family of Catholic Spain, traditionally regarded as the bulwark of Catholicism in Europe. Later, in the 1620s, Marie de Médicis became closely tied to a faction at court, the *parti dévot*, that advocated an uncompromising approach toward Protestants in France and unwavering support for Spain.[7] As we saw in chapter 2, the events of the 1610s thrust the kingdom once more into political and confessional instability, leading to conflict between the Crown and Protestants as well as princes of the blood and other grandees.[8] If most Huguenots maintained their allegiance to the Crown this time around, the unrest nevertheless posed a considerable challenge to Louis XIII when he reached the age of majority.

Louis XIII's approach to political and confessional instability lay somewhere between that of his parents. On the one hand, he readmitted the Jesuits to France (who had been banished in 1594), chose representatives of the church as his advisers, and extended legal and religious protections to the Catholic minority of staunchly Protestant Béarn, on the border with Spain, a measure that Henri IV had decided to forgo for fear of exacerbating religious tensions.[9] Having decided that the permission given to Huguenots in the Edict of Nantes to maintain fortified places was untenable, the king and his chief minister, Cardinal Richelieu, organized sieges of various Huguenot strongholds in the South of France in the 1620s.[10] On the other hand, Louis XIII chose to wage war against the Catholic Habsburgs and enter an alliance with the Protestant Dutch in the mid-1620s. Shortly thereafter, France entered negotiations with England for the marriage of Henri IV's daughter to Charles I. Much as the Spanish unions provoked protest on the part of Huguenots and those Catholics who favoured an autonomous French church, Louis XIII's foreign policy, viewed through the prism of these matrimonial and political alliances, appeared alarmingly anti-Catholic to some.[11] Combining a concern for the strong link between the French monarchy and Catholicism with political pragmatism, the king's strategy tended to antagonize one side or the other. The return to an adult king on the throne along with victories over the last Huguenot holdouts in the last years of the decade did, however, hold out hope for the long-sought re-establishment of stability.

While the terms by which stability would be achieved differed according to monarch, all three granted a central place to Catholicism in the reconstituted order, much like the New France assembly of 1621 and Le Caron's pamphlet. The Catholic Church emerged from the Wars of Religion engaged in its own process of restructuring and revitalization. If the Edict of Nantes affirmed the civil rights of Protestants, it also enabled the strengthening of the Catholic Church. At the most basic level, this entailed restoring infrastructure, reclaiming property and revenue, and reinstating Catholic worship where it had been eliminated during the Wars of Religion.[12] The Catholic Reformation, however, went well beyond the mere restoration of the church to pre-war conditions. On an institutional level, the church reaffirmed the principal tenets of the faith, established measures to tighten its control over both parishioners and clergy, and began a campaign to educate the populace about its faith, in accordance with the reforms of the Council of Trent (1545–63).[13] On a community level, a religious revival, resembling the Protestant Reformation in its energy and dynamism, swept through all levels of the church, galvanizing lay and clerical elites alike. The former, with the guidance of religious orders, created confraternities, while the latter undertook internal missionary work, following the example of François de Sales and Vincent de Paul. New religious orders also emerged during this period, and old orders were reformed and expanded. This included the Récollets, a reformed order of Franciscans.[14] All of these activities depended on *dévots*, or devout lay members. A particular phenomenon of the period, the dévots varied widely in their social, political, and religious aims. While some were propelled by the "crusading spirit" of the Catholic Reformation, others worked to roll back the civil rights granted Protestants, while some sought to advance a pro-Spanish foreign policy.[15] They did, however, have in common a strong antipathy toward Protestants, the desire to re-establish a unified Christendom, and the goal of Christianizing society through piety, charity, good works, and conversion. Among the activities sponsored by dévots were overseas missions. The lay congregations they established would become particularly instrumental in the financing and establishment of hospitals, schools, and seigneuries in New France in the 1630s and '40s.[16] A growing intensity characterized the trajectory of these interrelated phenomena – the religious policies of the Crown, Catholic reform, and lay and religious apostolic activities – over the course of the first few decades of the seventeenth century, a pattern replicated in New France.

Although the goal of spreading Christianity to Indigenous Peoples in North America featured in commissions from the start, it came to assume a central role in the enterprise only gradually. At the opening of the seventeenth century, the prevailing atmosphere of "tepid orthodoxy," reflecting the desire for peace in France, travelled overseas with those engaged in the New France enterprise and shaped its development.[17] On the eastern side of the Atlantic, while some ecclesiastics embraced the Tridentine reforms before their adoption by the Assembly of Clergy in 1615, most of the population, including royal officials and nobles, regarded the reformers' activities as overzealous and intrusive. Marc Lescarbot, the lawyer and author of the *History of New France* who accompanied Champlain and de Mons to Acadia in 1606, shared this view. He lamented the "fault-finders who observe and record all movements of your body and your heart, from whom even the greatest kings cannot defend themselves," and hoped that the evangelizing missions in New France would be free from such zealotry. Far removed from the reformers' perspective, de Mons's undertaking evinced a sort of "ecumenism" shaped by the humanism of its principal participants.[18] The members of his company and its agents came from both confessions and were accompanied by a Catholic and a Protestant minister on transatlantic crossings. His commission itself reflected this coexistence of faiths in its directive to convert the Indigenous inhabitants to Christianity, rather than to Catholicism specifically. Despite the evangelizing component, the parties involved implemented few concrete initiatives to realize this goal.[19]

The expansion of Catholic reform in the 1610s, coupled with a more aggressively Catholic queen regent, had immediate effects in New France. In the short term, the Protestant de Mons, as we have seen, lost his positions both at court and in the colony; for his part, Poutrincourt, a former member of the hard-line Catholic League, received the support of Marie de Médicis for his enterprise in Acadia. In the long term, missionaries imbued with the fervour of the Catholic Reformation came to tend to French inhabitants' spiritual needs at Quebec and to convert France's Indigenous allies in territories to the west. The arrival, first of the Récollets and then of the Jesuits, in the Saint Lawrence Valley introduced a new set of parties with their own visions of the proper direction for the New France enterprise.[20]

Due to a variety of factors, the evangelizing mission, heretofore in the background, moved to centre stage during the first half of the 1620s. The concept of spiritual geopolitics is useful here. Lauric Henneton defines the concept as "geopolitical decisions … that were at least partly dictated by confessional identities and agendas."[21] By examining the effects of the new evangelizing focus on the actions and rhetoric of the various parties in the colony, this chapter traces the concomitant shift in the balance of power among royal, religious, and commercial interests. The religious policies of the Crown, Catholic reform, and lay and religious apostolic activities interacted in their own particular way on the western side of the Atlantic, leading to a debate over, and then the transformation of, the terms of the sovereign project in North America.

Catholic Reform Comes to the Saint Lawrence Valley

The missionaries who arrived on the shores of the Saint Lawrence River at the habitation of Quebec in the spring of 1615 embodied both the religious revival among Catholics at all levels of society and the strict reforming spirit of the Council of Trent. As an order, the Récollets were literally born of these currents, having emerged in Spain in the sixteenth century and having only established themselves in French cities in the century's closing decades. They received financial support from the king and queen as well as other prominent figures in the church and at court. Known for their discipline and spiritual contemplation, they aimed to change the Franciscan order from within, an approach that tended to antagonize established members.[22] In the spirit of the time, a good part of their mission was devoted to pastoral activities. The Récollets, like other reformers, viewed all those ignorant of Catholicism – peasants, Protestants, heretics, Indigenous Peoples – as one group and, consequently, as objects of the same project of evangelization.[23]

By the time the order received the call to establish a mission in New France, the Récollets had long been active in the Protestant region of Saintonge, from which de Mons and Champlain hailed, as well as in South America. Indeed, it was a dévot from Saintonge, Louis Houel, Sieur du Petit-Pré, royal counsellor, and controller general of the salt works at Brouage, who made the proposal to the order, and it was from that same region that the four Récollets who arrived in 1615 came.[24] Drawing on the order's considerable experience, the missionaries lost no time in building a house and chapel at both Quebec and Trois Rivières during the year of their arrival. Denis Jamet, commissioner of the Récollets in New France, remained at Quebec while Jean Dolbeau and Joseph Le Caron went to winter among the Innu and the Wendats, respectively. By spring, Le Caron had concluded that "the time had not come to effect great conversions there."[25] If, in the eyes of the Récollets, the Wendats, Innu, Protestants, and peasants all suffered in the same ignorance, these initial experiences showed that different strategies were required in the diverse cultural, social, and political contexts of North America.

Just over a year after their arrival, the Récollets outlined a program for conversion. Armed with what they had learned over the winter, they held a meeting with Champlain and six other inhabitants in July 1616. The resulting articles assessed the readiness of various Indigenous groups for conversion and outlined the measures required to achieve this goal. The Récollets drew a relationship between the fertility of the land, the lifestyle of its inhabitants, and the chances of conversion. The more fertile the land and the more sedentary the inhabitants, went the argument, the more "susceptible of instruction" the people would be. By this logic, the Wendats were the most promising candidates. The meeting's participants were agreed that francization was necessary before conversion could take place: "They remark that none could ever succeed in converting them, unless they made them men before they made them Christians."[26] "Making them men" – a process also expressed through the terms *franciser*, *civiliser*, and *humaniser* – meant above all making the Indigenous inhabitants sedentary. Considering them without law or government, an assessment that recalls Champlain's own writings, the assembly also judged it necessary to "bring them up to our manners and laws." This process required a concerted program of colonization in order to gain "a greater number of settlers, mechanics [artisans] and farmers." Interaction among French and Indigenous inhabitants was to be encouraged, since "to civilize them it was necessary first that the French should mingle with them and habituate them among us."[27] To this end, trade in the colony would be opened up to all French inhabitants. There were two obstacles to this program, according to those assembled. The first was the CRSM, which, "to monopolize trade, did not wish the country to be settled, and did not even wish us to make the Indians sedentary." A second, overlapping obstacle was the Huguenots: "having the best share in the trade, it was to be feared that the contempt they showed for our mysteries would greatly retard the establishment of the faith." As a result, the latter should be excluded from the colony.[28] The program thus targeted three separate groups: the French, who were to colonize, the Huguenots, who were to be excluded, and France's Indigenous allies, who were to be made sedentary and *francisés*.

More than just a program for conversion, these articles proposed nothing less than to remake the colony in the Tridentine mould. In the interests of francization, the Récollets expected any and all new French inhabitants to fall under their authority. The articles noted that "even the bad example of the French might be prejudicial, if those who had authority in the country did not establish order." This view reflected the reforming spirit in France, whereby close supervision of behaviour and correction of beliefs was necessary to reform and strengthen a church and monarchy that zealous Catholics considered insufficiently orthodox.[29] But it also, if only implicitly, suggested a change in who would govern in the colony. Indeed, while the program called for more missionaries to be paid for by the company and more attention from "the associated gentlemen," the meeting's participants, and the Récollets in particular, set themselves and their vision in opposition to the traders. By presenting the company as an obstacle to two of the key elements of their program, colonization and sedentarization, they called into question its role in the governance of the colony. The Récollets went to the royal court every year from 1616 in order to obtain the king's approval for their program. The letters patent they received in March 1618 granted the provincial of the Saint-Denis Récollets exclusive permission to send missionaries to New France and "to build and construct there one or many convents and monasteries, as they shall deem proper."[30] Although the king did not explicitly approve all aspects of the proposed program, the Récollets' objectives converged with those of Champlain, presenting the possibility for collaboration in their mutual interest.

Champlain's personal attitude toward evangelization underwent significant evolution over the first two decades of his activity in New France, a shift particularly visible in the various editions of his travel accounts. Given his origins in Saintonge, coupled with a recently found baptismal record from the Protestant parish of Saint-Yon in La Rochelle, it is more than likely that he was born Protestant. By the time of his voyage to Acadia under de Mons in 1603, however, he was Catholic. A supporter of Henri IV during the last years of the Wars of Religion, he may very well have been one of the many people who converted during this period.[31] Whatever his confessional history, Champlain showed little interest in evangelization as a goal of the New France enterprise before 1615. The few mentions of missionizing included in his 1613 *Voyages* account depict it as a secondary activity: "In the course of time we hoped to pacify them, and to put an end to the wars they wage against one another, in order that in future we might derive service from them, and convert them to the Christian faith." Conversion's secondary status meant that it could be left for a later moment. When Champlain did evoke evangelization, it was usually for practical purposes, with the objective of gaining financial support for the enterprise.[32]

Six years later, Champlain's indifference gave way to a veritable plan for conversion in the 1619 edition. He concluded that the surest method was "to have patience … to continue both to explore the said country and also to learn their language and to form connections and friendships with the headmen of the villages and tribes, in order to lay the foundation of a permanent edifice both for the glory of God and also for the renown of the French." To this end, evangelization became one of the objectives of French interactions and alliances with Indigenous groups. In 1615, Champlain and Gravé Du Pont, the CRSM's agent, entered a military alliance with the Wendats, Algonquins, Innu, and Wolastoqiyik (Etchemins to the French) against the Haudenosaunee, "both to engage them the more to love us, and also to provide the means of furthering my enterprises and explorations which apparently could only be carried out with their help, and also because this would be to them a kind of pathway and preparation for embracing Christianity." Although Champlain put it third in his list of objectives, he nevertheless suggested that exposure to the lifestyle of the French would help advance the process of evangelization. If this position echoed that of the Récollets, so did the means by which it was to be achieved – namely, an increase in the colony's French population. Missionaries alone were insufficient: "inhabitants and families are needed to keep them [Indigenous converts] to their duty and by gentle treatment to constrain them to do better and by good example to incite them to correct living."[33] In short, Champlain drew the same links between colonization, francization, and conversion as did the participants in the 1616 meeting. By the 1632 edition of his *Voyages*, Champlain presented himself as the chief architect of the colony's evangelizing mission.[34]

The evolving role of evangelization in Champlain's vision of New France dovetails with the growing intensity of Catholic fervour during this period, both among the population and in royal circles in France. Although the precise reasons for Champlain's change in attitude are unknown, personal and professional factors alike favoured such a reorientation. On a personal level, Champlain's wife, Hélène Boullé, converted to Catholicism in 1612 and henceforth devoted herself to strict observance. On a professional level, there was the example of Acadia, where a secular priest had been active in 1610–11 under the auspices of Poutrincourt. Across the Atlantic in France, Champlain spent considerable time in the early 1610s seeking to broaden support for the enterprise among those with access to royal circles. The appointment of the Prince de Condé as viceroy (and thus protector) in 1613 was one step toward this goal, but it is likely that Champlain came into contact with dévots and influential churchmen as well. Indeed, the 1619 *Voyages* not only contains Tridentine elements, but is also infused with the dévot idea that laymen have an important role to play in Christianizing missions.[35] If Champlain was inspired by these methods, there were also plenty of pragmatic reasons for making the evangelizing mission more visible. Although he was particularly close to Henri IV, Champlain was a faithful royal servant in general. This commitment entailed adjusting himself and his program to the religious and political priorities of the current monarch. As we have seen, the arrival of the queen regent in 1610, among other factors, prompted a strategic reconsideration on the part of Champlain and de Mons. The particular emphasis put on the strengthening of Catholicism within and outside the kingdom during the regency may have encouraged Champlain to become directly involved in promoting evangelization. Finally, by the mid-1610s he had shown himself to be skilled at building networks, particularly among those influential at court, and at tailoring his message to particular audiences. Reading the prevailing mood among Catholics, he may have judged that the evangelizing mission could help advance his own objectives in New France.[36]

The interests of church and Crown converged in the visions of New France outlined by Champlain and the Récollets in the 1610s. They agreed, above all, on the need for a concerted colonizing program and on the related need to decrease the company's influence over the colony. If Champlain's approach to evangelization changed in the various editions of his *Voyages*, he consistently expressed his desire to create a populous colony. A secondary advantage to the introduction of more French inhabitants would be the diminishing proportion of company agents and employees in the overall population, a development that would help consolidate Champlain's own authority as the representative of both king and viceroy.

As we saw in the preceding chapter, the lieutenant was keenly aware of being outnumbered by the CRSM's representatives at the beginning of the trading season in 1621. The Récollets' call for all future French inhabitants to be brought under their authority in the 1616 program, while appearing as a potential challenge to Champlain's position, in fact served him well by settling the question of who wielded control over people in the colony to the company's detriment. Thus, we find Champlain accompanying the Récollets Jamet and Le Caron to France in 1616 to garner support for their program from viceroy and king. While the latter never granted the Récollets express authority over the inhabitants of New France, Champlain and the missionaries had discovered common ground on which they could work together for their own interests.[37]

During this period, Champlain was looking above all for a way to make the colony viable and to expand its population. He was open to various possibilities for how to achieve this. If he supported the Récollet program in 1616, he also put forth his own proposal for a new enterprise in 1618, one that would increase the population and reduce the power of the traders in the colony.[38] Finally, he supported the CRSM's commitment to transport and provide for a certain number of inhabitants, including artisans, labourers, and officers in 1619, and was hopeful that it would be carried out (it was not).[39] As Champlain's frustration with the company mounted in the late 1610s, his growing dedication to the evangelizing mission presented an alternative avenue by which to realize his vision for the colony. At the close of the decade, then, there were an increasing number of people in New France who favoured a conversion program according to Catholic reform methods, alongside those who continued to act according to the traditions of a mixed-faith enterprise.

The Twin Threats of Protestantism and Commerce

Such was the politico-religious backdrop of the 1621 assembly of inhabitants. The immediate catalyst for the meeting, the dispute between the CRSM and the Compagnie de Montmorency over trading rights, provided an opening for the Récollets, Champlain, and others to push their colonizing and evangelizing program to the forefront. Although the assembly was held in the name of the larger community, the documents and actions that followed reveal it to have been largely a Récollet endeavour.[40] Indeed, the *cahier* began with a memorandum by "the poor Religious

Récollets," who had "deemed themselves bound in conscience to inform Your Majesty of his interest in preserving that land."[41] Like others of the time, the memorandum highlighted the abundant resources and potential riches of New France, stated reasons for urgent action, and suggested remedies. What the colony needed, it argued, was "the order necessary to fend off so many misfortunes that threaten the future loss of these lands." Among the imminent dangers was the knowledge of the land's richness by foreign rivals, as a result of which "they [French inhabitants] were in a constant state of fear of surprise." Such threats could be averted through "the maintenance of Religion by the authority of Justice, when both are supported and maintained by the force of a garrison housed in a fort." The articles of the *cahier* then outlined the specific measures needed to secure the king's goal of evangelization, from which would follow an increase in his prosperity, glory, and dominion. In the area of religion, "interdiction will be made to all His Majesty's subjects of the so-called Reformed Religion to live there or to admit there any person of any nation whatsoever of the said so-called Reformed Religion." A seminary would also be established for fifty Indigenous children, each receiving fifty *écus* from the king, and an abbey built. Justice would be applied strongly "so as … not to allow under the authority of His Majesty any robberies, murders, assassinations, bawdiness, blasphemy, and other crimes, already too familiar among some French inhabitants of the said land, to be committed."[42] Finally, a fort and tower at Tadoussac with a garrison of fifty men, combined with an increase in the lieutenant's authority (and salary), would ensure the effectiveness of the above measures.

The memorandum draws on precedents from both sides of the Atlantic. Like the 1616 program, it recommends the exclusion of Protestants from the colony. However, where the program outlined a strategy of conversion for which the Récollets sought royal approval, the memorandum is a veritable call to action enjoining the king (and viceroy) to intervene in the colony. The change is most evident in the latter's evocation of the spectre of invasion. A threat commonly raised when seeking royal support, Champlain, too, used the tactic in his 1618 proposal. There were other echoes between these two appeals. Both aimed to strengthen the governmental apparatus, notably its judicial and defensive aspects, and increase the authority of the lieutenant. Long a concern of Champlain's, proper fortifications were to guarantee the proposed new order founded on justice and religion.[43] If the attention given to defence reflected local circumstances in New France, the basic elements of the new order were products of the Catholic Reformation in France. The central role accorded justice and religion recalls Henri IV's description of them as "the fundamental pillars of this kingdom." While just what constituted each was a matter of some debate, the two principles reflected the philosophy of the French monarchy in the following decades. The Récollets, like many Catholics galvanized by the religious and political renewal, had their own vision of what the new order would look like, a vision that reflected some collaboration with Champlain.[44] The aim of the new order was to eradicate disorder.

What set the memorandum apart from previous supplications was the location of the threat inside the colony itself and the radical nature of the proposed solution – namely, to eliminate an entire constituency of people from New France. The memorandum identifies two sources of disorder in New France: commerce and Protestantism. It is no coincidence that neither Protestants nor representatives of the two trading companies were present at the assembly. To those imbued with the spirit of the Catholic Reformation in New France, traders and Protestants were viewed equally as "human agents of sin and social disorder."[45] There is little doubt that they were the French inhabitants described in the memorandum as "already too familiar" with various crimes and moral transgressions. Commerce was not traditionally well regarded in France. Considered a base activity whose primary goal was economic gain, it was deemed unsuitable for people of rank. Those who hoped New France would become a populous colony, such as Champlain and Lescarbot, reproduced these views in their writings, depicting traders as greedy and only concerned with profit. Commerce had long been the foundation of the New France enterprise. As the evangelizing mission gained in importance from 1615, the nature of the relationship between the two activities came to be of more pressing concern.[46]

Behind the anxieties around disorder lies a struggle for control over New France. Both Champlain and Récollets such as Joseph Le Caron complained regularly about the companies' weight in the colony. On one occasion in 1619, the lieutenant opined that "a company ... holds the purse strings, it pays, gives, and assists whomever it likes: those who command for his Majesty are hardly obeyed, having no one to assist them, except under the good pleasure of the Company."[47] This passage expresses Champlain's frustration with his lack of success in obtaining more men to work on the habitation, more colonists to clear land, and more funds to cover the costs of fort construction under the CRSM. If he hoped this situation would change under the Compagnie de Montmorency, the trading dispute of 1621 revealed de Caën's preoccupation with his own commercial might and his willingness to ignore Champlain's claims to jurisdiction when it suited his purposes. Material concerns aside, the passage's comparison of "those who command for his Majesty" and company agents shows that Champlain chafed under the superior leverage of the company. It was he who, in his eyes, should have been in charge. Writing in *Au Roy sur la Nouvelle France* in 1626, Le Caron attributes the colony's "disorder" to de Caën's company, whose commercial preoccupations eclipsed the priorities of the enterprise – namely, the colonizing and evangelizing missions. His proposed solutions included allowing Catholics to travel freely to New France to trade: "all those who, under the aegis of Apostolic and Roman Catholics, would like to outfit a vessel to go trade in New France would be able to." Not an explicit ban on Protestants, this provision focused instead on extending access to the colony's commerce to French men and women outside the company, thus diminishing the companies' influence.[48] For both Champlain and Le Caron, the companies represented an obstacle to their own agendas. The memorandum, like Champlain's proposal of 1618 and Le Caron's pamphlet, sought to reduce the power of the companies relative to the other competing authorities in the colony.

Although the memorandum singled out Protestants for exclusion from the colony, in the minds of its signatories, trade and Protestantism were inextricably linked. In a letter to the provincial of the Récollets of Paris in 1618, Le Caron asserted that the traders' behaviour exposed the habitation to aggression from Indigenous inhabitants. He also complained of the dearth of Catholics in certain key positions: "Our merchants are always plunging into greater disorders. They give us a Huguenot as clerk and intendant of their stores; the powder magazine keeper is of the same religion as this Protestant who commands at this post. If possible, the king ought to put a Catholic lord in these parts, esteemed by him, who would give what is necessary to build a seminary."[49] While Le Caron's objective, the construction of a seminary, no doubt coloured his characterization of the employees of the company, the passage paints Protestants and traders as one and the same and hints at the consequences for the colony. Of course, Protestants had long been well represented in commercial activities in New France. Two of the major French ports involved in transatlantic commerce, Rouen and La Rochelle, boasted merchant communities composed predominantly of Protestants.[50] From de Mons's company in the early 1600s to the recently established Compagnie de Montmorency, many of the most prominent traders in the colony were Protestant, including de Mons himself, Samuel Georges and Jean Macain of La Rochelle, and Pierre Caulier, Lucas Legendre, and Guillaume de Caën of Rouen, with the latter two in important roles at the time the memorandum was drafted. Of course, this visibility aside, not all traders were Protestant. The partners of Legendre and his co-religionists in the CRSM were Catholics from Saint-Malo, a port that had produced associates (and interlopers) since Cartier's voyages in the mid-sixteenth century. In other words, if commerce and religion increasingly intersected after the Wars of Religion in some sectors, this was not the case in New France, where mixed enterprise prevailed.[51] It was, however, convenient for Le Caron and others to conflate traders and Protestants, two groups that were considered equally disruptive.

The loyalty of both groups was suspect. As the writings of Champlain and Le Caron show, company associates and agents were not to be trusted because they prioritized commercial profits over colonization, evangelization, and the habitation's security. The extensive international networks and, in some cases, foreign origins of traders made this indifference appear but one small step away from treason. In Dolu's defence of Montmorency's decision to replace the CRSM with de Caën's company in 1620, he suggested that certain associates were ready to give New France away to foreign rivals: "some of the said merchants are tempted to abandon it [the colony] and others of the same company to sell and take money from foreigners and put the said country in their hands, to the detriment of the honour of the said seigneur viceroy, Duc de Montmorency."[52] The basis for this accusation was the foreign origins – or in some cases, simply the foreign names – of certain associates or their affiliates, including Mathieu Duisterlo, of German extraction, Louis Vermeullen (or Vermeules), whose name was Flemish, and the Dutch-born Corneille de Bellois, a partner of Daniel Boyer.[53] If such a charge served Dolu's purposes, it also underscored the ambiguous attitude of French officials toward merchants in long-distance trade. To be competitive, France relied on these merchants' international connections and expertise, and yet at the same time such activity raised the possibility of foreign collaboration against the Crown.[54] Implicit in Dolu's concerns over the foreign origins of certain CRSM associates was their Protestant faith. Given that the French monarchy was itself Catholic, Catholic subjects were normally considered loyal by default and their connections to co-religionists in other nations, not to mention their affiliation with Rome, deemed unimportant. The reverse was true for Protestants. With ties to the Protestant centres of England and the Netherlands, it was assumed that French Protestants' allegiance was dictated by their faith rather than their place of birth or residence or their blood relations.[55] In this sense, Protestants posed a spiritual threat to the kingdom and colony, a corollary to the physical threat represented by de Caën's seizure of Gravé Du Pont's vessel.

To what extent were the threats evoked in the 1621 memorandum and elsewhere real? At the opening of the 1620s, events in both Europe and North America did give credence to anti-Protestant suspicions. In 1620, Louis XIII annexed Protestant Béarn and barred those of the majority confession from seeking public office, provoking a defiant declaration of political autonomy at a General Assembly of Protestants at La Rochelle. Considering this akin to open rebellion, Louis XIII led his army on several campaigns to force Protestant strongholds into royal submission throughout southern and southwestern France in 1621–22. English Protestants provided, if not direct military reinforcement, then at least financial and moral support. Although largely successful, the king fell short of taking control of La Rochelle. This conflict came to an end with the Treaty of Montpellier, which pardoned the commander of Protestant forces, Henri II, Duc de Rohan, an outcome that many Catholics regarded as far too lenient.[56]

Beyond France's borders, initiatives by the country's Dutch and English rivals heightened concerns. In 1621, the so-called Twelve Years' Truce between the young Dutch Republic and Spain came to an end. As these countries and their allies prepared for renewed fighting, both the States General of the Netherlands and the English Crown granted significant overseas commissions. The former established the West India Company, whose jurisdiction extended from New Netherland (in what is now the United States) to the West Indies and east to Africa. While its mandate covered both trade and colonization, it was primarily a war machine, designed to weaken Spanish power by targeting its treasure-laden ships and colonies in the Americas.[57] England, for its part, granted a commission to Sir William Alexander, poet, master of requests, and member of the Scottish Privy Council, to establish claims through colonization to "New Scotland," which encompassed Acadia and stretched as far north as the Saint Lawrence River. Despite several attempts to recruit settlers and found a colony over the next decade, the vision behind this grant did not come to fruition.[58] Viewed from France in 1621, however, these initiatives by France's main rivals in North America posed a credible threat to French possessions in general, and to New France in particular. When the 1621 memorandum evoked the possibility of foreign invasion and underscored the transgressions of certain (Protestant and merchant) inhabitants, then, it was no mere rhetorical device designed to win over its audience. Confessional issues within the colony heightened geopolitical concerns.[59] It is against this backdrop of war – potential and real, international and civil – that the memorandum finds its urgency and power.

Changing Definitions of Subjecthood: Protestant Traders

Faced with domestic and international dangers, French sovereignty needed to be rendered tangible in New France. While the construction of a fort at the Quebec habitation in 1620–21 was one step toward this goal, its reach was limited, as it was fixed in space. Subjects, however, whether traders, company agents, viceregal representatives, or missionaries, could function, as we have seen, as carriers of jurisdiction in their frequent travels along the waterways of North America. Any restriction on movement, such as barring entry to the habitation to de Caën's and the CRSM's agents when they arrived without papers, amounted to calling into question a subject's loyalty and legitimacy. Prior to the trading dispute of 1621, competing traders and title-holders had contested the rights and claims of their rivals but not their status as French subjects. By associating disorder (and the threat of the loss of New France) with Protestants and traders, the assembly of 1621, memorandum, and subsequent representations in France raised two related questions, both of which went to the core of French claims: Who constituted a legitimate subject? And who would define and police that status? The debate persisted over the next five years as the Récollets, in particular, attempted to redefine the nature of French subjecthood in the context of the increasingly central role accorded the evangelizing mission in the enterprise. In this quest, they targeted two groups: Protestant traders and France's Indigenous allies.

The activities of the Récollet Georges Le Baillif as the deputy of the 1621 assembly in France transformed the main conversation in the colony from one of trading rights to one of subjecthood. While his primary mandate was to obtain an audience before the king to present the inhabitants' list of grievances – which he did with Montmorency's help – Le Baillif was also granted the power to "name and appoint one or two lawyers to His Majesty's Council, Sovereign Courts and Jurisdictions" to represent their perspective in the lawsuit over trading privileges involving Montmorency, the CRSM, and de Caën's company then before the courts.[60] To this end, he appeared before the Conseil privé in December 1621 to request that the "putative charges and accusations made" at the Admiralty of Dieppe against Dolu, Villemenon, and associates be brought before the royal council, together with the assembly's list of grievances containing "the excesses and violence committed in the said country by the said associates." Le Baillif argued that the accusations and violence were "manifestations of one and the same reality."[61] This and other requests before the same court by other parties led to the appointment of commissioners to hear the representations of both companies before reporting to the council and interveners. By bringing the "disorders" in the colony to the attention of the courts and the king, Le Baillif and the assembly participants hoped to have their call to exclude Protestants from New France factor into the royal council's resolution of the trade dispute. The Récollet's intervention thus aimed to change the central issue from who had a legitimate claim to the trade of New France to who was a suitable leader of the enterprise.

The Récollets sought to make adherence to Catholicism a defining element of what it meant to be a subject under the king in New France. Catholic bona fides and commitment to the evangelizing mission had never been make-or-break conditions before 1620. After all, the New France enterprise had been mixed from the beginning. The Compagnie de Montmorency appeared to be following this trend when it formed under one Protestant, Guillaume de Caën, and one Catholic, Ézéchiel de Caën. The Récollets, however, took exception to Ézéchiel's recent conversion, seeing it as a calculated move to obtain royal contracts.[62]

That the Protestant faith of traders increasingly came to be seen as a problem and, more specifically, a source of disorder in the 1620s points to the growing influence of the Récollets in the colony's governance structure. Le Baillif's tenure in New France exemplifies this development. Having only arrived at the opening of the 1621 trading season as the procureur of the Récollet mission, he nevertheless quickly became an adviser to Champlain. Indeed, the lieutenant received instructions that spring from Montmorency, Dolu, and Villemenon "enjoining me not to do anything without communicating it to him [Le Baillif]." On several occasions over the summer, Champlain dispatched Le Baillif to mediate between de Caën and Gravé Du Pont over the trading rights accorded both companies, granting "full power from me [Champlain] to settle everything amicably."[63] It was perhaps not surprising, then, that Le Baillif was named the assembly's deputy to the king by summer's end. If the Récollet initially professed reluctance to take on such a role, as the negotiations it would entail "w[ere] not altogether suited to a missionary," he quickly embraced his new function. Indeed, he went so far as to publish an ad hominem attack on de Caën, in which he questioned the latter's loyalty, not only to God but to the king as well.[64]

While these over-the-top accusations were quickly discredited by others involved in New France, including Champlain, the presence of Protestant traders continued to draw criticism in the following years.[65] Among such opponents was the provincial of the Récollets of Saint-Denis, the province to which the missionaries in New France belonged. He requested in 1622 that the king forbid "those of the supposedly reformed religion from going there, either for trading or for living [*demeurer*], given the trouble that has already been unleashed by such people."[66] Framing the problem and solution in terms of subjecthood, the provincial argued that the advancement of the king's objectives, as well as the maintenance of his sovereignty, required a change in who constituted a legitimate traveller to and inhabitant of New France.[67] The concerns voiced by the provincial, the 1621 assembly, and Le Baillif stemmed, for many, from genuine bafflement as to how a mission devoted to the Catholicization of a population could proceed under a Protestant – a figure reformers regarded as in equal need of instruction himself. At the same time, the ability to shape the terms of belonging in New France was also one step toward consolidating civil authority over the colony's inhabitants in the hands of religious.

The argument that only Catholics could be subjects in New France amounted to nothing less than a redefinition of what it meant to be a French subject. In France, subjecthood was based on place of birth and blood relations, not religion.[68] Indeed, the Edict of Nantes attempted to separate religion from politics by establishing a civil definition of subjecthood. In the immediate aftermath of the Wars of Religion, there was a desire to create a renewed community to which all could belong, regardless of confession. Lawful and peaceful behaviour constituted the chief requirement. Subjects were first and foremost distinguished from foreigners through the enjoyment of various rights and privileges. Under the Edict of Nantes, the civil rights granted Protestants, including permission to enter the legal and scholarly professions, were comparable to those accorded naturalized foreigners.[69] This is not to say, however, that religion played no role in contemporaries' conceptions of subjecthood. It proved far harder in practice to separate politics from religion, especially as Protestants enjoyed certain legal protections as a corporation. On the one hand, many Protestants felt betrayed by Henri IV's conversion in 1593, and their numbers declined in France, particularly in the 1610s and 1620s, as confessional tensions reignited and their civil rights were undermined.[70] On the other hand, for staunch Catholics, Protestantism remained linked to treason. It was, however, only in the 1660s under Louis XIV that Catholicism came to be considered a criterion for subjecthood.[71]

By contrast, on the western side of the Atlantic, Catholic subjecthood became part of the articles of the Compagnie de la Nouvelle-France in 1627, almost sixty years before the Revocation of the Edict of Nantes. The second article of the company's edict stated, "Without however allowing the said associates and others to send any foreigner to the said places, thus peopling the said colony with native French Catholics."[72] Officials who allowed any contravention of this article risked being held legally responsible in their own name. Like Le Caron's letter and Dolu's appearance before the courts on Montmorency's behalf, the article draws an implicit link between foreigners and Protestantism. The CNF's establishment marked the official end to mixed enterprise. Unofficially, Protestants continued to be active in New France. The edict, then, presages, as some have argued, the "fiction of a Catholic France" that emerged in 1685. If the clause did not go as far as the Récollets demanded (a complete ban on Protestants), it was nevertheless in part the result of the sustained campaign launched by the Récollets to redefine the terms of the New France enterprise and those who could participate.[73]

As an indication of the significance of the shift in focus from trade to the evangelizing mission, the rival trading companies in turn changed the way they articulated their activities in the colony. While both were the target of criticism for their Protestant membership at least once between 1620 and 1626, their responses were notably different. The CRSM, for one, acceded to the new terms of subjecthood by adopting the Récollets' rhetoric. In response to Dolu's suggestion that foreign-born Protestant associates wanted to put New France in the hands of France's rivals, the company requested in March 1621 that an act be drawn up testifying to their good intentions. "In order to remove any suspicion that one could make to the said Sieur admiral and also to give His Majesty and the public all satisfaction on this subject, *they [the associates] do not intend to send [anyone] to live* [habiter] *in the said country who does not make profession of the Catholic, Apostolic, and Roman Religion*." They added that, should they contravene this promise, they would willingly accept any penalty, financial or otherwise, that the king cared to impose.[74] The CRSM thus professed its commitment, like the Récollets, to the foundation of a Catholic colony in New France. Coming as it did in the midst of a lawsuit against Montmorency, this request was without doubt a calculated move. The CRSM associates were, after all, trying to have their trading privileges confirmed under the new viceroy. At the same time, it attests to the rising prestige of the Récollets in the colony and in royal circles. What is notable is the relatively early date of the CRSM's articulation of the enterprise in Catholic terms. Occurring before the skirmishes between the rival companies and the assembly of 1621, it is likely as reflective of the tense confessional atmosphere in France at the close of 1620, as Louis XIII doubled down on his desire to bring Protestant regions fully under royal authority, as it is of conditions in New France.

If the CRSM associates fashioned themselves as the ones best suited to facilitate Catholic interests and objectives, de Caën and the associates of the Compagnie de Montmorency advanced their own vision for the colony by bringing trade and the evangelizing mission together. There is no extant record of any submission by de Caën on the subject in the context of the lawsuit between Montmorency and the CRSM in 1621. Three years later, however, de Caën responded to the frequent charges levelled by the Récollets of impropriety and obstruction of Catholic practices in New France.[75] Appearing before the Admiralty of France in 1624, he declared, "the country of New France [is] in such a good state by his [de Caën's] *order, industry, and diligence* and by the quantity of nations of natives which approach it before unknown to the French, that the great river Saint Lawrence by *the trade that takes place with the said natives the country being well managed and the natives kept in friendship*."[76] It was no accident that de Caën used the term "order" here. A direct challenge to the Récollets' portrayal of him individually, and of Protestant traders collectively, as sources of disorder, his statement went so far as to suggest that commerce had a role to play in the evangelizing mission. Simply put, it was a way to establish and maintain good relations with France's Indigenous allies. De Caën thus presented an alternative vision to that of the Récollets' in which commerce and evangelization were antithetical. De Caën was not alone in making the link between the two activities. Almost a year earlier, Champlain testified to Dolu of "the great friendship and connection of the natives with the said de Caën, which could bring them [the viceroy and his representatives] great advantage."[77] While the role of commerce is merely implicit here, the remark is in keeping with other statements made in Champlain's travel accounts that connect military alliances and commerce with exploration and evangelization. Activities like commerce helped to establish trust and amity between French and Indigenous inhabitants, a vital prelude to French goals of francization, conversion, and subjugation.[78] Coming at a time when his character was under attack, both statements in de Caën's favour countered the narrowing definition of subjecthood. By showing that his commercial activities and relations with Indigenous partners furthered French objectives, they portrayed him as a worthy colonial subject himself and even an appropriate leader in the enterprise.

De Caën's and Champlain's remarks provide a rare moment when Indigenous inhabitants of the Great lakes–Saint Lawrence region are visible as trading partners of the privileged companies. To a certain extent, such a focus was not unusual on Champlain's part, given his decades-long efforts to foster alliances with Indigenous Peoples for the purposes of exploration, trade, conversion, and occupation. As we saw in the previous chapter, one year prior to his letter to Dolu, Champlain had supported the Innu Miristou as chief in exchange for the promise to establish an Innu settlement near Quebec. His comments and, more often, complaints about traders' behaviour, however, typically concerned colonization and the construction and defence of the Quebec habitation, not their relationship to their Indigenous partners.[79] More unusual was de Caën's reference to the well-being of Indigenous Peoples as evidence of his good management of the colony. Indeed, company associates rarely made explicit mention of their trading partners, despite the fact that the success of each venture was utterly dependent on such relationships. While this silence may in part be a function of the limited sources that have survived, it was no coincidence that de Caën invoked the friendship of "the quantity of native nations" in his own defence at this particular moment. France's Wendat, Algonquin, and Innu trading partners were, after all, the object of the evangelizing mission. The bulk of the criticisms aimed at de Caën and his fellow Protestant traders pertained to their supposedly negative influence on these prospective Catholic converts, whether due to general "disorders" or to their practising their religion within hearing distance of the latter.[80] In response, de Caën aimed to show how his activities and relations with Indigenous traders served the goals of the evangelizing mission and the development of a stable colony. Whereas the CRSM associates appeared to bow to the Récollets' proposed new definition of subjecthood, de Caën countered it with his own colonial vision.

Changing Definitions of Subjecthood: Indigenous Inhabitants

If Protestants were to be excluded under the Récollets' proposed redefinition of subjecthood, the Indigenous inhabitants of North America were to be incorporated. In the 1620s, and indeed for much of the seventeenth century, the interests of the Catholic Church and the French monarchy converged in the bodies of Indigenous people in New France. The desire to incorporate the latter originated partly in the belief that the source of power of both institutions lay in people. As taxpayers and soldiers, people were the foundation of a state's standing in Europe. During the sixteenth and seventeenth centuries, royal policies aimed to maintain and increase France's population. One way was through the annexation of territory and incorporation of peoples on the kingdom's periphery, such as Brittany in 1532 and Navarre in 1589.[81] Notwithstanding France's status as the most populous kingdom in Europe, this demographic concern shaped approaches to colonization in North America. Ministers ranging from Sully to Richelieu to Jean-Baptiste Colbert wanted to avoid depopulating the kingdom in order to people New France with French subjects. In this context, conquest or incorporation of a peopled territory, rather than "virgin land," was imperative.[82] By making Indigenous inhabitants into Frenchmen, the Crown would strengthen its population and make visible its sovereign claims. (De Caën's emphasis on the "quantity of native nations" suggests that he grasped this demographic imperative.) The Catholic Church, for its part, was only as strong as the number of souls counted within it. In the context of the Catholic Reformation, ecclesiastics and lay members alike saw it as their mission to instruct all people in the Christian faith, both in Europe and overseas. Indigenous bodies, like those of the inhabitants of regions on France's periphery, thus represented potential souls to the church and subjects to the Crown.

The question was *how* to incorporate the Indigenous Peoples living in the territories claimed as New France. During the decade following the Récollets' arrival at Quebec, the terms of Indigenous subjecthood were being worked out. In 1627, the Crown articulated for the first time the conditions under which Indigenous inhabitants were to become French subjects. Article 17 of the edict establishing the CNF read as follows: "His Majesty orders that the descendants of the French who establish themselves in the said country, together with the natives who will be brought to knowledge of the faith, and in making such a profession, will be considered and reputed to be native French, and as such can come live in France when they would like to, and there acquire, bequeath, inherit, and accept donations and legacies just as subjects [*régnicoles*] and native French; without having to obtain any letter of registration or naturalization."[83] According to this definition, Indigenous subjecthood had both juridical and cultural components. Those who converted to Catholicism were to enjoy the same rights and privileges as natural-born French. In other words, they were not treated like foreigners in the kingdom who were subject to the *droit d'aubaine* and required letters of naturalization to acquire the privileges of subjecthood.[84] In this respect, the king granted converted Indigenous subjects the same juridical status as inhabitants of regions adjacent to France that came under his control.

What distinguished potential Indigenous subjects from the status of subjects in France was precisely what set French settlers apart: they had to be Catholic (converts). Baptism thus became the route by which Indigenous people were to be naturalized and gain entry to the French political community. Together with article 2, which stipulated that only French Catholics were allowed to settle in New France, article 17 created two new types of foreigner in law: French Protestants and unconverted Indigenous people.[85] These "foreigners" were, of course, not the same and, as a result, conversion had quite different consequences for each. Whereas French Protestants generally recognized French law and government, Indigenous nations like the Wendat, Algonquin, and Innu were sovereign in their territories and had their own legal and governmental systems. The Catholic Church and the Crown considered both, however, capable of improvement and thus admissible to the political, civic, and religious communities as Catholic converts.

This notion of an imminent possible belonging underscores the universal and inclusive ideologies of church and monarchy.[86] Considering all people equal before God, Catholic doctrine asserted that all were worthy and capable of salvation, regardless of social background, culture, or ethnicity. This universalist vision made the Catholic Church at once aggressively expansionist and accommodating, providing room for a variety of peoples, cultures, and languages. The universalism of the Catholic Church had its secular counterpart in royal approaches to rule. Within the realm of France, diversity reigned. Newly incorporated territories maintained their proper customs, laws, and institutions. What people in different provinces had in common was their status as subjects of the same king.[87] In this sense, the French realm and the Catholic Church provided space juridically, politically, and culturally for the Indigenous inhabitants of North America.

Admission to French political and religious/cultural communities could not be accomplished by baptism alone;[88] it also required *civilisation*. As we have seen, the Récollets considered this process a necessary prelude to conversion as early as 1616. Like that year's program and subsequent proposals, the CNF edict accorded French settlers a central role. While the four thousand settlers the company was responsible for transporting to New France over the following fifteen years aimed above all to strengthen the colony numerically, they would also serve as models of European lifestyle, manners, and behaviour.[89] But in order to "civilize" and, more specifically, *franciser* Indigenous Peoples, it was necessary to identify first what the qualities of "Frenchness" were. This question had no simple answer for there was no unifying French identity in the early seventeenth century. Linguistically and culturally diverse, the majority of French people identified most immediately with their village, parish, or region, rather than an overarching national entity.

What it meant to be "French," and even the concept of francization itself, were partly shaped in the context of French-Indigenous relations in New France.[90] Devised by colonial and imperial authorities, the resulting portrait was of an ideal subject who did not exist in the kingdom. This ideal subject spoke French, was Catholic, industrious, honest, disciplined, and dedicated to farming (i.e., sedentary).[91] Certain qualities were a function of the particular colonial context. For example, given the diversity of Indigenous nations, language groups, and cultures, it was not possible to have one group that had sufficient knowledge of French language and culture act as a go-between, and, consequently, French authorities wished for all Indigenous Peoples to learn French, a policy that contrasted with the official acceptance of multiple dialects in the metropole.[92] If metropolitan authorities wished that French subjects in the kingdom had the moral and behavioural characteristics described above, cultural assimilation was a feature of (Indigenous) subjecthood in New France alone.

Francization fit into a more general "disciplining" of society that characterized the period. Indeed, colonial and imperial authorities who defined *francité* tended to describe Indigenous people in the same terms as metropolitan officials used to refer to French peasants. Both were seen as lacking in civility.[93] Civility and *francité* reflected the social origins of these authorities, encompassing elite norms around morality, family, sexuality, and religion. Needless to say, only the lower strata of society and those on the margins were considered in need of reform and thus came to be the target of growing royal and ecclesiastical supervision. The poor, for example, became the object of relief programs administered first by the many newly established confraternities and lay associations and later by the state.[94] In the wake of the Council of Trent, reforming bishops and clergy attempted to separate sacred and profane spaces in their parishes. Churchyards and cemeteries, long sites of local civic celebrations and events, were to be confined to religious activities. By reducing the number of holidays, church authorities aimed to police more effectively the behaviours associated with such events, notably drinking, dancing, and extramarital sexual relations. The latter issue being of particular concern, the Tridentine reforms had strengthened the marriage sacrament, thus aiming to increase control not only over parishioners' souls but also over their bodies.[95] This general civilizing mentality helped to shape strategies to incorporate the Indigenous inhabitants of New France as subjects.

Indigenous Peoples had their own motivations for adopting Christian beliefs and French practices. Openness to both helped to strengthen alliances and could provide further protection in the context of demographic crises associated with war and disease. Indigenous groups did not, however, accept the totalizing character of Christianity and francization and the cultural superiority they implied. Instead, they experimented with and integrated select beliefs and practices into their own cultural and spiritual systems and lifeways. As Jean-François Lozier's study of mission settlements in the Saint Lawrence Valley convincingly demonstrates, Algonquian bands were open to experimenting with settlement near the French in the decades following the establishment of Quebec. Sources from the period refer to periodic requests from different Innu and Algonquin bands for the French to establish a post near what would become Montreal so that they could settle there without fear of the Haudenosaunee. While the French imagined permanent and fixed settlements, Indigenous bands had a more elastic and fluid definition. Members of Algonquian bands who took up residence and cultivated land near Quebec integrated this site into their seasonal migration patterns. The purpose of such settlements varied, ranging from subsistence needs to gaining favour with the French. The example of Miristou and his followers in 1622 is representative. While they did clear land and sow corn, their settlement proved temporary and was abandoned once its purpose had been served.[96]

Just as Indigenous bands tried out settlement near French posts in the context of traditional seasonal displacement, so their experimentation with Christianity was shaped by existing spiritual beliefs and practices. Indigenous cultures had an animistic approach to the world around them. All things, such as plants, animals, rocks, and rivers, were alive and had a spiritual essence. Endowed with supernatural powers that could be used for good or malevolent purposes, these spirits, or manitous, needed to be given offerings, notably tobacco, before particular activities such as a hunt or long voyage. In return, spirits offered their protection. The relationship between humans and supernatural forces was thus characterized by reciprocity.[97] Indigenous groups made sense of Christian teachings and their proselytizers through this world view. The Christian God was therefore considered another manitou who could be called upon for protection. Jesuit missionaries in the *pays d'en haut* described Indigenous men and women throwing tobacco around the perimeter of a chapel and speaking to the building directly, as they would their own spirits. In a similar vein, missionaries were seen as manitous themselves or as shamans who had particular powers to communicate with supernatural forces through rites and magic.[98] Indigenous groups sought to put these powers to use in subsistence activities and in war. For example, the Jesuit Allouez reported being asked by Fox warriors if they could sleep in the chapel so that God could speak to them and help them vanquish their enemies. Ojibway warriors asked another missionary to obtain the blessing of the "god of armies." Similarly, Indigenous participants endowed Christian rituals with meaning by drawing on their own spiritual traditions. Fasting was assimilated to a vision quest rather than understood as the expiation of sins. The cross and other Christian objects assumed the same significance as amulets and wampum and were worn for protection and strength.[99] In the Indigenous pluralist approach to spirituality, Christianity constituted another source of power.

If Christianization and francization led, in French eyes, to subjecthood, Indigenous groups understood their experimentation with Christian beliefs within the framework of alliance. The principles at the core of alliance – hospitality, openness, and tolerance – guided this experimentation. Some Indigenous men accepted baptism and participated in other Christian rites, not as a first step in the conversion process but as a gesture of openness toward the rituals of an ally.[100] Others who became converts did so in part as a demonstration of their commitment to the alliance. The mission settlement of Sillery, or Kamiskouaouangachit, founded in 1637–38, is instructive. Situated upriver from Quebec, it was created at the request of two Algonquians, Negabamat and Nenaskoumat, who were both already known to the French. While residents continued their seasonal displacements, Sillery departed from previous settlements in developing both a permanent infrastructure and a community identity based on Christian devotion and French alliance. An epidemic the year after its establishment had the effect of strengthening ties to the missionaries and among converts. Negabamat and others began to promote conversion and their own community to other bands. According to Lozier, they aimed to develop Sillery as a "diplomatic and ritual center." Over time, the community gained a certain prestige and attracted members of other bands who wished to develop relations with its members. The community's Algonquian leaders even made conversion a condition of strengthening alliances.[101] The need to maintain close ties with the French could also be a source of pressure on Indigenous groups. A year before Sillery was founded, an epidemic among the Wendats led some to accuse the resident Jesuits of sorcery. Although they were brought before the Grand Council, they were ultimately spared death due in part to the fear of losing trade connections and military support.[102] Considerations of alliance and adherence to the principles underlying it shaped Indigenous approaches to Christianization.

Intermarriage, a fundamental component of the French-Indigenous alliance, was for the French the principal route by which to create Indigenous subjects. Simultaneously fulfilling the royal and ecclesiastical objectives of evangelization, francization, and population growth, it was promoted from the beginning of French colonization, particularly by missionaries, and then later by royal officials in the 1660s under Louis XIV.[103] In the 1630s, for example, the Jesuits requested that the pope grant permission for marriages between French men and Indigenous women who were not yet baptized nor even much educated in Christianity. Champlain, for his part, promised the Innu in the same decade that "our young men will marry your daughters, and we shall be one people." Thirty years later, Minister Jean-Baptiste Colbert instructed Intendant Jean Talon to encourage Indigenous settlements near French habitations in order to facilitate such mixing.[104] As the three above-mentioned objectives suggest, the idea was not to create a new category of mixed people but, rather, to assimilate or even subsume the Indigenous subject into the European. The French had such confidence in their culture's superiority that they assumed that the French elements would prevail in a union.[105] Marriage policies targeted Indigenous women specifically. Due to the low numbers of European women in New France and European patriarchal beliefs about the institution of marriage, these unions were to take place exclusively between French men and Indigenous women, never Indigenous men and French women. Once Indigenous women were assimilated into the Catholic faith and French culture through marriage, French authorities hoped that they would also convert others in their communities.[106]

Indigenous groups were generally open to intercultural sexual relations and intermarriage as a means to cement alliances with the French. French chroniclers regularly commented on the greater sexual liberty enjoyed by Indigenous women compared to their European counterparts. Connected to the principle of hospitality, this liberty helped to foster bonds within a community as well as with allies. In matrilineal and matrilocal societies like the Wendats, women could engage in premarital sex with multiple partners. Extramarital sex was not forbidden, although once the couple had a child, the union tended to be monogamous.[107] French missionaries describe the custom by which male visitors to Indigenous communities in the *pays d'en haut* were offered a girl with whom they would spend the night. While the French mistook this practice for prostitution, in Indigenous societies it served to reinforce alliances and secure access to trade goods. In instances where Indigenous groups considered the French to be manitous, sexual relations were also a way to increase spiritual and military power to the benefit of the community as a whole.[108]

Marriage in the European Catholic mode could significantly curtail Indigenous women's traditional liberty, but it could also offer opportunities. In theory, it required them to submit to strict patriarchal norms, to obey their husbands, renounce extramarital sex, and never divorce. Missionaries aimed to confine sexual relations to monogamous marriage and to limit all sexual activity to reproductive purposes. These strictures went against the role of sexuality and marriage in Indigenous societies. As a result, some Indigenous men and women did refuse baptism.[109] For other Indigenous women, however, intermarriage could be a means to improve their positions. Among the Illinois and Great Lakes communities, for example, women significantly outnumbered men due to warfare. Polygamy was also practised. Both of these factors may have encouraged Illinois women to marry French men.[110] In the context of the fur trade, intermarriage could increase a woman's status within her community. The union provided improved access to trade goods, which increased her power as well as that of her household. As the wife of a fur trader, an Indigenous woman became a mediator between the two cultures and thus played a role in strengthening the alliance between her community and the French. Mixed unions were most common in the *pays d'en haut* and the *pays des Illinois*, where there were few French women and close relations with Indigenous communities were important for both the fur trade and general security. For a French trader, intermarriage made him part of his wife's kin network, which in turn facilitated his access to furs.[111] The advantages of these unions for both parties meant that they continued to grow in number, whether church-sanctioned or "in the custom of the country," at the beginning of the eighteenth century, even as French authorities began to ban intermarriage.[112]

While the aspiration of ecclesiastical and royal authorities was for Indigenous people to be subjects of the French king, commissions, treaties, and practice show that the French also considered them to be allies, just as Indigenous people themselves did. Throughout the seventeenth century, French documents reveal the ambiguous and complex nature of this relationship. De Mons's commission of 1603, for example, instructed him

> to subject, submit, and bring to obedience all the people of the said land … And by the means thereof, and all lawful ways, to call, make, instruct, provoke, and incite them to the knowledge of God, and to the light of the faith and Christian religion … To treat, and contract to the same effect, peace, alliance, and confederacy, good amity, correspondency, and communication with the said people and their Princes or others having power or command over them: To entertain, keep, and carefully to observe the treaties and alliances wherein you shall covenant with them: upon condition that they themselves perform the same of their part. And for want thereof to make open

> wars against them, to constrain and bring them to such reason as you shall think needful, for the honour, obedience, and service of God and the establishment, maintenance, and conservation of our said authority amongst them: at least to haunt and frequent by you, and all our subjects with them, in all assurance, liberty, frequentation, and communication, there to negotiate and traffic lovingly and peaceably.[113]

Although the aim was subjection, there was also a recognition of the sovereignty of Indigenous nations and, indeed, an assumption that they functioned in the same way as European polities. The emphasis in this passage is on pacific means (*voies douces*) with recourse to force only if contracting parties did not uphold their end of an alliance, a condition that derived from the law of nations, or *jus gentium*. Commissions before and after de Mons's varied in the importance placed on either a gentle approach or a more forceful conquest, making it difficult to discern an evolution from one to the other.[114] At the same time, the above passage, like similar ones in subsequent commissions, presents treaties and alliances as a principal way to expand French influence in North America.[115] More than half a century later, in the treaty concluding peace between the Haudenosaunee and the French, Wendats, and Algonquins in 1665, the latter two nations were described as "subjects of the said Seigneur King, or living under his protection," demonstrating that the uncertainty among the French regarding the status of Indigenous Peoples continued. Given that the French could not subjugate these nations by force, alliance – the primary framework within which Indigenous groups viewed their interactions with the French – could be an alternative, and more subtle, means of incorporation and extension of French sovereignty in North America.[116]

Catholicizing the Spaces of New France

The shift in the balance of power visible in the redefinition of subjecthood and responses to it was reinforced in the person of the new viceroy of New France, who arrived in 1625. Indeed, Henri de Lévis, Duc de Ventadour, Montmorency's nephew and lieutenant general of Languedoc, could be said to have embodied the growing rapprochement between royal and ecclesiastical interests over the previous decade. A devout Catholic, the new viceroy was active in dévot circles and, at the end of the 1620s, founded the Compagnie du Saint Sacrement, a secret and militant lay congregation whose aim was to eliminate Protestantism in the kingdom. Like other reformist organizations of its kind, it sponsored various evangelizing projects, both within and outside France, and was composed of a mix of lay and religious. One of the projects in which several of its members, including Ventadour, became involved was the establishment of Ville-Marie (later Montreal) through the Société de Notre-Dame de Montréal.[117] Married to a dévote, Ventadour and his wife both eventually entered religious life themselves. As lieutenant general of Languedoc during Louis XIII's campaign in 1621–22, the duke was also involved militarily in the struggle against Protestantism, even voluntarily raising a company of soldiers at his own expense. Five years later, in the midst of establishing the Compagnie du Saint Sacrement, he fought in the siege of La Rochelle.[118]

Ventadour's commitment to the ideals of the Catholic Reformation and service to "His Most Christian Majesty" shaped his approach to the viceroyalty of New France. His actions directly advanced the twin objectives of church and monarchy, the gaining of souls and subjects. Above all, Ventadour used his position to secure a prominent place for the Jesuits in the evangelizing mission, a mission that, by the Récollets' own admission, was in need of reinforcements. It was, in fact, his Jesuit spiritual director, Philibert Noyrot, who encouraged him to become viceroy in the first place. One of Ventadour's first acts in that role was to sponsor the transportation of six Jesuits to Quebec as well as their maintenance in the colony, thus beginning the order's activity in the Saint Lawrence Valley and Great Lakes region.[119] In a similar manner, the viceroy marked his departure – which occurred only two years later – with another initiative to strengthen the Jesuit presence in the colony: "a Jesuit house" would be established "in the name of the said seigneur duke, in which six priests will be maintained in perpetuity for the expansion of God's service and instruction of the natives of the said places." Indeed, Ventadour went so far as to make this a condition of his resignation.[120] Ventadour's initiatives and connections are suggestive of the ways in which the evangelizing mission and French claims to sovereignty were mutually reinforcing. While Récollet and, later, Jesuit missionaries helped to expand French influence through their conversion activities, which led them to take up residence within Indigenous communities, the integration of ecclesiastics and lay dévots into the government of New France – from Le Baillif as Champlain's adviser to Ventadour as viceroy – ensured that the evangelizing mission helped to shape the colony's direction.

If Ventadour did not attempt to implement the Récollets' new definition of subjecthood, he did contribute to a redefinition of the spaces of New France as Catholic. As we have seen, the role of Protestant traders was increasingly coming under attack in the early 1620s. Guillaume de Caën, in particular, was subject to certain constraints due to his faith. Champlain recounts his instructions from Montmorency on this issue: "As to the Sieur de Caen, although he was of the opposite religion, there were great hopes of his becoming a Catholic; and, as to the exercise of his religion, I was to tell him that *he was not to practice it either on land or on sea*; and as to anything further I was to use my own judgment."[121] The "great hopes" placed in de Caën's eventual conversion were perhaps due to his uncle's recent conversion (however incomplete or opportunistic it appeared to be, at least to the Récollets). They may also reflect, more generally, the optimism that attended the announcement of a new viceroy and company as well as reformers' confidence in the superiority and rightness of Catholicism. As for measures in the meantime, the proscription was at once categorical – no practice whatsoever – and vague, with no specification of *which* land or *where* at sea. Subsequent disputes show, however, that Protestant observance both continued and was, up to a point, accepted. In 1622, for example, a conflict arose between Raymond de La Ralde, brother-in-law of Guillaume de Caën, and one Hébert, ensign – both of whom were Catholic – over where Protestants and Catholics should gather for prayer on board de Caën's ship. Under de Caën's command, Protestants had typically worshipped in his cabin, Catholics in the bow – an arrangement that La Ralde wished to invert.[122] This incident may appear trivial (and certainly reveals the headstrong nature of both parties), but it testifies to the uneasy, fragile entente that obtained between the two confessions in a period of heightened tensions on both sides of the Atlantic.

Under the dévot Ventadour, Protestants continued to travel to and trade in New France, but they had to adhere to stricter rules governing their religious practice. It is notable that de Caën remained head of the enterprise after the change in viceroy and a subsequent reconfiguration of the company a year later, by which he won a bid to manage the trade on his own in return for 60 per cent of the profits.[123] Yet if a Protestant could still be considered the legitimate head of commercial activity in New France, he was nonetheless forbidden from setting foot in the colony in that capacity. Indeed, a condition of de Caën's continued leadership of the enterprise in 1626 was that a Catholic command the ships that made the transatlantic voyage; de Caën was henceforth to manage the enterprise from France.[124] Not only was access more limited but confessional practices were more spatially circumscribed as well. From the beginning of his viceroyalty, Ventadour forbade certain Protestant rites in particular areas of the colony. On one occasion, La Ralde relayed this to Émery de Caën, Guillaume's Catholic cousin, whom he had put in command of his vessel: "He also particularly charged Emery to tell the so-called Reformed sailors that he did not want them to sing their psalms in the river Saint Lawrence." Champlain continued his own narration of this event: "In the evening the said Emery assembled his crew and informed them that His Grace the Duc de Ventadour did not wish them *to sing their psalms in the Great River, as they had done at sea*. They began to murmur and say that they ought not to be deprived of that liberty. Finally it was agreed that they should not sing their psalms, but that they should assemble for prayer, since nearly two-thirds of them were Huguenots. And so out of a bad debt one gets what one can."[125] In contrast to Montmorency's generic land-and-sea ban, Ventadour made a distinction between the Saint Lawrence and the open sea. To a certain extent, this distinction is reminiscent of the division between the privileged trading zone of the Saint Lawrence River and the open trading zone of the Gaspé and Acadia under Viceroy Montmorency, as well as the general principle promoted by Grotius by which the sea was open to all by natural law but coastal waters could be managed and controlled by the adjacent countries. But whereas these divisions were about controlling *who* could go where, the limits imposed by Ventadour focused on *what* could be done in a particular space. The Saint Lawrence River thus became a privileged, but not exclusive, Catholic space. As the last part of the passage demonstrates, however, such restrictions decreed from France were still subject to negotiation on the ground, where numbers mattered far more than pieces of paper. The Protestant majority among the crew made this Catholic space an obvious fiction (as did the predominance of Indigenous inhabitants).

The numerous disputes that arose over Catholic and Protestant practices in the Saint Lawrence River confirm the shift in the terms of the sovereign project in the Saint Lawrence Valley in the 1620s. In 1626, the Jesuit Anne de Noue reported from Tadoussac that "since Emery [de Caën] had left there, the sailors had paid no attention to the restrictions that he had left at his departure in the matter of psalm-singing; they went on with it in spite of these, and in such a way that all the natives could hear them from the shore. There is no use in talking to them; it is their great zeal for their faith that impels them."[126] What particularly preoccupied de Noue, as it had the Récollet Le Caron in 1618, were the effects of the presence and practices of Protestants on Indigenous allies and prospective converts. Whereas Le Caron's proposed solution in 1626 was to allow Catholics to participate in the fur trade without restriction – thereby reducing the proportion of Protestants – de Noue seemed to imply that the only remedy to so intractable a problem was to exclude Protestants entirely from the colony. At the same time, the latter's recognition of the religious fervour of those he regarded as heretics underscores the complex navigation of confessional relations in this period. If the interaction between Catholics and Protestants was characterized by negotiation, clemency, threats, and outright violence, in colony and kingdom alike, the dynamic in New France took on a particular hue. The elimination of Protestantism may have been an objective on both sides of the Atlantic, particularly among Catholic reformers, but the possibility of its attainment seemed higher in the fledgling colony. Just as consequential was the convergence of royal and ecclesiastical interests in Indigenous bodies. The evangelization, francization, and incorporation of Indigenous people as souls and subjects and the gradual redefinition of subjecthood to restrict the Protestant presence in the colony (realized in 1627 with the CNF's edict) were two sides of the same coin and key components of spiritual geopolitics. People thus became the means through which to combat threatened sovereignty and render New France French and Catholic. In the mid-1620s, lobbying by the Récollets, the Jesuits, and Champlain at court converged with other political and commercial concerns to precipitate changes in the configuration of the New France enterprise.

5

The Consolidation of Maritime Authority and the Compagnie de la Nouvelle-France

In April 1628, a fleet of eight ships left Dieppe for New France under the command of the new Compagnie de la Nouvelle-France. Headed by Claude Roquemont de Brison, one of the company's founders, the ships carried four hundred people, including numerous artisans, along with provisions and tools to clear land and build shelter. The impressive size of the fleet was matched by the hundred investors behind the venture and from which the company got its nickname, the Cent Associés (One Hundred Associates). Thus, according to the traditional narrative of New France, the sustained colonization and development of the fledgling colony at last began.[1]

Contemporaries judged this development from multiple perspectives. When viewed from the western side of the Atlantic by the likes of Champlain and the Jesuit and Récollet missionaries, the CNF represented at long last a concerted effort to provide the numbers and support needed to put the colony on a solid footing. On the eastern side of the Atlantic, for fur traders in the ports of Saint-Malo and La Rochelle, the company's establishment may well have seemed like a defeat after years spent protesting against and breaking the exclusive privileges of smaller companies. In the eyes of Cardinal Richelieu and his many advisers on maritime affairs, it was a promising step toward commercial revitalization and a challenge to European rivals in the Atlantic and to personal and institutional rivals at home. To members of the Estates and Parlement of Brittany, the company probably looked like the lesser of two evils, in comparison to previous initiatives that threatened their control over naval power and all maritime commerce.

The CNF has served many purposes in early Canadian historiography. As mentioned above, it constitutes, for some, a welcome rupture with the previous history of the colony, a promising new beginning after a series of supposed failures to create permanent settlements. For others, it is above all a company with an evangelizing mission, the means to realize the original intentions of the noble project in New France. Indeed, the predominant motivations of the company have been the subject of some debate, with historians coming down on the side of either religious fervour or commercial and political calculation.[2] Finally, the large number of royal office-holders among its members has been used as evidence that French companies fell woefully short of their (successful) English and Dutch counterparts and were somehow inherently flawed.[3]

Resituating the CNF in an Atlantic frame changes our understanding of its emergence and configuration. Rather than a rupture, it reveals considerable continuity with previous periods in terms of objectives and methods. The CNF was part of the decades-long push to consolidate maritime authority under royal officers. In 1620, as we have seen, these efforts led Admiral Montmorency to become viceroy of New France, thereby linking control over trade routes to control over territory overseas, and to create a new company, inspired in part by foreign models. Drawing on the same methods, Cardinal Richelieu created the CNF seven years later as part of his bid to take over maritime affairs.

What distinguished the mid-1620s was that it was a particularly intense period of experimentation with the company form. In the two years prior to the CNF's first voyage, three other French companies were underway: the Compagnie de Morbihan, the Compagnie de la Nacelle de Saint-Pierre fleurdelisée, and the Compagnie de Saint-Christophe. Since the first two companies did not ultimately come to fruition due to their vast mandates – encompassing all commerce in France and overseas – scholars have argued that Richelieu made a conscious decision to focus instead on regional companies like the CNF and the West Indian Compagnie de Saint-Christophe.[4] A close examination of these different, and sometimes overlapping, creations, however, underscores the great variety of circumstances in which such companies took form. Looking generally for ways to consolidate maritime authority, Richelieu and Louis XIII approved initiatives for a variety of reasons: the desire to put all French commerce under a few large companies (the Compagnies de Morbihan and de la Nacelle de Saint-Pierre fleurdelisée), the necessity of dealing with specific problems in existing colonies (the CNF), the desire to encourage private enterprise that fit with royal interests (the Compagnie de Saint-Christophe), and, last but not least, Richelieu's own power ambitions.[5]

Looking at these companies together brings their experimental and contingent nature to the fore. There was not just one type of company. To consider these French enterprises as mere copies of their Dutch and English counterparts obscures the complexity and variability of such enterprises, including, at the most fundamental level, what a company was, how it could be applied in different circumstances, and how it would be received by others. Richelieu, Montmorency, and others may have borrowed the joint-stock model, but they adapted it to French legal, political, and commercial environments to meet particular maritime, political, and strategic objectives.[6] They also combined this innovative instrument with tools that had proven effective in the past. Attention to this context reveals, for example, that the CNF was both religious *and* commercial/political and, as such, was very much of its time.

This chapter explores the role of the CNF and other chartered companies in French state and empire formation. After presenting the broad strokes of the CNF in the first part, it takes in turn three simultaneous and interrelated developments. The second part examines discussions of diagnosed problems in the French economy and proposed remedies – especially the use of chartered companies overseas. The third part considers both the innovative and the traditional strategies deployed to consolidate maritime authority under Richelieu. Finally, the chapter closes with an exploration of the different experimentations with the company form that took place in the mid-1620s, comparing company configurations and the particular circumstances in which each emerged. Together, these developments demonstrate that the CNF was a particular example of the complex interactions among foreign models, metropolitan power struggles, and previous colonizing experiences that shaped French chartered companies.

The Terms of the Compagnie de la Nouvelle-France

Exactly one year prior to the company's inaugural voyage, Cardinal Richelieu, recently appointed *grand maître, chef, et surintendant de la navigation et du commerce*, entered a contract with six noblemen, de Roquemont among them, to form the CNF. Shortly thereafter, the king signed an act of establishment and subsequently ratified the articles of association among the members, thus legally bringing the CNF into being. This new association received in "full property, jurisdiction, and seigneury" the fort and habitation at Quebec and "all the said country of New France …

the length of the coasts from Florida … all the way to the Arctic Circle in latitude, and in longitude from Newfoundland, moving west, as far as the great lake, called the freshwater sea, and beyond," in return for the customary acts of allegiance to the Crown. The contract also granted the CNF regal powers, including defence, the manufacture of cannon and ammunition, the appointment of captains, and the distribution of lands. Tasked with "peopling the said colony," the company undertook to "send to the said country of New France two to three hundred men of all occupations starting next year 1628, and during the following years to increase that number up to four thousand of one and the other sex, in the fifteen years to come."[7] It promised to provide for these newcomers for the first three years, at the end of which it was to give them cleared land for their subsistence. In return for these considerable obligations, the king awarded the associates "for all time, the traffic in all hides, skins, and furs of the said New France." The contract allowed French colonists to trade with Indigenous Peoples on condition that they sell their furs for a fixed price to company clerks. In contrast to the fur trade, "all other commerce, either overland or seaborne, that can be conducted … in the expanse of the said country" would last for only fifteen years.[8] Only the fishery was left open to all subjects, as was customary. In short, the CNF's act of establishment maintained continuity with previous privilege-holders in New France with regard to the geographical area concerned, colonization, the presence of ecclesiastics, and the fur trading privileges granted, but it exceeded previous mandates in scale in all of these areas.

The CNF drew on foreign models in its privileges and exemptions, capital base, and governance structure. Beyond the exclusive rights to trade, Richelieu granted the company a range of other privileges, including tax exemptions on goods necessary to outfit voyages and on merchandise coming into the kingdom from New France; accession to master of all artisans who practised in New France for six years; protection from derogation of noble and ecclesiastical subscribers; ennoblement of twelve common associates; and a gift of four iron culverins, or heavy cannons. While these privileges had no particular strings attached, the Crown offered a second gift of "two warships of two to three hundred tons, armed, manned, and ready to set sail," conditional upon the associates' sending over at least fifteen hundred colonists during the first ten years.[9] In the spirit of encouraging enterprises on a larger scale than the typical partnerships among French subjects, the CNF's contract put forth a mixture of incentives aimed at individual as well as collective profit. Like the Compagnie de Montmorency (only more explicitly), the CNF resembled contemporary Dutch and English joint-stock enterprises in its organization. According to its own articles of association of 7 May 1627, there were to be one hundred associates, each furnishing 3,000 livres, for a total capital of 300,000 livres. Shares were divisible and transferable. For the first three years, no dividend would be distributed among the associates; thereafter, only one-third would be allocated. Twelve directors charged with managing the company's affairs were to be elected from among the associates for a term of two years. While merchants were to make up one-third, half were to come from Paris. The directors enjoyed complete decision-making power, except in the areas of the appointment of officers and the granting of land exceeding 200 arpents in size. Like the EIC, the company held an annual general assembly in which each member had a vote. With respect to the company's financial affairs, a receiver general was to keep the accounts and present them annually to the directors.[10] Bearing the hallmarks of its Dutch and English counterparts, the CNF was one of the pioneers of the *société de capitaux* in France.

The Revitalization of French Commerce and Navigation

The CNF and its contemporaries emerged in the context of discussions over how to tackle the economic problems afflicting France. Concern within and outside government centred on what was perceived as France's lagging standing in the areas of maritime commerce, navigation, and sea power. While the Netherlands prospered from its control of global commercial routes and Spain and England strengthened their navies, went the refrain, France ceded control of its international traffic to foreign rivals, particularly the Dutch, and had no naval force to protect what trade remained in the hands of its own merchants. Cardinal Richelieu solicited memoranda and proposals from men with first-hand knowledge of maritime affairs, including captains of naval and merchant ships, corsairs, and several Knights of Malta.[11] The role played by Richelieu in this discussion points to the necessity of distinguishing between the discourse around, and the reality of, the economic situation. The memoranda themselves had a particular political agenda, generally concerned with expanding maritime commerce and navigation through government-backed initiatives. Although the French economy had come out of the sixteenth-century

Wars of Religion somewhat diminished and with a higher number of foreigners active in its trades than previously, the effects of the unrest were not uniform throughout the kingdom. Agricultural regions and peasant populations were probably hit the hardest. By contrast, (some) urban areas and merchants profited from the increase in prices. The greatest obstacle to growth in the French economy lay in its division into isolated regional economies. Factors such as the poor condition of roads, the numerous tolls on overland and water routes, and the pattern of the river network hindered the development of an integrated national market.[12] At the same time, the final years of the Wars of Religion coincided with a shift in the centre of European trade from the Mediterranean to the Atlantic, a shift that allowed French ports to develop specialty trades within expanding international mercantile networks.[13] While the French economy certainly had its structural challenges, the problems and proposed remedies outlined in the memoranda were as much justifications for particular courses of action as reflections of the actual situation.[14]

The assumption behind all of these memoranda was that the current French approach to commerce, particularly maritime and foreign commerce, was utterly inadequate, leaving France far behind its rivals. The greatest obstacle to overcoming the status quo was widely considered to be the French contempt for, and suspicion of, commerce itself. Writing in 1620, Jean Le Cler remarked on the contrast between French and foreign attitudes: in England, Spain, Italy, Flanders, and Germany, "commerce and those who practise it, are they not [held] in honour and esteem, and do they not enjoy an infinity of exemptions, and privileges? Certainly."[15] And yet in France, he opined, commerce had been allowed to fall completely to ruin. Twenty years later, Jean Eon, a Carmelite in Nantes and author of the well-known *Le Commerce honorable*, lamented that "[the French] consider commerce to be the preserve of base souls and the object of men's greed rather than the generosity in which chance plays a bigger part than prudence."[16] The French, particularly nobles, did not want any part in this domain. Unlike in England, there was no tradition of one member from each noble family entering a maritime profession.[17]

Alongside commerce's bad reputation, as highlighted by Le Cler and Eon, there were far more attractive areas for the investment of time and money. Nobles and bourgeois alike preferred to put their money in offices and land, both means to increase family prestige and standing. At the same time as it resulted in few nobles entering commerce, this practice also led to the departure of merchants once they had sufficient funds. For Claude de Launay-Razilly, ship's captain and later vice admiral in the French Admiralty, frequent adviser to Richelieu on maritime affairs, and later seigneur in Acadia, it was this latter problem that was the most vexing: merchants "have sold their ships to throw themselves upon offices to which too much honour has been attached." This move to a less useful life cost France dearly on the international stage. The practical consequence of the lack of interest in and support for maritime commercial activities, the memoranda's authors observed, was that the bulk of French international trade rested with the Dutch. And while the French welcomed all manner of foreign trader, French traders were subject to harsh treatment in foreign ports, particularly in Spain.[18]

Proposed remedies to France's (perceived) maritime and commercial stagnation drew a relationship between sea power, colonies, and commerce. Memoirists suggested variously the building of a naval and merchant fleet through contributions by cities, an increase in duties imposed on foreign traffic, the ennoblement of merchants, and the exemption from derogation of nobles engaged in long-distance trade.[19] Given the widespread conviction in France that the prosperity and strength of its rivals derived from their sea power, many of the proposed solutions came from foreign models. Eon pointed to the colonies established by the Spanish, English, and Dutch, which had significantly increased these nations' riches and dominion. The poet, playwright, and author of the influential *Traité de l'économie politique*, Antoine de Montchrestien, recommended granting shipbuilders a subsidy per ton, as in England.[20]

The main tool borrowed from elsewhere was the chartered company. Those in charge of maritime affairs attributed Dutch commercial and military dominance of the sea to such vast enterprises as the VOC and its attendant privileges. By pooling their capital and sharing the risks, Dutch merchants dominated the rich spice traffic between the Indies and Europe and attracted foreign investment to their own ventures.[21] If France made companies a commonplace, writers suggested, it would achieve comparable success. The challenge was to overcome the proclivity of French merchants to trade on their own or in short-term associations with relatives, friends, and those with identical interests.[22] Incentives, such as ennoblement and exemption from derogation, were necessary to change the traditional patterns of French commerce.

If companies on foreign models were the vehicle for the rebuilding of French sea power and standing, royal material support and direction would be the method, according to commentators. The Crown had both a practical and symbolic role to play in mobilizing its subjects to reinvigorate traffic. On the most mundane level, the size of the undertaking necessitated royal funds: "it is something that seems to be reserved to his said Majesty as worthy of his vast and good fortune." It was too great to be left to individuals and required one head rather than several.[23] Advocates of chartered companies recommended the direct participation of the Crown in the hopes that its added weight and authority would overcome merchants' long-standing preference for undertaking their own ventures.[24] Further, the king needed to protect merchant traffic through the deployment of well-armed royal naval ships. Beyond the practical matter of security, the king's maritime presence would carry great symbolic power as both a deterrent to enemies at sea and a model for others.[25] For Isaac de Razilly, *chef d'escadre*, first captain in the French Admiralty, and, like his brother Claude, an important adviser to Richelieu, no sustained maritime program could be implemented without the engagement of the wealthy and powerful. "Following the example of the king, the queen, Monsieur, Your Greatness and the princes, dukes, and marshals of France will each have one [vessel] made, in order to enter into this royal company."[26] If the king himself participated, his status as the first among nobles would reassure others that such activities were perfectly in keeping with their station. These memoranda submitted to the Crown helped to fuel royal thinking on French maritime commerce and navigation in the 1620s.

The Maritime Program of the Assembly of Notables

The year 1626 was a particularly intense one for royal consultation, planning, and implementation of maritime initiatives. In October, Cardinal Richelieu became *grand maître, chef, et surintendant général de la navigation et du commerce de France*. While I will explore the motivations behind the creation of this office in more detail below, it is important to note here that it allowed Richelieu to cultivate a network of advisers with experience at sea. These contacts proved especially crucial in the government's preparations for the Assembly of Notables, convened between December and the following February. Assemblies were typically held to gain support among the ruling elites for government-proposed reforms. Members gave feedback on the proposals and presented their own. In 1626–27, the assembly's agenda was ambitious, ranging from the threat posed by the Huguenots and the unruliness of the great nobles to the urgent need for fiscal reform, all issues that shaped the policies of Louis XIII and Richelieu in the following decade. Related to these matters to varying degrees was the question of maritime security and commerce, both of which came to be, over the course of the assembly, a priority for the Crown.[27] In preparation, Richelieu drew upon a wide range of information, including the memoranda above, letters from his ambassadors in other European countries on the treatment of French merchants and the organization of foreign chartered companies, and reports on the state of the French war fleet. Part propaganda exercise, part quest to legitimate measures already decided upon – and, in some cases, already underway – the assembly and the briefs in preparation constitute a carefully crafted effort on the part of Richelieu and his advisers to steer French maritime consolidation.[28]

The brief that best encapsulates the aim to make France competitive on a global scale in commerce, navigation, and colonizing ventures was that of Isaac de Razilly, submitted to Richelieu in November 1626. Razilly was eminently qualified to provide such advice. With more than two decades in the navy, he had served in many parts of the world, ranging from North Africa (Barbary) to Brazil (Maragnan-Maranhão). In the years prior to writing his report, he had commanded ships in attacks against Huguenot ports, including that of La Rochelle in 1625. It was this last experience that convinced him of the desperate need to revitalize French naval forces. Like the authors of the memoranda discussed above, Razilly points to the low opinion of those involved in commerce and the lack of royal encouragement, all the while making comparisons to and drawing inspiration from the Dutch, English, and Spanish.

What distinguishes Razilly's brief from others is its breadth of vision. It presents a multi-faceted maritime program and outlines incentives for noble and merchant participation, the means by which to build a strong naval and merchant fleet, and the particular commercial, colonizing, and evangelizing goals to be pursued in each part of the globe.[29] Although Razilly later came to play an influential role in the colonization of Acadia (as its lieutenant general), his focus here was primarily on Africa and Asia.[30] In Africa, a colony established on the island of Mogador (off the coast of present-day Morocco) would be strategic: "it is to have one foot in

Africa in order to extend further." Geopolitics in North America likewise necessitated colonies to "limit the English as nearly as can be done" and to convert the Indigenous inhabitants. Asia, however, required a different approach: "one should not imagine planting colonies there," given the great distances involved. France should, instead, establish "a powerful company."[31] Confined neither to one sea or territory nor to one activity, the program brought all of these pieces together. Razilly, like Richelieu himself, viewed the navy, the merchant marine, overseas commercial and colonial expansion, and coastal security as intimately connected and vital elements in the strengthening of French maritime standing. Guided by the widely espoused principle that "whoever is master of the sea has great power over land," the naval commander aimed for nothing less than establishing a French universal monarchy through navigation and sea power.[32]

On the floor of the Assembly of Notables, royal officials eschewed a grand vision in favour of individual elements of Razilly's maritime program.[33] Correspondence between Richelieu and Michel de Marillac, the Keeper of the Seals, who would give the opening address, reveals a preoccupation with securing support for a naval fleet and commercial and colonizing companies. Echoing the authors of the memoranda, both men began their presentations with a portrait of the dismal state of France's naval capabilities and maritime traffic in comparison to those of its rivals. What was required, Richelieu argued, was the building up of a substantial fleet of warships to deter them from taking advantage of French merchants in their own ports, to protect French shipping from pirates, and to keep French subjects "within their proper limits."[34] The cardinal proposed thirty warships at a cost of 1.5 million livres annually, while the final statement from the notables to the king called for forty-five with a fund of 1.2 million livres. This outcome suggests a ringing endorsement from the assembly for increasing naval strength, but it also exposes the superficial nature of that support, as 1.2 million livres was an utterly unrealistic cost for such an undertaking. In accepting this outcome, Richelieu had avoided the hard question of finding funding sources.[35]

The proposal for commercial companies met with a similarly enthusiastic reception but no material support. In the preparations, propaganda, and assembly, the need to move from the traditional patterns of French merchant enterprise to big companies modelled on the highly successful English and Dutch ones gained wide recognition. The "Advis à Messieurs de l'Assemblée des Notables" – likely solicited by Richelieu himself – recommended that "in every capital city of his [the king's] provinces, merchants will form a company for navigation on the model of Amsterdam."[36] Addressing the assembly, Richelieu argued that the tendency among French merchants to work alone required "[us] like our neighbours ... to form large companies, obligate merchants to enter, [and] give them great privileges as they do."[37] Royal representatives and notables alike, however, did not move beyond a general approval of the form, in contrast to Razilly's brief. This may have been due in part to the fact that two companies on this model were already being established, but, like the proposed naval fleet, it also points to the limitations of the assembly itself.

Royal control of sea power was easier to accept in theory than in practice. Although the notables approved the Crown's maritime direction, they offered no firm commitment of funds and thus their endorsement cost them nothing. As a purely advisory body, the assembly was spared the delicate task of legislating or implementing these initiatives.[38] The rhetorical consensus in the memoranda and on the floor of the assembly belied the depth of opposition to companies and royal shipbuilding programs in several maritime provinces. As previous efforts to extend the Admiralty's authority to France's peripheries had demonstrated, there were multiple claimants to control over sea power within the kingdom. With the closing of the assembly, the real work began.

The Consolidation of Maritime Authority under Richelieu

Companies and the Contest for Maritime Control

In the mid-1620s, Richelieu experimented with various tools to put himself in control of maritime affairs. The fragmented nature of maritime authority in the kingdom required strategic flexibility and a combination of innovative instruments like chartered companies and traditional methods of exercising power. Events in the years leading up to the Assembly of Notables exposed the kingdom's vulnerability in the face of foreign and domestic challenges at sea. In the 1610s, countries throughout Europe strengthened their naval resources to prepare for a potential renewal of maritime conflict and to protect seaborne commerce as the Twelve Years' Truce between Spain and the Dutch Republic neared its end (1621). England began construction on a fleet of warships in 1618 to be completed within five years. Spain, for its part, created a series of laws and institutions designed to enforce its renewed embargo against Dutch trade. It introduced the "Pragmatica," which banned the entry of any foreign manufactured goods not absolutely necessary for domestic and imperial trade, developed the Flanders Armada, a traditional naval force, and actively encouraged privateering. The reform that touched France most closely, however, was the newly created Almirantazgo, or Seville Admiralty, which organized convoys for merchant ships, supervised Admiralty courts, and conducted inspections of ships to enforce the sanctions against the Dutch. No ships were exempt from such inspections, regardless of nationality or whether in Spanish ports or at sea.[39] French traders keenly felt these increased regulations.[40]

These international challenges to French maritime sovereignty had their domestic corollary in the person of the admiral and the Huguenot populations of the southwest. As we saw in chapter 3, Admiral Montmorency had a keen sense of the importance of maritime affairs to French standing in Europe and to his lineage's power within the kingdom. By the mid-1620s, his hard work to consolidate his authority as admiral had paid dividends. Through the mobilization of an extensive clientele network, the acquisition of governorships, and the aggressive pursuit of competitors, Montmorency had established a strong feudal hold over the Admiralty, in the sense that he had men in key positions who were personally loyal to him and would bear arms for him as a vassal to a seigneur. Whereas once the Crown had encouraged him in the construction of this power base, now Montmorency's command began to undermine the Crown's own interests and Richelieu's personal ambitions.

Like the admiral, the Huguenots posed a threat to sovereign control of the kingdom's coasts and coastal waters. Although religious in origin, the resurgence of Huguenot unrest in the 1610s and '20s was about far more than confessional differences. It concerned, at its heart, control over the sea. As we have seen, the centre of Huguenot strength, La Rochelle, boasted well-armed ships that effectively controlled the Atlantic coast, issued licences independent of the admiral's lieutenants, including to privateers, and was home to prominent merchants active in overseas commerce.[41] In effect, the port symbolized the weakness of royal naval power and control of maritime trade. Repeated conflicts with Huguenots along the Atlantic coast during this period provided concrete evidence of this vulnerability. In 1625, one year prior to the Assembly of Notables, Benjamin de Rohan, Duc de Soubise, launched with the support of just a few hundred men a bold and ultimately successful attack on newly acquired royal warships at Blavet in Brittany. Huguenot forces were subsequently able to take Île de Ré, one of two strategically important islands off the Atlantic coast at La Rochelle. Although royal forces retook the island a short time later under Montmorency's command, the French had to rely on Dutch naval support to do so.[42] Not only did France depend on foreign reinforcements, but it also faced the threat of imminent invasion by a formidable English navy in support of their fellow Protestants. Cardinal Richelieu suspected that the English – who had become alarmed at French efforts to strengthen its maritime power – would not stop at the defence of La Rochelle and the outer islands but would seize this opportunity to avail themselves of valuable commodities like salt in neighbouring provinces. By 1626, the Crown was desperately assembling a fleet for renewed fighting, which broke out the following year.[43] The combined threats from within and outside the kingdom convinced Louis XIII and Richelieu that the Crown's long practice of entrusting to individuals activities central to France's standing and security was no longer sufficient to protect royal interests.

In the quest to consolidate maritime authority under the Crown, the chartered company played a starring role. On 31 March 1626, Richelieu entered into a notarial contract in his name with Guillaume de Bruc, Jean-Baptiste du Val, Nicolas Le Mareschal, and Antoine Regnault de Montmort to establish the Compagnie de Morbihan for "general commerce in all sorts of manufactured merchandise and other possible and licit items ... on sea and on land, [in the] east, west, and [on] long-distance voyages ... everywhere inside and outside the kingdom."[44] We will return to the company's structure, powers, privileges, and obligations in the fourth part of this chapter. What is notable here is that, unlike other maritime enterprises, the Compagnie de Morbihan was not subject to the admiral's authority and received exemptions from paying the customary rights and obtaining licences. Instead, it fell under the supervision of "the superintendent general of commerce," the cardinal himself. Comprising a vast jurisdiction, this contract put all but the regulation of the fishery under the company's, and by extension Richelieu's, purview.[45] This last domain, as well as control over all new and existing manufactures, was granted in May to the (whimsically named) Compagnie de la Nacelle de Saint-Pierre fleurdelisée. Using the same terms as in the first company's contract, Richelieu, as superintendent general, pledged to "protect them [the associates of the company] and give them the necessary permission to facilitate the execution [of the contract]."[46] To both, the king reserved one or two ports in France to serve as the companies' headquarters, and with them, his powers of justice, administration, and taxation.

These two companies were designed to address simultaneously the three maritime challenges outlined above. The most striking aspect of the contracts is the way the companies bypass the admiral. In the Crown's quest to assume responsibility for maritime security, the cardinal considered the Admiralty a central obstacle. As an institution, the Admiralty presided, in theory, over all maritime traffic, rendered justice on matters occurring at sea, and commanded naval forces (such as they were). The person of the admiral was, also in theory, very powerful. As we saw in chapter 3, however, that power could be largely ephemeral in the face of governors, seigneurs, and other admirals. During his tenure, Montmorency, along with the king himself, had taken concrete steps to consolidate maritime authority under the admiral. The view from the mid-1620s, though, gave the king pause as to the wisdom of this strategy. With the princely revolts of the regency period still fresh in his mind, Louis XIII looked with suspicion upon the great nobles in top military positions. The Montmorency family was one of the foremost holders of maritime-military offices. The possibility that the admiral could mobilize a considerable force against the Crown encouraged the king to check this power.[47]

For Richelieu, the Montmorency family in general, and the admiral in particular, represented an obstacle to his own ambitions to become the most powerful man in the kingdom.[48] Control over sea power was essential to realizing this goal. As admiral, it was Montmorency who exercised maritime commercial, judicial, and naval jurisdiction. With the power to place people in positions of command, he extended his clientele networks to France's peripheries and pocketed his share of prizes and rights owed him in Admiralty proceedings. The chartered companies were one way to whittle away at the geographically and socially extensive authority of the admiral. Indeed, in August 1626, a revised royal edict for the Compagnie de Morbihan went so far as to suppress the position of admiral of France, Brittany, and Guyenne and transfer authority to the superintendent general of commerce.[49] Although this edict never took full effect, it betrayed Richelieu's intention to replace the admiral as the kingdom's point man on maritime affairs.

The Compagnies de Morbihan and de la Nacelle de Saint-Pierre fleurdelisée were also a response to the military and political pressure France was under from European rivals and rebellious subjects. Simply put, in 1626 Richelieu was looking for a source of warships for the next round against the Huguenots and their English co-religionists. Encompassing all commerce by land and sea as well as the fishery, the companies would be capable of producing a substantial fleet that could serve under the Crown in times of war. Indeed, according to a royal edict of July 1626, the Compagnie de Morbihan was to allocate a minimum of 400,000 livres for vessels and arms as well as merchandise. It was to build naval and other vessels, manufacture cannon, ammunition, and "other tools and manufactures necessary for war and commerce, to arm and equip vessels."[50] Bearing a seal under the authority of the king, it had the power to grant commissions for war. The Compagnie de Morbihan was, in short, a vehicle of war as much as commerce. In this respect, it strongly resembled the Dutch West India Company (Geoctrooieerde Westindische Compagnie, or GWC) that had emerged in 1621 with the reprise of hostilities between the republic and Spain. France supported the Dutch and had its own political and commercial reasons for opposing Spain. The Compagnies de Morbihan and de la Nacelle de Saint-Pierre fleurdelisée were, therefore, part of a larger campaign against the Habsburgs that involved several European countries.[51] In the event, with the companies stuck before the parlements, Richelieu was forced to cobble together a fleet of ships from various ports to rebuff an English attack on Île de Ré the following year. The military and political contexts in which these companies arose nevertheless explicitly shaped their parameters and purpose.

Putting the CNF alongside the Compagnies de Morbihan and de la Nacelle de Saint-Pierre fleurdelisée shows that the three played complementary roles in the cardinal's goal of reducing the maritime, commercial, and confessional strength of the Huguenots. In the CNF's case, the various steps toward the company's establishment took place in the shadow of a major stage in the struggle between the Huguenots and the Crown. Richelieu entered the contract for the CNF with the six noblemen three months before the English attack on the Île de Ré and renewed fighting at La Rochelle in 1627. The following year, the king ratified the company's articles in a military camp outside the besieged port. La Rochelle surrendered five months later. If the Compagnies de Morbihan and de la Nacelle de Saint-Pierre fleurdelisée were to provide military support in the conflict, the CNF would, it was hoped, become an instrument in the appropriation of La Rochelle's maritime resources, experience, and strategic position for royal ends by doing a key portion of its business and outfitting there.[52] In their respective ways, then, the three companies were to serve the purpose of asserting Catholic confessional and commercial power.

If companies were a route to increased maritime security in the eyes of Louis XIII and Richelieu, the perspective was, of course, altogether different beyond the towers flanking the entrance to La Rochelle's inner harbour (shown in figure 5.1). The consolidation of maritime authority, first under Montmorency and then under Richelieu, posed a real threat to the port's closely guarded political and economic independence. La Rochelle had long enjoyed the status of a "privileged enclave," a space – often urban – of legal exception where regulations and levies in place elsewhere did not apply.[53] The port's residents largely escaped the burden of paying royal taxes, including the notorious *gabelle*, or salt tax. Periodic attempts to introduce new levies in the sixteenth and early seventeenth centuries met with vehement opposition from the formidable *corps de ville*. Arguably the most important privilege, however, was La Rochelle's right to trade with any country, even adversaries of France. When the king ordered the cessation of all commerce with England in 1627, the Rochelais saw it as a denial of their long-held rights. The consequences of such extensive privileges were only too clear to the Crown: trade migrated to La Rochelle to avoid royal levies in adjacent towns, denying the royal treasury much-needed revenue. While the port's commercial prosperity and sea power were targets of royal initiatives ranging from naval attacks to chartered companies, the aim was not to destroy this strength but, rather, to appropriate it for royal – and Catholic – ends.[54] Political, commercial, and confessional issues came together in the Crown's response to internal and external struggles over control of the sea.

Richelieu Becomes grand maître de la navigation et du commerce

Richelieu's aim to assume control of maritime affairs gained momentum with the creation of a position that made him admiral in all but name and allowed him to pursue the development of companies. In October 1626, Richelieu obtained letters patent appointing him *grand maître, chef, et surintendant général de la navigation et du commerce de France*. The commission accorded the cardinal the traditional responsibilities of the admiral: to ensure "the safety of our subjects at sea, [in] ports, harbours, roadsteads and on its [France's] shores and adjacent islands" and

Figure 5.1 Entrance to the inner harbour of La Rochelle, flanked by the Tour Saint-Nicolas and the Tour de la Chaîne. Along with the fortified *hôtel de ville*, the towers were a strong symbol of La Rochelle's autonomy.

their compliance with naval ordinances, to eliminate corsairs and pirates, and assemble a fleet in peacetime to protect the coasts and long-distance commerce. It also pointed to the method by which French sea power and maritime commerce would be secured: the holder would "negotiate with all manner of people; consider and examine any proposals that have been or will be made to us on the subject of the establishment of commerce, and review and consider their merit, good and utility; resolve upon and guarantee all articles, treaties, contracts, or agreements with all those who wish to join together to form the said trading companies."[55] For Richelieu, as had been the case for Montmorency, these two elements – control of the Admiralty and promotion of companies – were inextricably intertwined, both essential to increasing French naval strength and challenging the commercial success of the English, Dutch, and Spanish.[56]

Two other developments in the same month reinforced the objectives of the new position. Richelieu acquired his first governorship, in the Norman port of Le Havre, and, at the end of the month, entered a contract for the establishment of the Compagnie de Saint-Christophe, in which he became an associate. The particular timing of Richelieu's becoming grand maître and governor of Le Havre was not accidental. Both occurred in the wake of the Chalais conspiracy, a plot to assassinate Richelieu implicating great nobles and members of the royal family, including the king's brother, Gaston d'Orléans. The conspiracy had the effect of felling men in key positions, most notably Montmorency, who was forced to resign as admiral of France, the governor of Le Havre, Georges de Brancas, Marquis de Villars, and the governor of Brittany and Louis XIII's half-brother, César, Duc de Vendôme. It was this event that allowed Richelieu to have his mandate as grand maître extended beyond commerce to include navigation.[57] Similarly, the cardinal was able to induce Villars to give up his governorship in exchange for a payment as well as another position and territory. Reflecting the goals of the *grande maîtrise*, Le Havre was to be an important commercial hub, becoming the headquarters of the Compagnie de Saint-Christophe and others like it. In reality, it came instead to resemble a military stronghold.[58] If Richelieu had been trying for some time to strengthen his hold on maritime affairs – as the Compagnies de Morbihan and de la Nacelle de Saint-Pierre fleurdelisée demonstrate – the period following the Chalais conspiracy provided a particularly opportune moment in which to do so.

The grandiose title of grand maître poorly masked the fact that the cardinal had taken control of the Admiralty in Montmorency's stead. Indeed, Richelieu adopted many of the measures used by his predecessor to assert his personal privileges and administrative authority. The difference lay in the systematic way in which he pursued these ends. One of the first steps he took was to send lieutenants general of the navy to the kingdom's ports to establish his position as well as naval commissioners to collect revenues owed him as grand maître, functions filled previously by

Montmorency's agents. In 1629, Richelieu commissioned Louis Le Roux, Sieur d'Infreville, *commissaire général de la marine*, to report on the state of coastal infrastructure, manpower, munitions, and Admiralty courts, the system of licences, and maritime rights claimed by other individuals on the Atlantic coast. The resulting document gave the grand maître a sweeping view of the physical, financial, and administrative conditions in ports as well as just how fragmented maritime authority was along the kingdom's coasts.[59] In his Conseil de la Marine, Richelieu expanded the mandate of Montmorency's Conseil des Prises, which judged prizes taken at sea, to include investigating allegations of abuse by Admiralty officials and evaluating commercial proposals. He also created the Conseil de l'Amirauté to ensure, among other things, that the revenue derived from wrecks and confiscated ships was divided properly, with the grand maître obtaining his fair share.[60] Montmorency's intendant, Villemenon, who ensured the recognition of the admiral's privileges by the provincial governors and seigneurs who frequently claimed judicial authority and Admiralty rights, had his counterpart under Richelieu first in Martin de Mauvoy and then in Julius de Loynes, Sieur de la Pontherie, a former commissioner of the navy in Picardy and Normandy.[61] As grand maître, the cardinal was above all concerned with enjoying the rights and privileges traditionally associated with the position of admiral. His preferred method for collecting revenues owed him was to farm them out in the form of leases. While the success of these tax farms varied considerably by province, Richelieu nevertheless reaped about 62,800 livres per year, almost twice the salary Montmorency had received as admiral of France.[62] As these examples demonstrate, the cardinal continued and extended the administration developed under Montmorency, rather than embarking in a new direction.

Apart from the creation of administrative positions, Richelieu primarily asserted his authority as grand maître by drawing on clientele and family networks and obtaining governorships. He placed relatives and clients in administrative positions, including his uncle, Amador de La Porte, *chef des escadres* and *intendant général de la marine et commerce*. From the start of his tenure, he steadily acquired governorships in key ports and provinces, among them Le Havre, Nantes, Île d'Orléans, Île de Ré, Aunis, and La Rochelle. Added to these were those held by his relatives and clients, which included Brest, Brouage, Calais, and Rouen. By the mid-1630s, the cardinal had effective control over most of the governorships of consequence from Normandy to the Gironde.[63]

This strategy of building regional strongholds reflected the political climate of the opening decades of the seventeenth century. Huguenots and rebellious nobles sought out and strategically used *places fortes*, or strongholds, in the 1610s and 20s. Ministers and members of the royal family worked to counter these bases with their own. It is no coincidence that Richelieu concentrated his efforts on the regions of Huguenot strength around La Rochelle. As grand maître, his control of maritime provinces helped secure the kingdom's coasts against rebels and rivals alike. On a personal level, it also facilitated the collection of revenues owed him in these regions.[64] If his authority was recognized in many Atlantic ports as a result, the situation was altogether different on the Mediterranean coast. The powerful Charles de Lorraine, Duc de Guise, from a family of Catholic League leaders and a rival of Richelieu, staunchly defended his claims to the Admiralty as governor of Provence. Even after Guise lost his position for political reasons in 1631, the only way for Richelieu to assert his presence as grand maître was to purchase positions, notably the *général des galères*, at considerable expense.[65] In short, Richelieu's authority varied widely by region and largely depended on his personal authority, exercised through the purchase of offices and the placement of relatives, much as Montmorency's had before him.[66]

The cardinal's need to secure a political base in order to exercise his powers as grand maître was nowhere more evident than in Brittany. The northwestern province viewed the growing intervention of the Crown in maritime commerce and navigation as an encroachment on its long-standing maritime, economic, and political autonomy. This was, after all, the province whose governor had frequently wrestled with the admiral of France over competing claims to maritime oversight. With Richelieu's appointment as grand maître coming mere months after the edicts establishing the Compagnies de Morbihan and de la Nacelle de Saint-Pierre fleurdelisée, the Estates and Parlement of Brittany viewed all three initiatives as part of Richelieu's broader intentions to create a uniform maritime jurisdiction across the kingdom under his command.[67] The provincial Parlement and Estates refused to register the companies' edicts and Richelieu's letters patent on various grounds. In the case of the Compagnie de Morbihan, the proposed site of which was in Brittany, the Estates argued that the edict violated the province's privileges by granting the port of Morbihan a host of immunities, notably from taxes and customs duties as well as from provincial legal jurisdiction. Traders in other ports – Saint-Malo foremost among them – protested that Morbihan would be at an unfair advantage. Much like their objections to previous New France enterprises, the *parlementaires* considered the company's right to seek redress before courts in Paris as undermining the provincial judiciary and establishing a dangerous precedent.[68] Richelieu's letters patent provoked other objections. The *parlementaires* repeated the long-standing argument that Brittany enjoyed a special status when it came to maritime affairs, with the governor standing in for the king as *grand amiral*. For their part, the Estates, having only recently ended a dispute with Admiral Montmorency over the judging of prizes, were particularly alarmed by the expanded powers granted the grand maître, such as the establishment of Admiralty courts.[69]

With all three acts stalled before the Breton Parlement and Estates, Richelieu (on the king's behalf) had to negotiate with these bodies for their registration over the following two years. Barely a month after the first royal edict establishing the Compagnie de Morbihan in July 1626, the Crown presented a revised version, which restored to the Parlement its customary right to hear appeals, among other changes. Unpacified, local and provincial bodies continued to oppose the company into 1627 and beyond, resulting in the enterprise's eventual abandonment.[70] As for Richelieu's letters patent, the Breton Parlement did finally register them in April 1627, but it rejected the powers to build up an arsenal for war, require licences for Breton ships, and establish Admiralty courts, recognizing only the grand maître's powers to grant licences for overseas voyages and to supervise coast guards.[71] The parties eventually reached a compromise in January 1629, by which the Parlement recognized Richelieu's power to grant licences for voyages outside the province and, in turn, the cardinal accepted the jurisdiction of the ordinary courts over maritime affairs.[72]

The way in which the two provincial bodies and Richelieu resolved two issues in the late 1620s and early 1630s highlights the importance of establishing a political base and clientele networks in the bid to centralize authority. Relations between the Crown and the province posed a particular challenge in this period. Even after the compromise of 1629 between Richelieu and the *parlementaires*, the cardinal had little success in collecting revenues owed him or in having orders executed. In addition, following the Chalais conspiracy and the imprisonment of the governor, the Duc de Vendôme, the governorship of this important province lay unoccupied.[73] Despite the tensions over jurisdiction, the Estates recognized

Richelieu's patronage on a few occasions during this period, most notably with a gift of 100,000 livres granted in 1630.[74] That same year, doubtless considering themselves at a disadvantage without a governor to advocate for the province's interests, they offered the governorship to Marie de Médicis, former queen regent, and the lieutenant generalship to Richelieu as her long-time adviser. This proposed arrangement mirrored several others already in place, including at Brouage and Oléron.[75] When Marie de Médicis went into exile following the Day of the Dupes in November 1630, it was perhaps only logical for the Estates to extend the offer of the governorship directly to Richelieu, an offer he readily accepted.[76] Following closely on his acquisition of the governorship of Nantes, these two positions considerably strengthened his base in the province.

Negotiations over the grande maîtrise and the companies were part of a larger pattern of concessions to Brittany in the king's and Richelieu's efforts to centralize maritime authority. As a strategically positioned sea power with effective control over the surrounding coasts, Brittany was an important source of naval and human resources for the Crown. The latter thus *needed* the northwestern province. If Richelieu's goal in becoming grand maître and founding the Compagnies de Morbihan and de la Nacelle de Saint-Pierre fleurdelisée had in part been to break the feudal character of maritime authority in the kingdom, his experiences in Brittany showed just how difficult this could be and the continued utility of traditional methods of exercising power.[77] It was only by becoming governor that the cardinal obtained any purchase there; indeed, even after 1631, the revenues he received as grand maître from the province's ports were very modest and his attempts to set up regional admiralties did not come to fruition.[78] Moreover, by accepting the offer of the governorship, Richelieu had in effect conceded that this office was inextricably linked with that of the admiral of Brittany. The fragmented nature of maritime jurisdiction in early seventeenth-century France shaped the methods by which the sea came more directly under the control of the Crown as well as the parameters of commercial and colonizing ventures overseas.

New France Is Incorporated into the Grande Maîtrise

The grand maître, like the admiral before him, viewed his maritime jurisdiction as co-extensive with French trading and colonizing ventures and, by extension, with New France. Just as Montmorency brought the fledgling colony into the institution of the Admiralty, so Richelieu made it a part of his mandate in his new position. The CNF and the Compagnies de Morbihan and de la Nacelle de Saint-Pierre fleurdelisée all shared the distinction of being under the protection of the cardinal as grand maître and of exercising a certain jurisdiction over the colony. The latter two companies were granted permission to "enjoy and possess the lands of New France both the continent and the islands and other places, that the said company is able to conquer and people."[79] For its part, the CNF, whose act of establishment was drawn up in April 1627 while the other companies were still before the provincial sovereign courts, had control over both existing settlements, most notably Quebec, as well as territory not yet claimed or inhabited by the French.

If the 1626 companies were partly designed to undercut the admiral of France, the CNF helped to eliminate another rival in Richelieu's bid to centralize maritime affairs under himself. As we saw in chapter 4, the Duc de Ventadour had governed New France through his lieutenant, Champlain, since 1625. He also enjoyed an annual income from the exclusive trading privileges he had delegated to the Compagnie de Montmorency. With the power to control traffic entering and leaving the colony, Ventadour represented an obstacle to the centralized supervision of the maritime movement of subjects and goods, in much the same way that Viceroy Condé had posed a challenge to Montmorency as admiral in the 1610s. As he was Montmorency's nephew, his elimination must also be seen as part of Richelieu's attack on the Montmorency family's power base.[80] By granting the CNF governmental jurisdiction and regal powers, the king and cardinal ostensibly put the colony under the control of a chartered company.

Despite appearances, Richelieu became de facto viceroy of New France. On 29 June 1627, Jean de Lauson, a royal counsellor and *maître des requêtes* at the Palais de Justice who was also one of the cardinal's creatures and had recently been appointed intendant of the CNF and New France, bought the viceroyalty and the attendant shares in the Compagnie de Montmorency from Ventadour.[81] For these, he paid 72,000 livres, which the duke received in the form of three offices. A letter sent from Lauson to Richelieu the following day announcing this shows that he was acting on his patron's instructions.[82] While this purchase may have been in the name of the company, evidence suggests that it was more likely on behalf of the cardinal as part of the consolidation of his authority as grand maître.[83] Indeed, the latter's jurisdiction extended to "the command of countries, islands, and lands conquered overseas … even in New France, for which country *under the authority of His Majesty and ours* there has been formed a new company."[84] Under the guise of grand maître, Richelieu assumed control of the colony.

Similar to his replacement of the admiral in France, Richelieu continued many of the practices of his predecessors in his supervision of activity in New France. His viceregal-like relationship to the CNF was evident in its administration. Recalling Montmorency's tenure, he re-established the position of intendant with the appointment of Jean de Lauson, at the request of the company associates.[85] As with Dolu before him, Lauson's responsibilities included hosting the CNF's annual general assemblies and reporting back to his patron. It was the cardinal who oversaw the granting of letters of nobility to common associates as well as duchies, baronies, and marquisates and who appointed, on the nomination of the company associates, captains of fortifications in the colony. And, again like the viceroys, he had people report to him in both official and unofficial capacities, was an associate, and authorized company voyages. His prerogatives as grand maître complemented these traditionally viceregal powers. Although the associates could name the commanders of the warships conferred by the Crown, these men were to receive a royal commission and serve "in the absence of my said Seigneur the Grand Maître."[86]

The extension of maritime authority to the colony under the Crown involved replacing one feudal-like authority with another. Just as Montmorency had established a new company upon his accession to the viceroyalty, so Richelieu replaced that same company with one of his own. Arguably one critical element in creating the CNF was the desire to exert control over its members. With strong ties to the Admiralty and Montmorency, Guillaume de Caën, the previous company's head, was connected to the institution and person capable of challenging the cardinal's personal and royal maritime ambitions.[87] If Richelieu blocked his rival's clientele networks, he also mobilized his own. The six representatives who came forward with a proposal for a company at the cardinal's request had close ties to him.[88] Apart from Richelieu himself, the most prominent associates were his clients, among them Isaac and Claude de Razilly, Philippe de Longvilliers, Sieur de Poincy, Sébastien Cramoisy, Gabriel Lattaignant, and Louis Houel, as well as highly placed officials in the naval and financial administrations, persuaded or pressured into supporting the project.[89] Some of the cardinal's clients served as informants in their travels around France; others received commissions to conduct particular business on his behalf. Many were also engaged in more than one company established under the grand maître.[90] Much like the web of clients and relatives that helped secure his presence in French ports as grand maître, clients in the CNF allowed Richelieu to keep close track of the company's and the colony's affairs and to influence their direction from afar.

The similar strategies used first by Admiral Montmorency and then by the cardinal to consolidate their hold on maritime authority underscore the existing tension between the Crown's reliance on personal authority to extend and maintain its control and the challenge such authority could pose to the king's own interests. The latter encouraged both men to consolidate their maritime authority through the installation of their own clients in administrative positions and the use of patronage to foster provincial and local connections. Eventually, Montmorency's authority came to extend over a larger geographic area and insinuated itself deeper into clientele networks than either the Crown's sense of security or Richelieu's personal ambitions could allow. The manner in which both men extended their jurisdictions overseas to New France – becoming viceroy in name or in fact, creating a new commercial and colonizing company, placing clients in key positions – highlights the intimate relationship between official functions and personal aggrandizement within early modern states. Viceroy and grand maître alike fortified their personal empire and tied the colony more closely to the Crown. For Richelieu, like Montmorency before him, New France fit strategically into many of his most pressing concerns – namely, maritime security, commercial revitalization, and Huguenot and rival European sea power.

Experimentations with Chartered Companies

The four chartered companies founded in the mid-1620s – the Compagnies de Morbihan, de la Nacelle de Saint-Pierre fleurdelisée, de Saint-Christophe, and de la Nouvelle-France – emerged during an age of companies in which various European countries embraced the company form to compete against each other in commercial and colonizing ventures overseas. Contemporaries, as Richelieu, Montmorency, and the various memoirists attest, attached considerable expectations to this form, having witnessed England's and the Netherlands' lucrative enterprises and growing sea power and commercial might in the East Indies since the turn of the seventeenth century. Speaking of these rival countries in 1646, Jean Eon remarked, "it is important to observe that all of their commerce is done in companies, and that as soon as they discover some way to profit from commerce, they set out at once to create a company, pool capital, and establish an order and economy which they wish to follow: and by this method they succeed at everything they undertake."[91] While this passage captures the optimism around the company form, it belies the great variety of factors that shaped an enterprise. In France, Richelieu and Louis XIII deployed companies as centralizing instruments in the struggle over control of the sea. If this objective united the four companies of the mid-1620s, the range of configurations and circumstances in which each emerged underscores their flexible, contingent, and complex nature. Each was a particular response to the challenges of the period.

Universal Companies

The view of the company form as a magic formula for commercial and maritime success was embodied in the Compagnies de Morbihan and de la Nacelle de Saint-Pierre fleurdelisée as well as the contemporaneous Compagnie royale de voyages de long cours, an initiative of François du Noyer de Saint-Martin, an economist and controller general under Louis XIII.[92] Together, they marked a shift in the magnitude and ambition of French ventures. The three companies exemplified the widespread and interrelated perceptions among memoirists and within government that commerce needed to be reformed in all its aspects and that the bigger the company chosen to do this, the better. All combined domestic and overseas commercial (and colonizing) activities in one enterprise.

The Compagnie royale de voyages de long cours was a multi-faceted enterprise that evolved considerably over twenty-four years to reflect contemporary preoccupations. François du Noyer submitted his first proposal for a royal company in 1612. That initial incarnation was a crusading company focused on reconquering "holy places" and seems to have also included the settlement of New France in partnership with Champlain.[93] Four years later, in 1616, du Noyer reoriented the project around the reorganization of commerce under the (long-winded) title of "Compagnie royale de voyages de long-cours, Levant, Midi et Ponant et autres effets et aménagements." The royal company was charged with organizing voyages to "Africa, Asia and America, New France, and in these places … be[ing] the first to plant the Cross, the instrument of our salvation, with French forts and colonies for the security of its [France's] commerce and possessions."[94] To be funded by the king, French cities, and individuals, it resembled the VOC in its organization. Capital was to be divided into shares and the company's affairs managed by directors chosen from among the associates as well as from the various municipal bodies throughout the kingdom. While the company would be under the king's protection and patronage, du Noyer himself was to be director general, governor in places under the company's jurisdiction, and vice admiral general outside France. Drawing on Italian precedents, this enterprise was but one aspect of a larger endeavour involving finances, administration, transportation, and public works.[95] The difficulty of mobilizing capital and support for such an extensive project so hindered the company's establishment that it was still in the planning stages when Richelieu began to organize the Compagnies de Morbihan and de la Nacelle de Saint-Pierre fleurdelisée ten years later.

The Compagnies de Morbihan and de la Nacelle de Saint-Pierre fleurdelisée constituted Richelieu's versions of the Compagnie royale, bearing a strong resemblance to the latter in inspiration, scope, objectives, and organization.[96] Where du Noyer's company focused primarily on the overseas dimension, Richelieu's companies prioritized their metropolitan operations. In the case of the Compagnie de Morbihan, all types of commerce in all regions were open to it. Similar to du Noyer's company, the enterprise enlisted the king's active support. The latter granted it, as mentioned above, the harbour and port of Morbihan in Brittany "for [its] permanent headquarters and residence."[97] There, the king derogated his powers of justice, administration, appointment of governors and lieutenants, and taxation. The company could found colleges, build vessels, manufacture cannon, and establish stores and agents in any town in France. The overseas corollary to these metropolitan powers and privileges was the enjoyment of exclusive privileges to, and permission to colonize, any lands in New France that it might discover. With a seal from the king, it could enter contracts and commissions for war and trade. The enterprise was to be organized with a permanent capital of 1.6 million livres, consisting of shares purchased by a hundred associates, with no threat of derogation to nobles or ecclesiastics.[98] Commercial regulator at home, colonizer abroad, the Compagnie de Morbihan integrated overseas activities into its primarily metropolitan mandate.

Like the Compagnie de Morbihan, the Compagnie de la Nacelle de Saint-Pierre fleurdelisée operated mainly in Europe. Its mandate covered a range of activities, allowing it to engage in "trade by sea and river as well as by land, establish fisheries, together with factories of all sorts of dishes, draperies both silk and wool, tapestries ... sow rice, plant sugar canes and refine [the sugar], manufacture ... arms ... soap, cheese, butter ... crystal glasses ... porcelain dishes."[99] The company received exclusive privileges for twenty-five years over all new manufactures it established. It proposed a vast European trade network, encompassing Norway, Denmark, Sweden, Hamburg, and Muscovy (Moscow). Like the Compagnie de Morbihan, it was to be granted its own ports, whose exact locations were yet to be determined: one on the Atlantic, close to a river route into the interior, and a second on the Mediterranean. While the king retained his rights to *lods et ventes*, the ports' inhabitants would be exempt from all other taxes and no officers of the Crown or the Admiralty would be permitted to levy fees based on customary rights.[100] The exercise of justice was to be entrusted to officers appointed by the company and approved by the king, their judgments having comparable force to those of royal officers, and the company was given complete discretion over the creation of regulations and statutes necessary to keep order in the ports, including those for particular trades. As with the Compagnie royale, it could provide loan services and open exchange offices. The company's colonizing functions overseas, like those of its Breton counterpart, were limited to New France and new lands in the West Indies.[101] There is no mention in the original contract of the size of the capital or the management structure, but it is likely, given the other similarities, that these terms resembled those of the Compagnie de Morbihan. Complementary in jurisdiction and focus, the Compagnies de Morbihan and de la Nacelle de Saint-Pierre fleurdelisée presided over all commerce and manufactures in the kingdom and overseas.

The three companies resembled their Dutch and English counterparts in their structures and in the powers and privileges granted. All had a capital fund organized around shares, made a distinction between investors and directors, and earmarked a certain portion of their capital for infrastructure, ranging from ships to fortifications. Like the foreign models on which they drew, the three companies also received royal charters, in which the king delegated substantial portions of his sovereign authority. While the royal company's proposal did not enumerate the powers delegated, the objective of building colonies and fortifications for the establishment of commerce overseas implied, at a minimum, some derogation of administrative and military authority as well as power over the distribution of land. In the case of Richelieu's two companies, the delegation was more specific and extensive: the king reserved one or more ports in France for their headquarters, and with them his attendant powers; and to the Breton company, he granted considerable military powers. Like the Dutch and English East India Companies, these were public enterprises funded by private capital, with the dual aim of strengthening French commerce and navigation and filling the pocketbooks of subscribers.

The vast scope of these companies highlights their role as a catch-all solution to weak commerce and naval forces and fragmented authority in the kingdom. If their general form recalled their Dutch and English counterparts, the Compagnies royale, de Morbihan, and de la Nacelle de Saint-Pierre fleurdelisée far exceeded the parameters of these foreign models, both geographically and in the range of activities under their purview. As the VOC and EIC demonstrate, the Dutch and English enterprises were typically confined to a specific geographic area of overseas trade. Richelieu's and du Noyer's creations, by contrast, had either transatlantic or global jurisdictions and, in the case of the former two, kingdom-wide supervision of commerce and manufactures.

The term accorded the Compagnies de Morbihan and de la Nacelle de Saint-Pierre fleurdelisée, *compagnies universelles*, or universal companies, aptly sums up this difference in scale. On the one hand, it underscores the limitless potential that the company form seemed to offer. The description of New France in the two companies' contracts is a good example. As mentioned previously, they were granted permission to "possess the lands of New France both the continent and the islands and other places."[102] Just what constituted "New France" – the Antilles seem to be included here – is not clear, in contrast to the more precise delineations in viceroys' commissions or in the CNF's edict. The emphasis in the contracts is instead on "conquests of lands outside those which are under the obedience of His Majesty."[103] In this sense, the companies were a hopeful expression of French claims to and occupation of North America and the Antilles. On the other hand, the term "universal companies" brings out the very impossibility of their coming to fruition. Political difficulties aside, the scale of these enterprises made them all but logistically impossible. Indeed, one historian has argued that *all* seventeenth-century companies combining commerce and colonization – never mind these global mandates – demanded more than any contemporary state's infrastructure could support.[104] Moreover, their projected capital was much smaller than that of the English or Dutch overseas enterprises. The Compagnie de Morbihan's was, for example, one-third that of the EIC and about one-quarter that of the VOC and GWC.[105] The aspirational quality of these companies reveals the optimism around the form as a quick route to increased French standing and lucrative maritime trade abroad and consolidated authority at home.

While the scale of the universal companies reflected the hope and ambition behind them, it also betrayed Richelieu's and the king's desire to break regionalized economies built on privileges, liberties, and custom. The Compagnie de Morbihan's control of all commerce within and outside the kingdom, for example, would eliminate regional particularities, especially those affecting the movement of goods, and help to direct revenue to the Crown. For Richelieu, the customs and privileges that parcelled up French commerce and encouraged small, local ventures prevented France from competing with its European rivals.[106] The companies, already designed to help create a uniform maritime jurisdiction, were also, therefore, intended to consolidate privileges. In this way, a host of privileges and liberties covering multiple jurisdictions would be replaced by two companies with exclusive privileges in particular areas of activity. The ultimate abandonment of the two companies was, as we have seen, in large part due to the strong reaction of ports and provinces against such standardization.

If the prospect of exclusive privileges was objectionable to those who would be directly affected, it also limited the Crown's and Richelieu's spheres of action. The establishment of the universal companies clearly made it difficult to accept any other company proposal. The drawback of their extensive mandates is suggested by a marginal note in the contract for the Compagnie de la Nacelle de Saint-Pierre fleurdelisée. In article 36, the king promised to refrain from establishing any similar company proposed by foreigners or allowing any individual ventures in the areas covered by the contract. The note, possibly written by Richelieu, deemed this condition "too rigorous" and the article was subsequently removed.[107] Although it concerned foreigners, not French, the comment points to the desire to keep possibilities open for other enterprises that could serve royal interests in the area of commercial and maritime revitalization. Richelieu may have ideally liked to reduce privileges, but they were nevertheless commercially and politically useful. The universal companies highlight simultaneously the potential of the company form and the limitations imposed on the scale of enterprises by contemporary methods of exercising power.

The CNF in Comparative Perspective: Universal Companies

Comparing the CNF to the Compagnie de Morbihan illuminates the different and particular role that the former played in meeting the domestic and international challenges of the time. If the edicts for both companies situated them in the context of the need to extend the Crown's influence outward, both in Europe and overseas, the nature of this extension was distinct for each. The edict for the universal company emphasized the value of "trade both by sea and by land with the remotest foreigners … [the Crown] having been duly informed that … the cessation of commerce in this kingdom is not so much due to the negligence of our subjects as to the lack of security for trading, and that it cannot be remedied but by the union of many people."[108] Encapsulating the views advanced in the memoranda and the Assembly of Notables, these excerpts make the case for the establishment of maritime trade routes, infrastructure, and naval forces.

The preamble to the CNF's edict instead underscored the Catholic ideology at the centre of the French monarchy: "as it is for the glory of God and the prosperity of this State, that the care we take to work for the advancement of the Catholic, Apostolic, and Roman Religion, is not limited to the breadth of France: but that in imitating this great Saint, from whom we bear both the scepter and the name, we act so that the renown of the French extends far into foreign lands and that their piety becomes known through the conversion of peoples buried in infidelity, and in barbarism."[109] As this preamble makes clear, overseas trade undertaken with the king's protection and moral and material support was not confined to commercial goals and activities. It spread the reputation of France and its monarch abroad and extended his dominion when traders discovered and claimed territory unknown to Europeans. It also helped to fulfill the special mission of the French to spread Catholicism.[110]

The different emphases in the preambles to the edicts for the Compagnies de la Nouvelle-France and de Morbihan were also visible in the body of each. On the one hand, provisions of a religious nature in the CNF's articles had no counterpart in the Compagnie de Morbihan's. The former company's second and third articles, respectively, limited settlement to "native French Catholics" and ensured the religious well-being of existing and future habitations by requiring the presence and maintenance of at least three ecclesiastics in each.[111] On the other hand, nowhere in the CNF's articles did the term "conquest" appear, in contrast to those of the universal companies.[112] The completely different frame given to each shows that the CNF and the Compagnie de Morbihan served different purposes in the quest to centralize authority under the Crown.

The CNF was simultaneously a religious, a commercial, and a political enterprise. The company's cast was shaped by the circumstances in which it emerged and traditional methods of mobilizing resources for royal projects. The religious emphasis in the CNF's articles reinforced the Crown's commitment to promoting Catholicism at a time when its foreign policies were under attack. In the mid-1620s, the cardinal and his policies enjoyed the support of two Catholic groups with opposing views, the parti dévot and the *bons Français*. The former, as we saw in the previous chapter, favoured strong ties with the Catholic Church and Catholic powers such as Spain along with an aggressive approach toward Huguenots within France. The *bons Français* advocated an independent foreign policy that reflected French interests, all the while maintaining a connection with Rome. Although Richelieu tried to keep this dual support for as long as possible, his policies provoked a break with the parti dévot in 1626.[113] That year, France decided to support its Protestant allies against Spain in a dispute over jurisdiction and entered a treaty with the Huguenots of La Rochelle in an effort to quell unrest there. Denouncing Richelieu as the "supreme pontiff of the Calvinists and the cardinal of La Rochelle," the parti dévot withdrew their support.[114] While the cardinal launched his own vigorous propaganda campaign, a letter to the king dated February 1626 shows that he was concerned about the Catholic bona fides of the Crown in the face of these attacks. Commenting on negotiations with the Assembly of Clergy on an unrelated matter, Richelieu observed that "the support and approbation of the clergy would be no small thing, *especially at this time when there are those who wish to slander the king and his ministers for lacking zeal for the good of religion*."[115] In this context, the CNF's religious preamble played a role in broader efforts to placate Richelieu's critics and bolster the Crown's position.[116]

While the religious objectives of the CNF may have served Richelieu's and the king's political interests, they also resonated with the growing segment of the population involved in the establishment of lay congregations in France. As we saw in chapter 4, dévots and religious alike extended their mission field to New France. It was there that the Duc de Ventadour, the former viceroy of New France and founder of the Compagnie du Saint-Sacrement in 1630, had financed the first Jesuit mission in 1625; the Société de Notre-Dame de Montréal founded Ville-Marie in 1642; and numerous female religious orders sponsored by wealthy dévotes – most notably Richelieu's niece, the Duchesse d'Aiguillon – established hospitals and schools in the 1630s and 40s.[117] The energy from this religious fervour was integral to the exploitation of New France as well as to the main vehicle chosen for this goal, the CNF.

The Crown's long-standing practice of seeking support from financial and ecclesiastical circles reinforced the CNF's politico-religious cast. The number of financiers and other government officials in the company has traditionally been used as evidence of the Crown's failure to attract merchants to the enterprise. With the latter making up only just over one-third of subscribers, the argument goes, Richelieu was forced to seek associates from within government administration.[118] This interpretation, however, ignores the traditional role of financiers as supporters of royal projects. The financier's primary function was to provide money to the king, perennially short of revenue, whenever he needed it, most often in times of war and at short notice.[119] With ready access to liquid funds, receivers and treasurers general, in particular, could easily reinvest a portion of what they collected in the form of advances and loans to the Crown or general farms.[120] Financiers' significant control over the king's revenue led naturally to participation in economic activities, ranging from agriculture to manufacturing and commerce, especially when the Crown was involved. The substantial amounts of capital demanded by the large commercial and colonizing companies favoured by Richelieu required investors who could afford to have liquid funds locked up for some time. Familiar with investments and the management of money, financiers brought valuable knowledge as well as their personal and professional networks, extending from high-ranking officials in government to prominent people in related areas. At the same time that their unique position afforded them the opportunity to participate, it made them subject to pressure from their superiors and patrons to join such ventures.[121] It is likely that at least some of the financiers who made up just over one-third of the CNF entered under obligation, with the aim of pleasing a patron such as Richelieu or improving their government position. That said, there were inarguably others who viewed their participation as simply another dimension of their role as furnishers of funds to the Crown.[122]

Similarly, the CNF bears the mark of the church's well-established role as both an institution and a network of individuals in providing financial and organizational support for royal ventures. The Crown relied heavily on the church for financial aid, ranging from the *don gratuit*, paid in acknowledgment of the clergy's continued enjoyment of privileges and exemption from taxes, to loans based on the clergy's exemplary credit.[123] Particular pressures, such as war, could prompt the Crown to seek further subsidies. During the siege of La Rochelle in 1627–28, Richelieu tried to obtain the pope's permission to fund the royal forces with ecclesiastical resources. The pope agreed, instead, to a fixed sum.[124] Like the financiers and other corporate groups, the church played a major role in maintaining the solvency of the French Crown. Equally important were the personal ties that helped the Crown draw on religious groups' skills as organizers and mobilizers of people and resources. As a former bishop and now a cardinal, Richelieu was very familiar with and connected to ecclesiastical networks, maintaining his own vast web of clients.[125] For example, the Jesuit Philibert Noyrot, the spiritual director of the Duc de Ventadour, influenced Richelieu's response to the situation in New France, eventually leading to the establishment of the CNF.[126]

Personal and institutional ties aside, the focus on colonization in the company's edict of 1627, coupled with the professed mandate to convert Indigenous people, encouraged collaboration among the company, religious orders, and lay societies. The practice of granting seigneuries to religious communities on the condition that they people the land suggests that the company saw these groups as an advantageous way to delegate its obligations, notably to bring four thousand people to New France. By the mid-1630s, the Jesuits, Ursulines, Sulpicians, and Hospitallers together had control over 800,000 arpents, or about 10 per cent of the land.[127] These orders provided invaluable aid through their dissemination of information about the colony, connections to wealthy donors, recruitment efforts, and contributions to the colony's infrastructure.[128] By mobilizing religious and financial circles, Richelieu changed the composition of the enterprise from the traders of previous companies to those with whom both he and the Crown had a well-established relationship.

The CNF's composition points to the complex intertwining of commercial, political, and religious interests in overseas expansion. The familial, political, professional, and social connections of three associates represent different variations of this relationship. Sébastien Cramoisy was the famous printer of the *Jesuit Relations*, king's printer from 1633, the official bookseller of Richelieu when the latter was bishop of Luçon, and the holder of various lucrative print monopolies, including the minting of money, received through his marriage to the granddaughter of the *général des monnaies*. He counted the cardinal, the Duchesse d'Aiguillon, and Chancellor Séguier, whose wife was an influential dévote, among his patrons. The grandson and nephew of Catholic Leaguers, he participated in several lay congregations, particularly those concerned with overseas missions. He entered the CNF as the thirty-seventh subscriber and became its procureur in 1633 before leaving the enterprise ten years later.[129] Another creature of Richelieu, Jean de Lauson, royal counsellor, *maître des requêtes*, and president of the Grand Conseil in 1630, participated in these networks in a different way. He was intendant of both New France and the company, the purchaser of a share for his son Jean around 1643, a dévot and an active member of the Compagnie du Saint-Sacrement, and the cousin of two treasurers general.[130] In contrast to these two men, Thomas Bonneau was himself a financier, one of the most influential of his time. He belonged to a complex network of these professionals, joined through blood and marriage alliances and radiating out from Tours, one of the hubs of dévot activity. Coming from an ultra-Catholic financial family, Bonneau was a cousin of the apostolic vicar of Tours and was connected through marriage to the pious Gault family, which included two bishops of Marseille. He was also the uncle of Madame de Miramion, an influential dévote later in the century, and of François Pallu, first bishop of China.[131] Bonneau subscribed to the CNF in his own name and that of his brother, Jacques, in 1628. Many of the financiers with whom he had professional or familial ties also became associates, in some cases through him.[132] While these examples cannot show how or whether one activity affected another, they do suggest that lay congregations in support of missions overseas and commercial and colonizing companies attracted many of the same people, motivated variously by economic, political, patrimonial, and religious considerations.[133] Distinct from other French companies of the mid-1620s, the CNF embodied the interconnections among commercial, religious, and political concerns at the time.

The CNF *in Comparative Perspective: Regional Companies*

Comparing the CNF to the Compagnie de Saint-Christophe reveals another dimension of this period of company experimentation. Created for a specific region in the Atlantic, each was a product of a particular combination of metropolitan and colonial commercial and political circumstances. The Compagnie de Saint-Christophe, established six months before the CNF, originated with a request from Pierre Belain d'Esnambuc, who had recently visited the island of Saint-Christophe, and Urbain de Roissey, a Rouennais *armateur* (shipowner), for permission to establish a colony in the West Indies. At the end of October 1626, Richelieu granted them a commission to this effect in his new capacity as grand maître. The same day, a contract of association and act of foundation created the Compagnie de Saint-Christophe.[134] The associates agreed to send d'Esnambuc and Roissey to "settle and populate the islands of Saint Christopher and Barbados and others" between the eleventh and eighteenth degrees of latitude, "to instruct the inhabitants of the said islands in the Catholic, Roman, and Apostolic religion … trade in foodstuffs and merchandise … and have them brought to France to Havre de Grâce to the exclusion of all other [subjects]" during a period of twenty years. They undertook to pool a capital of 45,000 livres with which to purchase three ships. While all associates were investors, only one was delegated responsibility for outfitting, recruitment, and general administration.[135]

The company, based originally on an unsolicited proposal, largely reflected the structure, organization, and objectives of previous overseas enterprises rather than the recent experiments with the company form. Its mandate to colonize, evangelize, and trade resembled the commissions of de Mons, Condé, Montmorency, and Ventadour for activities in New France over the previous three decades. Unlike these viceroys and lieutenants general, but comparable to the associations to which they delegated trading privileges, the Compagnie de Saint-Christophe had no regal powers. Indeed, it was not explicitly accorded either powers of administration or title to land.[136] The association's structure, in which there were investors and one manager, resembled a *sociéte en commandite*, just like the Compagnie de Montmorency in the Laurentian colony.[137] Finally, the relatively modest capital, comparable to the original capital of the Compagnie de Mons, recalled traditional small trading associations.

If the Compagnie de Saint-Christophe did not bear the imprint of the foreign joint-stock enterprises, it nevertheless signalled a new approach to commercial associations that sought to mobilize private initiative and capital for royal objectives. Newly minted as grand maître, Richelieu became a subscriber, entering for 10,000 livres, 8,000 livres of which came in the form of a ship. He also recruited other members, notably the Marquis d'Effiat and Martin de Mauvoy, who each invested 2,000 livres.[138] The subscription of well-placed officials, especially in the navy and finances, in overseas companies became common practice over the following decade, an indication of personal ties at court and in government on the part of an enterprise's leaders, Richelieu's personal involvement, and royal support for such initiatives.

While the CNF counted some of the same dignitaries among its membership, it emerged under very different circumstances from its West Indian counterpart. The French already had decades of experience in commercial and colonizing ventures to the region; after all, at least four companies with trading privileges, all of which were comprised primarily of merchants, had preceded the CNF. By the mid-1620s, habitations had existed for two decades at Quebec and longer in Acadia, albeit both with small populations and functioning largely as trading centres. While this decade saw the first seigneurial grants and the construction of fortifications, it also witnessed increasing conflict among the growing number of competing interest groups in the Saint Lawrence, as we saw in chapter 4. By 1626, the level of unrest had reached the attention of the Crown. Those with well-developed networks at court, notably Samuel de Champlain and the Jesuits, made personal representations to the king based on their perceptions of the present state of the Saint Lawrence colony and visions for the future. This situation gave Richelieu an opening to have six clients draw up a proposal for the CNF, as we saw earlier in the chapter.[139] It may be supposed, then, that it was crafted with greater direction than the more frequent unsolicited submissions by individuals, such as the Compagnie de Saint-Christophe. Like the universal companies, the CNF also reflected the innovations of the joint-stock form. The CNF and Compagnie de Saint-Christophe were distinct in structure, context, and inspiration, even as they both found a place in Richelieu's royal maritime program.

Examining these two Atlantic companies together also demonstrates the ways in which particular company iterations circulated in the 1630s and 40s. In 1635, colonial and metropolitan circumstances combined to favour the overhaul of the Compagnie de Saint-Christophe. The resulting Compagnie des îles de l'Amérique's edict and act of association closely resembled those of its Laurentian counterpart in its structure, organization, and obligations. There were, for example, to be four directors to manage the company's daily operations and a general assembly would be held annually. In exchange for exclusive privileges to commerce, associates committed to transporting four thousand French Catholics to the islands over a period of twenty years and establishing and maintaining missionaries. They had the power to distribute land and name magistrates and governors.[140] The Compagnie des îles de l'Amérique influenced, in turn, the powers, privileges, obligations, and structure of other companies during the following decades, including the Compagnie de Madagascar, founded in 1656.

Overlapping membership highlights the transmission of practices, experiences, and resources among these companies. From the establishment of the Compagnie de Saint-Christophe in 1626 to Richelieu's death in 1642, sixteen companies – ranging in regional focus from Cap-Vert in Senegal to Guyana to the East Indies – emerged with the grand maître's support. One-third of the associates of the Compagnie des îles de l'Amérique were already investors in the CNF. Well-connected merchants like Jean Rozée, highly placed office-holders like François Fouquet, and financiers like Pierre Chanut participated in several of these companies, taking on important roles such as director on many occasions.[141] By the early 1640s, then, the French had a substantial base of knowledge on which to draw, born of the various companies that had been tested since the mid-1620s.

Viewing the CNF alongside other French companies allows us to foreground the particular dynamism of this period of experimentation with the form. There was no such thing as a typical company. Indeed, the French companies proposed in 1626–27 alone covered the spectrum from the relatively modest Compagnie de Saint-Christophe to the all-encompassing Compagnies de Morbihan and de la Nacelle de Saint-Pierre fleurdelisée. In the CNF's case, interactions among foreign models, metropolitan power struggles, and local circumstances in the colony shaped its contours. Like Admiral Montmorency's assumption of the viceroyalty seven years previously, the company's establishment highlights, above all, the transatlantic nature of the growth of French maritime authority. Control of transatlantic traffic was linked to territorial control. Richelieu, like his predecessor, combined both innovative and traditional methods to strengthen royal control of maritime security, commerce, and navigation (at the expense of provinces and ports) as well as his personal power. Despite the CNF's ostensible governmental jurisdiction, the cardinal assumed the position of viceroy, delegating power in his absence to lieutenants, and kept a close eye on the company through numerous clients. There was, in this respect, strong continuity with the previous period. To have his position as grand maître recognized fully in Brittany, he resorted to the tried-and-true method of building a power base in the province. If these initiatives were part of royal attempts to centralize maritime commercial and navigational affairs since the late sixteenth century, the 1620s nevertheless saw the emergence of the chartered company as a preferred instrument. Experimentation with the structure and parameters of a company like the CNF did not end with its initial establishment but continued well beyond in an effort to realize its extensive mandate encompassing commerce, colonization, and governance.

6

Corporate Governance, Delegation, and Usurpation

As the longest-lasting French chartered company in the Atlantic, the Compagnie de la Nouvelle-France adopted various strategies over time in the execution of its mandate, with the dual goal of fulfilling its heavy obligations and reaping the rewards of its trading privileges. The range and evolution of these strategies underscores the experimental nature of this new tool of capital formation and governance. The CNF resembled other corporations in France in its constitution and governance. As we have seen, corporations were constituted by the king. By means of letters patent, they were granted legal personality, which allowed them to sue and be sued, own and manage property, as well as lend and borrow money. Their status as artificial persons was confirmed by a seal. When Louis XIII promulgated the CNF's edict of establishment, thereby confirming the earlier contract between Richelieu and the company's associates, he legally brought the CNF into being. A key feature of corporations lay in their responsibility for internal governance.[1] Following the contract and edict, CNF associates drew up articles of association that stipulated the functioning of the organization, ranging from the election of directors to the financial obligations of members, as well as their relations with outside individuals and groups.

Like other corporations, the company's relationship with the king was contractual. Louis XIII granted the CNF numerous privileges, such as tax exemptions on goods necessary to outfit voyages, as well as *dons*, or gifts, including royal ships and cannon. In exchange, the CNF pledged loyalty to the king and undertook to extend his and God's glory and reputation. As we saw in chapters 3 and 5, corporations, including chartered companies, played a role in the advancement of the public good by serving particular social functions. Those of the CNF were laid out in the edict's preamble. Its primary objective of peopling New France would serve God (through the evangelization of Indigenous inhabitants), the king (through the extension of royal power, increased population and industry, and glory and prestige), and subjects (through the development of commerce).[2] Company meetings were to take place in the presence of the intendant of the colony, in part to ensure the harmony between the public interest and the "good and utility of the said company." In keeping with the social character of corporations, the CNF's directors were charged with maintaining equality among members "of great or lesser quality." They also had the power to use up to 500 livres' worth of company profits toward "alms and charity," underscoring the company's obligation to serve the public interest.[3] The broad strokes of the company, its legal status, and relationship to the king echoed those of other corporations in France.

There were important differences between metropolitan and colonial corporations. As an overseas commercial and colonizing enterprise, the CNF was distinct in its dual status as a profit-seeking entity with responsibility to its investors and a means to extend French claims to sovereignty in North America. This latter role is particularly visible in the expansive seigneurial jurisdiction and the scale of delegated powers and privileges that the king granted the company. In return, the Crown demanded the customary symbolic acts of allegiance, including a gold crown with the accession of each new king. The company became seigneur, trader, commercial regulator, and governor. This combination of jurisdictions distinguished overseas corporations in general from their metropolitan counterparts. Enjoying exclusive privileges to the fur trade and other commerce, the CNF was responsible for policing the theoretically vast privileged trading area and catching any interloping vessels. In such an event, the confiscated ship and merchandise would accrue to the company. The delegation of regal powers, notably in the area of defence, aimed to ensure "the security of the said country [and] the conservation of commerce."[4] By far the company's heaviest responsibility, and the essence of its social function, was to transport, temporarily provide for, and distribute land to, four thousand men and women over the first fifteen years of its mandate. The nature of the CNF's privileges, social functions, and responsibilities – similar to those of colonizing companies of other empires – underscored its status as a vehicle to expand French dominion overseas.

If the CNF differed from other French corporations in scale and scope, it also departed from most of its rival Atlantic contemporaries in the area of colonial governance. Virtually all companies of the period, through the delegation of particular aspects of a ruler's authority, exercised sovereignty in the latter's name. The degree depended on the objectives of the enterprise, with some companies in the same country, such as the Dutch East and West India Companies, enjoying quite different relationships to the state. It could also change over time. During the first decades of its existence, the English East India Company was "often but not entirely coterminous with the regime"; only in the late seventeenth and eighteenth centuries did it become a "veritable state within a state."[5] The CNF's delegated sovereign powers made it more than a seigneur but less than a state. Compared to those of its Atlantic counterparts, its powers were circumscribed in the areas of defence, law, and diplomacy. While it could build military infrastructure, the company had no mandate to declare war or enter alliances. It could exercise seigneurial justice but could neither create laws nor tax the colony's inhabitants. Officials, including governors and lieutenants general of present and future habitations, officers of royal justice, and captains of forts, were to be "nominated and put forward by the said associates" to Cardinal Richelieu and subsequently granted a commission by the king.[6] By contrast, the Virginia and Massachusetts Bay Companies could name and remove governors, officers, and ministers, make and enact laws on land and sea, and, in the case of Virginia, the governor could impose martial law in the event of rebellion. The Dutch West India Company, for its part, could "make contracts, engagements and alliances with the princes and natives of the countries comprehended therein [i.e., the territory granted]," build an army, and declare war.[7] These companies received full powers of government, with the king and States General, respectively, retaining only suzerainty over the territory.[8] The CNF was, instead, firmly under the sovereignty of the king. It was not, then, a "company-state" as defined by Phillips and Sharman.[9] Indeed, the company was not the only body with governmental jurisdiction in America. As grand maître, Richelieu also enjoyed delegated sovereign powers. The CNF remained his project and under his patronage until his death. This configuration of authority set the CNF apart from its English and Dutch counterparts.[10]

What made commercial and colonizing companies like the CNF particularly novel was the fact that they were at once commercial associations and legally recognized corporations with responsibility for the public good. Unlike other commercial associations, they enjoyed the legal protection of incorporation and the grant of a charter; unlike other corporations, profit was a primary goal. They were, then, a particular form of corporation.[11]

This chapter explores the CNF as both a commercial and governmental entity. What strategies did it adopt to carry out its multi-faceted mandate? How did the relationship between its commercial and governmental jurisdictions evolve over its thirty-six-year tenure? What was the nature of its relations with the king, other French title-holders, and other corporate bodies? During the first fifteen years or so of its existence, the company delegated authority and privileges, and granted land in different permutations and combinations. In the 1640s, however, changes in personnel on the eastern side of the Atlantic and the establishment of new corporate bodies on the western side led to forced delegations and even usurpations of its authority, reconfiguring patterns of sovereignty, authority, and commercial jurisdiction in New France.

The Intertwining of Royal and Company Delegations

One distinguishing feature of the CNF compared to its English and Dutch contemporaries in the Atlantic was that there was already a trade and governance structure at the centre of its vast concession when the company was founded. The role that Richelieu played in the CNF demonstrates the continuing influence of previous practice. As chapter 3 showed, the position of grand maître effectively subsumed both the titles of admiral and viceroy. Noticeably present in the company's edict, Richelieu was to issue licences to the CNF's associates and agents and accorded the latter's request to name Jean de Lauson intendant of the company and colony. Commissioned by the king, commanders and captains of the company's ships served in his name.[12] But it is above all the naming of Champlain as his lieutenant that confirms Richelieu's assumption of the viceroyalty in all but name.[13] Sometime between June 1627, when the Duc de Ventadour sold the viceroyalty to Lauson, and April 1628, when the king sent Champlain news of the new company, the latter received a commission to "command in New France, in the absence of our dear and beloved cousin the Cardinal de Richelieu," as he had under all preceding viceroys.[14] It was not until March 1629 that the CNF presented Champlain with its own commission, having "nominated and presented him to His Majesty in conformity with the power that it pleased him to give us." Champlain was to serve "in the name of the Company" as Richelieu's substitute. In other words, he was both the cardinal's personal representative and charged with doing all that was possible for "the utility of the said Company."[15] This dual commission demonstrates that government in the colony, at least during the CNF's early years, was an amalgam of previous arrangements – viceroy, lieutenant, and trading company – and a proprietary company with governmental responsibilities. While this arrangement reflects the close ties between Richelieu and the CNF, it also attenuated the company's governmental prerogatives in creating two lines of authority and, by extension, the possibility of bypassing one in favour of the other.

The terms under which the CNF operated created a complex web of intra-imperial authority in New France. The company exercised varying degrees of influence when it came to the selection of governors and commanders of habitations. While Champlain acted as Richelieu's lieutenant as well as commander of Quebec under the company, first in 1628–29 and then again in 1632 following the restitution of Quebec by the English, his successors were named under a different procedure and were representatives of the king rather than the grand maître. The commission of the first governor general of New France, Charles Huault de Montmagny, appointed following Champlain's death in 1635, is not extant, but subsequent ones show that governors general (who were also governors of Quebec) were selected by the king from a list of three names put forward by the company.[16] In a general assembly in January 1651, the associates chose three of their members, Pierre Robineau de Bécancour, Guillaume Guillemot Duplessis-Kerbodot,[17] and Jean de Lauson, to be presented as candidates to the king. Lauson was then chosen governor and lieutenant general "following the presentation that was made to us of his person by the Compagnie de la Nouvelle-France, as it is shown from an excerpt of their deliberations."[18] Apart from administrative, defensive, and judicial responsibilities, each governor was directed to "take care that the said decrees and regulations of the Council, made for the establishment and operation of the Compagnie de la Nouvelle-France, are executed," a clause the company saw as a guarantee that its prerogatives would be respected.[19] Like Champlain, subsequent governors were to see to the welfare of the company and that of the inhabitants. The other two Saint Lawrence River habitations established during the CNF's tenure did not come directly under the government of the company. The governor of Trois-Rivières received his nomination from the governor of Quebec, who was also governor general of New France; in Montreal, which the CNF granted under seigneurial tenure to the Société de Notre-Dame in 1642, the latter chose that settlement's commander. While the situation in Trois-Rivières reflects the primacy of the Quebec habitation over all others, the arrangement in Montreal was partly in keeping with the common practice of granting governmental powers (from the king via Richelieu) to the bearer of a seigneurial concession from the company.

If the company had limited power to delegate authority, it enjoyed unrestricted power to grant land.[20] These two powers were continually intertwined in Acadia. The CNF's tenure marked the first time since the founding of Quebec that Acadia and the Saint Lawrence Valley fell under the same organization. Over the previous twenty years, the relationship between trading privileges and authority had developed differently in the two regions. In the Saint Lawrence, Condé and his successors delegated these two elements of their commissions separately. By contrast, subsequent title-holders in Acadia took direct charge of their powers and privileges, as had de Mons. In 1605–06, de Mons granted Jean de Biencourt de Poutrincourt land, fur-trading privileges, and rights to the fishery. The latter became commander of the Port-Royal habitation and lieutenant-governor in Acadia a year later, a title confirmed by royal commission in 1608. While Poutrincourt and his heirs continued their activities fitfully in Acadia over the following two decades, viceregal and royal attention focused on the habitation of Quebec. Indeed, the CNF's act of establishment made no reference to Acadia and its one remaining French habitation, Fort Lomeron near Cap de Sable under Charles Saint-Étienne de La Tour.[21] Previous patterns by which Acadia and the Saint Lawrence Valley were governed differently continued to obtain under the CNF.

To manage its obligations to provision, people, and govern Acadia, the company granted trading privileges and land and delegated authority to individuals, many of whom had previous ties to New France and an interest in the company. These concessions were then ratified in a commission from the king. The first such delegation was to La Tour, possibly an associate of the CNF. In February 1631, Richelieu, "with the consent of the said new company," nominated La Tour to the position of "lieutenant general of His Majesty in the said country of Acadia, fort Louis and port of la Tour [at Cap de Sable], and places under its government in New France"; the king then issued letters patent to this effect. In response, La Tour pledged to "be loyal to the King to Monseigneur the Cardinal and to the Compagnie de la Nouvelle-France, to uphold the ordinances and in particular the edict of the said Compagnie de la Nouvelle-France and its articles of association," underscoring the trio of authorities to which he owed his commission.[22] La Tour had been in Acadia since 1607, when he arrived with his father Claude. He subsequently served under Charles de Biencourt de Saint-Just, Poutrincourt's son and seigneur of Port-Royal, receiving his title in Acadia upon the latter's death.[23] After the capture of Port-Royal and Quebec by the English in 1629, La Tour's habitation at the southern tip of Acadia was all that remained of French possessions in northeastern North America. In 1635, the CNF, which had lent support to his efforts to create other habitations since its establishment, formally ceded the lands on which they stood and the surrounding area to the lieutenant general.[24] In a series of acts, La Tour received Fort Saint-Louis at Port de la Tour, Fort Sainte-Marie on the Saint John River, and rivière des Mines on the Minas Basin "in full property, justice, and seigneury and, as it pleased the king to give and grant the said country of New France to our said company, [to] hold them in fief of the fort of Quebecq."[25] Like all other commissions for lieutenants general and the grants of land from the CNF that usually preceded or followed, La Tour's were in recognition of services rendered to both king and company.[26]

The various permutations and combinations of delegated authority and concessions (as well as trading privileges) created a patchwork of legal, political, and personal relationships with the CNF, Richelieu, and the king. The complexity that resulted is visible in the commission and subsequent seigneurial concession to Isaac de Razilly in 1632. In March, Richelieu, on behalf of the king, commissioned his long-time adviser on maritime affairs and associate of the CNF to receive Port-Royal from the English, according to the terms of the treaty made between the two countries, and "put it in the possession of the Compagnie de la Nouvelle-France."[27] Shortly thereafter, Razilly was appointed "lieutenant general for the King throughout New France, all under the office of Monseigneur the Cardinal, Duc de Richelieu."[28] Two months after the first commission, the company granted Razilly the Sainte-Croix River, its islands, and the surrounding area in return for "fealty and homage," a golden link of chain mail with each change in ownership, and a year's revenue from the seigneurial dues Razilly would collect. These three delegations made the lieutenant general a vassal under both the sovereign authority of the king, via Richelieu, and the seigneurial authority of the company, with different degrees of responsibility to each.

The sweeping jurisdiction accorded Razilly as lieutenant general and seigneur resulted in a further layering of authority, ownership, and privileges as other title-holders came forward to defend their jurisdictions. Shortly after Razilly's commission was granted, Charles de La Tour sought confirmation of his own authority. In an agreement of February 1633 between La Tour and the CNF, the "governor and lieutenant general for His Majesty on the coast of Acadia" undertook to maintain and populate the two habitations at Cap de Sable and on the Saint John River "in place of … the company" in return for the right to half the furs traded throughout Acadia for six years. The second half would go to Razilly on behalf of the CNF.[29] There were, then, two lieutenants general in Acadia: La Tour, with no formal concession of his habitations but responsibility to people them, the expenses for which were to be met with half the profits from the fur trade; and Razilly, with the concession of Sainte-Croix, a fledgling habitation at La Hève (today LaHave) with no title, and obligations to colonize but no special trading privileges from the company.[30] The various combinations of land concessions, authority, and trading privileges accorded in Acadia highlights the CNF's strategy of delegating multiple parts of its commission in regions outside of the Saint Lawrence Valley. The individuality of arrangements between the company and each title-holder testifies to the close ties between the lieutenant generalship, though under the ultimate authority of Louis XIII and Richelieu, and the company's other prerogatives and obligations as seigneur of New France. While these ties no doubt aided the CNF in fulfilling its extensive mandate, they also point to the complementary nature of company and royal interests in the 1630s.

The CNF as Parent Company

Apart from individual concessions, the Compagnie de la Nouvelle-France created several regional subsidiaries beginning in the 1630s. These enterprises took various forms, depending on the CNF's finances, subscriber interest, and geography. While some were strictly commercial, others combined commercial and seigneurial jurisdictions, as did the company.[31] Subsidiaries were among a litany of strategies used by early modern organizations, ranging from corporations to the Crown itself, to remain solvent, maintain their credit, and share costs. Like tax farms, they could provide a sum up front or annually to the company and bear one or more of the costs associated with trading, provisioning, and peopling in exchange for profits from commerce. The creation of subsidiaries by company members was common practice among the CNF's contemporaries. Indeed, English plantation companies routinely created joint-stocks for a variety of types of commerce. In the 1620s, associates of the Virginia Company formed subsidiaries for a glassworks, fur trading, fishing, and the transportation of "maids to be made wives."[32] Where the CNF departed from its contemporaries was in the number of subsidiaries, their geographical spread, and the resultant sliding scale of privileges and obligations from the Saint Lawrence to Acadia.

The nature of the subsidiaries created under the CNF, their organization, scale, and extent, varied according to geographical area as well as the needs and interests of the parent company. In 1632, the company was recovering from heavy financial losses due variously to the capture of its ships by the English; shipwrecked, delayed, or aborted voyages during the previous four years; and the continued English occupation of Port-Royal and Quebec despite the peace treaty of 1629 between the two powers. Total losses amounted to over 300,000 livres, or the association's entire capital.[33] In addition, the company lost its exclusive trading privileges for 1632 to Guillaume de Caën of the former Compagnie de Montmorency in compensation for the revocation of his privileges as well as for losses suffered at the hands of the English. The associates were also simultaneously involved as defendants in two suits with de Caën, both of which sentenced them to substantial indemnities.[34] The deliberations from a company assembly in November of that year summed up the situation: "the funds of the Company having been so much altered, that it is impossible for its Directors, without loans, or without new contributions," to make the necessary arrangements for the following year's sail.[35] It was in this context that the CNF established the first *compagnie particulière* for the Saint Lawrence. The subsidiary was to be composed of any CNF associates who wished to join, with a capital of 100,000 livres to be used for the conduct of the fur trade in the Saint Lawrence and its tributaries, starting from Miscou on the Baie de Chaleur. Its privileges would last for five years, beginning in 1633. In all, about two-thirds, or sixty-odd associates, of the general company entered individually, while the CNF collectively subscribed for a third of the capital, bringing the total to 150,000 livres. The compagnie particulière undertook to transport munitions and supplies for the habitation at no cost and to give men passage for 20 livres. Its obligations were to stop there: "without the said subsidiary company being obliged in any way toward the maintenance of the colony." This clause notwithstanding, it committed to a *rente annuelle* of 10,000 livres to be paid to the CNF to go toward maintenance costs.[36]

The primary goal of the compagnie particulière was to finance each year's voyage. Over its five years of existence, the subsidiary met its obligations and produced a profit for investors, although the extant sources do not specify the amount.[37] Despite the favourable commercial returns for the general company, which bought all the furs from its subsidiary, the tone in the few extant CNF deliberations from early 1638 shows that the company still faced serious financial pressure, leaving it without the funds to meet annual outfitting costs. This situation, as well as the relative success of the first endeavour, prompted the creation of a second compagnie particulière, this time for four years. In contrast to the terms of the first one, subscriptions to the second subsidiary were virtually mandatory: "all associates of the general company are asked to contribute at least 1,000 livres each for each share they have in the said general company"; those who did not would be required to contribute 200 livres per share every year "for the maintenance of the said colony." The decision to create a second subsidiary came after the company had already tried to borrow 80,000 livres from its associates for the 1638 voyage, but few had come forward.[38] Although the second subsidiary comprised a comparable number of associates as the first and operated under the same terms, its directors had to request a second contribution from associates and take out several loans the following year, with the result that, by 1641, the enterprise had yet to make a return.[39]

The two subsidiaries established in the Saint Lawrence were distinct in their particularly close ties to the general company as well as their relatively narrow objective of funding the annual voyages. While they did contribute to the colony's upkeep costs, they did not assume responsibility for the "execution of the articles granted the Compagnie de la Nouvelle-France by the king and my said Seigneur Cardinal" in the general company's place. This feature set these two apart not only from the other regional subsidiaries, but also from the later Communauté des Habitants established at Quebec.[40] The particular cast of the subsidiaries in the Saint Lawrence was due in large part to the CNF's decision to manage directly this portion of its vast domain.

While the establishment of subsidiary companies in other regions was connected in part to the CNF's financial situation, the more extensive obligations, and in some cases privileges, suggest that different considerations were at play than in the Saint Lawrence Valley. At once seigneurial and commercial, like the CNF itself, two of these subsidiaries began as territorial concessions to individuals, while one was a company from the start (see figure 6.1). In 1633, the general company ceded Cape Breton

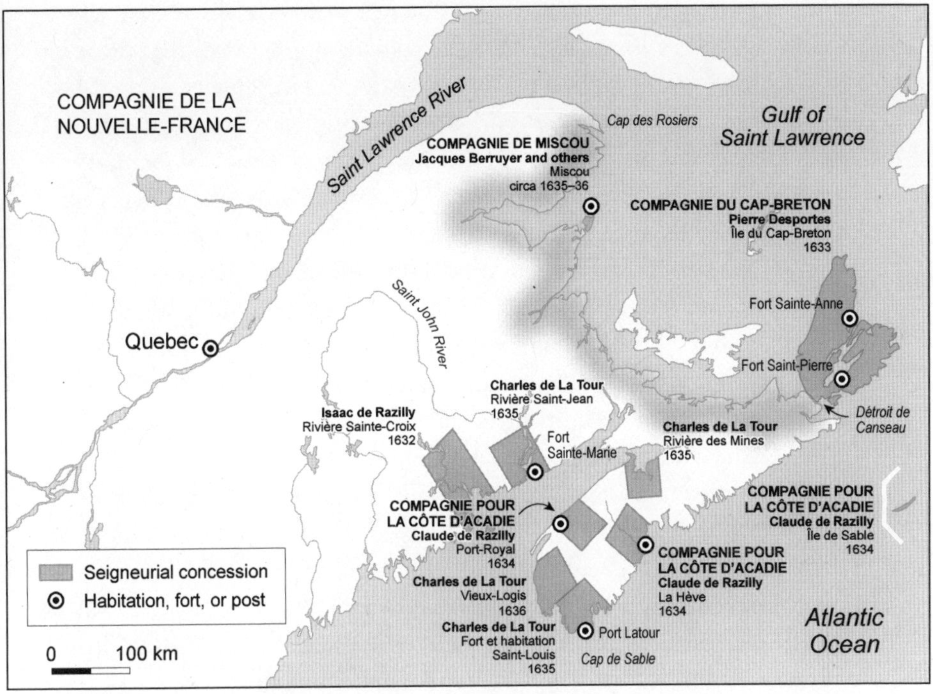

Figure 6.1 Seigneurial concessions accorded to associates of subsidiary companies and other title-holders in Acadia, 1632–36.

to one of its associates, Pierre Desportes, along with exclusive trading privileges. His responsibilities included maintaining Fort Sainte-Anne, established in 1629, and distributing land under seigneurial tenure. To this end, he entered an association, known as the Compagnie parisienne du Cap-Breton, with two merchants, Jean Belleteste and Nicolas Libert, and the royal navy captain who had founded Fort Sainte-Anne, Charles Daniel. Although they transported around fifty people to the island and made some land concessions in exchange for a portion of crop yields, much of their attention went into manning the fort and conducting the fur trade.[41] This company lasted two years, whereupon the associates divided up the company's assets and Desportes continued on his own, through his agent and fellow CNF associate Jean Tuffet, before the latter became his partner in 1639. This marked the end of CNF subsidiaries in Cape Breton. As the island was first and foremost a seigneurial concession to an individual, subsequent arrangements resembled those under Lieutenants General de Mons and Condé in the previous decades, ranging from direct participation in trade with partners to the delegation of privileges to others.[42]

The concession of two habitations in Acadia to Claude de Launay-Razilly, brother of Isaac, highlights the colonizing objectives that drove the establishment of certain regional subsidiaries. In January 1634, the CNF granted the naval captain Port-Royal and La Hève so that the two "be conserved and maintained and that the colony of French be increased as much as possible." In exchange, Launay-Razilly received trading privileges for ten years, to be shared with La Tour for the first six, in accordance with the agreement reached between Isaac de Razilly and the company one year earlier, and thereafter with the CNF "or others being in its rights."[43] Granted in recognition of his brother's colonial efforts, this concession also provided Launay-Razilly with the impetus to form a company. While initially composed of the brothers Razilly and Jean Condonnier, bourgeois de Paris,[44] the Compagnie pour la côte d'Acadie expanded a year later due, in part, to a need for further funds: "without assistance … they would have been forced to return the said settlements to the said Compagnie de la Nouvelle-France and lose expenses." The grateful and deferential tone no doubt also reflected the important position of their new associate, Cardinal Richelieu, a cousin of the Razillys. Two weeks later, the company added two more members, Jean Legrand, royal counsellor and president of the Chambre des Comptes in Dijon, and Louis Motin, controller of the salt storehouse at Mont-Saint-Vincent.[45] What distinguished this subsidiary from the Compagnie du Cap-Breton was the inclusion of the territorial concession in its assets. Although part of the purpose of the latter association was to increase the population of the island, Desportes remained the sole seigneur. A share in the Acadian company, by contrast, included "*the property of lands*, settlements, forts, buildings, rights, trade, and things granted by the said Compagnie de la Nouvelle-France." The associates, rather than Launay-Razilly alone, collectively owned the habitations and surrounding lands.[46]

Like the subscribers to the Compagnie pour la côte d'Acadie, those of the Compagnie de Miscou enjoyed both commercial and seigneurial rights in return for their investment. Founded sometime before January 1636, the Compagnie de Miscou's jurisdiction ran "from Canseau to Guaspe or cap des Roziers and as far inland as one can go."[47] It enjoyed control over both the habitation of Miscou on the Baie de Chaleur and the region's fur trade. In return, it sent provisions and men and provided an annual pension to the Jesuits living there. The associates, all members of the CNF, included Desportes, François Fouquet, Jacques Berruyer de Manselmont, Antoine Cheffault, and Jean Rozée, the last three of whom acted as *préposés*, or agents, for the subsidiary.[48] Few records remain of the company's activities, but evidence suggests that it was the largest such association beyond the Saint Lawrence, with at least thirteen members.[49] All three regional subsidiaries were formed in the service of the habitations ceded to one of their members or to the company as a whole. While less is known about the evolution of the Compagnie de Miscou, those for Acadia and Cape Breton expanded only gradually from a couple of associates and do not appear to have issued a general call within the CNF for more members, unlike the compagnies particulières in the Saint Lawrence Valley.[50] The development of these companies, then, was more ad hoc and informal than that of their Laurentian counterparts, a further testament to their differences in urgency and emphasis.

The experimentation with different types of subsidiaries, from partnerships among a handful of associates to smaller versions of the CNF itself, created further layers of participation in the enterprise, as associates took on a variety of roles in these smaller outfits. All of them were comprised predominantly of associates of the CNF, but only the Saint Lawrence companies appear to have had an explicitly members-only policy.[51] While most subscribers to the subsidiaries already had ties to the general company at the time of investment, some only became associates shortly before or upon entering a regional association. Among the latter were Jean Belleteste and Nicolas Libert, associates in the Compagnie du Cap-Breton, and Launay-Razilly and Philippe de Longvilliers de Poincy, both of the Compagnie pour la côte d'Acadie. There was no correlation between taking out a subscription on account of belonging to a subsidiary and dedication to the CNF: Launay-Razilly spent considerable amounts of capital and effort on his affairs in New France; Poincy, on the other hand, does not appear to have been actively involved beyond his initial investment.[52] A number of associates subscribed to several of the subsidiaries. For example, Launay-Razilly and Pierre Robineau were members of two, Desportes of at least three, and Berruyer, Rozée, and Cheffault were simultaneously in charge of affairs for two subsidiaries as well as for the general company. The multiple memberships make it difficult at times to know in what capacity an associate was acting; on more than one occasion, Cheffault entered contracts on the same day for two different entities.[53] To this participation in subsidiaries could be added the partnerships struck among CNF members for the purchase of furs from the general company or a subsidiary. In 1634, for example,

Desportes, Robert Godefroy, Robineau, and others "had associated to trade in all the said beaver coming from the said commerce," which they in turn sold to master hatters. In both the private partnerships and the subsidiaries, associates with the means and interest took the initiative, aware of the company's considerable financial and colonizing obligations and the potential profits to be had.[54] From the general company's point of view, the subsidiaries' composition allowed it to keep its privileges under its control, in contrast to its predecessors.

If the concession of trade to members was common among early modern companies, the creation of subsidiary joint-stock companies was much rarer. Of the five affiliates, four were smaller versions of the CNF, with a similar organization; only one, the Compagnie du Cap-Breton, was a more traditional partnership.[55] The four modelled on the parent company were capital-centred ventures in which associates pooled their funds, business was conducted under the name of the association, not the individual members, and management of the company's affairs fell to directors. Where the CNF selected twelve directors, the subsidiaries usually chose three.[56] Of the extant records, those of the Compagnie pour la côte d'Acadie are the most detailed regarding the conditions of operation. One share was equal to 17,000 livres; by the end of January 1635, the association had been divided into six.[57] The agreement among Launay-Razilly, Condonnier, and Cardinal Richelieu stipulated that individual associates could not be called upon to increase their contributions but could do so voluntarily. Launay-Razilly, responsible for the outfitting costs for the coming season, was permitted to borrow funds "at the risk and fortune of the sea or to commit the funds of the said company only." The following November, he would report to the directors in Paris. While associates could attend this meeting, they would have no deliberative voice. Finally, the first three years' profits would be put back into the company's capital, echoing the arrangement of the CNF itself.[58]

The first and last of the Compagnie pour la côte d'Acadie's articles highlight the uncertainties around the concept of "capital" in early modern enterprises. The expectation behind these types of association was that the capital would be self-sustaining, buoyed by annual profits. Alone among the subsidiaries in managing to do this was the first compagnie particulière. A cornerstone and major innovation of the joint-stock company, continuous capital developed only fitfully over the century, leading companies to use a combination of both temporary and permanent capital. The Virginia

Company's subsidiary for the sale of tobacco in England and the English East India Company had a distinct capital for each voyage.[59] The second Saint Lawrence subsidiary appears to have operated in this way, if only by necessity. With an initial capital of some 100,000 livres – barely enough for one season's voyage – it required new contributions the following year to raise the required 110,000 livres. In the 1640s, individual associates who contributed to each season's voyage expected the return of their contribution in the fall, a feature of distinct capital voyages; the royal council, however, decided to hold back the returns to finance the next season's preparations, turning these investments into a form of continuous capital.[60] At the same time that the blending of permanent and distinct capital ventures reflects the nascent form of the first, it also highlights the same creative flexibility that led big companies with vast mandates like the CNF's to establish various configurations, from smaller versions of themselves to trading partnerships and seigneurial concessions.[61]

A Unique Corporate Body in New France

As the second Saint Lawrence subsidiary wound up its business and the CNF associates decided how to finance the following season's voyage at the end of 1642, the company received news that would affect its ability to exercise its roles as governor, seigneur, and trader over the following decade. In December, Richelieu died. Patron, protector, and shareholder in both parent and subsidiary companies, the cardinal had viewed the CNF as the primary vehicle for the realization of royal objectives in New France. The number of his clients in the position of director or intendant of company and colony had afforded the CNF direct channels to the chief minister. Five months after this loss, Louis XIII died. While the king had supported the company associates through Richelieu, the greatest consequence of his death for them was the regency it ushered in. His son, Louis XIV, was only four years old; the latter's mother, Anne of Austria, accordingly became regent for almost a decade.[62] Like the regency that followed Henri IV's assassination, this one prompted changes in personnel, most notably on the royal council, where only the chancellor remained from Richelieu's tenure. It also encouraged jockeying among members of the nobility and corporate bodies hoping to take advantage of a weakened Crown to increase their own power. Where the previous regency had threatened the return to war between confessions, Anne of Austria's culminated in the civil unrest of

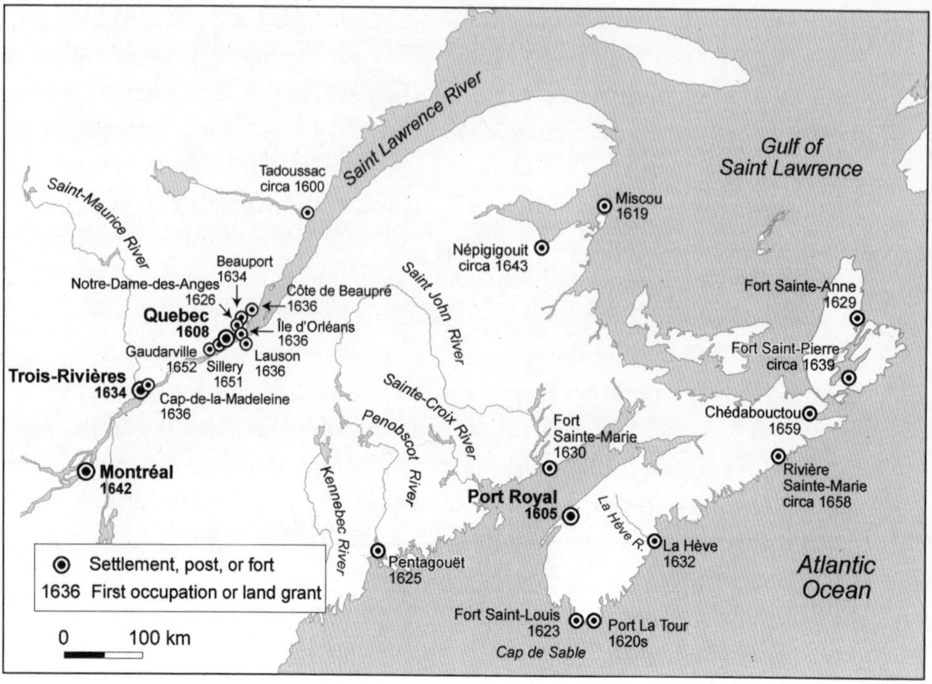

Figure 6.2 Principal French settlements in Acadia and the Saint Lawrence Valley, 1628–63.

the Fronde in the late 1640s. More immediately, however, with the loss of connections to the royal inner circle, the CNF found itself competing against other title-holders – some of whom it had put there itself – and new corporate bodies in New France.

By the time of Richelieu's death, fifteen years after the CNF's founding, the combination of delegated authority, trading privileges, and land concessions had had a visible, if modest, effect in the various regions under the enterprise's jurisdiction (see figure 6.2). The company had, from the beginning, granted land with the aim of off-loading part of its colonizing obligations and responsibility to distribute land to others. As land tenure was feudal, most was granted *en fief* or *en censive*.[63] It then fell to the seigneur to recruit settlers to clear and cultivate his estate. For example, Isaac de Razilly recruited three hundred men in 1632, assumed to be mostly labourers, soldiers, and sailors. It was only four years later that families were included among those transported to La Hève with the help of company agent Nicolas Denys at La Rochelle. The archival record gives only a partial view of concessions granted in Cape Breton, but Desportes did grant land to four individuals in 1633–34.[64] Given its status as the centre of the CNF's operations, the Saint Lawrence Valley saw the most subinfeudated land grants. Some seigneurial concessions preceded the company's arrival, such as that of Notre-Dame-des-Anges, granted to the Jesuits by the Duc de Ventadour in 1626. Both these and the first of the CNF's grants were concentrated around Quebec. During this period, recipients were primarily company associates or employees and religious orders.[65] In 1635–36, the CNF granted six fiefs to various associates. Among these was Beaupré, on the Saint Lawrence across from Île d'Orléans, granted to eight influential and active associates, including Cheffault, Rozée, Lauson, and Berruyer.[66] By 1645, the company had conceded a total of twenty-two tracts of land. The granting of land did not, however, translate necessarily into clearing, peopling, and cultivation. Of those twenty-two grants, sixteen remained more or less inactive. While religious orders and individuals could offset some of the CNF's colonizing obligations, their demand for workers was limited and thus they could not be a long-term source of recruits.[67] The mounting conflict with the Haudenosaunee also slowed settlement as those granted land west of Quebec were ordered to return. By Richelieu's death, the population in the Saint Lawrence Valley – if far from the four thousand envisioned – had nevertheless increased from around two dozen in 1632 to almost six hundred twelve years later.[68]

Like the colony's settlement, its infrastructure had developed gradually over the previous decade and a half. Quebec remained a small town with few concessions to individuals. Fort Saint Louis, on the heights overlooking the river, was not yet complete. In the developing Upper Town, religious and company establishments predominated. Here was the Ursuline convent, the headquarters of the CNF, and a makeshift Jesuit college, chapel, and presbytery in a company building, following a fire in 1640. Beyond Quebec, the most visible signs of French presence were the recently built forts at Trois-Rivières, Montreal, and the mouth of the Richelieu River. Governmental authority in the Saint Lawrence Valley, encompassing civil and military matters as well as justice, was concentrated in the hands of Montmagny, governor general since 1636.[69] This modest growth in infrastructure and settlement was to shape how the CNF fared in and responded to the new transatlantic political climate.

Besides external developments, the CNF was facing a fraught internal situation at the beginning of the 1640s. The company's financial burden had reached a critical point. From 1639 to 1645, it went through the process of debt liquidation. Royal commissioners assigned to investigate the company's finances concluded that the company owed a total of 410,796 livres, covering everything from salaries and wages to soldiers, officers, and the governor to loans from outside individuals and corporations, CNF members, and the two compagnies particulières. The king accordingly ordered each associate to pay a total of 4,527 livres 8 sols over a period of four years.[70] Entangled with the debt repayment were demands for new contributions to finance the annual voyage. In 1642, for example, the directors asked the associates for 1,500 livres. This financial pressure precipitated numerous suits. Both the CNF's directors and associates made multiple representations before the royal council for, respectively, condemnation of those with outstanding payments and permission to withdraw or confirmation of having done so. By the end of these proceedings, sixty-four associates remained in the company, a situation that rendered the task of raising funds for the annual voyage that much more difficult.[71]

It is in this transatlantic context that negotiations began for the transfer of control of the fur trade and administration in the Saint Lawrence Valley to the inhabitants themselves. With the support of the Jesuits, the newly formed Communauté des Habitants (CH) sent delegates to France to negotiate with the CNF's directors in 1644. Presenting the fur trade as the only means to entice current and future settlers to stay, delegates Pierre Legardeur de Repentigny, lieutenant to the governor, and Jean-Paul Godefroy, son of a CNF associate and a former interpreter under Champlain, reached an agreement with the company in January 1645, which was subsequently ratified by the regent. The company underscored the sacrifice of its interests for the good of the colony: "The said Company could have given no better demonstration than to deprive itself of the means to recover in future all the said expenses [it had made], as it did by relinquishing and abandoning the said trade to the profit of the said inhabitants, who desired and demanded it with great insistence, as the only way to increase and strengthen the said colony."[72] According to the articles, the CNF would retain "the names, titles, authorities, rights, and powers that were given to it by the Edict of its establishment … in full property, possession, justice, and Seigneury of all the countries and extent of land of New France," as well as the right to choose the governor, lieutenant general, and officers of justice, and grant licences to travel to the colony. It ceded to the CH, or the inhabitants collectively, the fur trade extending west from Miscou "as far as the limits of the said company extend." The community could not alienate any part of the trade without the company's permission. In return, the inhabitants undertook to pay annual seigneurial dues in the form of "a thousand weight of assorted beaver," provide for the colony's ecclesiastics, governor, lieutenant general, and soldiers, maintain forts and habitations, bring twenty people annually to New France, and recover debts owed the CNF. In short, the company kept its governmental powers but ceded those associated with the colony's administration.[73]

As with the company it was ostensibly under, the CH represented a new form of governance and capital formation, one without equivalence in France, even if it was an amalgam of several existing institutions. In some respects, the delegation of administration and trade to the CH resembled other grants by subinfeudation. It became a subordinate landlord, owing fealty and annual dues to the CNF as seigneur. Its sublease included responsibility for peopling and administering the land in exchange for the exercise of the company's trading privileges, an arrangement that recalls individual seigneurial concessions in Acadia. In other respects, the CH resembled a subsidiary trading company, in keeping with the long history of commercial associations in New France and the more recent history of the CNF's compagnies particulières. Like its predecessors, it was to enjoy exclusive privileges to the fur trade, the profits from which were to cover all expenses, including modest colonizing responsibilities and the payment of salaries of colonial officials; its members, the inhabitants, were to receive dividends; and twelve elected directors were to manage its affairs. Here, however, the similarities ended: the community had no pooled capital divided into shares; its members were not necessarily associates of the CNF; their eligibility derived from their status as residents of the Saint Lawrence Valley rather than a contribution to the capital fund; and the body bore full responsibility for the colony's administration and maintenance costs.[74] The organization's functioning, then, would not follow exclusively the logic of either a trading company or a subinfeudated land grant.

If the CH's focus on trade brings to mind a commercial company, its inclusion of all inhabitants recalls the communautés d'habitants in towns and rural areas throughout France.[75] These were corporate groups uniting all heads of household of a town or rural parish, thus excluding sons living under their father's roof, women (with the exception of widows), and servants. The community took charge of goods or property collectively owned, such as common pastures, maintained local order, managed the collection of the various taxes owed to the Crown, and was responsible for the community's relationship with the seigneur. In these functions, it played an indispensable local role and relieved the Crown of the responsibility for local government. When an issue needed to be addressed, the syndic elected by the inhabitants called an assembly; at the end of deliberations, the most prominent members signed the record.[76] These individuals tended to dominate a given community. As we have seen, in the port of Saint-Malo, where the wealthiest inhabitants were merchants, the community concerned itself primarily with the protection of its commercial privileges and the diminution of those of other ports. Its syndic lobbied frequently at court to overturn the exclusive trading privileges to New France granted to the viceroy and, through him, to other merchants.[77] The community thus served as an effective lobby group for the dominant interests in a given town or rural parish.

As "natural bodies," communautés d'habitants did not require royal letters patent to exist in law, but they did nevertheless enjoy certain protections under the king.[78] Like its metropolitan counterparts, the CH took charge of administration, collected outstanding debts, and assumed responsibility for common property, in this case the fur trade. The inhabitants petitioned the king on several occasions, including a request to be included under a more general decree granting protection from creditors to all communautés d'habitants in France.[79] The selective adoption of key elements of a familiar institution thus gave the inhabitants of New France a recognized legal status.

The main difference between the CH and its metropolitan counterpart lay in the nature of its property and source of revenue. Where the latter controlled pasture, salt marshes, and fuel and owned vineyards, houses, and woodland, the former managed the fur trade and provided for the habitations.[80] It was, in this sense, an original form of local government. Not wholly a communauté d'habitants, a trading company, or a subinfeudated lord, the CH's in-between status reflects the adaptation of metropolitan institutions to the colonial environment, the particular dynamics of the fur trade, and the intertwining of governance and commerce in the colony.[81]

The centrality of trade in the governance of New France demanded considerable commercial expertise and networks. The CH had to acquire and outfit ships, trade with its Indigenous partners, and sell the furs in France in exchange for merchandise and provisions. The notable-dominated organization largely lacked the knowledge crucial to the smooth running of this large-scale transatlantic commerce.[82] Whereas the CNF had merchant members like Jean Rozée of Rouen whose networks it could draw on to obtain the best rates, the CH depended largely on CNF associates and outside merchants. Unlike the company, it had no pooled capital through which to fund voyages; the intent was that profits from the fur trade would cover all expenses. It had, as a result, to take out multiple loans from the outset. In 1645, the community relied on loans from CNF associates at the modest rate of 5.5 per cent interest. From the second year of operations, however, the bulk of loans were *à la grosse aventure* (or bottomry) with much higher rates of interest, usually 20 to 30 per cent for an overseas voyage. Legardeur de Repentigny, for example, converted his loan granted at 5 per cent interest the previous year into a bottomry at 25 per cent interest in 1646; twenty years later, the community had paid only two-thirds of it back.[83] While Repentigny was himself a member of the CH, the majority of loans came from Rochelais merchants, who were accused of charging "excessive interest" in 1665.[84] Having borrowed more than 80,000 livres from forty-two creditors in 1649 alone, the community found itself owing over 200,000 livres in principal and interest by 1652.[85] This state of affairs made it difficult for the CH to carry out its administrative responsibilities in the colony and pay its annual seigneurial dues, a source of considerable friction with the CNF.[86]

Royal and Corporate Interests Realign in the Saint Lawrence

The new role of the CH prompted a shift in the balance of power across the Atlantic and within New France itself. The transfer of control over administration to a body based in a given colony was not singular to New France, of course, but was common among the plantation companies of English America in the same period. Both the Plymouth Company (established 1620) and the Somers Island Company (established 1612) saw a colonial government replace councils in England. While this shift occurred at a different point in the history of each – eight years after the Plymouth Company's founding compared to seventy years after that of Somers Island – both were prompted in part by changes in share distribution on the two sides of the Atlantic. By 1628 and the 1680s, respectively, the majority of shareholders resided in the colonies and owned shares in land.[87] In some ways, then, transfers of government from Europe to North

America reflected a certain stage of colonial development, particularly with regard to land distribution and settlement. As with the English companies, the establishment of the CH removed primary decision-making power from the metropole and placed it in the hands of a few groups in New France. It was up to the CH to make decisions on economic matters and the maintenance of fortifications and habitations, to choose when and how to distribute dividends from the fur trade among the inhabitants, and to manage the community's assets in such a way as to ensure financial solvency and provide for the colony's subsistence. Under the CNF to 1645, the directors and associates dealt with these matters at weekly meetings and general assemblies in Paris.[88] The CH's directors, for their part, met in the colony. They appointed a clerk to manage the French end of the community's business and a head of the fleet for the annual voyage and granted power of attorney as needed to enter contracts with merchants.[89] The CNF had a similar arrangement, but in the converse: it had a chief clerk in New France, the directors met regularly in Paris, and associates in Atlantic ports handled the company's operations there.

What distinguished the CNF-CH arrangement from that of the Plymouth and Somers Island Companies was the effect on the company. Whereas the transfer of government to colonists on the part of the latter led to the dissolution of the companies themselves, the CNF continued to exist as seigneur, parent company, and governor. Indeed, the same year that the CH obtained control of the fur trade, Montmagny was renewed for a fourth term as governor general at the request of the company. There were thus two bodies sharing authority in the Saint Lawrence.

With control of the fur trade under the CH, the CNF saw its seigneurial and governmental authority marginalized, highlighting the intimate relationship among these jurisdictions. The CH, anxious to assert its newfound privileges and powers, challenged the prerogatives of the CNF in several areas. In the spring of 1646, for example, the CH's head of the fleet, Pierre Legardeur, Sieur de Repentigny, refused to accept the CNF's chief clerk, Olivier Letardif, on board his vessel. Letardif had in hand a commission from the latter's directors "giving him the power to act in the recovery of all debts and other rights belonging to the said company."[90] Armed with letters and commissions for the colony's officials, Letardif was to be a passenger on the CH's ships according to the terms of the 1645 treaty. When Repentigny demanded that he hand over the letters, Letardif refused, protesting that "he had been appointed by Messieurs the directors of the Compagnie de la Nouvelle-France." In other words, he was a servant to the company, not to the inhabitants. Refused passage, Letardif and the CNF sought redress in the Admiralty court at La Rochelle; in the meantime, they were forced to find another ship to take him to New France.[91]

Although this incident could be seen merely as a typical flexing of muscle by a privilege-holder, it is more broadly reflective, together with the cession of trade to the CH, of new transatlantic political alignments and royal interests. The community's testing of how far it could use its newfound powers against the larger CNF recalls the Compagnie de Rouen et Saint-Malo's attempts to subordinate Champlain in the 1610s. But whereas in the latter case there was some overlap in areas of jurisdiction and the company paid the lieutenant's salary, the 1645 treaty left little ambiguity about the relationship between the CNF and the CH. The former ceded certain administrative powers and its trading privileges to the latter in exchange for annual seigneurial dues, modest colonizing obligations, and the transportation of CNF personnel, among other responsibilities. Under this arrangement, the CH was a subordinate landlord and subsidiary company. In the words of the company's representatives before the Admiralty court: "[Repentigny/the CH] depends on and is vassal of the said company and possesses nothing in the country except by its fief [*bénéfice*]."[92]

The role of the king in each power struggle points to the change in the CNF's transatlantic position since the deaths of its two patrons. Despite the murkiness of the line between Champlain's and the Compagnie de Rouen et Saint-Malo's respective jurisdictions, the former was able to obtain written confirmation of his commission from the king himself, while the latter had no avenues at court independent of the lieutenant.[93] In contrast, evidence suggests that the queen regent actively encouraged the CH in its marginalization of the CNF. A Rochelais merchant on board the ship at the time of Letardif's confrontation with Legardeur testified in the ensuing court proceedings that Legardeur claimed he was acting on orders from the community and the regent.[94] The cession of trade itself one year earlier appears also to have been politically motivated and made under duress. In a *mémoire* of 1663 outlining the considerable financial sacrifices made for the colony's development, the company opined that the 1645 agreement had "strip[ped] it of that which was most valuable and the only means to compensate it," but that this was done "to obey the will of the Queen mother of the King."[95] The pressure brought to bear on the company came only one year after the queen regent appointed a viceroy of New France for the first time since 1627. If Richelieu had been the colony's de facto viceroy, it was a position he nevertheless exercised through the company. The appointment of Viceroy François-Christophe de Lévis-Ventadour, Comte de Brion, Duc de Damville, the Duc de Ventadour's brother, clearly conflicted with and undercut the CNF's prerogatives and authority (even as it marked a return of the position to the Montmorency clan).[96]

These three developments together highlight a well-established pattern of transatlantic governance by which new monarchs, ministers, and viceroys replaced privilege-holders with their own clients, or at least those outside the client networks of their predecessors. Anne of Austria had perhaps particular reason to view with hostility those within the circle of her deceased husband and his minister. Having maintained close ties to her Spanish homeland and its court, she had long had tense relations with Louis XIII and Richelieu, particularly with the outbreak of war between the two countries in 1635, and she had fallen under suspicion for having passed information about French plans to Spain. The establishment of a new corporate body in New France aimed at the direct management of the fur trade fit well with the regent's assertion of authority overseas and at home and the pursuit of her own agenda.

The cession of trade in 1645 integrated another recently formed corporate body into the colony's governance structure. The Société de Notre-Dame de Montréal was founded in 1639 by dévot Jérôme Le Royer, Sieur de La Dauversière, and Pierre Chevrier, Baron de Fancamp and president-treasurer of France for the generality of Picardy, with the goal of establishing a colony in New France to convert Indigenous people to Christianity. Educated at the Royal College of La Flèche, both men were closely tied to Jesuit circles and had Jesuit confessors. Le Royer, as well as several subsequent members of the Société de Notre-Dame, were also connected to the Compagnie du Saint-Sacrement, the secret organization founded by Ventadour to re-Catholicize French society. The Montreal venture was thus part of the broader Catholic Reformation. At the end of 1640, the CNF ceded most of the island of Montreal to Le Royer and Chevrier "in full property, justice, and seigneury." According to the terms of the cession, the company retained the power to build and man forts as well as to appropriate land for this use within the ceded territory. The seigneury's courts were to fall within the appellate jurisdiction of a "Parlement or sovereign court that shall be hereafter established by the company at Quebec or elsewhere in New France" and, until that time, were under

Governor Montmagny at Quebec. Although the society's members could trade for furs for their own use, they could not do so commercially. As seigneur of Montreal, the Société de Notre-Dame could only grant lands to new arrivals from France. In keeping with the CNF's arrangements with individuals in Acadia and Cape Breton, any new settlers would count toward the company's quota of four thousand men and women.[97]

While this concession was a fairly straightforward seigneurial grant, the Société de Notre-Dame soon obtained much greater autonomy. It took the somewhat unusual move of seeking confirmation of the cession from the royal council. In addition to granting this request, the latter gave it the supplementary power to name its own governor, an act that removed the body from under the authority of the CNF. The society accordingly named Paul de Chomedey de Maisonneuve, a young military officer, to the position. It was in fact through Charles Lalemant, the procureur of the Jesuit mission in New France, that Maisonneuve, who was interested in contributing to the latter enterprise, met Le Royer and became a member of the society.[98] That Governor General Montmagny did not return to the island of Montreal after 1643 illustrates the considerable autonomy enjoyed by the new body and Governor Maisonneuve.[99]

When the Communauté des Habitants took over the administration of the fur trade in 1645, four years after the arrival of the first Montreal settlers, the Société de Notre-Dame became more integrated into the colony. As holders of concessions from the CNF, the two bodies entered an agreement a few days after the cession of trade. The terms included the establishment of a trading warehouse at Montreal maintained at the expense of the CH, which also committed to maintaining the island's forts and supporting its ecclesiastics from 1648 onward, in keeping with its obligations under the cession of trade. For the Société de Notre-Dame's part, it could participate and vote in CH assemblies at Quebec and review the community's annual report and the accounts of its clerks in France. A later addendum put the CH in charge of all transport on the part of the society, including the sending of goods to France free of charge, in exchange for a fixed sum.[100] If this agreement consolidated the CH's authority in the areas of administration and trade, it also gave it the burden of responsibility. The Société de Notre-Dame, conversely, emerged from the negotiations in a more influential position in the colony at little cost.

Reforms two years later aimed to address the shortfalls of the system established under the CH. By 1646, various interested parties, including *petits habitants*, the Jesuits, and associates of the CNF residing in the colony, were voicing complaints about the CH's management: the inhabitants were no longer allowed to trade individually with their Indigenous allies, as had been customary under the CNF; in a breach of its obligations, the CH was not covering all of the Jesuits' maintenance costs; and the CH's directors were keeping all the power and benefits to themselves.[101] These protests culminated in a delegation of three – Montmagny's secretary, Guillaume Tronquet, Montreal governor Chomedey de Maisonneuve, and Robert Giffard, seigneur and CH director – to France in order to "pursue some regulation for a resolution to their business." In response, the queen regent appointed three commissioners, Élie Laisné, Sieur de la Marguerie, Jean-Antoine de Mesmes, Sieur d'Irval, and Antoine Barillon, Sieur de Morangis, to study the situation in New France. Appointed to the royal council since the deaths of Richelieu and Louis XIII, all three were members of or closely tied to the Compagnie du Saint-Sacrement and the Société de Notre-Dame.[102] Their report led to a "regulation for the establishment of a good order and police in Canada," which created the Conseil de Québec in 1647.[103]

The first of its kind in New France, the council consisted of three members, Governor General Montmagny, Governor Chomedey de Maisonneuve, and the superior of the Jesuits, Jérôme Lalemant, brother of Charles. Syndics elected by the inhabitants of Quebec, Montreal, and Trois-Rivières could attend when the council discussed matters concerning the CH but had no vote. The body was charged with regulating the fur trade, managing the colony's finances, ensuring public safety, and making appointments; in other words, it assumed the responsibilities formerly undertaken by the CH's directors. Addressing directly the complaints voiced against the CH, the regulation reopened the fur trade to all inhabitants, specified the amount of money to be spent on the support of garrisons and missionaries, and limited the terms of directors.[104] If the CH was now under the stewardship of the council, the continuation of the community's directors in prominent roles and the limited representation of inhabitants led to renewed lobbying the following year. The royal commissioners accordingly expanded the council to include the governor of Trois-Rivières, any former governor general residing in the colony, and two or three inhabitants chosen by the syndics and the other counsellors; each member now had a vote. While the composition and doubling of council members suggests an attempt to balance various interests, representation remained narrow, as the queen regent chose the first three inhabitants, all of whom were former directors of the CH.[105]

The year 1648 likewise saw changes to the governor general's term and confirmed the CNF's marginalization within the colony's government. Following Montmagny's twelve-year tenure, appointments were limited to three years. Anne of Austria replaced him with Louis D'Ailleboust, Sieur de Coulonge. A dévot and member of the Société de Notre-Dame since its formation, D'Ailleboust had served as Chomedey de Maisonneuve's lieutenant on the island of Montreal since 1641 and had commanded the annual fleet in 1647. The CNF associates had originally approached the governor of Montreal about the position, but the latter declined in favour of his subordinate. Although D'Ailleboust was subsequently put forward as one of the CNF's nominees, as per the company's prerogatives, the customary statements mentioning the latter's nomination and the governor general's obligation to ensure the execution of the CNF's edict were absent from the letters patent. Worried about the "recognition of the rights of the said company," the CNF protested these omissions and "asked that such provisions be reformed when they are sent every three years."[106] The absence of the customary clauses, in contrast to Montmagny's prolongation three years earlier, reflected more broadly the company's diminished position in the colony since 1645.

At the same time that the developments of 1647–48 arguably helped to streamline the administration of New France, they also consolidated the position of authority of ecclesiastical and dévot interests that aligned with the queen regent's agenda. Both the Société de Notre-Dame and the Compagnie du Saint-Sacrement enjoyed considerable access to the regent. As the commissioners assigned to address the complaints against the CH attest, members of one or both organizations served on the royal council. The Compagnie du Saint-Sacrement had another connection through Vincent de Paul, who sat on the regent's new Conseil de Conscience.[107] Together with Chomedey de Maisonneuve's and D'Ailleboust's presence on the Conseil de Québec, the choice of commissioners points to Anne of Austria's receptivity to the mandate and ambitions of the Société de Notre-Dame in New France. Even the Jesuits, who, having been particularly close to Richelieu, were more critical of the Crown following his death, played an important role in the colony's reorganized government.[108] Jérôme Lalemant, one of three (and eventually seven) counsellors, enjoyed considerable say in the day-to-day management of the colony's affairs. Indeed, in 1651, those entrusted with outfitting ships, obtaining merchandise, and entering agreements with merchants were not to make any decisions without his consultation. If an agent borrowed money without the Jesuit's express consent, he would be liable "in his proper and private name."[109] The influence of the three religious companies is evident in the stated end of the fur trade in a decree of 1649. First and foremost, it ensured "the maintenance of the mission."[110]

The collaboration between the Catholic Church and the Crown in New France during the 1640s had strong echoes with the 1620s. Then, too, a missionary was to be consulted on all matters affecting the colony's governance. Indeed, both Le Baillif and later Lalemant initially expressed reluctance to take on such a political role before relenting.[111] Transatlantic events provided an opening for the strengthening of ecclesiastical influence. In the 1620s, the renewal of conflict between the monarchy and Huguenot subjects in the kingdom and the establishment of Récollet and Jesuit missionaries in New France contributed to this development. Two decades later, the change in monarch, chief minister, and other members of the royal circle, as well as the creation of new corporate bodies across the Atlantic, led to a similar result. The evangelizing objectives of dévots and religious orders combined with those of the Crown in both periods to lead to a shift in the balance of power among groups and a new program in the colony.[112] Unlike in previous years, however, the CNF found itself on the losing end in the 1640s. It was notably absent from the Conseil de Québec and its nominated governor had less power than he did in 1645. The particular nature of colonial institutional development in both decades underscores the importance of the link between royal connections and the exercise of effective authority in New France.

Sovereign Interests and Feudal Authority in Acadia

The CNF's outsider status in the Laurentian colony was reproduced in Acadia during the same period. Since 1632, the two lieutenants general for Acadia, Isaac de Razilly and Charles de La Tour, developed their habitations, recruited settlers, and shared the profits from the fur trade. Sometimes arranging for the transport of provisions on the same ship, they exercised their shared jurisdiction over the region in a general spirit of co-operation.[113] With Razilly's death at the end of 1635 and his replacement by Charles Menou d'Aulnay, his cousin and a naval captain, this entente began to unravel. Menou had been present in Acadia since 1632, when he participated under Razilly's command in the restitution of Port-Royal from the English. He subsequently became his lieutenant. In 1635, on Razilly's orders, he successfully recaptured the post at Pentagouet between the Penobscot and Kennebec Rivers (in present-day New Brunswick and Maine), which the English had continued to possess following the conflict between the two powers. Razilly's death gave Menou the opportunity to pursue his ambitions to bring all authority in Acadia under himself. Sometime between 1636 and 1638, Menou became the king's lieutenant general in Razilly's stead, with the consent of Claude de Launay-Razilly, who continued to manage the Compagnie pour la côte d'Acadie from France. Menou was named chief clerk of the company in 1636. While the competition between him and La Tour did not date from the former's succession to Razilly's title, Menou's newfound authority heightened existing tensions between them. Louis XIII's attempt to clarify these jurisdictions in 1638 was hopelessly confused and only served to exacerbate the situation. Confirming La Tour as seigneur of Fort Saint-Louis at Cap de Sable and Fort Sainte-Marie on the Saint John River and Menou as seigneur of Port-Royal and La Hève, the king proceeded to appoint each the lieutenant general in the area surrounding the other's concessions.[114] He also transferred Pentagouet, which the CNF had put under the command of Claude de La Tour, Charles's father, in 1636, to Menou at the latter's request and without the permission of the company.[115]

The decree's maladroitness transformed simmering tensions into outright aggression in Acadia. In 1640, La Tour's forces attacked Menou's ships in the Annapolis Basin as the latter were returning to Port-Royal from Pentagouet. Withstanding the assault, Menou seized the opportunity to make his case against La Tour at court, assembling testimonials from his men, the Capuchins of Port-Royal, and some of La Tour's men who had been captured in the standoff.[116] La Tour, for his part, refused to heed a summons to Paris to explain his actions. On this and subsequent occasions, Menou returned with royal letters authorizing him to arrest La Tour and seize his property. Skirmishes between the two continued over the next five years, with the violence on both sides and the charges against La Tour – who sought reinforcements from the English in Boston on several occasions – escalating in equal measure.[117] In the meantime, Menou had consolidated his position in the Compagnie pour la côte d'Acadie in 1641–42, having received an honorary share from the associates as well as those of Launay-Razilly, become the steward of the shares owned by the Capuchins in the colony, and entered an agreement with a wealthy and prominent Rochelais merchant, Emmanuel Le Borgne, to outfit ships, provide loans, and serve as his representative in the port.[118] By 1645, La Tour had long since retreated to Fort Sainte-Marie on the Saint John River, having abandoned Fort Saint-Louis at Cap de Sable to Menou, who burned it down. In the spring of that year, while La Tour was away in Boston, Menou's force took the Saint John River fort, imprisoning La Tour's wife and killing or hanging the garrison. The latter fled to Quebec, where he spent the next four years. Menou, for his part, was richly rewarded with a commission of governor and lieutenant general over all of Acadia in 1647. The defeat of La Tour had led to nothing less than the installment of a viceroy in the region.[119]

The CNF became directly involved in the feud between La Tour and Menou in its capacity as the parent company of regional subsidiaries. Following the sea battle between the two adversaries in the Annapolis Basin in 1640, the widow of one of La Tour's men killed in the conflict had a ship belonging to the Compagnie pour la côte d'Acadie seized upon its arrival in La Rochelle. This action brought both Menou and the CNF directors before the Admiralty of La Rochelle and the Conseil privé to request the release of the ship and its merchandise as well as the payment of damages.[120] Five years later, the company again found itself in court in support of a subsidiary, only this time the directors were fervently against Menou. Having captured La Tour's fort on the Saint John River and forced him to flee, Menou had ordered a ship, *Le Cardinal*, to patrol the coasts of the Gulf of Saint Lawrence for any ships illegally trading in furs. On the Richebouctou River, located on the western coast of present-day New Brunswick, *Le Cardinal* came upon a ship, *La Madeleine*, belonging to the Compagnie de Miscou, which had received the CNF's trading privileges in the area in 1635. Acting on Menou's orders, *Le Cardinal*'s captain seized the ship, its crew, and merchandise. This aggression prompted the Compagnie de Miscou and the CNF to appear before the Admiralty of La Rochelle to request permission to seize *Le Cardinal* and its contents. Once granted, the sentence was appealed by Menou before the Parlement of Paris. The requests and counter-requests continued over the next two years.[121] In both disputes, the CNF came to its subsidiaries' aid in a comparable way to past viceroys when a privileged company faced challenges from without.

It was in this highly charged context that the queen regent accorded Menou his extensive and generous commission of 1647. Granted jurisdiction from the Saint Lawrence River to Virginia, Menou received substantial regal powers, including "to commit, establish, and appoint all Officers, both of War and of Justice and Order (*Police*) … have established Laws, Statutes, and Ordinances … negotiate and contract peace, alliance, and confederation with the said Peoples, their princes or others having power and command over them, make open war upon them to establish and conserve our authority … have built and constructed Cities, Forts, Ports, Harbours, and other places … and generally do for the conquest, settlement, habitation, and conservation of the said countries, lands, and coasts of la Cadie … in our Name and Authority all that we would do, if we were there in person."[122] The commission resembled those of previous viceroys of New France like Condé and, more recently, Damville – indeed, it even reproduced whole passages from those earlier documents. Like Damville's commission, this one undermined the CNF's prerogatives in a variety of respects, ranging from its geographical extent to its regal powers. The company's response was fast and furious. In a factum, it outlined its case against Menou, accusing him of illegitimately holding the title of lieutenant following Razilly's death, usurping the company's authority in having himself named lieutenant general and governor in 1641 and 1647, and committing "piracy."[123] While this latter charge referred to the seizure of the Compagnie de Miscou's ship, it may also have encompassed Menou's subsequent sacking of the settlements of other CNF-appointed title-holders, notably Desportes in Cape Breton and Nicolas Denys in the Gulf of Saint Lawrence.[124] Following this public denunciation, the CNF's directors continued legal proceedings against Menou and, after his death in 1650, his widow and heirs. In 1652, they demanded that the latter be "declared stripped of all and any rights by them claimed in the said lands and settlements of the said New France, which will be and remain reunited under the domain of the said company … this being done without regard to the letters patent in the form of a declaration of His Majesty of the month of February 1647 that will be declared void."[125] Swept aside by the politicking, connections, and chutzpah of Menou, the CNF was only able to regain this portion of its jurisdiction after the death of its redoubtable rival.

The conflict pitting Menou against first La Tour and then the CNF highlights the ways in which subjects overseas fought for ascendancy by linking their actions with sovereign interests and concerns. The extant decrees and correspondence show that Menou invoked royal sovereignty, portraying himself as the sole champion of French dominion in Acadia and his opponent as an accessory to a possible English takeover. Writing in September 1647 to his well-placed protector at court, Chancellor Pierre Séguier, Menou declared that, if it were possible, "I would soon return them [the lands of his commission] to the obedience of His Majesty notwithstanding all the resistance that foreign Protestants could make who have usurped them from France by the negligence or the Powerlessness of the French who have been here before me." The presence of Protestants in La Tour's entourage, including his wife, and his probable conversion no doubt helped Menou's cause.[126] The latter's loyalty and service to the king were frequently juxtaposed against La Tour's "open rebellion" and acts of treason. In 1645, following the fall of La Tour's Saint John River fort, both Anne of Austria and the young Louis XIV praised Menou for having foiled "the evil designs and collusion that the Sieur de La Tour had with some foreigners to the detriment of the King."[127] One year earlier, a royal decree had forbidden any subjects in the forts from helping La Tour "on pain of being declared rebels and accused of treason."[128] Charges of treason levelled at fellow countrymen and competitors were not unusual in the far reaches of empire. Areas accessible only by river posed a particular danger to authority, putting those who frequented them "beyond reach of patronage and punishment."[129] It is no coincidence that, as the conflict between La Tour and Menou escalated, the former retreated to his fort on the Saint John River, an area far from Port-Royal and much easier to defend – and, not incidentally, especially rich in furs.

Apart from its remoteness, the Saint John River region held particular significance for French sovereignty in North America and, as such, was a place where charges of treason were particularly potent. Lying to the northeast of New England, it was the part of Acadia most accessible from that English colony. The security of the region had been a particular concern since 1621, when William Alexander had received his grant of "New Scotland," extending from the Sainte-Croix to the Saint Lawrence Rivers, thereby directly challenging French claims. In collaboration with the Kirke brothers, who had a commission to capture Quebec, Alexander and his son took over Port-Royal in 1629, establishing a fort and small colony. Although they remained there for three years, the treaty between the English and French monarchies in 1632 returned both settlements to the

French.[130] The earlier English capture of the region fuelled concern among the French about future attempts, particularly from Massachusetts. When La Tour sent emissaries, and then went himself, to Boston to seek both a trading alliance and ships and men to fight Menou, the latter skilfully used these supplications to heighten existing fears of English Protestant encroachment.[131] If the English took the Saint John River fort, it would not only deprive the colony – and Menou personally – of much-needed profits from the most lucrative region of the fur trade, it would also give the English a clear path to the peninsula and Port-Royal. That La Tour's father, Claude, had previously collaborated with the English on plans for the colonization of Acadia after his capture by the Kirke brothers in 1628 only seemed to confirm Charles's disloyalty.[132] As in the 1620s, confessional issues shaped geopolitical concerns.

Charges of treason overseas were serious in any context, but they had particular force during times of rebellion in France. When Menou appeared before the royal council in 1642 with his story of La Tour's attack in collaboration with a group of Bostonians, the Crown had just put down the Cinq-Mars rebellion, which was an attempt on the part of a favourite of the king, Henri Coiffier de Ruzé, Marquis de Cinq-Mars, to wrest power from Richelieu. Six years later, following the end of the Thirty Years' War, *parlementaires*, princes, and nobles engaged in a series of civil wars known as the Fronde. Menou capitalized on the anxieties at court over the loyalty of French subjects to consolidate his authority. When he exceeded his instructions, such as when he set fire to La Tour's fort and surrounding settlement at Cap de Sable in 1641, or challenged other commissions, there were no repercussions.[133] The domestic context may explain in part why Menou received more or less carte blanche from the king and queen regent to apprehend La Tour and reaffirm royal control over the region.

Menou was not the only colonial commander to take advantage of the political instability in France to bolster his own authority. Putting New France in an Atlantic frame allows us to see that, along with the West Indian islands, it was a site of experimentation with a single repertoire of tools of privilege granting, governance, and capital formation. Title-holders faced the same challenges of building and maintaining royal support and of countering the pretentions of competing or subordinate claimants. The CNF's counterpart in the Antilles, the Compagnie des îles de l'Amérique, appointed a captain general in each island but exerted little control over them in practice. From 1648 onward, these men engaged in their own conquests of neighbouring islands. If these acquisitions appeared to extend the company's jurisdiction, the captains general considered themselves independent of any other authority.[134] The Compagnie des îles de l'Amérique had, in short, several Menous who ruled in the islands in close proximity to one another. This volatile situation erupted into an islands-wide civil war in the mid-1640s, what one historian has labelled a "colonial Fronde."[135] The initial power struggle involved two island governors. Since 1639, Philippe de Longvilliers de Poincy, Knight of Malta and one-time associate of the Compagnie pour la côte d'Acadie, had held the position of the king's lieutenant general of the islands and governor (or captain general) of Saint-Christophe on behalf of the Compagnie des îles de l'Amérique.[136] From the start of his mandate, Poincy attempted to build up a personal power base by putting the government of other islands under those close to him. In the early 1640s, the company appointed one of its own members, Charles Houel, son of a founding director of the CNF, governor of Guadeloupe. Houel and Poincy, both ambitious men who wielded their authority with a heavy hand, came into conflict almost immediately. When the two parties sought resolution from the company and royal council in France, Poincy took advantage of Houel's absence to try to install another governor in Guadeloupe.[137]

Having received complaints about Poincy's conduct from various quarters, and worried about his hold on power, the company associates requested that the queen regent recall him. She replaced him with one of her clients, Patrocles de Thoisy, and sent a *lettre de cachet*, or secret royal order, often of a disciplinary nature, to Poincy, ordering him to relinquish his post and return to France to defend his actions. When Thoisy arrived in the islands, however, he was unable to land at Saint-Christophe.[138] Poincy prepared to defend himself by force, entering an agreement with the English, who inhabited part of the island, banning all company personnel and anyone who sided with Thoisy, and ensuring continued provisions through trade with the Dutch.[139] This open defiance precipitated a full-out battle between the two men and their supporters over the next two years; the conflict also expanded to other islands as inhabitants took the opportunity to voice their own grievances. Although Thoisy initially received asylum at Guadeloupe, he and Houel soon fell out over their respective jurisdictions, leading to the former's expulsion and refuge at Martinique.

This protracted state of civil war prompted the royal council to intervene. In a decree of 25 February 1647, the council permitted Poincy to remain as lieutenant general for one year; his nephew, who had been governor of Saint-Christophe since the mid-1640s, would retain his position for six months. Thoisy would then take over as lieutenant general and put someone in charge on Saint-Christophe. In the meantime, he was to exercise his position in the rest of the islands from his base in either Martinique or Guadeloupe. The council also ordered Poincy to restore the seized belongings of company personnel and any inhabitants who had fled Saint-Christophe. To ensure that these orders were followed, a commissioner would be sent to the islands.[140] The council's attempt to strike a compromise between entrenched rivals was, however, overtaken by events. While the council had been deliberating, Martinique's inhabitants had handed Thoisy over to Poincy, who had him imprisoned before sending him back to France. Poincy continued as lieutenant general; Thoisy never returned to the islands.[141]

While the circumstances surrounding the struggles in the two colonies were not identical, the comparison is revealing for what it says about the means to claim and enforce authority in the context of competing title-holders. At first glance, the greatest parallel is between Poincy and La Tour. Both attacked their rivals' positions and then defied royal orders to return to Paris to explain their conduct. Certain of punishment at home, La Tour and Poincy dug in and put up a formidable fight. Armed revolt on the part of princes or nobles was not uncommon in France, particularly when royal power was weak. As we saw in the case of Condé, it did not automatically lead to charges of treason and imprisonment; it could, instead, be a route to negotiation.[142] The decree of 1647, which gave Poincy a way to leave honourably, was, to a degree, evidence of the success of the defiant lieutenant general's actions. Here, according to conventions of noble revolt, was an opportunity for the latter to surrender and admit his wrongs. But Poincy was not interested in compromise, much less surrender; he intended, rather, to keep his lieutenant general's position. That this break with convention did not result in armed action on the king's behalf likely reflects the descent into civil war in France. For La Tour's part, he left his refuge at Quebec and returned to France to defend himself and seek a pardon following Menou's death in 1650. In the battle of charges and counter-charges, there were endless possibilities for resurrection. What had been "the evil designs" of a "very bad Frenchman" became "accusations and conjectures that they [La Tour's enemies] could not prove." La Tour's contrition, the lack of an obvious successor to Menou in Acadia, and the weakness of a regency beset by civil and foreign war all contributed to the restitution of his title.[143]

Disobedience of royal orders aside, Poincy drew on a set of strategies that were similar to Menou's. Both assembled their own forces, which they used against their rivals and any who dared to side with them. They frequently stretched the boundaries of their commissions. For example, Poincy used his lieutenant general's commission to appoint a governor in Houel's stead, a power he did not possess. Menou, for his part, claimed jurisdiction beyond the region granted when he ordered the seizure of ships trading in the Gulf of Saint Lawrence. Through these and other actions, the two men declared war on the company with seigneurial, commercial, and governmental authority in their respective regions. While the two had different relationships to each company – Poincy had been appointed by the Compagnie des îles de l'Amérique's associates; Menou had no connection to the CNF other than as lieutenant of the Razillys – they both refused to recognize the companies' authority. Poincy capitalized on existing discontent to incite the inhabitants of Saint-Christophe and neighbouring islands against the associates and agents of the Compagnie des îles de l'Amérique.[144] Just as Poincy punished supporters of the company, Menou targeted the settlements of the CNF's lieutenants and long-time collaborators in Acadia. If Menou fashioned himself as the protector of sovereign interests and made frequent appearances at court while Poincy hunkered down and disobeyed orders, both were ultimately working to expand their own feudal power base in their respective regions.

The CNF and the Compagnie des îles de l'Amérique found themselves in a similarly defensive position in the 1640s. Founded under Richelieu, peopled with his clients, and with overlapping personnel, both companies suffered from the loss of their patron in 1642. In the CNF's case, the changes to authority in both the Saint Lawrence and Acadia reveal a systematic undermining of the company's jurisdiction. Unlike Richelieu and Montmorency, Anne of Austria looked outside the company form to other types of corporate bodies, such as the Société de Notre-Dame, whose goals fit with her own. She also rewarded the strong-arm tactics of Menou, who could count on the support of Chancellor Séguier, second only to Cardinal Mazarin in power.[145] The Compagnie des îles de l'Amérique, for its part, had to contend with captains general who routinely exceeded their powers and treated the islands as their own private fiefs, a typical enough behaviour on the part of officers in early modern France. In contrast to the CNF's experience, the queen regent backed its Antilles counterpart in its dispute with Poincy. The reasons for this difference are various. While the strategic importance of Acadia and proximity of the English favoured tolerating Menou's indiscriminate use of force, Poincy's tightening hold on the islands threatened royal authority and stability. The replacement of the lieutenant general also gave the regent an opportunity to appoint one of her own clients to the highest position in the islands. Royal support of the company did not, however, last beyond the decree of 1647. When it became clear that Poincy had no intention of ceding his authority, the associates looked to the regent to enforce the decree, but no action was taken.[146]

The consequences of the companies' marginalization were of different degrees and duration in each case. For the Compagnie des îles de l'Amérique, the 1647 decree failed to resolve the conflict with Poincy. The latter continued to act independently while the company continued to struggle to control various island governors. In the long-term, Poincy's actions and the absence of royal enforcement of the decree contributed to the associates' decision to sell the islands in the early 1650s.[147] The royal letters patent confirming the sale of Saint-Christophe to the Order of Malta even praised Poincy's governance of the island. Like La Tour, therefore, the lieutenant general eventually obtained a pardon and continued as governor until his death in 1660.[148] Faced with simultaneous attacks on their authority in Acadia and the Saint Lawrence, did the CNF associates adjust their strategies to meet the changed circumstances? Extant sources show that they pursued judicial avenues, submitting remonstrances, issuing a factum, and fighting lawsuits throughout the decade. It is difficult to know, however, whether they also tried unofficial routes to negotiate with the queen regent. Did they offer her something in return for upholding their privileges and authority? Did they make overtures to new members of the royal council or others at court, as Champlain and de Mons had during the previous regency? The available evidence suggests that the CNF associates stuck to the same strategy, continuing to favour and rely on those long associated with the enterprise, such as Nicolas Denys. While it is difficult to say what role this strategy played in the outcome, the CNF's loss of authority proved to be short-term and reversible, in contrast to the experience of the Compagnie des îles de l'Amérique.

The same year that La Tour returned to the position of lieutenant general of Acadia, the CNF began to regain its footing in government and the administration of trade in the Saint Lawrence. In 1651, the process for selecting a new governor of New France respected the company's prerogative to nominate three candidates, from which Lauson was ultimately chosen. One of the new governor's first measures was the establishment of a *sénéchaussée* court, a type of seigneurial tribunal, in keeping with the CNF's rights to exercise high, middle, and low justice. A royal decree at the end of the decade confirmed the *sénéchaussée* courts of Quebec and Trois-Rivières as courts of first instance, with appeals to be heard by either the governor or the Parlement of Paris, depending on each case's importance.[149] More significantly, the company established a presence and power on the government council from which it had originally been excluded.

In the mid-1650s, vocal representations by the CNF led to further reorganization of trade management in the colony. Appearing before the royal council, company representatives presented the associates' grievances: the cession of trade to the inhabitants in 1645 had not had the beneficial effects they had intended, notably the growth of the colony; the inhabitants "did not have more liberty in the said trade than they had before it was left to them"; nor was the Conseil de Québec able to pay all of the colony's routine expenses or the seigneurial dues owed the company. They accused the council, "established unbeknownst to the said supplicants," of reserving all the merchandise, and thus benefits, to only the most powerful inhabitants. In response, royal counsellors created a new set of regulations for the council, henceforth named the Conseil de la Traite, which largely reflected the company's requested reforms.[150] The council would be composed of the governor, a CNF director (for a three-year term), four elected councillors (two from Quebec and one each from Trois-Rivières and Montreal), and the company's *procureur fiscal*. All decisions were to be made by plurality. While half of the merchandise for the trade would be distributed to inhabitants, the other half would go in the public storehouse and the profits subsequently put toward the colony's annual expenses. Besides its representation on the council, the company would receive all accounts relating to trade as well as government, and annual seigneurial dues were to be paid just after all ordinary expenses.[151]

The 1650s saw the CNF retrieve its place in the supervision of trade and the colony's finances. Adopting a confident tone in its appeals to the royal council, it was now the instigator, rather than the casualty, of changes in governmental structures. If this transformation was helped by the end of the regency in 1651, the measures taken in the 1650s were part of the decades-long search for viable ways to fulfill the company's extensive mandate and render the venture profitable. From de Mons's commission, title-holders, whether individual or corporate, had tried to cover expenses with profits from the fur trade. The CNF's tenure was a particularly rich period of experimentation with different forms of delegation to achieve this goal. While in Acadia the company (and Crown) granted various combinations of trading privileges, land concessions, and authority to individuals, the Saint Lawrence was a site of corporate and institutional experimentation. In the latter case, proposed solutions to the thorny question of financial viability reveal that trade and governance were not simply intertwined but that a large part of governance *was* the problem of fur trade management. This question would continue to shape approaches to governance and patterns of authority in the following decades.

EPILOGUE

The Struggle to Shape French Imperial Expansion

The opening of the 1660s brings us full circle to a set of circumstances remarkably similar to those that led to the establishment of the Compagnie de la Nouvelle-France in the mid-1620s. In February 1663, the company associates, following a request from King Louis XIV, returned New France to the royal domain: "as undeniable proof of [the] profound respect and complete deference of the said Company to the will of His Majesty, its directors and secretary hereby relinquish to His Majesty the property and seigneury of the said country."[1] On a domestic level, Louis XIV had reached his majority in 1651, bringing the regency to a close. The end to the Fronde two years later gave the Crown the opportunity to restore order and stability to the realm, just as the siege of La Rochelle had twenty-five years earlier. At the same time, the death of Chief Minister Cardinal Mazarin in 1661 precipitated a succession battle between two of his favourites, Nicolas Fouquet, *surintendant des finances* and attorney general, and Jean-Baptiste Colbert, *intendant des finances*.[2] On an international level, the 1660s were another important moment of consolidation and reconfiguration in the areas of sea power and commerce across European empires in the Atlantic. While England founded the Royal African Company at the start of the following decade, Denmark and the Netherlands created or reorganized their respective West India Companies.[3] Renewed attention to French maritime security, commerce, and navigation in this period was at once propelled by and part of these larger European and Atlantic contexts.

As in the 1620s, the sea was a key site for the power struggles among royal ministers and other office-holders motivated by both royal and personal ambitions. Much as Admiral Montmorency had spent the 1610s strengthening his supervision of maritime traffic by buying out rival admirals and governors and sending agents to French ports to collect dues owed him, Nicolas Fouquet, son of François, Richelieu's primary representative in several commercial and colonizing enterprises, embarked on a program of maritime regeneration, investing in overseas companies, acquiring strategically important islands, and placing clients in important maritime posts.[4] From Colbert's perspective, Fouquet's maritime activities looked more like a threat to the king's authority than a renewal of coastal infrastructure on his behalf. They also made the junior official jealous of his influence. Colbert's engineering of Fouquet's fall is well-known. Through regular reports of the latter's latest maritime activities from his cousin and *intendant de la marine* at La Rochelle and his own close study of the surintendant's accounts, he assembled a substantial dossier with which to condemn his rival.[5] Like Richelieu, after whom he modelled himself, Colbert aimed to standardize and consolidate fragmented maritime authority under himself. Believing, too, that the security and prosperity of king and realm lay in a strong navy and merchant marine, Colbert considered companies and colonies essential to realizing these objectives.

The late 1650s and early 1660s saw growing financial, military, and socio-political challenges in New France. The heavily indebted Communauté des Habitants was unable to meet the substantial annual expenses associated with the colony's administration. Exacerbating the situation, increasing warfare with the Haudenosaunee had cut off French access to the most lucrative areas of the fur trade and precipitated repeated calls for reinforcements from France that largely went unanswered. The CNF, faced with a dwindling membership, lacked the funds itself for such an expensive operation. As was the case forty years previously, internal conflict among colonial authorities, this time between missionaries and governor, led to pilgrimages to the royal court to seek redress.[6] In 1660, however, New France was not the only colony that found itself in a difficult situation. The West Indian islands that had been under individual and corporate proprietors since the early 1650s were facing similar and multiple challenges, including irregular access to goods and provisions, internal conflicts – ranging from revolts over high taxes to disputes over land claims and family feuds – and external competition from the English and Dutch. Meanwhile, further to the south, repeated attempts to establish a settlement at Cayenne on the coast of South America, as a site from which to launch attacks on Spanish shipping, had ended in disaster.[7] The critical junctures at which several colonies found themselves encouraged the implementation of the ambitious plans for maritime and commercial renewal underway as a result of the new metropolitan circumstances.

When the associates of the CNF tendered their resignation in 1663, they requested compensation in proportion to the money they had spent on the colony's establishment and maintenance over the previous thirty years. Reimbursement, however, was not forthcoming, in contrast to the substantial sums granted to West Indian proprietors in exchange for giving up their titles.[8] The associates and their heirs appealed to the royal council to distribute the compensation owed on several occasions over the following two decades. While their initial requests totalled between 900,000 and 1,200,000 livres, the associates saw the amount reduced to a fraction of that in 1687: 60,000 livres in principal and 73,000 livres in interest, for a total of 133,000 livres. It is worth recalling that de Caën and the Compagnie de Montmorency, whose operations had been much smaller, had received 150,000 livres from the CNF. Almost thirty years after the associates resigned, the remaining associates or their heirs received barely more than the sum they had originally invested for a share in the enterprise.[9]

The year 1663 has long been seen as a turning point in early Canadian historiography. It is the moment when, New France having fallen into disarray yet again – due in part to the negligence of the Crown – Louis XIV and Colbert take over administration, funnelling much-needed military, financial, and material resources and transplanting provincial institutions to the colony.[10] This book thoroughly challenges this narrative of rupture. Comparing the 1660s with the 1620s demonstrates that the concerns, plans, ambitions, and strategies of king and minister would have been recognizable to predecessors forty years previously – and, indeed, even earlier. New France's becoming a royal colony can only be understood as part of the longer history of the developing repertoire of tools of governance, capital formation, and privilege granting of the previous half century. Seen in this context, it becomes a story of continuity, of continued experimentations rather than a fresh start. More significantly, the circumstances of the early 1660s are emblematic of several aspects of the story of the developing repertoire told in this book: they are transatlantic and international; they are linked to struggles over sea power; they involve personal and institutional rivalries; and they highlight the entangled processes of state and empire formation.

This book demonstrates the imperative of going beyond the national histories of early Canada and early modern France. New France and France were interconnected spaces. To contemporaries, overseas colonizing and commercial activities were a domestic issue, one that had a direct impact on fishermen's customary rights, ports' standing, and provincial autonomy. New France was in turn connected to larger developments in both France and Europe. As the sea became increasingly important to building and maintaining power at home and abroad, control over the colony was a means to strengthen control over Atlantic trade routes. New France thus became a site of experimentation with the company form, by which the innovations of the Dutch and English models were combined with previous experiences in the colony. Resituating New France in these currents foregrounds the maritime and colonial dimensions of state formation in France. At the same time, this frame highlights the dynamism that characterized empire formation in New France.

The Atlantic was a meaningful legal and geographical space in which legal and governmental practices and commercial and colonizing instruments circulated. While this book has focused particularly on transatlantic linkages, it has also illuminated the interconnections between New France and the French West Indies, a subject that deserves more attention from scholars. Both were sites of a developing repertoire of tools of governance, privilege granting, and capital formation in the same period. In their unique ways, the Compagnie de la Nouvelle-France and the Compagnie de Saint-Christophe both fit into Louis XIII's and Richelieu's maritime objectives in the mid-1620s. When the CNF became the model for the revamped Compagnie des îles de l'Amérique, the same investors supported both enterprises. Closely tied to Richelieu, both companies had to contend with the strong-arm tactics of competing title-holders following his death. The two regions were, of course, not identical; their colonizing histories as well as the structure, objectives, and outcomes of their colonizing and commercial enterprises varied. Putting New France and the West Indies into the same frame, however, underscores the role of local circumstances, metropolitan political, commercial, and legal contexts, and international experimentations with the company form in shaping the constellation of authority, power, and privileges in the Atlantic.

The study of this evolving constellation destabilizes existing understandings of the early modern French Empire, specifically, and Atlantic empires, more generally. The empire portrayed here is quite different from the one described in existing histories of the French Atlantic.[11] Always in the making, this empire was a messy, ramshackle enterprise, one that responded to pressures from within and without, was composed of multiple visions, and that was negotiated and contested among French subjects themselves. This conception highlights the dynamism and experimentation that characterized the first half of the seventeenth century. When put alongside other Atlantic empires, the developing French Empire resists easy categorization. It shared a similar repertoire of tools with its Dutch and English counterparts. At the same time, it resembled its Iberian neighbours in its strong Catholic ideology and centralizing monarchy. By looking at the evolving forms of power and authority that developed in transatlantic political, legal, and commercial contexts, this book has presented the French Empire on its own terms as another variation on imperial forms.

Studying the full range of French actors involved in the colonization of New France foregrounds the multiple agendas that shaped the developing repertoire of tools of privilege granting, governance, and capital formation. In the eyes of contemporaries, royal commissions, privileges, and legal documents and institutions were all instruments to be leveraged in the service of particular interests. Rather than a plan to be followed to the letter, royal commissions set the terms for negotiation over the nature and duration of the powers, authority, and privileges contained therein. Both Chauvin and de Mons negotiated exclusive privileges to the fur trade and, in the latter's case, a reduction in the number of settlers he was required to transport. At the same time, other title-holders came forward to have their own jurisdictions confirmed, as Charles de La Tour did in response to Isaac de Razilly's becoming lieutenant general of New France in 1632. Negotiations aside, commissions encouraged title-holders to push their authority as far as they could. In the 1640s, Charles Menou d'Aulnay seized ships and demanded dues far beyond the boundaries of his, albeit extensive, commission in Acadia. De Mons and his agents, for their part, aggressively pursued suspected interlopers (sometimes to a fault), while the latter defiantly and openly flouted the ban on trade. Although it is tempting to see such actions as evidence of the inefficacy or abuse of commissions, this type of armed negotiation was at their heart. Royal responses varied widely, depending on such factors as domestic and international political circumstances. While Menou saw his strong-arm tactics rewarded, the terms of de Mons's commission became increasingly restricted.

The fundamentally relational character of privileges led to regular changes in their boundaries and terms. Always for someone and against someone else, privileges had to be weighed against each other. Exclusive privileges to the fur trade may sound absolute, but in the context of the culture of privilege in France, contemporaries – king, title-holders, and opponents alike – understood them to be elastic. Thus, the inhabitants of Saint-Jean-de-Luz requested an exemption within the privileged trading zone of the Compagnie de Montmorency in 1620, brandishing in support previous royal confirmations of its privileges to travel to that area. Fifteen years earlier, the royal council chose not to enforce the fine of 30,000 livres in contravention of de Mons's privileges as a way to enjoy the continued support of provincial corporate bodies on whom the king depended. De Mons, for his part, submitted several proposals to the king, each with a different circumscribed trading zone, in an effort to respond to the opposition that had led to the revocation of his privileges in 1609. If all parties involved actively shaped their parameters, privileges needed to be constantly (re-)earned. The Compagnie de la Nouvelle-France thus found itself paying compensation to de Caën and the Compagnie de Montmorency despite its close ties to Richelieu.

In these contests over privileges and power, the French legal system became an integral forum for the construction of sovereignty and authority across the Atlantic. Litigation over company compensation, trading privileges, and the respective jurisdictions of title-holders functioned as a sort of second act to events overseas. Claimants rarely launched just a single suit; rather, they were involved in several at once, one sometimes in retaliation for another. The costs notwithstanding, litigants like Guillaume de Caën and Samuel Georges used their intricate knowledge of judicial procedure and the justice system to prolong and delay suits in court. A popular strategy, it was designed to wear down and bankrupt an adversary. Indeed, in most cases the goal was to *not* resolve a dispute, even when it was internal to a company. Courts, then, were another tool in claimants' repertoires, just like commissions or force. The stakes were high. Not merely disputes over the seizure of ships or merchandise, these suits constituted struggles for supremacy over the fur trade of New France, inter-port standing, and the direction and administration of the fledgling colony. French courts of justice thus played an important role in the struggle to shape imperial expansion.

Traditional and innovative methods combined to influence empire and state formation. On the one hand, the inability of any one party to hold on to their privileged claims for long highlights the quintessentially personal nature of power in the early modern French Atlantic. Each new viceroy, minister, or monarch wished to install their own clients in existing positions and create or support a different set of institutions than those of their predecessors. Both Montmorency and Richelieu as admiral/grand maître and viceroy also bought out rival claimants to consolidate their power. On the other hand, new instruments, like the chartered company, developed alongside these traditional forms. While the company form allowed Montmorency, Richelieu, and later Colbert to supervise the circulation of subjects and goods along major trade routes, it was also a vehicle to wrest naval, commercial, and political power from strategic ports like La Rochelle and provinces like Brittany. The first chartered company in the Atlantic, the CNF combined previous arrangements in the colony – viceroy, lieutenant, and trading company – with the joint-stock structure. A second corporate body that emerged during the company's tenure, the Communauté des Habitants, was an original form of local government, merging a traditional communauté d'habitants in France, a trading company, and a subinfeudated lordship. If the new body suited Queen Regent Anne of Austria's desire to assert her newfound authority at the expense of the company, it was also a creative way for notable families of New France to put governance and control of the fur trade in their hands. In this way, thoroughly traditional metropolitan forms of privilege and legal, political, and commercial structures gave rise to novel arrangements in the spaces of New France.

This book has offered an expanded conception of what companies were in the seventeenth century. Participants in the New France enterprise (and in the French Atlantic more broadly) experimented with different scales and types of organization and degrees of involvement, ranging from the loose partnerships among ports of the Compagnie de Mons and the Compagnie de Rouen et Saint-Malo to the *société en commandite* of the Compagnie de Montmorency to the chartered universal companies and the Compagnie de la Nouvelle-France. Companies also assumed varying configurations of sovereignty, authority, and privileges. While the Compagnie de Rouen et Saint-Malo had no seigneurial or administrative responsibilities and retained its commercial jurisdiction only as long as the particular viceroy with whom it had contracted remained in his position, the CNF delegated its seigneurial, judicial, and commercial powers and privileges to varying degrees in the Saint Lawrence Valley and Acadia over its thirty-five-year existence. These different arrangements among and within companies created a patchwork of legal, political, and personal relationships among associates, title-holders, subsidiaries, and the king. The study of French enterprises highlights the range of possibilities in the company form and in the role of companies in imperial visions.

The difference between the French, Spanish, Dutch, and British Empires lay in the nature of state involvement in overseas enterprises and the corporate groups the state called upon for resources and organizational support.[12] Royal regulation of traffic to and activity in New France increased over the period covered by this book. It was neither linear nor inevitable. During the first two and a half decades of the seventeenth century in particular, dependence on certain corporate bodies – communautés d'habitants, parlements, and estates – led the king to abruptly restrict, revoke, or dilute powers and privileges granted. Protest against the CNF was milder than against previous companies, in part because Richelieu had become the principal protector and governor of Brittany, traditionally home to the most vocal opposition. From the 1620s, other corporate bodies emerged as key enablers of projects to strengthen royal control of maritime security, commerce, and colonization. Prominent among CNF associates and those to whom the company delegated a portion of its colonizing obligations were financiers, religious orders, and lay societies, all of whom had a long history of supporting royal initiatives. The story of the CNF is just the most prominent example in this book of the overlapping of commercial, political, and religious/Catholic interests that lay at the heart of French empire (and state) formation, overturning the all-too-common tendency to put these elements in opposition. They may not have always been complementary, but their interactions helped to shape the forms of power and authority that developed.

While the legal, political, and commercial institutions in which the French negotiated and contested claims among themselves did not recognize Indigenous sovereignty, the latter had an important impact on the forms of French power and authority that developed in early seventeenth-century North America. Beyond the Saint Lawrence River, French mobility was limited and depended on Indigenous knowledge and guidance. Champlain's expeditions along interior waterways only went as far north and west as the Algonquins and Wendats permitted.

Wishing to preserve their own role as intermediaries in diplomatic and trade relations with the French, the latter controlled French knowledge of interior waterways, lands, and peoples. French power and authority were concentrated in a few trading posts. While the French aimed to incorporate Indigenous Peoples as subjects through Christianization and francization, Indigenous bands understood their interactions with the French within the framework of alliance. They adopted select Christian beliefs and French practices in a spirit of openness and tolerance toward an ally's culture, to strengthen the alliance, and to acquire further protection for war, subsistence, and other activities. Similarly, mixed unions could increase the status of women and their kin networks within their own community. If the French had to conform to the Indigenous logic of alliance, alliance presented its own advantages. It provided the means to expand French sovereignty through Indigenous territorial control in the context of a lack of material power and authority.

Although this book ends in 1663, the story of experimentation with tools of governance, capital formation, and privilege granting does not end there. While the Compagnie de la Nouvelle-France wrapped up its affairs, the king, via Colbert, established the Compagnie des Indes occidentales with commercial, seigneurial, and governmental jurisdiction over not only New France but also the West Indies and slave trading posts in West Africa. In New France, the company joined existing institutions unique to the colony like the Communauté des Habitants as well as newly established ones comparable to those in a French province, notably an intendant and a parlement-like Conseil souverain. Each of these authorities had their own claims to commercial, judicial, and political jurisdiction. As had been the case during the first half century of French colonization, the king and his ministers had to work with these individuals and institutions and vice versa. It was this collaborative and conflictual relationship that shaped the contours of royal involvement in overseas enterprises throughout the seventeenth century.

Notes

Abbreviations

ADCM: Archives départementales de la Charente-Maritime
ADIV: Archives départementales d'Ille-et-Vilaine
ADSM: Archives départementales de Seine Maritime
AN: Archives nationales
Arch. mun. de Saint-Malo: Archives municipales de Saint-Malo
BnF: Bibliothèque nationale de France
Coll. mss: *Collection de manuscrits contenant lettres, mémoires, et autres documents historiques relatifs à l'histoire de la Nouvelle France, recueillis aux Archives de la Province de Québec, ou copiés à l'étranger, mis en ordre et édité sous les auspices de la législature de Québec, avec tables, etc.*
Corresp. gén.: Correspondance générale
Dépt de mss: Département de manuscrits
Docs inédits: *Relation originale du voyage de Jacques Cartier au Canada en 1534: Documents inédits sur Jacques Cartier et le Canada*
EO: *Édits, ordonnances royaux, déclarations et arrêts du Conseil d'état du roi concernant le Canada*
HNF: *Histoire de la Nouvelle France*, Marcel Trudel
LAC: Library and Archives Canada
MC: Minutier central des notaires de Paris
Mém des comm.: *Mémoires des commissaires de Sa Majesté Très-Chrétienne et de ceux de Sa Majesté brittannique* [*sic*]
NAF: Fonds nouvelles acquisitions françaises
Nouv. docs: *Nouveaux documents sur Champlain et son époque*

Introduction

1 Champlain, *Works*, 5:6–7. In the final stages of this project, a new French-language edition of Champlain's writings appeared: *Oeuvres complètes de Champlain*, edited by Éric Thierry (Quebec: Septentrion, 2019).
2 A recent example is Fischer, *Champlain's Dream*.
3 For a discussion of recent literature that takes this approach, see Dewar, "Agents, Institutions and French Empire/State Formation," 89–94.
4 Church, *Constitutional Thought in Sixteenth-Century France*; Piant, "Encadrement judiciaire des populations locales et concurrence des juges sous l'Ancien Régime," 125–6.
5 Desbarats and Greer, "North America from the Top Down," 133; Tomlins, *Freedom Bound*, quotation at 5–6. On the application of metropolitan judicial institutions to the New France context from 1663 onward, see Gilles, "Les acteurs de la norme coloniale face au droit métropolitain"; Wenzel, "'Afin que ceux qui aspirent aux charges de judicature puissent estre instruits,'" 67–78.
6 Benton, *A Search for Sovereignty*, 33.
7 For the perspective that they were petty quarrels among greedy merchants, see Biggar, *The Early Trading Companies of New France*. For the argument that they disrupted the supposedly linear process of colonization, see Trudel, *HNF*, vol. 2. For their omission from discussion altogether, see Fischer, *Champlain's Dream*, chap. 17, esp. 377–8.
8 On the development of this institution in the Eurasian trade, see Harris, "Trading with Strangers," 88–118.
9 The beginnings of this revised view may be traced to Elliott, "A Europe of Composite Monarchies," 48–71. For examples of the literature on the early modern French state, see Collins, *The State in Early Modern France*; Hildesheimer, *Du siècle d'or au grand siècle*; Cornette, *Affirmation de l'État absolu*; Drévisson, *Les rois absolus*; Carrier, *Le Labyrinthe de l'État*; Aubert et al., *États, pouvoirs et contestations dans les monarchies française et britannique*.
10 Beik, *Absolutism and Society in Seventeenth-Century France*, 31–2, 219, 281; Brewer, *The Sinews of Power*, 12–17.
11 Braddick, *State Formation in Early Modern England*, 6.
12 Hindle, *The State and Social Change in Early Modern England*; Hardwick, *Family Business*.
13 Descimon and Cosandey, *L'Absolutisme en France*; Hurt, *Louis XIV and the Parlements*. Revisionist examples include Parrott, *Richelieu's Army*; Rowlands, *The Dynastic State and the Army under Louis XIV*.
14 Breen, "Law, Society, and the State in Early Modern France," 377. In 1989, David Parker urged French historians to pay more attention to legal practice. See "Sovereignty, Absolutism and the Function of the Law in Seventeenth-Century France," 36–7.

15 Among these studies are Breen, *Law, City, and King*; Debordes-Lissillour, *Les Sénéchaussées royales de Bretagne*; Hardwick, *Family Business*; Lanza, *From Wives to Widows in Early Modern Paris*; Schneider, *The King's Bench*.

16 See, among others, Mancke, "Empire and State," 193–213; Mancke and Reid, "Elites, States, and the Imperial Contest for Acadia," 25–47; Muldoon, *Empire and Order*, esp. 8, 145–6. For a recent critique of this approach, see Roper, *Advancing Empire*, 8–9.

17 Benton, *A Search for Sovereignty*, 31, quotation at 56; Mancke, "Empire and State," 200.

18 See, for example, Swingen, *Competing Visions of Empire*.

19 Burbank and Cooper, *Empires in World History*, 17; Sheehan, "The Problem of Sovereignty in European History," 1–15; Stoler, "On Degrees of Imperial Sovereignty," 125–46.

20 Tomlins, *Freedom Bound*, 5–6; Tomlins, "Law's Empire," 26–45; MacMillan, *The Atlantic Imperial Constitution*, 1–2; MacMillan, *Sovereignty and Possession in the English New World*.

21 Roper and Van Ruymbeke, "Introduction," 10.

22 Another major approach to chartered companies has been economic, evaluating how well they performed as firms. This literature tends to see seventeenth-century chartered companies as part of the developments leading to the modern corporation. See, among others, Carlos and Nicholas, "Giants of an Earlier Capitalism," 398–419; Ekelund and Tollison, "Mercantilist Origins of the Corporation," 715–20; Gelderblom, de Jong, and Jonker, "The Formative Years of the Modern Corporation," 1050–76; Jones and Ville, "Efficient Transactors or Rent-Seeking Monopolists?," 898–915; North, "Institutions, Transaction Costs and the Rise of Merchant Empires," 22–40. For a work that attempts to put these two approaches together, see Wagner, *The English Chartered Trading Companies*.

23 Scammell, "English Chartered Trading Companies and the Sea," 24; Pettigrew, *Freedom's Debt*; Swingen, *Competing Visions of Empire*. See also Antunes and Miranda, eds., "Bankruptcies in the Context of Empire." This literature builds on an older one that examined these enterprises in the context of European expansion. See Erikson and Assenova, "Introduction: New Forms of Organization and the Coordination of Political and Commercial Actors," 5–6. On the need to explore economic institutions in their social and political contexts, see Stern and Wennerlind, "Introduction," 4–5; Røge and Reinert, "Introduction: The Political Economy of Empire," 5–6.

24 Adams, *The Familial State*, 4, 20. For the role of Dutch companies in state warfare, see Brandon, *War, Capital and the Dutch State*, esp. chap. 2.

25 Stern, "'Bundles of Hyphens,'" 21; Phillips and Sharman, *Outsourcing Empire*, 7–9. See also Barkan, *Corporate Sovereignty*, 4–6.

26 Desbarats, "La question de l'État en Nouvelle-France," 187–98. See also Hodson and Rushforth, "Absolutely Atlantic," 111.
27 Dechêne, *Power and Subsistence*, 5, 97.
28 Greer, *Property and Dispossession*, 18–19.
29 Havard, *Empire et métissages*; Lozier, *Flesh Reborn*. See also Morrissey, *Empire by Collaboration*; Cook, "Onontio Gives Birth," 165–93; Cook, "'Vivre comme frères.'"
30 Delâge, "L'alliance franco-amérindienne 1660–1701," 1–15; White, *The Middle Ground*; DuVal, *The Native Ground*.
31 Desbarats and Greer, "Où est la Nouvelle-France?," 31–62; Desbarats and Greer, "North America from the Top Down," 109–36; Lennox, *Homelands and Empires*.
32 Comparative works that give the French Empire attention, however cursory, include Benton, *In Search of Sovereignty*; Pagden, *Lords of All the World*. More sustained attention is given in Greer, *Property and Dispossession*; Burnard and Garrigus, *The Plantation Machine*.
33 Bosbach, "The European Debate on Universal Monarchy," 87–8, 92–8.
34 Due to the constraints of this study, the first two modes will be the primary focus.
35 For the argument that they were not in fact representative of the chartered companies of the time, see Roulet, "Introduction," 8–9.
36 Trudel, *HNF*, 3.1:18–9; Bonnassieux, *Les grandes compagnies de commerce*; Chailley-Bert, *Les compagnies de colonisation sous l'Ancien Régime*.
37 Harris, *Going the Distance*, 326–7; Phillips and Sharman, *Outsourcing Empire*, 104. For a deeper analysis of the different groups the state called upon for resources and organizational support, and the effect of this relationship on chartered companies in the Dutch Republic, France, and England, see Adams, *The Familial State*, chaps. 2 and 4. For a recent study that foregrounds the role of non-state actors, and especially company directors, in French chartered companies of the late seventeenth and early eighteenth centuries, see Heijmans, *The Agency of Empire*.
38 On the role of English and Dutch municipalities in overseas enterprises, see Adams, *The Familial State*, 54, 122–32.
39 Stern, *The Company-State*. A growing literature on the developing British Empire is challenging the notion that chartered companies did not play a role in the imperial policy of the state. See, for example, Mishra, *The Business of State*; Pettigrew, *Freedom's Debt*; Swingen, *Competing Visions of Empire*.
40 Adams, *The Familial State*, 32–6.
41 In 1608, for example, Champlain, along with François Gravé Du Pont, a loyal agent of de Mons, and other officers, sentenced to death Jean Duval, locksmith, and his three accomplices for their plot to assassinate Champlain.

While Duval was executed at Quebec, the three others were sent to France for execution. See Thierry, *La France de Henri IV en Amérique du Nord*, 291–3.

42 See, for example, Biggar, *The Early Trading Companies of New France*; Trudel, HNF, vol. 2.

43 For the ultimate sentences in these cases, see Arrêt de Parlement de Rouen, 25 June 1633, 1B 981, ADSM; Arrêt de Parlement de Rouen, 12 July 1633, Extraits des diverses séries, LAC.

44 Kagan, *Lawsuits and Litigants in Castile*; Carrier, "Virtuosité procédurière."

45 Benton, *A Search for Sovereignty*, 24.

46 Braddick, "State Formation and Social Change in Early Modern England," 10.

47 Cis-Atlantic history is "the history of any particular place – a nation, a state, a region, even a specific institution – in relation to the wider Atlantic world" and allows for the transcending of "artificial, but nonetheless enduring, divisions between histories usually distinguished from each other as internal and external, domestic and foreign, or national and imperial." See Armitage, "Three Concepts of Atlantic History," 24, 25.

48 For two seminal works on the French Atlantic, see Banks, *Chasing Empire Across the Sea*, and Pritchard, *In Search of Empire*. For recent special issues on the French Atlantic, see Vidal, ed., "L'Atlantique français," special issue, *Outre-mers* 96, nos. 362–3 (2009); Desbarats and Wien, eds, "La Nouvelle-France et l'Atlantique," special issue, *Revue d'histoire de l'Amérique française* 64, nos. 3–4 (Winter–Spring 2011); Le Glaunec, Fick, and Furstenberg, eds, "L'Atlantique français et ses frontières: Résistances, circulations, savoirs," special issue, *Revue d'histoire de l'Amérique française* 71, nos. 1–2 (Summer–Fall 2017).

Chaper One

1 "Edit du Roy contenant le pouvoir et commission … au Marquis … de la Roche," 12 January 1598, Extraits des diverses séries, LAC. All translations are my own unless otherwise noted. "Norumbega" was a term used to designate a region in what is today New England. Hochelaga refers to the village of the Saint Lawrence Iroquoians, where Montreal now is.

2 On the geographical ambiguity of the term "Canada" (as well as "New France") throughout the sixteenth, seventeenth, and eighteenth centuries, see Desbarats and Greer, "Où est la Nouvelle-France?," 31–62. On the similarity between these commissions and those for newly incorporated provinces in France, see Ruggiu, "Colonies, Monarchy, Empire and the French *Ancien Régime*," 197–8.

3 Biggar, ed., *A Collection of Documents Relating to Jacques Cartier and the Sieur de Roberval*, 181–2, quotation at 181.

4 The exceptions are Roberval's commission, which related the ban to evangelizing goals, and La Roche's commission granted by Henri III in

1578, which granted him the title of lieutenant general in exchange for the obligations undertaken. See *A Collection of Documents Relating to Jacques Cartier and the Sieur de Roberval*, 182–3; appendix 2 in Champlain, *Des Sauvages*, 202.

5 "Edit du Roy contenant le pouvoir et commission … au Marquis … de la Roche," 12 January 1598, Extraits des diverses séries, LAC.

6 "Privilege" in Nicot, *Thresor de la langue françoyse, tant ancienne que moderne* (emphasis added).

7 Bossenga, *The Politics of Privilege*, 5.

8 Appendix 3 in Champlain, *Des Sauvages*, 209. Coujugon does not appear in other letters patent nor on maps of the period. Its exact location is unknown.

9 Registre des délibérations des États de Bretagne, 16 March 1588, C 2642, ADIV. A *communauté d'habitants* was a corporate group uniting all the keepers of a hearth in a town or rural parish. In *pays d'état*, the estates were a body comprising the province's three orders (clergy, nobility, and commoners).

10 Appendix 3, Champlain, *Des Sauvages*, 212–13.

11 Appendix 5, Champlain, *Des Sauvages*, 218–25, quotations (in order of appearance) at 219, 222; Biggar, *The Early Trading Companies of New France*, 44–6; Liebel, *Pierre Dugua, sieur de Mons*, 72–4.

12 "Articles proposés au roi par le sieur de Monts," 6 November 1603, C11D, LAC. A gentleman in ordinary of the king's chamber (*un gentilhomme ordinaire de la chambre du roi*) was one of thirty to forty noblemen in this position in the king's household since Henri III (1551–1589). The gentlemen ordinary served either three months per year or one out of every two years. See Marion, *Dictionnaire des institutions de la France aux XVIIe et XVIIIe siècles*, 348; Mousnier, *Les institutions de la France*, 2:117–18.

13 The full text of the vice admiral's commission is found in Lescarbot, *History of New France*, 2:219; Liebel, *Pierre Dugua, sieur de Mons*, 75–7.

14 "Articles proposés au roi par le sieur de Monts," 6 November 1603, 28v, 30v, C11D, LAC; Fischer, *Champlain's Dream*, 152; Binot, *Pierre Dugua de Mons*, 65–7.

15 Lescarbot, *Nova Francia*, 2–5, quotation at 5; Thierry, *La France de Henri IV en Amérique du Nord*, 42–4, 46–7. There is an earlier commission dated 8 January 1603; however, scholars agree that the date must be wrong, as it is out of sequence with the other documents. See "Lettre par laquelle le roi Henri IV nommait le sieur de Monts son lieutenant-général en Acadie," 8 January 1603, fol. 32–8, C11D, LAC; Trudel, *HNF*, 2:11n6; Le Blant, "Henri IV et le Canada," 47; Binot, *Pierre Dugua de Mons*, 67n9.

16 "Monopole de la traite avec les Indiens accordé par le roi à Pierre Du Gua de Monts et ses associés," 18 December 1603, fol. 49v–50, C11D, LAC. The title, which was given by LAC, is not accurate in its use of the term "monopole" – not used in any contemporary French document examined – and in its

emphasis on the privileges accorded de Mons rather than on the ban imposed on other traders, the actual focus of the decree. See also "Lettre patente du roi portant nouvelle défense à tous ses sujets," 22 January 1605, fol. 52–7, ibid.

17 "Remontrances faites au roi par le sieur de Monts," 18 December 1603, fol. 38v, ibid. On the king's condition, see Liebel, *Pierre Dugua, sieur de Mons*, 82.

18 On the delegation of responsibilities in exchange for privileges and the use of the feudal system for colonization, see Roper and Van Ruymbeke, "Introduction," 3, 7.

19 While Aymar de Chaste, vice admiral and governor of Dieppe, did not have his own commission, he took over Chauvin's upon the latter's death in early 1603. Chauvin, de Chaste, and de Mons were all in service to Henri IV in Normandy during the Wars of Religion, particularly around Honfleur and Dieppe. See Bréard, *Le vieux Honfleur et ses marins*, 57.

20 Trocmé, "La Rochelle protestante," 103–4, 107–9, 134–7; Parker, *La Rochelle and the French Monarchy*, 34–5, 64–6; Lespagnol, *Messieurs de Saint-Malo*, 43–5, 52, 110; Lespagnol, "Saint-Malo, port mondial," 67; Brunelle, *New World Merchants of Rouen*, 11, 33–4, 57–8, 67.

21 Lespagnol, *Messieurs de Saint-Malo*, 94.

22 Ibid.; Trocmé, "La Rochelle protestante," 108; Brunelle, *New World Merchants of Rouen*, 28, 28n73.

23 Rouen and La Rochelle surpassed Saint-Malo in the fur trade in the first few decades of the seventeenth century. Rouen was the headquarters of the associations accorded trading privileges until 1627, when primary decision-making moved to Paris under the Compagnie de la Nouvelle-France. Commerce and recruitment of settlers and indentured servants (*engagés*) continued to be organized from Rouen, with ships sailing from Dieppe, and, increasingly, from La Rochelle, particularly from the 1640s. See Lespagnol, "Saint-Malo, port mondial," 101; Carpin, *Le Réseau du Canada*, esp. chaps. 4–6, 9.

24 Robbins, "Families and Politics of La Rochelle," 58–60; Trocmé and Delafosse, *Le commerce rochelais*, 135–6, 166, 168–9, 187; Le Blant and Delafosse, "Les Rochelais dans la Vallée du Saint Laurent," 336; Liebel, *Pierre Dugua, sieur de Mons*, 85.

25 Commerce was traditionally considered to be beneath a noble's rank and thus participation could cost nobles their privileges, an act called derogation. While royal edicts promulgated periodically throughout the early modern period forbade nobles to engage in the retail trade, wholesale and long-distance commerce was permitted and even encouraged in a bid to invigorate French maritime trade. See Mousnier, *Les institutions de la France*, 1:109–11, 137–8, 183.

26 Brunelle, *New World Merchants of Rouen*, 2–4.

27 Trocmé and Delafosse, *Le commerce rochelais*, 192.

28 *Nouv. docs*, 80–1, 82–3, quotation at 80.

29 See the act of association, 10 February 1604, in Gosselin, *Nouvelles glanes historiques normandes*, 24–9.

30 See the entries for Pierre Ribertière, Jehan Sarcel, Étienne Goret, François Martin, and Luc Sere in Paris-Jallobert, *Anciens registres paroissiaux de Bretagne*.

31 *Nouv. docs*, 87–8.

32 Ibid., 84–5.

33 Harris, "Trading with Strangers," 92–3; Phillips and Sharman, *Outsourcing Empire*, 7; Davies, *The Royal African Company*, 25–7; Griffiths, *A Licence to Trade*, xii–xiii.

34 This arrangement was in contrast to a *société de capitaux*, in which shares were transferable and members easily replaced. See Lévy-Bruhl, *Histoire juridique des sociétés de commerce en France*, 32, 141–2, 180–3.

35 Trocmé and Delafosse, *Le commerce rochelais*, 185. On the characteristics of the *société générale* and solidary liability, see Lévy-Bruhl, *Histoire juridique des sociétés de commerce en France*, 31–2, 50–1, 141–2.

36 For the 10 February 1604 arrangement, see *Nouv. docs*, 82–3; Liebel, *Pierre Dugua, sieur de Mons*, 171–2; Binot, *Pierre Dugua de Mons*, 110. The agreement among the remaining associates is no longer extant. There is considerable confusion around the number of shares into which de Mons's company was divided. Based on the primary evidence, it appears that it was at first divided into three, and then, with the withdrawal of Saint-Jean-de-Luz in 1605, reorganized into fifths. If the share size remained the same, 18,000 livres, then the total capital of the second company would have been 90,000 livres. For the view that it was first divided into thirds, see Liebel, *Pierre Dugua, sieur de Mons*, 87–8; Binot, *Pierre Dugua de Mons*, 81–2; Gosselin, *Nouvelles glanes historiques normandes*, 24–9. For the suggestion that it had always been divided into fifths, see Biggar, *The Early Trading Companies of New France*, 53–4; Trudel, HNF, 2:14–15.

37 Bossenga, "Estates, Orders, Corps," 146–7, 150; Bien, "Offices, Corps, and a System of State Credit," 91, 98; Revel, "Les corps et communautés," 1:225, 227.

38 Bossenga, *The Politics of Privilege*, 7.

39 Collins, *Classes, Estates and Order in Early Modern Brittany*, 154–8, quotation at 154; Hoffman, "Early Modern France," 227–9.

40 The exact date of registration is unknown. See the letter, dated 17 February 1604, from the Palais de Justice to the Parlement de Rouen in response to the latter's objections in Gosselin, *Nouvelles glanes historiques normandes*, 21–3; Liebel, *Pierre Dugua, sieur de Mons*, 84.

41 "Lettres patentes pour l'enregistrement des pouvoirs et commissions donnés au Sieur de Monts," 29 January 1605, fol. 61, C11A, LAC; Liebel, *Pierre Dugua, sieur de Mons*, 166.

42 Table des registres secrets du Parlement de Bretagne, 3 June 1605, Rég. 104, fol. 39, 1B b 869, ADIV.

43 Délibérations de la communauté de ville, 22 March 1605, SMBB10, Arch. mun. de Saint-Malo; Lespagnol, *Messieurs de Saint-Malo*, 45–7.

44 *Docs inédits*, 30; Trudel, *HNF*, 2:66; Liebel, *Pierre Dugua, sieur de Mons*, 166.

45 Moote, "The French Crown versus its Judicial and Financial Officials," 149.

46 Gosselin, *Nouvelles glanes historiques normandes*, 22–3.

47 De Waele, *Les relations entre le Parlement de Paris et Henri IV*, 403–5, 410–11, 415; Holt, "Henri IV et les privilèges municipaux à Dijon"; Carpi, "Une réconciliation ratée? Amiens au sortir de la Ligue." For the argument that Henri IV intended, in fact, to impose his authority on towns and provincial bodies, see Major, "Henry IV and Guyenne."

48 Collins, *Classes, Estates and Order in Early Modern Brittany*, 158.

49 Darsel, *L'Amirauté en Bretagne*, 204.

50 Registre des délibérations des États de Bretagne, 5 October 1585, C 2642, ADIV; Darsel, *L'Amirauté en Bretagne*, 191–206.

51 Darsel, *L'Amirauté en Bretagne*, 206, 210–12.

52 *Nouv. docs*, 94.

53 Trudel, *HNF*, 2:65–6.

54 "King's declaration concerning the exemption of New France merchandise from customs," 8 February 1605, in Lescarbot, *History of New France*, 223–6, quotation at 224–5; *Nouv. docs*, 94n3.

55 This time, the acquittal was granted at Avranches. See *Nouv. docs*, 101. It seems likely that the incidents at Condé-sur-Noireau and Avranches were part of the same case, as the amount of merchandise in question was the same and Buffé was involved in both. For this interpretation, see Liebel, *Pierre Dugua, sieur de Mons*, 164; Trudel, *HNF*, 2:65. For the view that they were two separate events involving different merchandise, see Biggar, *The Early Trading Companies of New France*, 56–7.

56 *Nouv. docs*, 89–90.

57 Le Blant, "Henri IV et le Canada," 51.

58 Allaire, *Pelleteries, manchons et chapeaux de castor*, 136–8, 141–2. On the role of the king's furriers in the fur trade of New France from the 1580s, see Turgeon, *Une histoire de la Nouvelle-France*, 136–7.

59 The situation was hardly better in France itself. It was not until Richelieu's tenure that officials conducted a systematic survey of the ports along the coast and made an effort to establish an effective patrol.

60 See, for example, *Nouv. docs*, 113, 128–30, 139–43, 169–72.

61 Thierry, *La France de Henri IV en Amérique du Nord*, 19–28; Turgeon, *Une histoire de la Nouvelle-France*, 96–134; Biggar, *The Early Trading Companies of New France*, 54–5; Innis, *The Cod Fisheries*, 84–5.

62 Lescarbot, *Nova Francia*, chap. 2.

63 See, for example, Champlain, *Works*, 2:11–12. On the numbers of interlopers, see Biggar, *The Early Trading Companies of New France*, 55; Fischer, *Champlain's Dream*, 233.

64 Champlain, *Works*, 3:323; Fischer, *Champlain's Dream*, 233, 240–1, 241n47; Trudel, *HNF*, 2:67, 153n9; Biggar, *The Early Trading Companies of New France*, 57, 63.

65 *Nouv. docs*, 169–72, quotations at 171. For the terms of compensation for de Mons and his associates in the event of illegal trading, see his commission in Lescarbot, *Nova Francia*, 1–6. On the use of the term "Florida" to designate the coast of northeastern North America, at least as far north as Maine, see Turgeon, *Une histoire de la Nouvelle-France*, 104–5.

66 *Nouv. docs*, 128.

67 Le Blant, "Les prémices de la fondation de Québec," 49; Liebel, *Pierre Dugua, sieur de Mons*, 171.

68 *Nouv. docs*, 129–30.

69 Thierry, *La France de Henri IV en Amérique du Nord*, 207–8, 212; James, *The Navy and Government in Early Modern France*, 38, 40.

70 On French kings' use of exemptions from existing privileges, see Horn, *Economic Development in Early Modern France*, 7, 14.

71 Rent-seeking is defined as "the attempt to obtain a greater share of existing wealth through manipulation of the sociopolitical environment rather than by creating new wealth." See ibid., 25–6, 38; Bossenga, "Estates, Orders, Corps," 149–50.

72 Kwass, *Privilege and the Politics of Taxation in Eighteenth-Century France*, 28; Hoffman, "Early Modern France," 227–9.

73 "Monopole de la traite avec les Indiens accordé par le roi à Pierre Du Gua de Monts et ses associés," 18 December 1603, fol. 48v, C11D, LAC. See also "Lettre par laquelle le roi Henri IV nommait le sieur de Monts son lieutenant-général en Acadie," 8 January 1603, fol. 34v, ibid.

74 The only extant information concerning a sum for the lieutenant generalship is the transaction between the Prince de Condé and the Duc de Montmorency in which the latter paid 30,000 livres for the position in 1620. See chapter 3, this volume.

75 Liebel, *Pierre Dugua, sieur de Mons*, 192–5; Biggar, *The Early Trading Companies of New France*, 63.

76 *Nouv. docs*, 132; Kupp, "Quelques aspects de la dissolution de la compagnie de Monsieur de Monts, 1607," 362. For Dutch jurist Hugo Grotius's arguments in favour of freedom of navigation, see chapter 3, this volume.

77 One lengthy trial as a result of these attacks concerned a Black man, Mathieu de Coste, who was brought to Canada for de Mons by one of the defendants; this facet of the dispute was not resolved until 1619. See Liebel, *Pierre Dugua, sieur de Mons*, 193–5; *Nouv. docs*, 135–6, 194–5, 196, 212–15, 388–93.

78 Champlain, *Works*, 3:323.
79 Ibid., 3:324. See also Lescarbot, *History of New France*, 2:351–2.
80 *Nouv. docs*, 137–8, and see also 222.
81 The commission is reproduced in Liebel, *Pierre Dugua, sieur de Mons*, 221, and see also 219; Trudel, *HNF*, 2:82.
82 Champlain, *Works*, 4:33.
83 *Nouv. docs*, 191–3, quotations at 191; Biggar, *The Early Trading Companies of New France*, 68.
84 "Déclaration du corps général de la communauté qu'il ne payera pas 6,000 livres au Sieur de Monts," 26 March 1609, register 6, Arch. mun. de Saint-Malo. The date of the royal council's decree is not known.
85 *Nouv. docs*, 192–3, quotation at 192. For the progression of suits in this case, see also ibid., 210–11, 231, 303–4, 336; registration of the ban on trade issued by Condé, 22 November 1612, in register 6, Arch. mun. de Saint-Malo. There was no Admiralty in Saint-Malo until 1681; there was, however, likely a representative of the Admiralty of France in the port at this time.
86 Binot, *Pierre Dugua de Mons*, 125.
87 Thierry, *La France de Henri IV en Amérique du Nord*, 258–9, 261–2; Trudel, *HNF*, 2:82; Binot, *Pierre Dugua de Mons*, 130; Liebel, *Pierre Dugua, sieur de Mons*, 219–20.
88 Allaire, *Pelleteries, manchons et chapeaux de castor*, 144n107.
89 Ibid., 141–2, 143–4.
90 At least eleven Parisian hatters later also became members of the Compagnie de la Nouvelle France. See appendix A in Trudel, *HNF*, 3.1:415–25; Carpin, "Migrations to New France in Champlain's Time," 169n7; Carpin, *Le Réseau du Canada*, 94, 110.
91 *Nouv. docs*, 213–14; Champlain, *Works*, 3:324.
92 *Nouv. docs*, 162; Barbiche, "Henri IV and the World Overseas," 29–30, 32.
93 Campbell, "Sully, Maximilien de Béthune, Baron de Rosny, Duke of." On the role of what later became known as the controller general of finances, see Root, *The Fountain of Privilege*, 23–6.
94 *Nouv. docs*, 222; "Monopole," in *Dictionnaire de l'Académie française* (1694) and Féraud, *Dictionnaire critique de la langue française* (1787).
95 The terms "privilege" and "liberty" were not clearly distinct from one another in the seventeenth century and were often used interchangeably. Both privilege and liberty conferred rights. I generally use the term "liberty" to mean exemption from privilege, which did not denote a complete absence of regulation, in contrast to its modern meaning.
96 For a more explicit statement to this effect, see appendix 5 in Champlain, *Des Sauvages*, 224.
97 Hirsch and Minard, "'Laissez-nous faire et protégez-nous beaucoup,'" 144.

98 27 June 1624, fo. 386, vol. 79a, Conseil d'Etat du Roi, Série E, LAC. King Louis XIII had renewed Saint-Jean-de-Luz's privileges in 1614 and 1620. On the active role of privilege-holders, see Horn, *Economic Development in Early Modern France*, 4.

99 Collins, *Classes, Estates and Order in Early Modern Brittany*, 135–8, 139–41, 153.

100 Horn, *Economic Development in Early Modern France*, 17, 27–8.

101 Champlain, *Works*, 2:216; Le Blant and Delafosse, "Les Rochelais dans la vallée du Saint-Laurent," 341–4.

102 Champlain, *Works*, 4:35.

103 *Nouv. docs*, 210–11, quotation at 210, and see also 191, 303–4.

104 Champlain, *Works*, 2:111; Biggar, *The Early Trading Companies of New France*, 34–5; appendix 3 in Champlain, *Des Sauvages*, 209. For evidence that Basque and Breton traders had already penetrated the Saint Lawrence probably as far as Montreal as early as the 1580s, see Turgeon, *Une histoire de la Nouvelle-France*, 120–3.

105 The exact number of Rouennais in the company is not clear.

106 Brunelle, *New World Merchants of Rouen*, 39, 42; Liebel, *Pierre Dugua, sieur de Mons*, 102.

107 *Nouv. docs*, 124; Liebel, *Pierre Dugua, sieur de Mons*, 179. On captains and crews owning a share in the ship or voyage, see Brunelle, *New World Merchants of Rouen*, 38.

108 *Nouv. docs*, 86; Trocmé and Delafosse, *Le commerce rochelais*, 62–5; Brunelle, *New World Merchants of Rouen*, 39–42.

109 *Nouv. docs*, 142.

110 28 December 1607, no. 17, étude XV, vol. I, MC, LAC.

111 In 1606, de Mons uncovered an illegal trading venture and fraud on the part of the Rouennais Bellois, the receiver general of the company, which led to the dissolution of the Rouennais partnership formed in 1604. See Liebel, *Pierre Dugua, sieur de Mons*, 177–92; Gosselin, *Nouvelles glanes historiques normandes*, 31; Trudel, *HNF*, 2:67.

112 Brunelle, *New World Merchants of Rouen*, 74; Le Blant, "Les prémices de la fondation de Québec," 52. For the view that Caulier and Legendre were old partners of de Mons, see Biggar, *The Early Trading Companies of New France*, 66.

113 Le Blant, "La première bataille pour Québec," 115; Liebel, *Pierre Dugua, sieur de Mons*, 225; Fischer, *Champlain's Dream*, 236.

114 For the suggestion that Georges and Macain had been planning to join de Mons's new company but withdrew when Legendre, whom they saw as a competitor for furs, joined, see Thierry, *La France de Henri IV en Amérique du Nord*, 265.

115 *Nouv. docs*, 219–24, quotation at 221; Le Blant, "La première bataille pour Québec," 125.

116 Champlain, *Works*, 2:12. On the Basques' refusal to hand over the merchandise to Gravé du Pont, see *Nouv. docs*, 186.

117 *Nouv. docs*, 185–7, 219–24, 289–91, quotation at 224.

118 Ibid., 178, 173, 178 (quotations in order of appearance), also 178–80; Liebel, *Pierre Dugua, sieur de Mons*, 225–6. *Table de marbre* was used to refer to the jurisdiction of the Admiralty, *Connétablie*, and *Eaux et Forêts*.

119 *Nouv. docs*, 144, 147, 174–7.

120 On the practice of traders "plundering from within" a company, see Boulle, "French Mercantilism, Commercial Companies and Colonial Profitability."

121 Having returned to France with the rest of the colonists in 1607, Poutrincourt did not sail again for Port-Royal until 1610. See Huia Ryder, "Biencourt de Poutrincourt et de Saint-Just, Jean de."

122 *Nouv. docs*, 153.

123 De Mons may also have gone to court to push the Malouins to settle. On this tactic, see Hardwick, *Family Business*, 76.

124 For the argument that they had significant financial difficulties that season, see Trudel, *HNF*, 2:168. Biggar suggests that they succeeded in making some profit, due to the absence of colonizing obligations. See *The Early Trading Companies of New France*, 68. There was no "typical" cost of a court case. Fees were charged for every document written, copied, and registered, as well as for any supporting documents sent from other jurisdictions (the cost of which depended on the type of act). Other costs included the compensation of legal officials, including sergeants and bailiffs, and legal representatives such as *procureurs* and *avocats*. Total costs depended heavily on the complexity and length of a case, the number of jurisdictions involved, and the financial means of the litigants. Members of the elite, for example, may have been more likely to appeal a ruling or to prolong litigation, and therefore costs and complexity were greater. See Hardwick, *Family Business*, 64–6, 87; Carrier, "Virtuosité procédurière," 81–3.

Chapter Two

1 For more on the assassination of Henri IV and subsequent events, see Greengrass, *France in the Age of Henri IV*, 252–6.

2 Henri IV was an important patron to Champlain's family and, especially, to Samuel. See Thierry, "Introduction," 1:5–12. For possible explanations for this close relationship, including that Samuel may have been the king's illegitimate son, see Fischer, *Champlain's Dream*, 43–7.

3 Breen, *Law, City, and King*, 12, 67, quotation at 12; Breen, "Patronage, Politics, and the 'Rule of Law' in Early Modern France," 101.

4 Carrier, "Virtuosité procédurière," 33. The type of case, the particular court, and the socio-economic position of the litigants all affected the unfolding of a suit and whether an appeal was likely. See Hardwick, *Family Business*, 87.

5 Breen, "Patronage, Politics, and the 'Rule of Law' in Early Modern France," 95–113; Breen, "Law, Society, and the State in Early Modern France," 375, 380, 384; Lanza, *From Wives to Widows*, 9–11, 22–7; Piant, "Encadrement judiciaire des populations locales et concurrence des juges," 134–6, 138.

6 Champlain, *Works*, 4:207–8; Fischer, *Champlain's Dream*, 300–3; Galland, *Pour la gloire de Dieu et du roi*, 59; Ruggiu, "Colonies, Monarchy, Empire and the French *Ancien Régime*," 198–9.

7 Bitsch, *Vie et carrière d'Henri II de Bourbon, prince de Condé*, chaps. 1 and 2. On the role of the Spanish marriages in the rebellion of great nobles in the 1610s, see Bergin, *The Politics of Religion in Early Modern France*, 90–1.

8 Condé later added viceroy to his lieutenant general's title. When exactly this occurred is not clear, as all of the versions of his letters patent from 1612 identify him only as lieutenant general.

9 Liebel, *Pierre Dugua, sieur de Mons*, 109–60.

10 Champlain, *Works*, 2:112; Grenon, "Pierre Dugua de Mons: Lieutenant General of New France," 146. For a list of commanders of Acadia and Quebec from 1604 to 1628, see Trudel, *HNF*, 2:485–500.

11 Champlain, *Works*, 4:210–12. Both quotations are from the Comte de Soissons's commission to Champlain. The substance was the same under Condé's viceroyalty.

12 Ibid., 4:214. For those who took Champlain to be governor, see Le Clercq, *First Establishment of the Faith in New France*, 1:150–1; Lanctôt, *L'administration de la Nouvelle-France*, 21. For the suggestion that he hoped to receive such a title, see Fischer, *Champlain's Dream*, 440–1. For the argument that Champlain was governor de facto if not de jure, see Thierry, "Champlain and Lescarbot: An Impossible Friendship," 133.

13 Champlain, *Works*, 4:214; *Docs inédits*, 36–7; Gosselin, *Nouvelles glanes historiques normandes*, 34; Trudel, *HNF*, 2:191–2. On Champlain's preference for one large company, see Biggar, *The Early Trading Companies of New France*, 85.

14 Among those who had participated in the Compagnie de Mons were de Mons, Lucas Legendre (Rouen), Samuel Georges, and Jean Macain (La Rochelle). At the last minute, the latter two ended up not joining, along with other traders from La Rochelle. Veteran trader François Gravé Du Pont (Saint-Malo) continued to work under the new company.

15 *Nouv. docs*, 316–17. For the full texts of the three agreements, see 250–1, 256–61, 310–21.

16 Ibid., 251 (emphasis added).

17 Sharon Kettering quoted in Breen, *Law, City, and King*, 69–70.

18 Hanley, "Social Sites of Political Practice in France," 32–6, quotation at 34.

19 The description of Champlain as painter may have been a reference to the drawings contained in *Des Sauvages* (1603) and *Brief Discours*. See *Nouv. docs*, 245, as well as the editor's comments in 245n3.

20 *Nouv. docs*, 248.

21 Ibid., and see also 246.

22 Arrêt de Parlement de Rouen, 14 December 1613, 1B 981, ADSM. See also *Nouv. docs*, 263–4, 267–70, esp. 270. On the royal pressure applied to the Parlement, see Trudel, *HNF*, 2:192.

23 Berenger, "Les États de Bretagne et la colonisation nord-américaine," 13.

24 For Condé's role in the Estates General, see Hayden, *France and the Estates General of 1614*, chap. 4.

25 Champlain, *Works*, 4:225; see also 347.

26 Schaeper, "Colonial Trade Policies Late in the Reign of Louis XIV," 210–11; Horn, *Economic Development in Early Modern France*, 4. For the context in which the king usually accorded privileges, see Olivier-Martin, *Histoire du droit français des origines à la Révolution*, 347.

27 Hirsch and Minard, "Laissez-faire nous et protégez-nous beaucoup," 144, 146–7; Horn, *Economic Development in Early Modern France*, 14–15.

28 De Waele, "Conflict Resolution under the First Bourbons," 141–9.

29 James, *The Origins of French Absolutism*, 11–12; James, *The Navy and Government in Early Modern France*, 23–4; Hildesheimer, *Richelieu*, 65; Sawyer, *Printed Poison*, chaps. 2 and 6; Bitsch, *Vie et carrière d'Henri II de Bourbon, prince de Condé*, 132–89.

30 *Nouv. docs*, 355–60, quotation at 359.

31 This sum was 1,500 livres above the viceroy's habitual annual revenue and was part of a scheme to deprive Champlain of the lieutenant's position. See Trudel, *HNF*, 2:240–1; Fischer, *Champlain's Dream*, 345–6, 349; Champlain, *Works*, 4:345. On the agreement between the company and Thémines and the ensuing dispute, see *Nouv. docs*, 371–2; 17 May 1618, fo. 122, vol. 58b, Conseil d'État du roi, Série E, LAC.

32 Champlain, *Works*, 4:341–5, quotation at 341.

33 The company successfully petitioned to have the annual fee lowered to the amount it had paid previously. See Trudel, *HNF*, 2:240–1.

34 Among the Malouins who had decided to cut their losses were Thomas Porée, Guillaume Le Breton, and Richard Boulain, all of whom entered the company negotiations with Champlain in the middle of 1613.

35 *Docs inédits*, 46. See also *Nouv. docs*, 372n3.

36 *Docs inédits*, 47–9; Berenger, "Les États de Bretagne et la colonisation nord-américaine," 13.

37 Champlain, *Works*, 4:348.

38 *Docs inédits*, 47–8; see also resolutions to the same effect of 23 October 1618 and 3 October 1619, 49–51.

39 The exact date of the council's ruling in favour of the CRSM is unknown. Berenger suggests that it occurred as early as 27 May 1617, but records in *Docs inédits* show that this was merely the date of the company's request.

The case was still unresolved in November of that year. See Berenger, "Les États de Bretagne et la colonisation nord-américaine," 13; *Docs inédits*, 47–9; *Nouv. docs*, 371–2.

40 *Docs inédits*, 49–51.

41 Cornette, *Histoire de la Bretagne et des Bretons*, 1:426–8, 547.

42 James, *The Origins of French Absolutism*, 13–14; Fischer, *Champlain's Dream*, 346–8.

43 Champlain, *Works*, 4:343–4.

44 The documents as presented in Champlain's *Works* are out of order: the proposal to the Chamber of Commerce preceded that to the king and his council. See Trudel, *Beginnings of New France*, 125n25. Despite the timing of the proposal, there is no evidence that Champlain was reacting directly to the incident of 1617. Berenger intimates, incorrectly, that Champlain's proposal came in 1617, between the decree in favour of free trade and the request by the company to have its privileges restored. See "Les États de Bretagne et la colonisation nord-américaine," 13.

45 Champlain, *Works*, 2:339. The phrase "prospective inventory" comes from Tomlins, "Law's Empire," 31.

46 Champlain, *Works*, 2:343.

47 Ibid., 2:345, 349 (quotations in order of appearance).

48 The letter sent by the Chamber of Commerce to the king also couched its message in these terms. See ibid., 2:346–51.

49 Ibid., 2:326–7, quotation at 327. A similar emphasis on the threat posed by France's rivals in North America can be found in "Lettre de Monsieur Potrincourt aux authorités de la ville de Paris," 1 September 1618, *Coll. mss*, 1:58.

50 Champlain, *Works*, 2:328.

51 Champlain's writings abound with laments for the lack of royal assistance and calls for financial and administrative support from "those that have the power to attend to it and to contribute towards it of their abundance." See ibid., 3:147; see also 2: 221; 3:14, 176; 4:300; 5:72–3. Among those who shared Champlain's view, see "Lettre de Monsieur Potrincourt aux authorités de la ville de Paris," 1 September 1618, *Coll. mss*, 1:58–9; Sagard, *Histoire du Canada*, 84; "Mémoire du Chevalier de Razilly," in Deschamps, ed., *Un colonisateur du temps de Richelieu, Isaac de Razilly*, 22, 25; François du Noyer de Saint-Martin's proposal for a "compagnie royale de voyages de long cours," 1623, fo. 215, vol. 17329, dépt de mss, fonds français, BnF.

52 Champlain, *Works*, 2:338, 339 (quotations in order of appearance).

53 Benton, *A Search for Sovereignty*, 30–1.

54 Champlain, *Works*, 4:364–5.

55 While the proposal was never implemented, it may have influenced a plan for colonization drawn up by the CRSM in 1618. It, too, did not come to fruition,

although the company did send over some settlers the following year. See ibid., 4:353–6; Trudel, *HNF*, 2:262–3.

56 Champlain, *Works*, 4:361–7, quotation at 365 (emphasis added). On the king as arbitrator, see Parker, "Sovereignty, Absolutism and the Function of Law," 69–70.

57 *Nouv. docs*, 394–6, quotation at 396.

58 Breen, *Law, City, and King*, 70–1; Hayden, *France and the Estates General of 1614*, chap. 4.

59 Champlain dedicated his writings to various patrons. His first work, *Des Sauvages* (1603), was dedicated to Henri IV. The *Voyages* of 1613, 1619, and 1632 were dedicated to the Prince de Condé, Louis XIII, and Cardinal Richelieu, respectively.

60 On early modern French commercial law and the security of incorporated companies, see Lévy-Bruhl, *Histoire juridique des sociétés de commerce en France*, 141–2, 151, 280–1.

61 *Nouv. docs*, 250–5, 256–61, 310–21.

62 20 December 1624, no. 1, c. 50, Conseil privé, v6, LAC; Arrêt de Parlement de Rouen, 25 June 1633, 1B 981, ADSM. There are two decrees from the Parlement of Rouen of this date, one concerning the Rochelais merchants' participation in the CRSM, the other their alleged contravention of the trading ban. For the purposes of citation, they will hereafter be distinguished as (1) and (2), respectively.

63 Champlain, *Works*, 4:220–1, quotation at 221; Acte de Chesneau, 27 October 1618, 3 E 261, ADCM.

64 On the three ports' privileges, see André Lespagnol, *Messieurs de Saint-Malo*, 43–5, 52, 94, 110; Trocmé, "La Rochelle protestante," 103–4, 107–9, 134–7; Parker, *La Rochelle and the French Monarchy*, 34–5, 64–6; Brunelle, *New World Merchants of Rouen*, 11, 28n73, 33–4, 57–8, 67.

65 Beaulieu, "'L'on n'a point d'ennemis plus grands que ces sauvages,'" 375–6.

66 Arrêt de Parlement de Rouen, 25 June 1633 (2), 1B 981, ADSM.

67 For Champlain's version of events, see *Works*, 4:222.

68 The Rochelais had an agent at Biencourt's seigneury of Port-Royal from 1615 to 1621. See Parker, *La Rochelle and the French Monarchy*, 72.

69 See chapter 3, this volume.

70 Arrêt de Parlement de Rouen, 25 June 1633 (1), 1B 981, ADSM.

71 The settlement is quoted in a decree of 20 December 1624. See no. 1, c. 50, Conseil privé, v6, LAC.

72 On the appeal by Georges and associates, see *Nouv. docs*, 386; Acte de Chesneau, 27 October 1618, 3 E 261, ADCM. On that by Boyer et al., see Arrêt de Parlement de Rouen, 25 June 1633 (1), 1B 981, ADSM; 20 December 1624, no. 1, c. 50, Conseil privé, v6, LAC.

73 Arrêt de Parlement de Rouen, 25 June 1633 (1), 1B 981, ADSM. The Rochelais were still prepared to join at the end of October 1618. See Acte de Chesneau, 27 October 1618, 3 E 261, ADCM.

74 For the numerous rulings on this subject, see, among others, 20 December 1624, no. 1, c. 50, Conseil privé, V6, LAC; Arrêt de Parlement de Rouen, 25 June 1633 (1), 1B 981, ADSM. On the phenomenon of cases splitting into multiple suits, see Carrier, "Virtuosité procédurière," 48.

75 Arrêt de Parlement de Rouen, 25 June 1633 (1), 1B 981, ADSM. The CRSM was awarded compensation of 10,000 livres in 1622 – which they in fact exchanged for entry into the new privileged trading company.

76 Arrêt de Parlement de Rouen, 25 June 1633 (2), 1B 981, ADSM.

77 Arrêt de Parlement de Rouen, 25 June 1633 (1) and (2), 1B 981, ADSM. For a contrary view of the impact of the ruling on the respective parties, see Le Blant, "Les arrêts du Parlement de Rouen du 25 juin 1633 et les premières compagnies du Canada," 49; Delafosse and Trocmé, *Le commerce rochelais*, 168.

78 Kagan, *Lawsuits and Litigants in Castile*, 115, 118. On the advantages and disadvantages of lawsuits and arbitrated settlements, see ibid., 77–8; Carrier, "Virtuosité procédurière," 59–63.

79 Breen, *Law, City, and King*, 15, 67; Parker, *Class and State in Ancien Régime France*, 185.

80 See acts of 18 and 27 June and 11 July 1631 described in Arrêt de Parlement de Rouen, 25 June 1633 (1), 1B 981, ADSM.

81 See descriptions of acts of 24 August 1624 and 14 and 26 November 1630 in ibid.

82 Such, at least, was the rhetoric at the time. As Julie Hardwick points out, while some types of courts and litigation bear this out, it is less true for others, including lower royal courts like the *sénéchaussée* of Lyons and the *prévôté* of Nantes. See *Family Business*, 59, 87.

83 *Nouv. docs*, 379. On Biencourt's use of his vice admiral's commission and status as seigneur to claim duties from fishermen-traders in the area, see Dewar, "Litigating Empire," 58–9.

84 For contracts between the two parties, see Arrêt de Parlement de Rouen, 12 July 1633, Extraits des diverses séries, LAC; 11 March 1625, no. 42, c. 52, Conseil privé, V6, LAC; *Nouv. docs*, 379. On the many similar arrangements the Rochelais merchants entered with others, see Delafosse and Trocmé, *Le commerce rochelais*, 136.

85 For the final sentence in the Saint John River dispute, see Arrêt de Parlement de Rouen, 12 July 1633, Extraits des diverses séries, LAC.

86 *Nouv. docs*, 340–3. On the manipulation of jurisdictions by opposing parties, see Parker, "Sovereignty, Absolutism and the Function of Law," 58; Kagan, *Lawsuits and Litigants in Castile*, 35, 42.

87 Parker, "Sovereignty, Absolutism and the Function of Law," 56; Olivier-Martin, *L'organisation corporative de la France d'Ancien Régime*, 497–8.

88 *Nouv. docs*, 265.

89 Arrêt de Parlement de Rouen, 25 June 1633 (2), 1B 981, ADSM. This request was turned down. See "Arrêt ordonnant que les differends entre les deux parties seront procédés à l'admirauté de Rouen et en appel au Parlement de Rouen," 11 March 1625, no. 42, c. 52, Conseil privé, v6, LAC. On the strength of local and regional legal institutions, see Tomlins, "Law's Empire," 39.

90 For contrasting findings in lower royal courts, see Hardwick, *Family Business*, 67.

91 Carrier, "Virtuosité procédurière," 96. Piant argues that jurisdictional competition encouraged judges to work hard and thus compensated for venality of office, which discouraged it. See "Encadrement judiciaire des populations locales et concurrence des juges," 136–8.

Chapter Three

1 Desbarats and Greer, "Où est la Nouvelle-France?," 43; Mancke, "Early Modern Expansion and the Politicization of Oceanic Space," 229; Mollat du Jourdin, *Europe and the Sea*, 114–15.

2 Steinberg, *The Social Construction of the Ocean*, 77–84.

3 Mancke, "Empire and State," 199.

4 Armitage, introduction to Hugo Grotius, *The Free Sea*, xi–xiii. As Armitage observes, Grotius's defence stemmed from a controversy around the Dutch seizure of the Portuguese ship the *Santa Catarina* and its extremely lucrative merchandise in the Singapore Strait in 1603.

5 Ibid., xv–xvii; Steinberg, *The Social Construction of the Ocean*, 91–4, 97; Benton, *A Search for Sovereignty*, 135.

6 Steinberg, "Lines of Division, Lines of Connection," 259–60; Steinberg, *The Social Construction of the Ocean*, 95–8; Armitage, introduction to Grotius, *The Free Sea*, xvii–xviii.

7 Steinberg, *The Social Construction of the Ocean*, 98.

8 Mancke, "Spaces of Power in the Early Modern Northeast," 32.

9 Dessert, *Les Montmorency*, chaps. 4–6.

10 The origin of regional admirals was on account of the distance between what were considered the separate seas surrounding France. See Du Voisin de La Popelinière, *L'Amiral de France, et par occasion, de celuy des autres nations*, 64–5.

11 Valin, *Nouveau commentaire sur l'ordonnance de la marine du mois d'août 1681*, 38–40.

12 Darsel, *L'Amirauté en Bretagne*, chap. 5, esp. 212–16.

13 James, *The Navy and Government in Early Modern France*, 34–6; Parker, *La Rochelle and the French Monarchy*, 74–6. *Droits d'ancrage et du guet* refers to

rights levied on dropping anchor in a harbour and on the patrol of the sea that coastal inhabitants were required to undertake.

14 James, *The Navy and Government in Early Modern France*, 58, and see also 24, 40, 50, 62, 76. The strengthening of the French admiral's authority appears to have been the reverse of the trend in England at the beginning of the seventeenth century. There, the Admiralty's jurisdiction was in decline amid competition from the common law courts. See Baker, *An Introduction to English Legal History*, 106–8; Sanborn, *Origins of Early English Maritime Law*, 303; Carter, *History of English Legal Institutions*, 172, 173–4; De Luca, "Beyond the Sea," chaps. 4 and 5.

15 By the time he was finished, Provence was the only province officially outside his jurisdiction. See Valin, *Nouveau commentaire sur l'ordonnance de la marine du mois d'août 1681*, 38.

16 In Brittany's case, admirals of France were given separate letters patent for this position, a practice that continued in the late seventeenth century. See ibid., 37.

17 Dessert, *Les Montmorency*, 163–4.

18 On Condé's relationship to Louis XIII and his royal service following his release from prison, see Bitsch, *Vie et carrière d'Henri II de Bourbon, prince de Condé*, 222–5.

19 Desbarats and Greer, "Où est la Nouvelle-France?," 42, 46–7.

20 Though a commission from the king, the viceroyalty became venal with Montmorency's purchase of it from Condé. On the practice of venality, or the sale of offices, see Mousnier, *Les institutions de la France*, 2:457.

21 *Nouv. docs*, 233, 234.

22 Ibid., 308 (emphasis added).

23 Ibid., 235 (emphasis added); Steinberg, *The Social Construction of the Ocean*, 93; De Luca, "Beyond the Sea," 275–6.

24 The number of those who stayed over the winter varied between two and twenty-three in the habitations of Port-Royal and Quebec during the 1610s. See appendix E in Trudel, *HNF*, vol. 2. On the impact of the tradition of the "fishing commons" on later arrangements when the state became involved, see Greer, "La pêche, les communs maritimes et l'empire français en Amérique du Nord," 179.

25 Gillis, "Islands in the Making of an Atlantic Oceania," 21, 27–9; Desbarats and Greer, "North America from the Top Down," 121.

26 Desbarats and Greer, "Où est la Nouvelle-France?," 42–3.

27 Steinberg, *The Social Construction of the Ocean*, 48.

28 Lescarbot, *Nova Francia*, 2. De Mons's commission from the admiral is no longer extant. This clause does not appear in Condé's letters patent.

29 "Procuration de Montmorency à Dolu," 24 February 1620, no. 495, étude LIV, MC, LAC; Trudel, *HNF*, 2:265–6. A *grand audiencier* worked in the Chancellery. See Mousnier, *Les institutions de la France*, 2:138.

30 Champlain, *Works*, 4:368; Trudel, *HNF*, 2:488–97.

31 Trudel, *HNF*, 2:277–8; Fischer, *Champlain's Dream*, 367–8.

32 When Dolu took out a share in the Compagnie de Montmorency in November 1622, he had already resigned from his position as intendant and emphasized his status as an ordinary subject of the king. This suggests that he did not want to appear to be Montmorency's man in the company; however, he may have continued to report to the viceroy in an informal capacity. See 5 November 1622, fo. 190–1v, vol. 9269, Collection Margry, dépt de mss, BnF.

33 Champlain, *Works*, 5:6–7.

34 Ibid.

35 MacMillan, *Sovereignty and Possession in the English New World*, 108–15, quotation at 111; Benton, *A Search for Sovereignty*, 54–7; Seed, *Ceremonies of Possession in Europe's Conquest of the New World*, esp. 1–15.

36 *Nouv. docs*, 406.

37 For the two sides' positions, see ibid., 417–19.

38 On the importance of the scale of activity in the North Atlantic compared to the South, see Turgeon, "Pêches basques du Labourd en Atlantique Nord," 169.

39 Steinberg, *The Social Construction of the Ocean*, 72–3, 98. For Steinberg, the goal of the mercantilist state was to control the "channeled paths of circulation," rather than territory. See ibid., 73.

40 On the role of chartered companies in the merchant capitalist period, see ibid., 68.

41 Montmorency did, however, approach them with more caution than some of his contemporaries, including Henri IV. Given the scale and risks of overseas enterprises, the admiral advocated a probationary period of two to three years before issuing formal letters patent. There is no evidence that this practice was ever implemented. See Boiteux, *Richelieu, grand maître*, 79–80.

42 Harris, *Going the Distance*, 251–4; Harris, "Trading with Strangers," 91–4.

43 Davies, *The Royal African Company*, 32–7; Scott, *The Constitution and Finance of English, Scottish and Irish Joint-Stock Companies*, 1:153.

44 Griffiths, *A Licence to Trade*, x; Scammell, "English Chartered Trading Companies and the Sea," 3; Coornaert, "European Economic Institutions and the New World," 247.

45 Phillips and Sharman, *Outsourcing Empire*, 5–6, 8–9; Stern, "History and Historiography of the English East India Company," 1157; Cavanagh, "A Company with Sovereignty and Subjects of Its Own?," 27–8.

46 Brandon, *War, Capital and the Dutch State*, 93–114.

47 Coornaert, "European Economic Institutions and the New World," 245–7, quotation at 246; Scott, *The Constitution and Finance of English, Scottish and Irish Joint-Stock Companies*, 1:126.

48 By contrast, the passive investors in the VOC had no vote and no access to the company's accounts. See Harris, *Going the Distance*, 279–80, 307–8.

49 The EIC, for one, did not establish a permanent capital until the 1650s. Scammell, *The World Encompassed*, 481; Davies, *The Royal African Company*, 27; Coornaert, "European Economic Institutions and the New World," 243; Griffiths, *A Licence to Trade*, 84–5; Scott, *The Constitution and Finance of English, Scottish and Irish Joint-Stock Companies*, 1:146. Limited liability was not recognized by courts in France or England until the nineteenth century. See Streichenberger, *Sociétés anonymes de France et d'Angleterre*, 33, 38, 41; Freedeman, *Joint-Stock Enterprises in France*, 5.

50 Lévy-Bruhl, *Histoire juridique des sociétés de commerce en France*, 136–8, 255.

51 This organizational form may have been based on the Italian *commenda*. See Harris, "The Institutional Dynamics of Early Modern Eurasian Trade," 609–11.

52 Kessler, *A Revolution in Commerce*, 175; Kessler, "Limited Liability in Context," 519–23; Lévy-Bruhl, *Histoire juridique des sociétés de commerce en France*, 33–9, 105–51; Freedeman, *Joint-Stock Enterprises in France*, 1–4.

53 The term "joint-stock" was not used in France during the period. The use of the term *société anonyme* to denote companies along the lines of joint-stocks only developed toward the end of the eighteenth century. I use the term "joint-stock" to refer generally to companies on Dutch and English models. I use *société de capitaux* in reference to French companies, which drew on both the joint-stock and existing French forms of association in practice. See Streichenberger, *Sociétés anonymes de France et d'Angleterre*, 29–31. For the definition of a *société anonyme* in the seventeenth and eighteenth centuries, see Lévy-Bruhl, *Histoire juridique des sociétés de commerce en France*, 40–2.

54 Hilaire, *Introduction historique au droit commercial*, 199, 205; Davies, "Joint-Stock Investment in the Later Seventeenth Century," 292. *Sociétés de capitaux* were not formally recognized in law until the Napoleonic Code of 1807. See Szramkiewicz, *Histoire du droit des affaires*, 156, 162–3.

55 Lévy-Bruhl, *Histoire juridique des sociétés de commerce en France*, 180–248. The first attempt to codify associations occurred during Jean-Baptiste Colbert's tenure with the ordinance of 1673, also known as the Code Savary. On the blurred lines between various types of association, see Coornaert, "European Economic Institutions and the New World," 251–2; Lévy-Bruhl, *Histoire juridique des sociétés de commerce en France*, 52–3.

56 "Lettres patentes par Louis XIII pour la première Compagnie des Indes Orientales, 2 Juillet 1615," in *Histoire de la Compagnie des Indes*, 164.

57 Ibid., 162–6, quotation at 165; Haudrère, *La Compagnie française des Indes au XVIIIe siècle*, 1:19–23. The CIO may have originally been christened "of Montmorency" when it fell under the protection of Charles in 1611. See James, *The Navy and Government in Early Modern France*, 41–2.

58 *Nouv. docs*, 407–14, quotations (in order of appearance) at 412, 411. A *toise* is a unit of measurement roughly equivalent to six feet or a little less than two metres.

59 Ibid., 412–13. This clause was added in the margin of the November 1620 contract after a 1 April 1622 royal decree folded the rival companies into one. See ibid., 440. The practice continued under the Compagnie de la Nouvelle-France after 1627.

60 Ibid., 432. Although nobles had certainly participated in ventures to New France – most notably de Mons and his partners from Saint-Malo – they had all shared the responsibilities of outfitting, recruiting, and trading. See chapter 1, this volume. On the long-standing goal of noble participation in long-distance commerce, see Brunelle, "Narrowing Horizons: Commerce and Derogation in Normandy," 63–79.

61 *Nouv. docs*, 408 (emphasis added). On the public good as the raison d'être of corporations, see Revel, "Les corps et communautés," 226–7.

62 When the Compagnie de la Nouvelle-France was established in 1627, it followed the same practice in its assemblies. See chapter 5, this volume.

63 On the geography of the French state's mercantilist policy, see Lespagnol, "État mercantiliste et littoral dans la France des XVIIe–XVIIIe siècles," 354.

64 *Nouv. docs*, 408, 409 (quotations in order of appearance).

65 Ibid.

66 Ibid., 409, 411 (quotations in order of appearance).

67 For a list of those who had commanded and wintered at Quebec when he was in France, see Trudel, *HNF*, 2:488–97.

68 *Nouv. docs*, 411.

69 Champlain, *Works*, 5:103–8.

70 Ibid., 5:14, 16, 17 (quotations in order of appearance).

71 Ibid., 5:18, 22–3. De Caen and his associates intervened in the suit sometime after assigning a procureur to represent them in April 1621. See "Procuration en blanc par Guillaume de Caen pour intervenir au procès pendant entre le duc de Montmorency et le Sieur Legendre et ses associés," 1 April 1621, no. 48, étude XVI, MC, LAC.

72 Champlain, *Works*, 5:25–8, quotation at 26.

73 Ibid., 5:28, 30–1 (quotations in order of appearance); see also 35.

74 *Nouv. docs*, 435. On these representations, see Trudel, *HNF*, 2:279–80.

75 Champlain, *Works*, 5:35–47, quotations (in order of appearance) at 43, 46, 46–7.

76 The royal council "resolved" the trading dispute between the two companies in April 1622 by awarding trading privileges to the Compagnie de Montmorency in exchange for allowing the CRSM associates to enter the company. See *Nouv. docs*, 438–43, 466–7; Champlain, *Works*, 5:83–4, also 61. The two sides continued their dispute inside the company over the next four years. See 10 May 1624, c. 47, no. 12, Conseil privé, v6, LAC; 13 March 1626, c. 58, no. 10, ibid.; 3 April 1626, c. 59, no. 13, ibid.; 28 April 1626, c. 59, no. 30, ibid.;

and 19 November 1626, c. 61, no. 1, ibid.; 26 March 1626, fo. 374, vol. 86, Conseil d'Etat du Roi, Série E, LAC; 9 July 1626, fo. 244, vol. 87b–88a, ibid.

77 On forts as symbols of imperium, see Macmillan, *Sovereignty and Possession in the English New World*, chap. 4, esp. 122, 144–5; Benton, *A Search for Sovereignty*, 8–9.

78 Champlain, *Works*, 5:46.

79 Ibid., 5:19. For similar frustration on the part of British authorities in eighteenth-century Acadia, see Mancke, "Spaces of Power in the Early Modern Northeast," 44.

80 Champlain, *Works*, 5:91; Benton, "Spatial Histories of Empire," 26.

81 Champlain, *Works*, 5:37.

82 On the practice of using one decree against another, see Carrier, "Virtuosité procédurière," 79.

83 Benton, *A Search for Sovereignty*, 23–33, quotation at 24; Macmillan, *Sovereignty and Possession in the English New World*, 13, 41–2, 79, 115, 206; Tomlins, "Law's Empire," 27–8.

84 Champlain, *Works*, 5:28.

85 Ibid., 5:126 (emphasis added). See also 5:8.

86 Ibid., 5: chaps. 3, 4.

87 Ibid., 5:3, 50–1, 178. For examples of other French interlopers, see 5:101, 208.

88 Ibid., 5:90.

89 On the geographic, demographic, and technological factors that combined to prevent the Innu from regulating access to the river, see Beaulieu, "L'on n'a point d'ennemis plus grands que ces sauvages," 379–80, 380n60.

90 Mancke, "Spaces of Power in the Early Modern Northeast," 37.

91 Bohaker, "*Nindoodemag*," 39–40; Greer, *Property and Dispossession*, 43–8; Morin, "Propriétés et territoires autochtones en Nouvelle-France," 131.

92 Bohaker, "*Nindoodemag*," 39, 42–3. Champlain, for example, describes Indigenous groups' lifestyles as "a wandering life over the land, not tilling the soil … and hunt now in one place, now in another." See Champlain, *Works*, 3:117–18.

93 Trigger, *Natives and Newcomers*, 141, 172–3; Beaulieu, "L'on n'a point d'ennemis plus grands que ces sauvages," 370.

94 Trigger, *Natives and Newcomers*, 174–5, 178; Bohaker, "*Nindoodemag*," 39, 42.

95 Champlain, *Works*, 2:255, 264–5.

96 Ibid., 2: chaps. 2, 3, 4; 3: chap. 1, esp. 100–5; Trigger, *Natives and Newcomers*, 177–81, 197.

97 Lozier, *Flesh Reborn*, 38–9.

98 Champlain, *Works*, 5:62, 70 (quotations in order of appearance).

99 Ibid., 5:70–1.

Chapter Four

1 Sagard, *Histoire du Canada*, 1:80; Trudel, *HNF*, 2:281. Some historians have suggested that this was the occasion on which the posts of *procureur du roi*, provost's lieutenant, and law clerk of the Jurisdiction of Quebec were established. See Dickinson, "Champlain, Administrator," 117.

2 Sagard, *Histoire du Canada*, 1:80, 81 (quotations in order of appearance).

3 Le Caron, *Au Roy sur la Nouvelle France*, 3.

4 For examples in English North America, see MacMillan, *Sovereignty and Possession in the English New World*, 103; Benton, *A Search for Sovereignty*, 97.

5 Wolfe, *The Conversion of Henri IV*, 189.

6 Diefendorf and Reinberg, "Catholic Reform and Religious Coexistence," 178.

7 Bergin, *The Politics of Religion in Early Modern France*, 89–91; Wolff, *Histoire des protestants en France*, 124–5; Larin, *Brève histoire des protestants en Nouvelle-France et au Québec*, 38. On the growing influence of Catholic reformers and the parti dévot over the course of Henri IV's reign, see Stephan, *Histoire du Protestantisme français*, 140–1; Tapié, *France in the Age of Louis XIII and Richelieu*, 26–7.

8 On the power and influence wielded by a number of Protestant nobles, including the brothers the Duc de Rohan and the Duc de Soubise, within Protestant circles, see Tapié, *France in the Age of Louis XIII and Richelieu*, 20, 26–7, 69.

9 Béarn was part of the kingdom of Navarre in the Basque Country. Louis XIII sent his army there in 1620 to unite the province with France and apply the Edict of Nantes, under which the Catholic minority would enjoy freedom of worship and have its property restored. See James, *The Origins of French Absolutism*, 13–14; Stephan, *Histoire du Protestantisme français*, 144–5; Tapié, *France in the Age of Louis XIII and Richelieu*, 87–8, 95.

10 Holt, "Redrawing the Lines of Authority," 206–7.

11 Bergin, *The Politics of Religion in Early Modern France*, 95.

12 Diefendorf and Reinberg, "Catholic Reform and Religious Coexistence," 177–8.

13 Deslandres, "Samuel de Champlain and Religion," 192n1. In France, the reforms of the Council of Trent were not ratified by the Assembly of Clergy until 1615.

14 Diefendorf and Reinberg, "Catholic Reform and Religious Coexistence," 182, 186; Diefendorf, "Henri IV, the Dévots and the Making of a French Catholic Reformation," 170–1. On François de Sales and Vincent de Paul, see Allier, *La Cabale des dévots*, 17; Secret, "Saint François de Sales et les missions à l'intérieur," 304–15; Chalumeau, "Saint Vincent de Paul et les missions en

France au XVIIe siècle," 317–27; Rapley, *The Dévotes*, 10–12, 19–22; Crowley, "The French Regime to 1760," 3–4.

15 Diefendorf and Reinberg, "Catholic Reform and Religious Coexistence," 177; Holt, "Redrawing the Lines of Authority," 208; Gutton, *Dévots et société au XVIIe siècle*, 5; Rapley, *The Dévotes*, 10–11. Tapié has characterized those born around 1600 as a generation of dévots. See *France in the Age of Louis XIII and Richelieu*, 85.

16 Bergin, *The Politics of Religion in Early Modern France*, 88, 92, 97–8. On these organizations' various activities in New France, see chapter 5, this volume.

17 The phrase comes from Deslandres, "Samuel de Champlain and Religion," 193.

18 Ibid., 197, 193 (quotations in order of appearance). On Lescarbot as a disillusioned ultra-Catholic, see Thierry, *Marc Lescarbot, vers 1570–1641*.

19 Deslandres, "Samuel de Champlain and Religion," 193, 196–7; Codignola, "Competing Networks," 540–3. La Roche's commission of 1598 is notable for the use of the term "Catholicism" rather than "Christianity." See "Edit du Roy contenant le pouvoir et commission … au Marquis … de la Roche," 12 January 1598, Extraits des diverses séries, LAC.

20 The Jesuits had already missionized in Acadia from 1611 to 1613.

21 Henneton, "Spiritual Geopolitics," quotation at 216; Lachenicht, Henneton, and Lignereux, "Spiritual Geopolitics in the Early Modern Imperial Age," 181–7.

22 Galland, *Pour la gloire de Dieu et du roi*, 62, 69; Diefendorf, "Henri IV, the Dévots and the Making of a French Catholic Reformation," 170–1; Dompnier, "Les Franciscains entre fidélité à leur héritage et défis religieux de l'âge moderne, " 61–97.

23 Greer and Mills, "A Catholic Atlantic," 5; Deslandres, *Croire et faire croire*, 48–9, 55–6, 61.

24 Deslandres, "Samuel de Champlain and Religion," 200; Galland, *Pour la gloire de Dieu et du roi*, 54n2, 55.

25 Le Clercq, *First Establishment of the Faith in New France*, 1:106, and also 87, 90, 92–3. For a biography of the Récollets who went to New France in 1615, see Galland, *Pour la gloire de Dieu et du roi*, 71.

26 Le Clercq, *First Establishment of the Faith in New France*, 1:110.

27 Ibid., 110–11. When the Jesuits arrived a decade later, they attributed the Wendats' suitability for conversion in part to their "civilizational resources," including a council. See McShea, *Apostles of Empire*, 168.

28 Le Clercq, *First Establishment of the Faith in New France*, 1: 111. For the entire program, see 109–12. This paragraph draws on Deslandres, *Croire et faire croire*, 246–8; Deslandres, "Samuel de Champlain and Religion," 199–201; Codignola, "Competing Networks," 545.

29 Le Clercq, *First Establishment of the Faith in New France*, 1:111; Wolfe, *The Conversion of Henri IV*, 189–90.

30 Le Clercq, *First Establishment of the Faith in New France*, 1:112, 79; Jaenen, "The Persistence of the Protestant Presence in New France, 1541–1760," 31.

31 Ritch, "Discovery of the Baptismal Certificate of Samuel De Champlain"; Deslandres, "Samuel de Champlain and Religion," 192; Fischer, *Champlain's Dream*, 23–4, 56–7.

32 Champlain, *Works*, 1:272; Deslandres, "Samuel de Champlain and Religion," 194–5.

33 Champlain, *Works*, 3:14, 30, 145 (quotations in order of appearance).

34 Deslandres, "Samuel de Champlain and Religion," 201; Thierry, "Introduction," 1:63–4.

35 Deslandres, "Samuel de Champlain and Religion," 195–7, 199–200; Trudel, *HNF*, 2:91–102.

36 The three previous paragraphs are heavily indebted to Deslandres, "Samuel de Champlain and Religion," 191–204, esp. 197–201. See also Galland, *Pour la gloire de Dieu et du roi*, 50–1.

37 On the convergence of the Récollets' evangelizing program and Champlain's "political project," see Galland, *Pour la gloire de Dieu et du roi*, 288.

38 See chapter 2, this volume.

39 Champlain, *Works*, 4:353–6.

40 For a different view, see Galland, *Pour la gloire de Dieu et du roi*, 291–2.

41 Le Clercq, *First Establishment of the Faith in New France*, 1:168, 171 (quotations in order of appearance).

42 Sagard, *Histoire du Canada*, 1:82, 87, 89, 92 (quotations in order of appearance).

43 Champlain, *Works*, 5:6, 135.

44 Diefendorf, "Henri IV, the Dévots and the Making of a French Catholic Reformation," 165; Wolfe, *The Conversion of Henri IV*, 189–90.

45 Barnes, "'Playing the Part of Angels,'" 173.

46 Brazeau, *Writing a New France*, 107–9. Brazeau describes commerce as the "historically negative Other" of Christianity (107).

47 Champlain, *Works*, 5:18.

48 Le Caron, *Au Roy sur la Nouvelle France*, 22–3.

49 Le Clercq, *First Establishment of the Faith in New France*, 1:134–5.

50 Trocmé, "La Rochelle protestante," 85–154; Brunelle, *New World Merchants of Rouen*, 53; Rambeaud, "L'Amiral à La Rochelle, l'union du ciel et de la mer," 135, 137.

51 Brunelle, *New World Merchants of Rouen*, 81.

52 *Nouv. docs*, 418–19; Bosher, "The Counter-Reformation in France," 49.

53 *Nouv. docs*, 418n3.

54 For an example of the royal solicitation of foreign commercial expertise, see Thomson, "France's Grotian Moment?," 407–27.

55 Bosher, "The Counter-Reformation in France," 48–52.

56 Ibid., 39–40.

57 *Charter of the Dutch West India Company*, 3 June 1621; James, *The Navy and Government in Early Modern France*, 43; Davies, *The Royal African Company*, 17.

58 Reid, "Sir William Alexander and North American Colonization," 25–6; Harvey, "Alexander, William, Earl of Stirling." In the late 1620s, Alexander came into competition with the Kirke brothers, who requested exclusive trade in Canada from the English king. His son collaborated with them to capture Port-Royal in 1629.

59 For a similar situation in the 1670s and '80s, see Henneton, "Spiritual Geopolitics," 225–6.

60 Sagard, *Histoire du Canada*, 1:82.

61 10 December 1621, no. 5, c. 36, Conseil privé, v6, LAC.

62 Miquelon, "Le commerce huguenot entre la France et la Nouvelle-France," 448. Ézéchiel's son, Émery, was born a Catholic. He later commanded Quebec from 1624 to 1626 in Champlain's absence and took back Quebec from the English in 1632 under Richelieu's orders. See Trudel, "Caën, Émery de."

63 Champlain, *Works*, 5:15–16, 39–40 (quotations in order of appearance). Already upon de Caën's arrival in New France in 1621, he was in conflict with two religious, Paul Huet and Guillaume Poullain, who had accompanied him on the voyage. In what seems an ironic action in retrospect, Champlain sent Le Baillif to settle the matter, along with the more serious one of the sharing of trade between the two companies. See ibid., 40–1.

64 Le Clercq, *First Establishment of the Faith in New France*, 1:162–3; Deslandres, *Croire et faire croire*, 250, 254; Trudel, *HNF*, 2:283–5. For the suggestion that Le Baillif's motivation stemmed from the denial of the Récollets' request to build a seminary in 1622, see Galland, *Pour la gloire de Dieu et du roi*, 90.

65 See the list of letters for and against de Caën dating from 1621 in "Extraits des Registres du Conseil d'Etat," 27 August 1634, vol. 16738, fonds français, dépt de mss, BnF; Trudel, *HNF*, 2:283n53. For positive assessments of Georges Le Baillif's actions, see Le Clercq, *First Establishment of the Faith in New France*, 1:163–4; Dumas, "Le Baillif, Georges." For a more critical view, see Trudel, *HNF*, 2:283–7. For the argument that Le Baillif was ultimately successful in his representations, despite failing to secure a ban on Protestant participation in the New France enterprise, see Fischer, *Champlain's Dream*, 377–8.

66 *Nouv. docs*, 437.

67 On the definition of subjecthood as one of the primary preoccupations of sovereign powers overseas, see Benton, *A Search for Sovereignty*, 37; Herzog, *Defining Nations*, chap. 3.

68 Sahlins, *Unnaturally French*, 59–62.

69 Ibid., 22–4; Havard, "'Les forcer à devenir Cytoyens,'" 989–90; Wells, *Law and Citizenship in Early Modern France*, 89–92, 115.

70 Diefendorf and Reinberg, "Catholic Reform and Religious Coexistence," 196. On the increasing exclusion of Protestants from civil offices and public functions during Louis XIII's reign, see Bosher, "The Counter-Reformation in France," 42–3.
71 Wells, *Law and Citizenship in Early Modern France*, 113–20.
72 "Acte pour l'établissement de la Compagnie des Cent Associés pour le commerce du Canada," in EO, 7.
73 Belmessous, "Être français en Nouvelle-France," 512–13.
74 *Nouv. docs*, 436 (emphasis added).
75 Deslandres suggests that the majority of inhabitants harboured no ill feeling toward de Caen on account of his religion; if any existed, it was due to his economic power. See *Croire et faire croire*, 251.
76 23 March 1624, fo. 122, vol. 10, Amirauté de France, série Z1D, LAC (emphasis added).
77 "Extraits des Registres du Conseil d'Etat," 27 August 1634, vol. 16738, fonds français, dépt de mss, BnF. In 1626, certain travellers to New France made an act affirming the good character of de Caën at the Admiralty of Dieppe. See ibid.
78 For the connections among these elements, see, for example, Champlain, *Works*, 3:30.
79 See, for example, Champlain, *Works*, 5:199, 236–7, 256–7, 268.
80 For example, ibid., 5:206–7.
81 Deslandres, "… alors nos garçons se marieront à vos filles, & nous ne ferons plus qu'un seul peuple," 22n69. Brittany was first incorporated through the marriage between Anne of Brittany and Charles VIII of France in 1492 before being officially integrated into the kingdom through treaty in 1532; Navarre became part of France upon Henri of Navarre's accession to the French throne as Henri IV.
82 Slattery, "French Claims in North America, 1500–59," 141; Bourguet, "Le sauvage, le colon, le paysan," 234; Havard, "Nous ne ferons plus qu'un peuple," 91; Deslandres, "Et loing de France, en l'une & l'autre mer, Les Fleurs de Liz, tu as fait renommer," 104. On the Catholic French and Spanish emphasis on peopled territory in contrast to the Protestant English, see Greer, *Property and Dispossession*, 197.
83 "Acte pour l'établissement de la Compagnie des Cent Associés pour le commerce du Canada," in EO, 10.
84 Havard, "Les forcer à devenir cytoyens," 989–90; Deslandres, "… alors nos garçons se marieront à vos filles, & nous ne ferons plus qu'un seul peuple," 24–5. The *droit d'aubaine* was the right by which the personal and real property of a foreigner who died in France became the property of the king.
85 Deslandres, "… alors nos garçons se marieront à vos filles, & nous ne ferons plus qu'un seul peuple," 24–5.

86 Morin, "Des nations libres sans territoire?" 24–5.

87 Havard, "Nous ne ferons plus qu'un peuple," 95–6; Greer and Mills, "A Catholic Atlantic," 9–10.

88 Religious disagreed among themselves over whether baptism was sufficient for conversion. When the Jesuits Pierre Biard and Énemond Massé arrived in Acadia in 1611, they were critical of the secular priest Jessé Fléché's conversion of more than a hundred Mi'kmaq who had not learned any of the fundamental Christian teachings. See Vachon, "Fléché, Jessé," and Campeau, "Biard, Pierre."

89 "Acte pour l'établissement de la Compagnie des Cent Associés pour le commerce du Canada," in *EO*, 6–7.

90 On the ways in which the disputes over the appropriate place of commerce and religion in the colony also contributed to this development, see Brazeau, *Writing a New France*, 113.

91 Havard, "Les forcer à devenir Cytoyens," 997, 999–1000; Bourguet, "Le sauvage, le colon, le paysan," 237–40. On the linguistic challenge of teaching Christian precepts to Indigenous groups in Acadia, see Guillorel, "Gérer la 'confusion de Babel,'" 178–87.

92 Belmessous, "Être français en Nouvelle-France," 515.

93 Havard, "Les forcer à devenir Cytoyens," 995–6.

94 Norberg, *Rich and Poor in Grenoble*; Schneider, *Public Life in Toulouse*, 308–10.

95 Deslandres, "… alors nos garçons se marieront à vos filles, & nous ne ferons plus qu'un seul peuple," 32; Greer and Mills, "A Catholic Atlantic," 4–5.

96 Lozier, *Flesh Reborn*, 39–43.

97 Havard, *Empire et Métissages*, 483–6, 489; Delâge, *Le pays renversé*, 82–3.

98 Havard, *Empire et métissages*, 483, 487, 489; Delâge, *Le pays renversé*, 179. In the first encounters between French and Indigenous Peoples of the Great Lakes region, all French were considered to be spirits on account of their technology. See Havard, *Empire et métissages*, 276–80.

99 Ibid., 488–9, 492–4, quotation at 488. On the French assumption that Indigenous men and women would worship God in the same way as they did, see Jaenen, "The Frenchification and Evangelization of the Amerindians in Seventeenth-Century New France," 36.

100 For examples among the societies of the *pays d'en haut*, see Havard, *Empire et métissages*, 494–5; on the Wendats, see Delâge, *Le pays renversé*, 190.

101 Lozier, *Flesh Reborn*, 53–72, quotation at 69.

102 Delâge, *Le pays renversé*, 180–2. On the growing conflict between traditionalists and converts within Wendat communities, see ibid., 210–11.

103 Both the Jesuits and the Ursulines came to adopt a more flexible policy toward francization, with the Jesuits notably advocating the establishment of separate communities for Indigenous converts, like Sillery above. See Deslandres, "… alors nos garçons se marieront à vos filles, & nous ne ferons plus qu'un

seul peuple," 33; Cowan, "Education, *Francisation* and Changing Colonial Priorities," 6–7, 11–13, 22–3.

104 *Jesuit Relations and Allied Documents*, 5:210–11; Havard, "Les forcer à devenir Cytoyens," 1001–2. Champlain saw the proposal by which three young Indigenous women would come live with the French through a similar lens. See Champlain, *Works*, 5:252. On the divergence between the Jesuits' and Colbert's approaches to intermarriage, see McShea, *Apostles of Empire*, 162–83.

105 This policy was not limited to North America or colonial spaces but also frontier areas of France. See Deslandres, "… alors nos garçons se marieront à vos filles, & nous ne ferons plus qu'un seul peuple," 16–17.

106 Havard, "Les forcer à devenir Cytoyens," 1002; McShea, *Apostles of Empire*, 180–1; Deslandres, "… alors nos garçons se marieront à vos filles, & nous ne ferons plus qu'un seul peuple," 29.

107 Delâge, *Le pays renversé*, 80, 208–9.

108 Havard, *Empire et métissages*, 444–7, 456–7.

109 Delâge, *Le pays renversé*, 209–10; McShea, *Apostles of Empire*, 174; Havard, "Nous ne ferons plus qu'un peuple," 100. On the constraints of European Catholic marriage, see Deslandres, "… alors nos garçons se marieront à vos filles, & nous ne ferons plus qu'un seul peuple," 25. On Jesuit acceptance, and even encouragement, of non-Catholic marriages, see McShea, *Apostles of Empire*, 180–1.

110 Havard, *Empire et métissages*, 455; Morrissey, *Empire by Collaboration*, 99–100; Belmessous, *Assimilation and Empire*, 39–40.

111 Havard, *Empire et métissages*, 455; Sleeper Smith, "Women, Kin, and Catholicism," 429–30. On regional differences, see Deslandres, "… alors nos garçons se marieront à vos filles, & nous ne ferons plus qu'un seul peuple," 31; Havard, "Nous ne ferons plus qu'un peuple," 102.

112 Havard, "Les forcer à devenir Cytoyens," 1003; Havard, *Empire et métissages*, 457–61. For the argument that official policies – whether ecclesiastical or royal – had little effect on the nature of relations between Indigenous and French individuals, see Codignola, "The Issue of Tridentine Marriage in a Composite North Atlantic World," 201–70.

113 Lescarbot, *Nova Francia*, 2–3.

114 Morin, "Des nations libres sans territoire?," 18–19; Morin, "La dimension juridique des relations entre Champlain et les Autochtones de la Nouvelle-France," 399–404.

115 Slattery, "Paper Empires," 63–4.

116 Morin, "Des nations libres sans territoire?," 18–19; Havard, "Les forcer à devenir Cytoyens," 1014, 1017–18; Slattery quotation in Jaenen, "French Sovereignty and Native Nationhood during the French Régime," 34. On the advantages to the French of keeping the status of Indigenous Peoples

ambiguous, see Morin, "Des nations libres sans territoire?," 37 for the Saint Lawrence Valley, and Lennox, *Homelands and Empires*, 79 for Acadia. On Indigenous-controlled spaces as an "instrument of empire," see Desbarats and Greer, "North America from the Top Down," 126–8, quotation at 127.

117 Tallon, *La Compagnie du Saint-Sacrement*, 19–20; Allier, *La Cabale des dévots*, 10–18, 143–50; Codignola, "Competing Networks," 547–8, 547n29; Deslandres, *Croire et faire croire*, 82–3; Bergin, *The Politics of Religion in Early Modern France*, 105–6; Barnes, "Playing the Part of Angels," 168–9, 173. On the Société de Notre-Dame's social and political influence in New France, see chapter 6, this volume.

118 Bosher, "The Counter-Reformation in France," 40–1; Bergin, *The Politics of Religion in Early Modern France*, 105.

119 Champlain, *Works*, 5:139–40; Codignola, "Competing Networks," 547–8, 547n29; Trudel, *HNF*, 2:298; Monet, "Noyrot, Philibert." On the Jesuits' solicitation of Ventadour's support, see Galland, *Pour la gloire de Dieu et du roi*, 86–7. On competition among orders over the version of the "Most Christian" nation that was to be transplanted in New France, see Brazeau, *Writing a New France*, 106. For an emphasis on the co-operation between the Jesuits and the Récollets, see Deslandres, *Croire et faire croire*, 275–6; Deslandres, "Ils ont toujours conservé un même esprit," 109–22.

120 "Vente par le duc de Ventadour à Jean de Lauson de la charge de viceroi au Canada," 29 June 1627, no. 86, étude LI, MC, LAC. On the resignation, see chapter 5, this volume. He also attached similar conditions to a proposed sale of the viceroyalty in 1625. See "Procuration par Henry de Lévy, duc de Ventadour pour la cession de sa charge de vice-roi du Canada," 29 April 1625, no. 431, étude VI, MC, LAC.

121 Champlain, *Works*, 5:15–16 (emphasis added).

122 Ibid., 5:85–6.

123 7 March 1626, fo. 66, vol. 86, Conseil d'Etat du Roi, Série E, LAC; 26 March 1626, fo. 406, vol. 86, ibid.; 4 April 1626, fo. 41, vol. 87a, ibid. The other associates were also to pay their share of the outfitting costs in return for 36 per cent – later 40 per cent – of the profits. See "Cautionnement par Jean-Jacques Dolu pour Guillaume de Caen," 16 January 1626, no. 267, étude CV, MC, AN; "Cautionnement par Salomon Langlois pour Guillaume de Caen," 4 April 1626, ibid.; 4 April 1626, fo. 41, vol. 87a, Conseil d'Etat du Roi, Série E, LAC. On the dispute that arose regarding this new arrangement, see 19 January 1626, fo. 36, vol. 7, Amirauté de France, série Z1D, LAC; 7 February 1626, fo. 50–51v, ibid.; 20 February 1626, fo. 52v-3v, ibid.; 24 March 1626, fo. 55–6.

124 Champlain, *Works*, 5:151.

125 Ibid., 5:194–5 (emphasis added). On Ventadour's reaction, see 5:150.

126 Ibid., 5:206–7.

Chapter Five

1 See Trudel, *HNF*, vol. 3, *La seigneurie des Cent-Associés, 1627–1663*.

2 For the view that the CNF was a dévot-led missionary endeavour, see, for example, Campeau, *Les Cent-Associés et le peuplement de la Nouvelle France*, 10; Campeau, *Les finances publiques de la Nouvelle France*, 58; Trudel, *HNF*, 3.1: 5–6, 16–17; Bosher, "The Political and Religious Origins of La Rochelle's Primacy in Trade with New France," 291–8. For the view that it was political and commercial, see Carpin, *Le Réseau du Canada*, 80–1, 94–5, 105–8, 115–16.

3 See, for example, Trudel, *HNF*, 3.1:18–19.

4 See, for example, Roulet, *La Compagnie des îles de l'Amérique*, 34. Several authors have incorrectly stated that the Compagnie de Morbihan was the predecessor of the CNF. Part of the confusion between the Compagnies du Morbihan and de la Nouvelle-France arose because they shared the same moniker, "les Cent Associés." See Castagnos, *Richelieu face à la mer*, 73; Thomson, "France's Grotian Moment?," 383, 389; Carmona, *La France de Richelieu*, 186.

5 Marion Godfroy-Tayart de Borms has noted the same experimentation with various methods in the case of companies for Guyana. See "Les premières compagnies françaises de Guyane dans le contexte de la rivalité franco-hollandaise du premier XVIIe siècle," 142.

6 For a different view of the reasons behind the adaptation of the Dutch and English joint-stock model in France, see Heijmans, Antunes, and Svalastog, "Essai de comparaison des compagnies néerlandaise, anglaise et française traitant sur la côte occidentale de l'Afrique au XVIIe siècle," 161–87, esp. 182–4.

7 "Acte pour l'établissement de la Compagnie des cent Associés pour le commerce du Canada," in *EO*, 7, 6 (quotations in order of appearance).

8 Ibid., 8.

9 Ibid., 8–9.

10 "Articles et conventions de société et compagnie, du 7e mai 1627, pour l'exécution des articles accordés, le 29e avril 1627, à la compagnie du Canada," in *EO*, 12–17.

11 See, among others, Le Cler, "Advis et tres humbles remonstrances au roy sur l'establissement du commerce en France," 30 December 1620, fo. 228, vol. 18781, fonds français, dépt de mss, BnF; "Mémoire pour les conjonctions des mers," fo. 514, vol. 17329, ibid.; "Mémoire pour l'establissement du commerce en France," fo. 24v–25, vol. 7287, NAF, dépt de mss, BnF; Montchrestien, *Traité de l'économie politique*; "Mémoire de Chevalier de Razilly," 24–32; "Remèdes aux déprédations des marchands et moyens de restablir le commerce," in *Les Papiers de Richelieu*, 569–70; "Mémoire pour faciliter le commerce de France avec les estrangers," in ibid., 576–8.

12 Horn, *Economic Development in Early Modern France*, 127–9; Hoffman, "Rural, Urban, and Global Economies," 74–7; Collins, *The State in Early Modern France*, 52–3; Parker, *La Rochelle and the French Monarchy*, 58–61.

13 Hoffman, "Rural, Urban, and Global Economies," 89–90.

14 Indeed, it is no coincidence that memoranda espousing this same constellation of ideas appeared during the century's other great period of discussion of overseas trade, Jean-Baptiste Colbert's tenure, 1661–83.

15 "Advis et tres humbles remonstrances au roy sur l'establissement du commerce en France," 30 December 1620, fo. 228, vol. 18781, fonds français, dépt de mss, BnF. I have not been able to identify this Jean Le Cler.

16 Eon, *Le Commerce honorable*, 44. For similar comments on the state of commerce in the 1640s, see Hauser, *La pensée et l'action économiques du Cardinal de Richelieu*, 126. A Carmelite's interest in the subject of French commerce requires some explanation. Eon, who wrote his treatise anonymously in 1646, had several powerful patrons. The prior of a Carmelite house in Nantes, he was under the patronage of the *commissaire général* of the Order of Mont-Carmel, Antoine de la Porte, who in turn was related to La Meilleraye, the governor and lieutenant general of Brittany and a relative of Richelieu. Eon became an adviser to La Meilleraye. An attempt by Nantes merchants to establish a *bourse commune* in the 1640s along the lines of earlier companies attempted under Richelieu met resistance from the Parlement of Rennes as well as in an anonymous publication. La Meilleraye, a supporter of the above project, probably suggested Eon, whom he knew to be one well positioned to formulate a riposte. See Dugast-Matifeux, *"Le Commerce honorable" et son auteur*, 6–27.

17 Castagnos, *Richelieu face à la mer*, 119. When speaking of the absence of noble engagement in commerce, contemporaries made a distinction between the Levant, where all classes were engaged in maritime and long-distance trade, and western France, where Atlantic commerce was growing. See Boiteux, *Richelieu, grand maître*, 200. For similar views in contemporary England, see Glaisyer, *The Culture of Commerce in England, 1660–1720*, 17–19.

18 Memorandum by Claude Razilly to Richelieu, n.d., fo. 1, vol. 4826, fonds français, dépt de mss, BnF. See also Castagnos, *Richelieu face à la mer*, 119; Horn, *Economic Development in Early Modern France*, 13–14; Hoffman, "Rural, Urban, and Global Economies," 94–5; Parker, *La Rochelle and the French Monarchy*, 59–60.

19 "Advis et tres humbles remonstrances au roy sur l'ordre et retablissement du Commerce et Navigation en suite de la proposition cy devant faicte a sa Majeste sur ce mesme subject," 19 March 1626, fo. 234, vol. 18781, fonds français, dépt de mss, BnF; "Mémoire pour les conjonctions des mers," fo. 514 vol. 17329, ibid.; "Mémoire de Chevalier de Razilly," 24–32; Eon, *Le Commerce honorable*, 170–5, 294–5; "Remèdes aux déprédations des

marchands," in *Les Papiers de Richelieu*, 569–70; "Mémoire pour faciliter le commerce de France," in ibid., 576–8.

20 Eon, *Le Commerce honorable*, 294–5; Montchrestien, *Traité de l'économie politique*, 311–12. On the origin of shipbuilding subsidies in England, see Loades, *England's Maritime Empire*, 30. In contrast to Eon, Montchrestien had no strong political connections, but became interested in commerce and industry through his own travels. He lived for a time in England, where he witnessed the industry of his fellow Frenchmen and became familiar with the operation of various industries. He also travelled to the Netherlands, where he was introduced to the large commercial companies of the Dutch. Returning to France, he set up his own steelworks and a tool factory. He wrote his treatise on political economy in 1615 and dedicated it to Louis XIII and the queen regent. Although he obtained an audience before the monarch and regent, he did not succeed in convincing them to follow his program. Disillusioned, he later joined the Huguenots in revolt. See Funck-Brentano "Introduction," x–xxi. On Montchrestien's religion, see Brazeau, *Writing a New France*, 106, 111–12.

21 Like their French counterparts, English thinkers and merchants engaged in a close study of the Dutch economy in order to imitate the patterns that had led to its success. This included attempts to create a West India company along Dutch lines in the 1620s. See Appleby, *Economic Thought and Ideology in Seventeenth-Century England*, chap. 4; Appleby, "An Association for the West Indies?," 213–41; Wagner, *The English Chartered Trading Companies*, 45–51.

22 Eon, *Le Commerce honorable*, 295; Boiteux, *Richelieu, grand maître*, 204.

23 "Mémoire pour l'establissement du commerce en France," fo. 27, vol. 7287, NAF, dépt de mss, BnF. See also "Pour obéir au Commandement de Monseigneur le Cardinal," fo. 54, vol. 4826, ibid.; "Mémoire pour les conjonctions des mers," fo. 514, vol. 17329, ibid.

24 Petit, "Mémoire sur le commerce et les avantages de la marine," 287–8.

25 For an outline of the practical advantages, see "Pour obéir au Commandement de Monseigneur le Cardinal," fo. 54–54v, vol. 4826, fonds français, dépt de mss, BnF. See also Claude de Launay-Razilly, fo. 1, ibid.

26 "Mémoire du Chevalier de Razilly," in Deschamps, ed., *Un colonisateur du temps de Richelieu, Isaac de Razilly*, 24–5, quotation at 25. The royal company referred to was one that the king would make with his "beloved [nobles at court]." Many of Razilly's contemporaries were of the same opinion. See, for example, Champlain, *Works*, 3:147.

27 Thomson, "France's Grotian Moment?" 385–6; Collins, *The State in Early Modern France*, 56–9, esp. 56–7.

28 Petit, *L'Assemblée des Notables*, 37, 39, 40–1; Boiteux, *Richelieu, grand maître*, 105, 108.

29 "Mémoire du Chevalier de Razilly," in Deschamps, ed., *Un colonisateur du temps de Richelieu, Isaac de Razilly*, 24–35.

30 While Razilly's report is usually presented in Canadian historiography as the precursor to the CNF's establishment, it devoted, in fact, very little space to North America. For a similar view, see Carpin, *Le Réseau du Canada*, 68–70. For the more traditional view, see Trudel, *HNF*, 3.1:5.

31 "Mémoire du Chevalier de Razilly," in Deschamps, ed., *Un colonisateur du temps de Richelieu, Isaac de Razilly*, 30, 32, 31 (quotations in order of appearance).

32 Ibid., 18; see also 20.

33 Petit, *L'Assemblée des Notables*, 173.

34 Parker, *La Rochelle and the French Monarchy*, 79.

35 "Mémoire touchant la Marine, envoyé à M. le Garde des Sceaux, le 18 novembre 1626," in *Les Papiers de Richelieu*, 531; Petit, "Mémoire sur le commerce et les avantages de la marine," 288; James, *The Navy and Government in Early Modern France*, 45, 49; Levot, "La Marine française et le Port de Brest sous Richelieu et Mazarin," 10–11. There were ten vessels reportedly built by 1630. See ibid., 14. In a proposal to the king also submitted in 1626, Richelieu advocated for forty ships at a cost of 2.5 million livres. See Vergé-Franceschi, *Chronique maritime de la France d'Ancien Régime*, 317–18.

36 Ardier, *L'Assemblée des notables tenue à Paris ès années 1626 et 1627*, 9. Ardier was the clerk of the assembly, appointed by the king, as well as a royal counsellor, secretary, treasurer, and principal clerk to the *secrétaire d'État des affaires étrangères*.

37 Deschamps, "La question coloniale en France au temps de Richelieu et de Mazarin," 371. Others, including Mathieu Molé, *procureur général*, and the king in his statement echoed this sentiment during the assembly. See Ardier, *L'Assemblée des notables*, 227; Petit, *L'Assemblée des Notables*, 175.

38 Collins, *The State in Early Modern France*, 56–7.

39 James, *The Navy and Government in Early Modern France*, 43–6; Hauser, *La pensée et l'action économiques*, 54–6; Tapié, *France in the Age of Louis XIII and Richelieu*, 141–2; Briggs, "Richelieu and Reform: Rhetoric and Political Reality," 86. Historians disagree on the relative weight Richelieu accorded to English and Spanish threats. For the former, see James, *The Navy and Government in Early Modern France*, 53–4; for the latter, Thomson, "France's Grotian Moment?," 378.

40 In 1625, the seizure of Spanish ships by the Duc de Guise in Genoa prompted counter seizures by Spain and a ban on trade between the two countries. See 13 May 1625, 1Bb 864, Table des Registres du Parlement de Bretagne, ADIV; Thomson, "France's Grotian Moment?," 381.

41 For the history of Protestant mercantile activity in La Rochelle, see Rambeaud, "L'Amiral à La Rochelle, l'union du ciel et de la mer," 131–43.

42 This was Montmorency's first naval battle. See Dessert, *Les Montmorency*, 172–3.

43 Parker, *La Rochelle and the French Monarchy*, 14, 71–82; James, *The Navy and Government in Early Modern France*, 28; Holt, *The French Wars of Religion*, 190–1; Bonney, *Political Change in France under Richelieu and Mazarin*, 387–9.

44 "Contrat de la Compagnie du Morbihan, 31 mars 1626," in *Les Papiers de Richelieu*, 305.

45 "Edit du roi pour l'établissement de la Compagnie des Cent-Associés," July 1626, corresp. gén., C11A, LAC; Boiteux, *Richelieu, grand maître*, 87, 90–1.

46 "Contrat fait par Monsieur Le Cardinal de Richelieu comme Surintendant général du Commerce avec une compagnie de Flamens [*sic*] et autres associés," 19 May 1626, vol. 318, Collection Dupuy, LAC.

47 Dessert, *Les Montmorency*, 76, 86, 143, 160–1. On similar checks to the power of the other top three military officers, see Collins, *The State in Early Modern France*, 57–9.

48 On Richelieu's efforts to destroy the power of the Montmorency family, see Dessert, *Les Montmorency*, chap. 6, esp. 164–91.

49 Carpin, *Le Réseau du Canada*, 53–4.

50 "Edit du roi pour l'établissement de la Compagnie des Cent-Associés," July 1626, fo. 74, corresp. gén., C11A, LAC; see also 72v.

51 Thomson, "France's Grotian Moment?," 380, 384, 392; Dunkley, "Trading Companies and Privilege in Richelieu's France," 5; Vergé-Franceschi, *Chronique maritime de la France*, 317.

52 On the convergence of royal objectives in New France and the port of La Rochelle from 1628, see Bosher, "The Political and Religious Origins of La Rochelle's Primacy in Trade with New France," 286–312. In actual fact, Normandy remained the main centre of trade and recruitment under the CNF until the 1640s, when La Rochelle eclipsed it for a decade. See Carpin, *Le Réseau du Canada*, 122, 151, 181–2.

53 Horn, *Economic Development in Early Modern France*, chap. 2, quotation at 24; Parker, *La Rochelle and the French Monarchy*, 65.

54 Parker, *La Rochelle and the French Monarchy*, 65–7; James, *The Navy and Government in Early Modern France*, 46. On the maritime history of the Wars of Religion, see Vergé-Franceschi, "L'amirauté de France dans la deuxième moitié du XVIe siècle," 35–43, esp. 38.

55 "Lettres patentes de création de la charge de Grand Maître Chef et surintendant général de la navigation et commerce de France et provision d'icelle en faveur de Monsieur le Cardinal de Richelieu en octobre 1626," fo. 203, vol. 203, Cinq Cents de Colbert, dépt de mss, BnF.

56 For a different emphasis, see James, *The Navy and Government in Early Modern France*, 53–4.

57 Bergin, *Cardinal Richelieu*, 95.

58 Ibid., 82–4, 95–6; Roulet, *La Compagnie des îles de l'Amérique*, 24–6, 30–2.

59 "Voyage et inspection maritime de M. D'Infreville sur les côtes françaises de l'océan," in *Correspondance de Henri D'Escoubleau de Sourdis*, 3:171–221; James, "Voyage et inspection maritime de M. D'Infreville sur les côtes françaises de l'océan, 1631," 448–53; Bergin, *Cardinal Richelieu*, 100–2. For other examples of this type of report submitted to Richelieu, see "Rapport de Nicolas Langlois sieur du Collemoulins … sur les ports et havres de Normandie," 22 March 1627, vol. 18596, fonds français, dépt de mss, BnF; James, *The Navy and Government in Early Modern France*, 62, 69–70.

60 On Richelieu's creation of a database to shore up royal claims to shipwrecks, see Thomson, "Commerce, Law and Erudite Culture," 418.

61 Bergin, *Cardinal Richelieu*, 49, 100, 115; James, *The Navy and Government in Early Modern France*, 57–9, 62–3; Boiteux, *Richelieu, grand maître*, 114–17. Other variations of Martin de Mauvoy's name in the literature include Mauroy and Maunoy.

62 Bergin, *Cardinal Richelieu*, 96, 104–7, 112.

63 Ibid., 82–9; Boiteux, *Richelieu, grand maître*, 115–16, 133, 150–1; James, *The Navy and Government in Early Modern France*, 65; Castagnos, *Richelieu face à la mer*, 68–70.

64 Bergin, *Cardinal Richelieu*, 102.

65 Ibid., 81–4, 94, 112–13; Thomson, "Commerce, Law and Erudite Culture," 419–20.

66 For the view that Richelieu's grande maîtrise created a sort of ministry of marine, commerce, and colonies, see Boiteux, *Richelieu, grand maître*, 99–100. For the traditional view of Richelieu as a reformer with a coherent, long-term program, see Tapié, *France in the Age of Louis XIII and Richelieu*; Elliott, *Richelieu and Olivares*; Castagnos, *Richelieu face à la mer*. For recent examples that challenge this view, see Briggs, "Richelieu and Reform," 71–97; Parrott, *Richelieu's Army*; James, *The Navy and Government in Early Modern France*; Dessert, *Les Montmorency*, 164; Thomson, "Commerce, Law and Erudite Culture," 421–2; Dewar, "Souveraineté dans les colonies, souveraineté en metropole," 63–92.

67 Thomson, "France's Grotian Moment?," 388; Dunkley, "Trading Companies and Privilege in Richelieu's France," 10.

68 Darsel, *L'Amirauté en Bretagne*, 217–19. The Estates did eventually register the edict in January 1628 but with conditions so severe as to completely undermine its intent.

69 Ibid., 219nn3–4.

70 The Compagnie de Morbihan was definitively abandoned in 1628. See Carpin, *Le Réseau du Canada*, 55, 57, 58; Dunkley, "Trading Companies and Privilege in Richelieu's France," 5–9. The Compagnie de la Nacelle de Saint-Pierre

fleurdelisée, which also encountered considerable opposition, continued until at least March 1627, when Richelieu was preparing to bring its edict before the parlements once more. See Boiteux, *Richelieu, grand maître*, 100–1; *Les Papiers de Richelieu*, 2:124–5.

71 Bergin, *Cardinal Richelieu*, 108; Boiteux, *Richelieu, grand maître*, 103. The letters had been registered by the Parlement of Paris on 18 March and by the Parlement of Rouen on 16 April. The sovereign court in Bordeaux did not register them until the end of May. See Carpin, *Le Réseau du Canada*, 72.

72 Darsel, *L'Amirauté en Bretagne*, 220–2.

73 Pons de Lauzières, sieur de Thémines, erstwhile viceroy of New France, had been appointed as governor in Vendôme's place, but he died in 1627. See Bergin, *Cardinal Richelieu*, 87n87.

74 Darsel, *L'Amirauté en Bretagne*, 224; Collins, *The State in Early Modern France*, 62; Collins, *Classes, Estates and Order in Early Modern Brittany*, 117, 176, 184; Bergin, *Cardinal Richelieu*, 93. This gift, which became an annual pension, has sometimes been mistaken for a salary received as governor.

75 Bergin, *Cardinal Richelieu*, 85, 87.

76 The Day of the Dupes refers to the day in November 1630 when Louis XIII decided to keep Cardinal Richelieu in his position against the advice of his mother, Marie de Médicis, and the latter went into exile.

77 Darsel, *L'Amirauté en Bretagne*, 224.

78 Bergin, *Cardinal Richelieu*, 108; Darsel, *L'Amirauté en Bretagne*, 227; Valin, *Nouveau commentaire sur l'ordonnance de la marine du mois d'août 1681*, 40–1.

79 "Edit du roi pour l'établissement de la Compagnie des Cent-Associés," July 1626, corresp. gén., C11A, LAC. See also "Contrat fait par Monsieur Le Cardinal de Richelieu comme Surintendant général du Commerce avec une compagnie de Flamens [*sic*] et autres associés," 19 May 1626, vol. 318, Collection Dupuy, LAC.

80 Ventadour had, however, supported Richelieu's policies as viceroy. See Ruggiu, "Colonies, Monarchy, Empire and the French *Ancien Régime*," 200–1.

81 In seventeenth-century France, clients tended to refer to themselves as *créatures* in correspondence with their patron. Patron-client relationships were reciprocal, with the client receiving positions and other forms of patronage in return for service. While Richelieu had his creatures, he was also the creature of Louis XIII. See Kettering, *Patrons, Brokers, Clients in Seventeenth-Century France*, 16.

82 "Vente par le duc de Ventadour à Jean de Lauson de la charge de viceroi au Canada," 29 June 1627, no. 86, étude LI, MC, LAC; "Convention entre le duc de Ventadour et Jean de Lauson pour le paiement de la charge du vice-roi du Canada," 29 June 1627, ibid.; Lauson to Richelieu, 30 June 1627, fo. 178, vol. 785, Mémoire et documents, France, Fonds du Ministère des affaires étrangères, LAC.

83 A royal decree concerning the liquidation of the CNF's debts included a substantial sum due to the Compagnie de Montmorency to compensate for the loss of trading privileges. It listed Richelieu as having renounced his right to the viceroy's share in the earlier company, which he had purchased from Ventadour. See 24 July 1643, fo. 144–52, vol. 181c, Conseil d'Etat du Roi, Série E, LAC; Campeau, *Les finances publiques de la Nouvelle France*, 41; Boiteux, *Richelieu, grand maître*, 148, 278.
84 Letters patent to Charles de La Tour as governor and lieutenant general of Acadia, 8 February 1631, in Couillard-Després, *Charles de Saint-Etienne de La Tour*, 191 (emphasis added).
85 "Articles et conventions de société et compagnie, du 7e mai 1627, pour l'exécution des articles accordés, à la Compagnie du Canada," in *EO*, 16.
86 Ibid., 13.
87 On Richelieu's desire for control over the company, see Carpin, *Le Réseau du Canada*, 78. De Caën had another well-placed ally at the Admiralty of France in the Sieur de Saint-Martin, who had been a guarantor for him in the agreement concerning the new configuration of the Compagnie de Montmorency in 1626.
88 These were François Castillon; Simon Dablon, syndic of Dieppe; David Duchesne, counsellor and alderman of Havre-de-Grâce; Louis Houel, sieur du Petit-Pré, the royal counsellor and controller general of the salt works at Brouage who had proposed to the Récollets that they make New France their mission field; Gabriel Lattaignant, former mayor of Calais; and Claude Roquemont de Brison, future head of the company's fleet.
89 Philippe de Longvillliers, Sieur de Poincy, a Knight of Malta, served later as governor in the West Indies; Sébastien Cramoisy was a prominent printer, bookseller, and publisher of the *Jesuit Relations*. Among the royal officials in the CNF were the superintendant of finances, the Marquis d'Effiat, and the intendant of the navy, Martin de Mauvoy. For the full membership list, see appendix A in Trudel, *HNF*, 3.1:415–25. For a social portrait of the CNF's associates, see Beaudin, "Les membres de la Compagnie des Cent-Associés: Étude d'histoire sociale."
90 Carpin, *Le Réseau du Canada*, 63–4, 73, 98; Castagnos, *Richelieu face à la mer*, 129–41.
91 Eon, *Le Commerce honorable*, 295.
92 On du Noyer de Saint-Martin, see Boiteux, "Un économiste méconnu," 3–8, 36.
93 Boiteux, "Un économiste méconnu," 9, 9n2.
94 "Compagnie royale de voyages de long cours," 1623, fo. 306v, vol. 17329, fonds français, dépt de mss, BnF. In addition to its ambitious overseas mandate, it was to include an insurance service and a "Royal and General Bank" to provide credit and bottomry loans. The company would also control the registers of

the *État civil* (a remarkable power since civil registration was not established in France until the Revolution), passports, and industrial manufactures.

95 Boiteux, "Un économiste méconnu," 50–2; Verlinden, *The Beginnings of Modern Colonization*, 7.

96 Indeed, du Noyer went so far as to accuse Richelieu of having stolen his idea. See Boiteux, "Un économiste méconnu," 55.

97 "Contrat de la Compagnie du Morbihan ou des Cent Associés," in *Les Papiers de Richelieu*, 1:306.

98 Ibid., 1:303–13.

99 "Contrat de la Compagnie de la Nacelle de Saint-Pierre fleurdelysée, 19 mai 1626," in ibid., 1:323–4. What follows is based on the text of the contract at 321–38.

100 *Lods et ventes* refers to the right of the seigneur – in this case, the king – to a one-twelfth part of the sale price of a building on his seigneury.

101 There is some confusion in the historiography as to whether the company enjoyed any exclusive privileges outside of France. Articles 23 and 41 in the contract granted the company exclusive trading privileges only in lands they "discovered" and claimed for France. "Contrat de la Compagnie de la Nacelle de Saint-Pierre fleurdelysée, 19 mai 1626," in *Les Papiers de Richelieu*, 1:331, 335; Trudel, HNF, 3.1:3–4; Carmona, *La France de Richelieu*, 186.

102 "Edit du roi pour l'établissement de la Compagnie des Cent-Associés," July 1626, corresp. gén., C11A, LAC.

103 "Contrat de la Compagnie de la Nacelle de Saint-Pierre fleurdelysée, 19 mai 1626," in *Les Papiers de Richelieu*, 1:331, and see also 335; "Contrat de la Compagnie du Morbihan ou des Cent Associés," in ibid., 1:311.

104 Davies, *The Royal African Company*, 21.

105 Calculations based on Harris, *Going the Distance*, 323; Phillips and Sharman, *Outsourcing Empire*, 72; McCusker, *Money and Exchange in Europe and America*, 88.

106 On the fragmented nature of French markets, see Horn, *Economic Development in Early Modern France*, 129.

107 "Contrat de la Compagnie de la Nacelle de Saint-Pierre fleurdelysée," in *Les Papiers de Richelieu*, 1:334n1.

108 "Edit du roi pour l'établissement de la Compagnie des Cent-Associés," July 1626, corresp. gén., C11A, LAC.

109 "Edit du roi pour l'établissement de la compagnie de la Nouvelle France," May 1628, fo. 91, corresp. gén., C11A, LAC.

110 On French claims to universal monarchy, see Bosbach, "The European Debate on Universal Monarchy," 87–8, 92–8. On the contemporary conviction that France was the natural heir to Rome and the Holy Roman Empire, see Yates, *Astraea: The Imperial Theme in the Sixteenth Century*, 121; Haran, *Le lys et le globe: Messianisme dynastique et le rêve imperial*, 180.

111 "Acte pour l'établissement de la Compagnie des cent Associés pour le commerce du Canada," in EO, 7. The second article's use of the verb *faire passer* (to send over/transport) has caused some debate among scholars. Here is the full article: "faire passer aucun étranger ès dits lieux, ains peupler la dite colonie de naturels François catholiques." Although foreigners were categorically excluded, it is possible that Protestants could travel to New France but not live there. See Carpin, *Le Réseau du Canada*, 82–3; Trudel, *HNF*, 3.1:13.

112 The frequency of commercial terms also varies substantially between the two universal companies and the CNF. Terms such as "commerce," "trade," "merchandise," and "profit" are used only four times in the edict of 29 April 1627 and seven times in the company's articles and conventions of 7 May but appear thirty-six times in the July 1626 edict of the Compagnie de Morbihan and forty-two times in the Compagnie de la Nacelle de Saint-Pierre fleurdelisée's May 1626 contract.

113 Tapié, *France in the Age of Louis XIII and Richelieu*, 143; Gutton, *Dévots et société au XVIIe siècle*, 9.

114 Tapié, *France in the Age of Louis XIII and Richelieu*, 145–6, 148–50, 152–3, quotation at 152.

115 "Advis sur les affaires présentes qu'a le Roy en février 1626," in *Les Papiers de Richelieu*, 1:296 (emphasis added).

116 Philip Boucher has suggested that a similar consideration was at play when the Compagnie des îles de l'Amérique was established in 1635, the year France formally entered the Thirty Years' War against Spain. See "French Proprietary Colonies in the Greater Caribbean," 171.

117 On dévot connections and other religious linkages among members of the CNF, see Frostin, "Vogue canadienne et milieu métropolitain de soutien à la mission lointaine au XVIIe siècle," 420–4; Bosher, "The Political and Religious Origins of La Rochelle's Primacy in Trade with New France," 291–4, 297–8; Gutton, *Dévots et société au XVIIe siècle*, 18, 30, 84–5.

118 Trudel, *HNF*, 3.1:18–19.

119 Bayard, *Le monde des financiers au XVIIe siècle*, 302.

120 Dessert, *Argent, pouvoir et société au Grand Siècle*, 203–4; Dent, *Crisis in Finance*, chap. 3; Bien, "Offices, Corps, and a System of State Credit," 103, 110–11.

121 Dessert, *Argent, pouvoir et société au Grand Siècle*, 207, 379, 389; Dent, *Crisis in Finance*, chap. 5. Indeed, Razilly recommended exploiting this state of dependence in his memorandum and favoured drawing on church revenue to cover colonization costs. See "Mémoire du Chevalier de Razilly," in Deschamps, ed., *Un colonisateur du temps de Richelieu, Isaac de Razilly*, 26.

122 On the various reasons a financier might feel compelled to subscribe to the CNF, see Carpin, *Le Réseau du Canada*, 105–8.

123 For examples of such loans, see McManners, *Church and Society in Eighteenth Century France*, 142–3, 160.

124 Bonney, *The King's Debts*, 147–8.

125 Bergin, "Crown and Episcopate in the Age of Henri IV and Louis XIII," 71–2.

126 Trudel, *HNF*, 3.1:6. For another example, see Frostin, "Vogue canadienne et milieu métropolitain de soutien à la mission lointaine au XVIIe siècle," 421.

127 Not all of this land, it should be noted, was granted by the CNF. See Trudel, *HNF*, 3.2:105–6, 3.1:154–8.

128 Carpin, *Le Réseau du Canada*, 200, 205; Boiteux, *Richelieu, grand maître*, 250–1; Bosher, "The Political and Religious Origins of La Rochelle's Primacy in Trade with New France," 292.

129 Frostin, "Vogue canadienne et milieu métropolitain de soutien à la mission lointaine au XVIIe siècle," 420–1; Jacquet, "Cramoisy (Famille)," 9:1161–3.

130 Frostin, "Vogue canadienne et milieu métropolitain de soutien à la mission lointaine au XVIIe siècle," 422; Bosher, "The Political and Religious Origins of La Rochelle's Primacy in Trade with New France," 294; Bergin, *The Politics of Religion in Early Modern France*, 105.

131 Frostin, "Vogue canadienne et milieu métropolitain de soutien à la mission lointaine au XVIIe siècle," 423–4; "Notices biographiques," in Dessert, *Argent, pouvoir et société au Grand Siècle*, 543.

132 These associates included Pierre Aubert, Charles Fleuriau d'Armenonville, Claude de Chastellain, Quentin de Richebourg, and Etienne Pavillon. See Carpin, *Le Réseau du Canada*, 100–3; Trudel, *HNF*, 3.1, appendix A.

133 François Fouquet and Pierre Chanut are two other examples of these interconnections. See, respectively, Dessert, *Fouquet*, 129–30, 130n20, and Roulet, *La Compagnie des îles de l'Amérique*, 129–31.

134 The Compagnie de Saint-Christophe only took this title after the establishment of its successor, the Compagnie des îles de l'Amérique in 1635, in order to distinguish the two companies. The original act of association was for "les seigneurs de la Compagnie des îles de l'Amérique." See "Contrat d'association de la Compagnie de Saint-Christophe," 31 October 1626, in *Les Papiers de Richelieu*, 1:508; Roulet, *La Compagnie des îles de l'Amérique*, 19. On the evolution of the company's terms over time, see Roulet, "L'évolution des statuts de la Compagnie des îles de l'Amérique de 1626 à 1642," 109–25.

135 "Contrat d'association de la Compagnie de Saint-Christophe," in *Les Papiers de Richelieu*, 1:509–10, quotation at 509.

136 On the absence of any territorial concession, see Chailley-Bert, *Les compagnies de colonisation sous l'Ancien Régime*, 38. Carpin notes that one secondary source cites an earlier document dated 2 October 1626, which specified that the company was to bring settlers to the island, conduct all types of commerce, and give the king one-tenth of the profits. See Carpin, *Le Réseau du Canada*, 58n53.

137 On the *société en commandite*, see Lévy-Bruhl, *Histoire juridique des sociétés de commerce en France*, 33–9.
138 "Contrat d'association de la Compagnie de Saint-Christophe," 31 October 1626, in *Les Papiers de Richelieu*, 1:510n2.
139 On the clientele ties between the proponents and Richelieu, see Carpin, *Le Réseau du Canada*, 97.
140 Roulet, *La Compagnie des îles de l'Amérique*, 126–7. For the act of foundation, see Servant, *Les Compagnies de Saint-Christophe*, 29–32. For the articles among members, see "Articles accordés entre les associés de la Compagnie des îles de l'Amérique," Roulet, *La Compagnie des îles de l'Amérique*, 224–7.
141 Roulet, *La Compagnie des îles de l'Amérique*, 119–21, 123–4, 129–31, 157–62. On the exceptional case of the Compagnie du Sénégal, see Steiner, "La première Compagnie du Sénégal (1633)," 152–6.

Chapter Six

1 Revel, "Les corps et communautés," 225; Vincent, *Les confréries médiévales dans le royaume de France*, 148–50.
2 "Acte pour l'établissement de la Compagnie des Cent Associés pour le commerce du Canada," in EO, 5–7.
3 "Articles et conventions de société et compagnie, du 7e mai 1627, pour l'exécution des articles accordés, à la Compagnie du Canada," in EO, 17, 15 (quotations in order of appearance). For the suggestion that the CNF was generous toward "poor and sick Natives," see McShea, *Apostles of Empire*, 120. Although Henri Lévy-Bruhl suggests it was not an uncommon clause in *actes de sociétés* in general, I did not find this clause in charters of any other companies created in the period. See *Histoire juridique des sociétés de commerce en France*, 73.
4 "Acte pour l'établissement de la Compagnie des Cent Associés pour le commerce du Canada," in EO, 8.
5 Mishra, *The Business of State*, 8; Coornaert, "European Economic Institutions and the New World," 245–8, 261, quotation at 246; Ogborn, "Wherein Lay the Late Seventeenth-Century State?," 96–101; Royle, *The Company's Island*, 156.
6 "Acte pour l'établissement de la Compagnie des Cent Associés pour le commerce du Canada," in EO, 8, 9. This practice was also a feature of the later Compagnie des îles de l'Amérique, although the king reserved to himself the power to appoint a lieutenant general for all of the islands. See Servant, *Les Compagnies de Saint-Christophe*, 30–1.
7 *First Charter of Virginia*, 10 April 1606; *Second Charter of Virginia*, 23 May 1609; *Third Charter of Virginia*, 12 March 1611; *Charter of Massachusetts Bay*, 1629; *Charter of the Dutch West India Company*, 1621.

8 Stern, "Bundles of Hyphens," 28. "Sovereignty" refers to the supreme authority exercised by a ruler and reflects their complete independence from external control. "Suzerainty" refers to the condition by which a territory enjoys domestic sovereignty but is ultimately answerable to an outside authority. From *Canadian Dictionary of the English Language*. On the similarities between the CNF and the Massachusetts Bay Company with respect to territory granted, see Greer, *Property and Dispossession*, 194.

9 Phillips and Sharman, *Outsourcing Empire*, 7–9.

10 Dewar, "Government by Trading Company?," para. 12–13.

11 On the need to examine French corporations in a comparative and Atlantic context, see Dewar, "Agents, Institutions and French Empire/State Formation," 98–106.

12 "Articles et conventions de société et compagnie, du 7e mai 1627, pour l'exécution des articles accordés, à la Compagnie du Canada," in *EO*, 13.

13 Contemporaries in fact considered him to be viceroy of New France; Isaac de Razilly addressed him as "your eminence with the charge of viceroy in this new world." See Isaac de Razilly to Richelieu, 25 July 1634, vol. 4, Mémoires et documents, Amérique, Fonds du ministère des Affaires étrangères, BnF.

14 Champlain, *Works*, 5:288; also 6:360.

15 Ibid., 6:151–2. The company appointed Champlain only "provisionally" at this time. See Vachon, "The Administration of New France."

16 For Montmagny's reappointment in 1645 – his fourth and last – see *Mém. des comm.*, 2:397–9; Trudel, *HNF*, 3.1:142; Vachon, "The Administration of New France"; Lanctôt, *L'administration de la Nouvelle-France*, 22.

17 Robineau was a nobleman, royal counsellor, and treasurer of the light cavalry of France. The only reference to Duplessis Kerbodot as a member of the company is his nomination of 1651. See Trudel, *HNF*, 3.1:435.

18 *Mém. des comm.*, 2:399–401, quotation at 400. For the CNF assembly at which the three were nominated, see "Provision de gouverneur de la Nouvelle France pour le sieur de Lauzon," 2 January 1651, vol. 1, Deuxième Série, Nouvelle-France. Correspondance officielle, LAC.

19 *Mém. des comm.*, 2:398. While this clause appeared in the renewal of Montmagny's commission accorded in June 1645, it is worth noting that it was absent in Lauson's commission.

20 This power was common among chartered companies in the Atlantic. The form of land tenure differed, with the Dutch West India Company granting patroonships and English companies enjoying the same terms as the bishops of Durham. See MacMillan, *Sovereignty and Possession in the English New World*, 97; Jacobs, "Dutch Proprietary Manors in America," 301–26. For the exceptional case of New England, where townships, rather than the Massachusetts Bay Company, granted land, see Greer, *Property and Dispossession*, 202–12, 377.

21 Baudry, "Charles d'Aulnay et la Compagnie de la Nouvelle France," 221; MacBeath, "Saint-Étienne de La Tour, Charles de."

22 Letters patent to La Tour as governor and lieutenant general of Acadia, 8 February 1631, in Couillard-Després, *Charles de Saint-Etienne de La Tour*, 192. For La Tour's request for a royal commission, see ibid., 149–52. The only reference to La Tour as a company associate is found in his commission from Richelieu. See Trudel, *HNF*, appendix A, 3.1:428.

23 Couillard-Després, *Charles de Saint-Etienne de La Tour*, 149; MacBeath, "Saint-Étienne de La Tour, Claude."

24 Champlain, *Works*, 6:172–3; Le Blant, "La Compagnie de la Nouvelle-France et la restitution de l'Acadie," 77. One of the vessels in the first fleet sent by the CNF in 1628 was to go to Cap de Sable with supplies but was intercepted by an English force under the Kirke brothers. See Carpin, *Le Réseau du Canada*, 122–3; Claude Massé, "Jean Tuffet et ses activités en faveur de la Nouvelle-France," 6, 11–13.

25 Couillard-Després, *Charles de Saint-Etienne de La Tour*, 252; *Mém. des comm.*, 2:388–90. La Tour later received Vieux-Logis at the southern tip of Acadia, near Fort Saint-Louis at Port de la Tour, in 1636. See Carpin, *Le Réseau du Canada*, 232, 240–1. For La Tour's concessions, see figure 6.2 below.

26 In a concession to Nicolas Denys in 1653, the CNF promised to name him governor and lieutenant general, provided that he met his obligations as seigneur; he became governor the following year. See "Concession à N. Denys," 3 December 1653, C11D, LAC; *Mém. des comm.*, 2:401–7.

27 *Coll. mss*, 1:85–6, quotation at 86. For the king's commission, see 110.

28 12 August 1635, no. 156, vol. 5654, Série B, Amirauté de La Rochelle, LAC. Razilly's governor's commission is no longer extant.

29 Couillard-Després, *Charles de Saint-Etienne de La Tour*, 206. Razilly received the furs for the CNF rather than for his private person. See Carpin, *Le Réseau du Canada*, 246.

30 Carpin, *Le Réseau du Canada*, 240; Couillard-Després, *Charles de Saint-Etienne de La Tour*, 203–4; Le Blant, "La Compagnie de la Nouvelle-France et la restitution de l'Acadie," 82–3. For La Tour's request to have his and Razilly's respective concessions registered, see Couillard-Després, *Charles de Saint-Etienne de La Tour*, 250–1.

31 The historiography has tended to attribute the subsidiaries to either the commercial or colonizing dimensions of the CNF without considering how the two were intertwined. For a commercial explanation, see Fischer, *Champlain's Dream*, 512; Trudel, *HNF*, 3.1:60. For a colonizing one, see Campeau, *Les Cent-Associés et le peuplement de la Nouvelle France*, 10–11.

32 Scott, *The Constitution and Finance of English, Scottish and Irish Joint-Stock Companies*, 2:276–7; Griffiths, *A Licence to Trade*, 153. In 1612, the Virginia

Company established a subsidiary, the Somers Island Company, with the objective of beginning a new colony. See Scott, *The Constitution and Finance of English, Scottish and Irish Joint-Stock Companies*, 2:260, 262–6.

33 Trudel, *HNF*, 3.1:56–7; Carpin, *Le Réseau du Canada*, 120–1, 126, 128–9.

34 The year 1632 was not the first time de Caën's quest for compensation disrupted the CNF's trade. In 1628, four clerks were sent to trade for him but were captured by the English; in 1629, three ships were allowed to voyage to New France in advance of the CNF to trade in his name, and in 1631 he was again allowed to trade at Quebec. See fo. 9–15, vol. 16738, fonds français, dépt de mss, BnF; Carpin, *Le Réseau du Canada*, 131–3. On the lawsuit over compensation between de Caën and the Compagnie de Montmorency and the CNF, see 27 August 1634, fo. 44–67, vol. 16738, fonds français, dépt de mss, BnF; "Transaction entre Guillaume de Caën et les directeurs de la Compagnie de la Nouvelle-France," 23 February 1636, no. 72, étude XVI, MC, LAC; "Promesse de garantie par Guillaume de Caen envers les directeurs de la Compagnie de la Nouvelle France," 7 March 1646, no. 92, ibid.

35 "Extrait des délibérations de la Compagnie de la Nouvelle France sur l'établissement d'une compagnie particulière," 15 November 1632, vol. 381, Collection Clairambault, dépt de mss, BnF.

36 Ibid. There is no extant list of participating associates. See Trudel, *HNF*, 3.1:118. An earlier association among six members of the CNF and two foreigners for a voyage to Acadia in 1630 had established a precedent for a subcontracting company. See Carpin, *Le Réseau du Canada*, 129.

37 "Récit véritable de la Compagnie de la Nouvelle France," 1663, vol. 11, Compagnies de Commerce, F2A, LAC; Carpin, *Le Réseau du Canada*, 145.

38 27 January 1638 vol. 16738, fonds français, dépt de mss, BnF; 9 January 1638, ibid. To satisfy its capital needs, the compagnie particulière's directors were permitted to borrow sums that would then have to be paid back with interest by the associates who were slow to pay. See 11 January 1638, ibid.

39 "Récit véritable de la Compagnie de la Nouvelle France," 1663, vol. 11, Compagnies de Commerce, F2A, LAC; Carpin, *Le Réseau du Canada*, 149–50.

40 "Extrait des délibérations de la Compagnie de la Nouvelle France sur l'établissement d'une compagnie particulière," 15 November 1632, vol. 381, Collection Clairambault, dépt de mss, BnF.

41 Carpin, *Le Réseau du Canada*, 238.

42 Le Blant, "Les compagnies du Cap-Breton," 81–94; Carpin, *Le Réseau du Canada*, 233–7.

43 "Concession pour dix années, par la Compagnie de la Nouvelle-France à Claude Razilly," 15 January 1634, no. 98, étude LXXXVIII, MC, LAC.

44 Condonnier was acting for Philippe de Longvilliers de Poincy, member of the Order of Malta and future governor in the Antilles. As members of the

order, neither Isaac de Razilly nor Poincy could act in their own name in a commercial association. Claude de Launay-Razilly thus engaged for both himself and his brother. See Carpin, *Le Réseau du Canada*, 246–7.

45 "Association du Cardinal de Richelieu avec Claude de Launay-Razilly et Jean Condonnier pour les affaires de l'Acadie," 16 January 1635, vol. 9281, NAF, dépt de mss, BnF. For the Legrand and Motin agreement, see 25 January 1635, ibid.; Carpin, *Le Réseau du Canada*, 248.

46 16 January 1635, vol. 9281, NAF, dépt de mss, BnF (emphasis added).

47 "Cession par les associés de la compagnie de Miscou à Nicolas Denys, de l'habitation de Miscou," 25 April 1645, no. 208, étude XC, MC, LAC; Le Blant, "La première Compagnie de Miscou," 363–70, esp. 368.

48 Fouquet was a royal counsellor and client of Richelieu. Succeeding Lauson as the CNF's intendant in all but name, he was a member of, and the cardinal's representative in, several companies founded during the latter's tenure; Jacques Berruyer was a royal counsellor; Cheffault was a nobleman and *avocat* in the Parlement of Paris; Jean Rozée was a Rouennais merchant.

49 "Cession par les associés de la compagnie de Miscou à Nicolas Denys, de l'habitation de Miscou," 25 April 1645, no. 208, étude XC, MC, LAC.

50 On the solicitation of new members for the Compagnie pour la côte d'Acadie, see Carpin, *Le Réseau du Canada*, 248–9.

51 The Compagnie pour la côte d'Acadie, for example, included two non-CNF members, Motin and Legrand.

52 Carpin, *Le Réseau du Canada*, 234, 247; Trudel, *HNF*, 3.1:415, 428, 430.

53 Le Blant, "La première Compagnie de Miscou," 366.

54 16 September 1636, fo. 265, vol. 133b, Conseil d'Etat du Roi, Série E, LAC. In 1652 and then again in 1659–60, two associations involving Norman associates contracted with the Communauté des Habitants to provide merchandise in exchange for furs. See "Articles accordés entre René Robineau … Et le Sieur Toussaint Guenet … ," 18 October 1659, fo. 352, vol. 9269, Collection Margry, dépt de mss, BnF; Carpin, *Le Réseau du Canada*, 181–2.

55 In the Compagnie du Cap-Breton, all associates were outfitters and each was responsible for subsidizing the transportation and provisioning costs of the labourers and settlers they sent over. See Carpin, *Le Réseau du Canada*, 234–5.

56 "Articles et conventions de société et compagnie, du 7e mai 1627, pour l'exécution des articles accordés, à la Compagnie du Canada," in *EO*, 12–17; Le Blant, "La première Compagnie de Miscou," 363; Scott, *The Constitution and Finance of English, Scottish and Irish Joint-Stock Companies*, 1:151.

57 With the awarding of a share to Charles Menou d'Aulnay, chief clerk, for his service to the company in 1641, the number of shares increased to seven. See 27 February 1641, vol. 9281, NAF, dépt de mss, BnF.

58 16 January 1635, ibid.

59 Scott, *The Constitution and Finance of English, Scottish and Irish Joint-Stock Companies*, 1:155–7, 160; Coornaert, "European Economic Institutions and the New World," 256–7. On the VOC's establishment of a permanent capital in 1612, see Gelderblom, de Jong, and Jonker, "The Formative Years of the Modern Corporation," 1059–64.

60 14 February 1643, fo. 530, vol. 177a, Conseil d'Etat du Roi, Série E, LAC; 24 July 1643, fo. 144–52, vol. 181c, ibid. On the second subsidiary of the Saint Lawrence, see 11, 18 January 1639, vol. 16738, fonds français, dépt de mss, BnF. According to a document from 1663, members of the second subsidiary collectively contributed 243,500 livres during its four years of operation. See "Récit véritable de la Compagnie de la Nouvelle France," 1663, vol. 11, Compagnies de Commerce, F2A, LAC.

61 For the idea that the goal of such companies was to allow individual subscribers to profit, rather than the company itself, see Kennedy, "Protecting Their Investments," 275–91. For the view that these practices constituted "plunder from within," see Boulle, "French Mercantilism, Commercial Companies and Colonial Profitability," 97–117.

62 She also became grand maître in 1646, following the death of Richelieu's nephew, the Marquis de Brézé, who had succeeded the cardinal.

63 The grantee of a fief became a seigneur, bound in vassalage to his lord, the granter. A *grant en censive* was within a fief and came with various obligations, notably the annual dues, or *cens*. See Greer, *Property and Dispossession*, 159–60. On the seigneury in Acadia, see Kennedy, *Something of a Peasant Paradise?*, chap. 4.

64 Kennedy, *Something of a Peasant Paradise?*, 136–7; Carpin, *Le Réseau du Canada*, 239, 250–1.

65 Greer, *Property and Dispossession*, 162–3, 166–9.

66 A ninth grantee of Beaupré was not a member of the CNF. See Carpin, *Le Réseau du Canada*, 160.

67 Ibid., 160–3; Greer, *Property and Dispossession*, 164.

68 Trudel, *HNF*, 3.1:164.

69 Ibid., 159–65; Dubé, *The Chevalier de Montmagny*, 203–4.

70 5 February 1642, fo. 291, vol. 167a, Conseil d'Etat du Roi, Série E, LAC; 15 October 1644, fo. 140, vol. 195b, ibid; "Etat général des debtes passives de la Compagnie de la Nouvelle France," 1641–42, fo. 195–209v, corresp. gén., C11A, LAC.

71 "Récit véritable de la Compagnie de la Nouvelle France," 1663, vol. 11, Compagnies de Commerce, F2A, LAC; Trudel, *HNF*, 3.1:169. For examples of requests for the condemnation of associates, see 15 October 1644, fo. 140, vol. 195b, Conseil d'Etat du Roi, Série E, LAC; 14 January 1645, fo. 402, vol. 198a, ibid. For examples of requests from associates to renounce their

shares, see 11 May 1644, fo. 378, vol. 190a, ibid.; 23 June 1644, fo. 320, vol. 191b, ibid. The Compagnie des îles de l'Amérique, which found itself in a similarly difficult financial situation in the 1640s, had recourse to the same strategies. See Roulet, *La Compagnie des îles de l'Amérique*, 149–51.

72 "Articles accordés entre les directeurs et associés en la Compagnie de la Nouvelle France et les deputés des habitants dudit Pays," 14 January 1645, fo. 7–11v, corresp. gén., C11A, LAC; "Arrêt par lequel Sa Majesté approuve la délibération de la Compagnie de la Nouvelle France et le traité fait en conséquence entre ladite compagnie et le député des habitants de la Nouvelle-France," 6 March 1645, fo. 12–13v, ibid.

73 "Articles accordés entre les directeurs et associés en la Compagnie de la Nouvelle France et les deputés des habitants dudit Pays," 14 January 1645, fo. 7–11v, corresp. gén., C11A, LAC. Governmental powers refer to those associated with justice, law, and the military; administration is concerned with the day-to-day tasks that keep a government functioning. For more on this distinction, see Mousnier, *Les institutions de la France*, 2:456–7.

74 Horguelin, *La Prétendue République*, 33. The inhabitants were to receive dividends in accordance with their placement in one of three classes: "principals" (or nobles), "middling," and "commoners." Note that this classification departs from the traditional language of privilege and division of society into three orders. See Trudel, *HNF* 3.1:176–7; Campeau, *Les finances publiques de la Nouvelle France*, 65; Carpin, *Le Réseau du Canada*, 172.

75 Historians of New France have all but ignored this strong transatlantic connection. See, for example, Campeau, *Les finances publiques de la Nouvelle France*, 63–6; Trudel, *HNF*, 3.1:167–8. The exception is Horguelin, *La Prétendue République*, 33.

76 Mousnier, *Les institutions de la France*, 1:428–31. The *corps de ville*, a form of municipal government, was distinct from the communauté d'habitants. For comparisons between the communauté d'habitants in France and New France, see Lavallée, *La Prairie en Nouvelle-France*, 164–81; Kennedy, *Something of a Peasant Paradise?*, 187–97. For Montreal, see Robichaud, "Les origines d'une élite créole," esp. 14, 18, 21.

77 Lespagnol, *Messieurs de Saint-Malo*, 45, 110.

78 Mousnier, *Les institutions de la France*, 1:428.

79 3 March 1649, fo. 255, vol. 234a, Conseil d'Etat du Roi, Série E, LAC; "Arrêt pour la liquidation des dettes de la communauté du Canada," 31 March 1665, fo. 163–7, corresp. gén., C11A, LAC.

80 Mousnier, *Les institutions de la France*, 1:431.

81 There were also instances of inhabitants of other American colonies taking on the responsibilities of administration and trade, each delegation under its own particular arrangements. See Griffiths, *A Licence to Trade*, 184–5, 191; Trudel, *HNF*, 3.1:179; Servant, *Les Compagnies de Saint-Christophe*, 46.

82 In remonstrances concerning the colony's financial state submitted to the royal council twelve years later, the CNF's directors stated that the inhabitants "did not have all the necessary experience" to manage such an operation. See "Arrêt du Conseil d'Etat portant règlement sur le commerce et traite de Canada," 7 March 1657, fo. 323, vol. 9269, Collection Margry, BnF.

83 "Estat au vray des charges et despenses, debtes actives et passives de la Communauté des habitans de la Nouvelle France," 1652, fo. 318–19v, vol. 9269, Collection Margry, dépt de mss, BnF; Campeau, *Les finances publiques de la Nouvelle France*, 63–5, 75.

84 "Arrêt pour la liquidation des dettes de la communauté du Canada," 31 March 1665, corresp. gén., C11A, LAC.

85 "Estat au vray des charges et despenses, debtes actives et passives de la Communauté des habitans de la Nouvelle France," 1652, fo. 318–19v, vol. 9269, Collection Margry, dépt de mss, BnF; Carpin, *Le Réseau du Canada*, 177. See also "Convention entre la Communauté des Habitants et ses créanciers," 1 April 1651, fo. 255–65v, corresp. gén., C11A, LAC; "Etat des dettes esquelles la Communauté des habitans de la Nouvelle France est engagée en France et qui ont été contractées les années précédentes," 1652, vol. 1, Deuxième Série, Nouvelle-France. Correspondance officielle, LAC.

86 17 April 1655, fo. 445, vol. 276a, Conseil d'Etat du Roi, Série E, LAC; "Extrait des Registres du Conseil d'Estat," 15 March 1656, fo. 321, vol. 9269, Collection Margry, dépt de mss, BnF.

87 Scott, *The Constitution and Finance of English, Scottish and Irish Joint Stock Companies*, 2:293–7, 310. This feature highlights one of the most significant differences between English plantation companies and French companies like the CNF: in the former, investment in the company was closely intertwined with colonization. Each share had a value in acres of land, which shareholders then received as a dividend. See ibid., 2:257, 262, 310.

88 Campeau, *Les finances publiques de la Nouvelle France*, 71.

89 Jean-Paul Godefroy and Pierre Legardeur were heads of the fleet; the chief clerk in France was first Noël Juchereau, Sieur des Chastelets, and then his nephew, Jean Juchereau, Sieur de La Ferté. See 3 March 1649, fo. 255, vol. 234a, Conseil d'Etat du Roi, Série E, LAC; "Convention entre la Communauté des Habitants et ses créanciers," 1 April 1651, fo. 255–65v, corresp. gén., C11A, LAC.

90 "Protestation d'Olivier Letardif et des directeurs de la Compagnie de la Nouvelle France contre le sieur de Repentigny," 27 July 1646, no. 93, étude XVI, MC, LAC.

91 Ibid.; Campeau, *Les finances publiques de la Nouvelle France*, 73; Horguelin, *La Prétendue République*, 72. For the CNF's claims to damages for the costs of Letardif's voyage, see "Compromis entre les directeurs de la compagnie de la Nouvelle France et l'envoyé des habitants," 22 February 1647, no. 94, étude XVI, MC, LAC.

92 "Protestation d'Olivier Letardif et des directeurs de la Compagnie de la Nouvelle France contre le sieur de Repentigny," 27 July 1646, no. 93, ibid.

93 See chapter 2, this volume.

94 Carpin, *Le Réseau du Canada*, 166–7.

95 "Mémoire montrant les dépenses et les pertes de la Compagnie de la Nouvelle France depuis 1628," 1663, fo. 59, corresp. gén., C11A, LAC. Historians of New France have not traditionally delved into the significance of Anne of Austria's involvement in the creation of the CH. See Campeau, *Les finances publiques de la Nouvelle France*, 65–6; Trudel, *HNF*, 3.1:170–1; Horguelin, *La Prétendue République*. A recent exception is Carpin, *Le Réseau du Canada*, 165–7.

96 Dionne, "Vice-rois et lieutenants généraux de la Nouvelle-France," 43.

97 For the longer history behind this concession, see Trudel, HNF, 3.1:154–6; "Concession d'une grande partie de l'île de Montréal," fo. 190–4, corresp. gén., C11A, LAC. On the number of settlers that the society transported, see Carpin, *Le Réseau du Canada*, 213–26.

98 Daveluy, "Chomedey de Maisonneuve, Paul de."

99 Dubé, *The Chevalier de Montmagny*, 220.

100 "Accord entre Pierre Le Gardeur de Repentigny et Le Royer de la Dauversière pour l'exécution du traité du 14 janvier 1645," 20 January 1645, Série II, Fonds du Séminaire de Saint-Sulpice, Montreal, LAC; Trudel, *HNF*, 3.1:172.

101 On the favours distributed to the family members of the CH's directors, see ibid., 3.1:186.

102 *Jesuit Relations and Allied Documents*, 28:238; Trudel, *HNF*, 3.1:187; Carpin, *Le Réseau du Canada*, 168, 168n20.

103 "Règlement de 1647 pour établir un bon ordre et police au Canada," 27 March 1647, fo. 173–9, vol. 2, Deuxième série, Nouvelle-France. Correspondance officielle, LAC.

104 Ibid.; Trudel, *HNF*, 3.1:187–9; Vachon, "The Administration of New France."

105 The chosen inhabitants, all seigneurs, were François Chavigny de Berchereau, Robert Giffard, and Jean-Paul Godefroy, controller general and admiral of the fleet. See "Arrêt portant règlement en faveur des habitants de la Nouvelle France," 5 March 1648, vol. 1, Deuxième série, Nouvelle-France. Correspondance officielle, LAC; Trudel, *HNF*, 3.1:192–4; Vachon, "The Administration of New France."

106 "Acte de protestation de la Compagnie de la Nouvelle-France relative aux lettres de provisions expédiées par le roi pour la commission de gouverneur de la Nouvelle-France à Louis d'Ailleboust," 22 March 1649, fo. 380–2, vol. 4, Mélanges, Fonds de l'Hôtel-Dieu de Québec, LAC; Carpin, *Le Réseau du Canada*, 169–70.

107 Carpin, *Le Réseau du Canada*, 167. On the Compagnie du Saint-Sacrement's influence in the Antilles, see Roulet, *La Compagnie des îles de l'Amérique*, 128, 144–5.

108 McShea, *Apostles of Empire*, 85.

109 "Ordre pour le voyage de France en 1650 par le Conseil," 29 October 1650 and 26 May 1651, Minutes Teuleron, 1651, in Delafosse, "Documents inédits: La Communaulté des habitans de la Nouvelle France," 118–20, 120–1.

110 "Arrêt par lequel Sa Majesté en interprétant l'art. 12 de la déclaration du 22 octobre dernier déclare n'avoir entendu révoquer les privilèges accordés aux membres de la Compagnie de la Nouvelle-France et le monopole de la traite des fourrures accordé aux habitants du Canada," 2 March 1649, 254–254v, corresp. gén., C11A, LAC.

111 On Lalemant, see Trudel, *HNF*, 3.1:189. For Le Baillif, see chapter 4, this volume.

112 For a different interpretation of the increase in ecclesiastical authority in the 1640s, see Horguelin, *La Prétendue République*, 41.

113 Carpin, *Le Réseau du Canada*, 241–2.

114 For the rationale behind Louis XIII's division of jurisdiction, see Kennedy, "À la recherche de sa propre voie," 147–76.

115 *Mém. des comm.*, 2:391–3; Couillard-Després, *Charles de Saint-Etienne de La Tour*, 203–6; Baudry, "Menou D'Aulnay, Charles de"; MacBeath, "Saint-Étienne de la Tour, Charles de."

116 Carpin, *Le Réseau du Canada*, 244; MacDonald, *Fortune and La Tour*, 85–7; Mahaffie, *A Land of Discord Always*, 69. There is some debate over whether Menou or La Tour made the first aggressive move in 1640.

117 For examples, see *Mém. des comm.*, 2:393–4; 21 February 1642, vol. 9281, Collection Margry, dépt de mss, BnF; 6 March 1644, fo. 19–21v, vol. 1688, Conseil d'Etat du Roi, Série E, LAC. Richelieu revoked La Tour's commission on 23 February 1641 and replaced him with Menou five days later. While Menou was making his representations, La Tour's wife went to seek support for her husband from the CNF and others. See MacDonald, *Fortune and La Tour*, 98–101.

118 Carpin, *Le Réseau du Canada*, 256; Baudry, "Charles d'Aulnay et la Compagnie de la Nouvelle France," 228; Trudel, *HNF*, 3.1:77; Baudry, "Menou D'Aulnay, Charles de." Le Borgne replaced the company's long-time representative, Nicolas Denys, who was closely associated with the CNF.

119 *Coll. mss*, 1:120–5, 125–6; Baudry, "Charles d'Aulnay et la Compagnie de la Nouvelle France," 231; Kennedy, "À la recherche de sa propre voie," 167.

120 1 February 1641, no. 53, c. 154, Conseil privé, v6, LAC; 19 March 1641, no. 3, c. 155, ibid.

121 No. 95–6, 99–100, vol. 192, Série B, Amirauté de La Rochelle, LAC; no. 23, 26–9, vol. 5656, Série B, Amirauté de La Rochelle, LAC; no. 1, vol. 5657, Série B, Amirauté de La Rochelle, LAC; Carpin, *Le Réseau du Canada*, 260–1.

122 *Coll. mss*, 1:120–4, quotation at 122–3.

123 "Factum par les directeurs et associés de la Compagnie de la Nouvelle France, demandeurs et complaignants contre le Sieur d'Aunay Charnizay deffendeur

et accusé," 1647, pc. 33, vol. A 15444, Bibliothèque Mazarine, BnF; Baudry, "Charles d'Aulnay et la Compagnie de la Nouvelle France," 218–41.

124 Carpin, *Le Réseau du Canada*, 261; Baudry, "Menou d'Aulnay, Charles de"; Baudry, "Charles d'Aulnay et la Compagnie de la Nouvelle France," 232–3; Trudel, *HNF*, 3.1:83–4.

125 "Arrêt obtenu par la Compagnie de la Nouvelle France … contre la veuve et les heritiers de Charles de Menou d'Aulnay," 16 February 1652, no. 50, c. 263, Conseil privé, v6, LAC. Some historians have claimed that the CNF directors did not pursue the initial charges. See Baudry, "Charles d'Aulnay et la Compagnie de la Nouvelle France," 232; Trudel, *HNF*, 3.1:83.

126 D'Aulnay to Séguier, 10 September 1647, fo. 218v, vol. 17387, fonds français, dépt de mss, BnF; also 16 February 1652, no. 50, c. 263, Conseil privé, v6, LAC; Kennedy, "À la recherche de sa propre voie," 168. For denunciations of La Tour as a heretic by both the Capuchins and Récollets present in Acadia, see, respectively, *Coll. mss*, 1:117–18, and Galland, *Pour la Gloire de Dieu et du roi*, 135.

127 *Coll. mss*, 1:121, 119–20 (quotations in order of appearance).

128 6 March 1644, fo. 19–21v, vol. 1688, Conseil d'Etat du Roi, Série E, LAC.

129 Benton, *A Search for Sovereignty*, 59.

130 Reid, "Sir William Alexander and North American Colonization," 25–33; Reid, "Champlain: Longevity and Commemoration," 210–11; Moir, "Kirke, Sir David"; Harvey, "Alexander, Sir William"; Henneton, "Spiritual Geopolitics," 219–20.

131 On La Tour's and Menou's relations with New England, see Peterson, *The City-State of Boston*, 76–8; Bremer, *John Winthrop*, 343–5; Mahaffie, *A Land of Discord Always*, chaps. 8, 9; MacDonald, *Fortune and La Tour*, 144–53, 159–63. On Boston leaders' fears of reprisal from Menou as a result of La Tour's overtures, see Henneton, "Spiritual Geopolitics," 221–2.

132 While his father may have been a turncoat on that occasion, Charles repelled the English forces and his father from Cap de Sable in 1630. See MacBeath, "Saint-Étienne de La Tour, Claude."

133 21 February 1642, vol. 9281, Collection Margry, dépt de mss, BnF.

134 Roulet, *La Compagnie des îles de l'Amérique*, 359–63.

135 Boucher, *France and the American Tropics to 1700*, 84.

136 "M. Le Cardinal de Richelieu présente au Roy M. le Commandeur de Poincy pour Lieutenant General de Sa Majesté aux isles de l'Amérique," 14 February 1638 in Du Tertre, *Histoire générale des Antilles habitées par les François*, 1:123–4; "Commission de Lieutenant General de S.M. aux Isles de l'Amerique, donnée à M. de Poincy," 15 February 1638 in ibid., 125–6; Oath of loyalty to the Seigneurs of the Compagnie des îles de l'Amérique by Poincy, 6 January 1645, in ibid., 1:237–8.

137 "Commission de Gouverneur de la Guadeloupe à M. l'Intendant [Leumont] par M. de Poincy," 17 October 1644, in Du Tertre, *Histoire générale des Antilles habitées par les François*, 1:243–5; Letter from the Seigneurs of the Compagnie des îles to Houel in France, c. 1645, in ibid., 1:263–6.

138 "Nomination de Lieutenant General de Sa Majesté aux Isles de l'Amérique, pour le Sieur de Thoisy," 26 December 1644, in Du Tertre, *Histoire générale des Antilles habitées par les François*, 1:252–8; "Lettre de Cachet à M. le Commandeur de Poincy," 18 August 1645, in ibid., 1:276; Letter from the Seigneurs of the Compagnie des îles to Houel concerning Thoisy's arrival, 26 August 1645, in ibid., 1:279–80; "Acte de la prise de possession à la Guadeloupe, de la Charge de Lieutenant General pour sa Majesté ez Isles de l'Amerique, par le sieur Lambert, au nom de M. de Thoisy Patrocles," 2 June 1645, in ibid., 1:269.

139 Roulet, *La Compagnie des îles de l'Amérique*, 546–7.

140 "Extrait des Registres du Conseil d'Etat," 25 February 1647, in Du Tertre, *Histoire générale des Antilles habitées par les François*, 1:379–86; "Lettre de cachet à M. le Commandeur de Poincy," 26 May 1647, in ibid., 1:386–7.

141 Boucher, *France and the American Tropics to 1700*, 83–6, 85n55. For a full discussion of events, see Roulet, *La Compagnie des îles de l'Amérique*, chap. 20.

142 De Waele, "Conflict Resolution under the First Bourbons," 142, 149.

143 *Coll. mss*, 1:119, 118; "Confirmation de gouverneur et lieutenant général … au sieur Charles de Saint Etienne et Chevalier de La Tour," 27 February 1651, vol. 2, Deuxième Série, Nouvelle-France. Correspondance officielle, LAC. Claude de La Tour had also enjoyed a second chance under the French. See MacBeath, "Saint Étienne de La Tour, Claude."

144 Roulet, *La Compagnie des îles de l'Amérique*, 549–50, 551–3.

145 On the similarity of Menou's behaviour with that of medieval lords in France, see Kennedy, *Something of a Peasant Paradise?*, 138.

146 Roulet, *La Compagnie des îles de l'Amérique*, 564.

147 Servant, *Les Compagnies de Saint-Christophe*, 91–8; Boucher, *France and the American Tropics to 1700*, 86–7; Boucher, "French Proprietary Colonies in the Greater Caribbean, 1620s–1670s," 181. Among other factors were the company's ongoing financial difficulties.

148 Roulet, *La Compagnie des îles de l'Amérique*, 559–64, 574–6.

149 "Arrêt du roy en son conseil en response des remonstrances faites par la Compagnie de la Nouvelle France au sujet de l'arrêt du 7 mars 1657," 13 May 1659, vol. 1, Deuxième Série, Nouvelle-France. Correspondance officielle, LAC. On the governor's corresponding loss of power over justice, see Trudel, *HNF*, 3.1:251–2. The Société de Notre-Dame and other seigneurs had their own seigneurial courts, appeals from which were heard by the courts in Trois-Rivières or Quebec. See Vachon, "The Administration of New France."

150 "Extrait des Registres du Conseil d'Estat," 15 March 1656, fo. 321, vol. 9269, Collection Margry, dépt de mss, BnF; "Arrêt du Conseil d'Etat portant règlement sur le commerce et la traite de Canada," 7 March 1657, fo. 323, ibid.

151 "Arrêt du Conseil d'Etat portant règlement sur le commerce et la traite de Canada," 7 March 1657, fo. 323, vol. 9269, Collection Margry, dépt de mss, BnF. For Governor Voyer d'Argenson's suggested improvements to the decree, see "Double des advis que j'ay envoye à Messieurs du Conseil," 1658, fo. 325, vol. 9269, Collection Margry, BnF.

Epilogue

1 "Cession par les membres de la Compagnie de la Nouvelle France au Roi," 24 February 1663, fo. 14, corresp. gén., C11A, LAC.

2 Collins, *The State in Early Modern France*, chap. 3.

3 Brandon, *War, Capital and the Dutch State*, 107–14; Swingen, *Competing Visions of Empire*, chap. 4.

4 Dessert, *Fouquet*, 131, 134. On François Fouquet's overseas activities, see Vergé-Franceschi, *Colbert*, 149–50; Roulet, *La Compagnie des îles de l'Amérique*, 120–5.

5 Boucher, "Comment se forme un ministre colonial," 432–5. On the *affaire Fouquet* more generally, see Dessert, *Fouquet*, chaps. 9, 10; James, *The Origins of French Absolutism*, 86–9; Vergé-Franceschi, *Colbert*, chaps. 4, 5. For a skeptical view of the threat Fouquet posed, see Dessert, *Fouquet*, 136–9.

6 "Convention entre la Communauté des Habitants et ses créanciers," 1 April 1651, fo. 255–65v, corresp. gén., C11A, LAC; "Estat au vray des charges et despenses, debtes actives et passives de la Communauté des habitans de la Nouvelle France," 1652, fo. 318–19v, vol. 9269, Collection Margry, dépt de mss, BnF; "Extrait des Registres du Conseil d'Estat," 15 March 1656, fo. 321, ibid.; "Etat des dettes esquelles la Communauté des habitans de la Nouvelle France est engagée en France et qui ont été contractées les années précédentes," 1652, vol. 1, Deuxième Série, Nouvelle-France. Correspondance officielle, LAC; 17 avril 1655, fo. 445, vol. 276a, Conseil d'Etat du Roi, Série E, LAC; "Mémoire pour Monsieur le Chancellier," 1657, fo. 136–7v, vol. 17871, fonds français, dépt de mss, BnF; Horguelin, *La Prétendue République*, 74–82.

7 Boucher, *France and the American Tropics to 1700*, 93–103.

8 On the compensation granted West Indian proprietors, see Boucher, *France and the American Tropics to 1700*, 175; Mims, *Colbert's West India Policy*, 73–4, 74n8.

9 For the original sum requested, see "Cession par les membres de la Compagnie de la Nouvelle France au Roi," 24 February 1663, fo. 14–21, corresp. gén., C11A, LAC; "Récit véritable de la Compagnie de la Nouvelle France," 1663,

vol. 11, Compagnies de Commerce, F2A, LAC; 5 July 1687, vol. 569a, Conseil d'Etat du Roi, Série E, LAC. For continued appeals over the following decades, see "Requête présentée 'au roi étant en son Conseil' par les membres de l'ancienne Compagnie de la Nouvelle-France," 9 November 1683, fo. 214–214v, corresp. gén., C11A, LAC; letter from the CNF to "Monseigneur," 24 November 1683, fo. 213, ibid.; 15 June 1688, vol. 574b–575a, Conseil d'Etat du Roi, Série E, LAC. For the settlement, ensuing compensation dispute, and payments, see 15 June 1688, vol. 574b–575a, ibid.; "Main levée par François Roy à la Compagnie de la Nouvelle France," 3 December 1688, no. 262, étude LXVI, MC, LAC; "Quittance faite par demoiselle Marguerite Thiboutot, femme et procuratrice de Jean Berruyer," 31 July 1690, no. 144, étude CXIII, MC, AN.

10 See, for example, Eccles, *France in America*.

11 Banks, *Chasing Empire across the Sea*; Pritchard, *In Search of Empire*.

12 For a comparison of these aspects among the French, Dutch, and British Empires in the second half of the seventeenth century, see Adams, *The Familial State*, 32–6, 116–17, 122–32.

Bibliography

Primary Sources

MANUSCRIPT SOURCES

Archives départementales d'Ille-et-Vilaine (Rennes)
1Bb 864. 1Bb 869. Table des Registres du Parlement de Bretagne.
C 2642. Registre des délibérations des États de Bretagne.

Archives départementales de la Charente-Maritime (La Rochelle)
3 E 261. Actes de Chesneau.

Archives départementales de Seine Maritime (Rouen)
1B 981. 1 B 946. Parlement de Rouen.
2E1/1072. Tabellionage de Rouen.

Archives municipales de Saint-Malo (Saint-Malo)
Registre 6.

Archives nationales de France (Paris)
Minutier Central des notaires de Paris. Études CI, CXIII.

Bibliothèque nationale de France, Département de manuscrits (Paris)
Cinq Cents de Colbert. Vol. 203.
Collection Clairambault. Vol. 381.
Collection Margry. Vols. 9269, 9281.
Fonds français. Vols. 4826, 4870, 16738, 17329, 17387, 17871, 18592, 18596, 18781.
Fonds nouvelles acquisitions françaises. Vols. 7287, 9281.

Bibliothèque Mazarine. Vol. A 15444. Pc. 33. "Factum par les directeurs et associés de la Compagnie de la Nouvelle-France, demandeurs et complaignants contre le Sieur d'Aunay Charnizay deffendeur et accusé." 1647.

Library and Archives Canada (Ottawa)
Amirauté de La Rochelle. B 192, 5654, 5655, 5656, 5657, 5659.
C11A. Correspondance générale.
C11D.
Collection Dupuy. Vol. 318.
Nouvelle-France. Correspondance officielle. Deuxième Série. Vols 1, 2.
Extraits des diverses séries.
F2A. Compagnies de Commerce. Vol. 11.
Fonds de l'Hôtel-Dieu de Québec. Mélanges. Vol. 4.
Fonds du ministère des Affaires étrangères. Mémoires et documents. Amérique. Vol. 4.
Fonds du ministère des Affaires étrangères. Mémoires et documents. France. Vol. 785.

Minutier Central des notaires de Paris. Études VI, XVI, LI, LIV, LXVI, LXXXVIII, XC.
Série E. Conseil d'État du roi.
Série Z1D. Amirauté de France. Vols. 7, 10.
V6. Conseil d'Etat privé.

PUBLISHED SOURCES

"Acte pour l'établissement de la Compagnie des Cent Associés pour le commerce du Canada, contenant les articles accordés à la dite Compagnie par M. le Cardinal de Richelieu, le 29 avril, 1627." In *Édits, ordonnances royaux, déclarations et arrêts du Conseil d'État du roi concernant le Canada*, 5–11. Quebec: E.R. Fréchette, 1854.

Ardier, Paul. *L'Assemblée des notables tenue à Paris ès années 1626 et 1627*. Paris: C. Besongne, 1652.

"Articles accordés entre les associés de la Compagnie des Îles de l'Amérique (1635)." In *Le monde des compagnies. Les premières compagnies dans l'Atlantique, 1600–1650. I. Structures et modes de fonctionnement*, edited by Éric Roulet, 224–7. Aachen, DE: Shaker Verlag, 2017.

"Articles et conventions de société et compagnie, du 7 mai 1627, pour l'exécution des articles accordés, à la Compagnie du Canada, etc." In *Édits, ordonnances royaux, déclarations et arrêts du Conseil d'État du roi concernant le Canada*, 12–17. Quebec: E.R. Fréchette, 1854.

Biggar, H.P., ed. *A Collection of Documents Relating to Jacques Cartier and the Sieur de Roberval*. Ottawa: Public Archives of Canada, 1930.

Champlain, Samuel de. *Des Sauvages*. Edited by Alain Beaulieu and Réal Ouellet. Montreal: Éditions Typo, 1993.

Charter of the Dutch West India Company. 3 June 1621. The Avalon Project: Documents in Law, History and Diplomacy. Yale Law School. https://avalon.law.yale.edu/17th_century/westind.asp.

Charter of Massachusetts Bay. 1629. The Avalon Project: Documents in Law, History and Diplomacy. Yale Law School. https://avalon.law.yale.edu/17th_century/mass03.asp.

Collection de manuscrits contenant lettres, mémoires, et autres documents historiques relatifs à l'histoire de la Nouvelle France, recueillis aux Archives de la Province de Québec, ou copiés à l'étranger, mis en ordre et édité sous les auspices de la législature de Québec, avec tables, etc. 4 vols. Quebec: Imprimerie A. Coté et cie., 1883–85.

Delafosse, Marcel. "Documents inédits: La Communaulté des habitans de la Nouvelle France." *Revue d'histoire de l'Amérique française* 5, no. 1 (June 1951): 118–25.

Dictionnaire de l'Académie française. 1694. The ATFL Project: Dictionnaires d'autrefois. University of Chicago. http://artfl-project.uchicago.edu/content/dictionnaires-dautrefois.

Du Tertre, Jean-Baptiste. *Histoire générale des Antilles habitées par les François*. 4 vols. Paris: Chez Thomas Iolly, 1667–71.

Eon, Jean. *Le Commerce honorable, ou Considérations politiques contenant les motifs de nécessité, d'honneur et de profit qui se trouvent à former des Compagnies de personnes de toutes conditions pour l'entretien du Négoce de mer en France*. Nantes: Guillaume Le Monnier, 1646.

Féraud, Jean-François. *Dictionnaire critique de la langue française*. 1787. The ATFL Project: Dictionnaires d'autrefois. University of Chicago. http://artfl-project.uchicago.edu/content/dictionnaires-dautrefois.

First Charter of Virginia. 10 April 1606. The Avalon Project: Documents in Law, History and Diplomacy. Yale Law School. https://avalon.law.yale.edu/17th_century/va01.asp.

Grillon, Pierre, ed. *Les Papiers de Richelieu. Section Politique intérieure. Correspondance et papiers d'État*. Vols. 1 (1624–26) and 2 (1627). Paris: Éditions A. Pedone, 1975–77.

Jesuit Relations and Allied Documents. Edited by Reuben Gold Thwaites. 73 vols. Cleveland, OH: Burrows Bros, 1896–1901.

Le Blant, Robert, and René Baudry, eds. *Nouveaux documents sur Champlain et son époque*. Vol. 1 (1560–1622). Ottawa: Publications des Archives publiques du Canada, 1967.

Le Caron, Joseph. *Au Roy sur la Nouvelle France*. 1626.

Le Clercq, Chrestien. *First Establishment of the Faith in New France*. Translated by John Gilmary Shea. 2 vols. New York: J.G. Shea, (1691) 1881.

Lescarbot, Marc. *Histoire de la Nouvelle France*. Paris: Adrien Perier, 1618.

– *History of New France*. 3 vols. Translated by W.L. Grant. Toronto: Champlain Society, (1618) 1907–14.

– *Nova Francia: A Description of Acadia*. Translated by Pierre Erondelle. London: George Routledge and Sons, (1609) 1928.

"Lettres patentes de Louis XIII pour la première Compagnie des Indes Orientales, 2 juillet 1615." In *Histoire de la Compagnie des Indes*, edited by Jacques du Fresne de Francheville, 162–6. Paris: Chez De Bure, 1746.

"Mémoire du Chevalier de Razilly." In *Un colonisateur du temps de Richelieu, Isaac de Razilly: Biographie et mémoire inédit*, edited by Léon Deschamps, 15–35. Paris: Charles Delagrave, 1887.

Mémoires des commissaires de Sa Majesté Très-Chrétienne et de ceux de Sa Majesté brittannique [*sic*]*: Sur les possessions & les droits respectifs des deux couronnes en Amérique: Avec les actes publics & piéces justificatives*. Paris: Imprimerie royale, 1755–57.

Montchrestien, Antoine de. *Traité de l'économie politique*. Edited by Théophile Funck-Brentano. Paris: E. Plon, Nourrit, (1615) 1889.

Nicot, Jean. *Thresor de la langue françoyse, tant ancienne que moderne*. 1606. The ATFL Project: Dictionnaires d'autrefois. University of Chicago. http://artfl-project.uchicago.edu/content/dictionnaires-dautrefois.

Petit, Jeanne. "Mémoire sur le commerce et les avantages de la marine." In *L'Assemblée des Notables de 1626–1627*, edited by Jeanne Petit, 187–8. Paris: A. Margraff, 1937.

Popelinière, Henri Lancelot Du Voisin de La. *L'Amiral de France, et par occasion, de celuy des autres nations*. Paris: T. Périer, 1584.

Relation originale du voyage de Jacques Cartier au Canada en 1534: Documents inédits sur Jacques Cartier et le Canada. Edited by H. Michelant and A. Ramé. Paris: Librairie Tross, 1867.

Sagard, Gabriel. *Histoire du Canada et voyages que les frères mineurs recollects y ont faicts pour la conversion des infidels: depuis l'an 1615*. 4 vols. Paris: Libraire Tross, (1636) 1866.

Second Charter of Virginia. 23 May 1609. The Avalon Project: Documents in Law, History and Diplomacy. Yale Law School. https://avalon.law.yale.edu/17th_century/va02.asp.

Third Charter of Virginia. 12 March 1611. The Avalon Project: Documents in Law, History and Diplomacy. Yale Law School. https://avalon.law.yale.edu/17th_century/va03.asp.

Valin, René-Josué. *Nouveau commentaire sur l'ordonnance de la marine du mois d'août 1681*. Vol. 1. La Rochelle: Chez Jérôme Legier et Pierre Mesnier, 1760.

"Voyage et inspection maritime de M. D'Infreville sur les côtes françaises de l'océan." In *Correspondance de Henri D'Escoubleau de Sourdis, augmentée des ordres, instructions et lettres de Louis XIII et du Cardinal de Richelieu*. Vol. 3. Edited by Eugène Sue, 171–221. Paris: L'imprimerie de Crapelet, 1839.

The Works of Samuel de Champlain. Edited by H.P. Biggar. 6 vols. Toronto: University of Toronto Press, (1922–35) 1971.

Secondary Sources

Adams, Julia. *The Familial State: Ruling Families and Merchant Capitalism in Early Modern Europe*. Ithaca, NY: Cornell University Press, 2005.

Allaire, Bernard. *Pelleteries, manchons et chapeaux de castor: Les fourrures nord-américaines à Paris, 1500–1632*. Sillery, QC: Septentrion, 1999.

Allier, Raoul. *La Cabale des dévots, 1627–1666*. Paris: Librairie Armand Colin, 1902.

Antunes, Cátia, and Susana Münch Miranda, eds. "Bankruptcies in the Context of Empire." Special issue, *Itinerario* 43, no. 1 (April 2019): 47–172.

Appleby, John C. "An Association for the West Indies? English Plans for a West India Company 1621–29." *Journal of Imperial and Commonwealth History* 15 (1987): 213–41.

Appleby, Joyce Oldham. *Economic Thought and Ideology in Seventeenth-Century England*. Princeton, NJ: Princeton University Press, 1978.

Armitage, David. Introduction to *The Free Sea*, by Hugo Grotius, xi–xx. Edited by David Armitage, translated by R. Hakluyt. Indianapolis, IN: Liberty Fund, 2004.

– "Three Concepts of Atlantic History." In *The British Atlantic World, 1500–1800*, 2nd ed., edited by David Armitage and Michael J. Braddick, 13–29. New York: Palgrave Macmillan, 2009.

Aubert, Gauthier, Olivier Chaline, David Chaunu, Edmond Dziembowski, Marie-Laure Legay, Jean-Pierre Poussou, François-Joseph Ruggiu, and Éric Suire. *États, pouvoirs et contestations dans les monarchies française et britannique*. Malakoff, FR: Armand Colin, 2018.

Baker, J.H. *An Introduction to English Legal History*. 2nd ed. London: Butterworths, 1979.

Banks, Kenneth J. *Chasing Empire Across the Sea: Communications and the State in the French Atlantic, 1713–1763*. Montreal and Kingston: McGill-Queen's University Press, 2006.

Barbiche, Bernard. "Henri IV and the World Overseas: A Decisive Time in the History of New France." In *Champlain: The Birth of French America*, edited by Raymonde Litalien and Denis Vaugeois, translated by Kathe Roth, 24–32. Montreal and Kingston: McGill-Queen's University Press, 2007.

Barkan, Joshua. *Corporate Sovereignty: Law and Government under Capitalism*. Minneapolis: University of Minnesota Press, 2013.

Barnes, Andrew E. "'Playing the Part of Angels': The Company of the Holy Sacrament and the Struggle for Stability in Early Modern France." In *Early Modern France: From Crisis to Stability*, edited by Philip Benedict and Myron P. Gutmann, 168–96. Newark: University of Delaware Press, 2005.

Baudry, René. "Charles d'Aulnay et la Compagnie de la Nouvelle-France." *Revue d'histoire de l'Amérique française* 11 (1957): 218–41.

– "Menou d'Aulnay, Charles de." In *Dictionary of Canadian Biography*, vol. 1, edited by Frances G. Halpenny and Jean Hamelin. Toronto: University of Toronto Press, 1966. http://www.biographi.ca/en/bio/menou_d_aulnay_charles_de_1E.html.

Bayard, Françoise. *Le monde des financiers au XVIIe siècle*. Paris: Flammarion, 1988.

Beaudin, René. "Les membres de la Compagnie des Cent-Associés: Étude d'histoire sociale." Master's thesis, Université de Montréal, 1997.

Beaulieu, Alain. "'L'on n'a point d'ennemis plus grands que ces sauvages.' L'alliance franco-innue revisitée (1603–1653)." *Revue d'histoire de l'Amérique française* 61, nos. 3–4 (Winter–Spring 2008): 365–95.

Beik, William. *Absolutism and Society in Seventeenth-Century France: State Power and Provincial Aristocracy in Languedoc*. Cambridge: Cambridge University Press, 1989.

Belmessous, Saliha. *Assimilation and Empire: Uniformity in French and British Colonies, 1541–1954*. Oxford: Oxford University Press, 2013.

– "Être français en Nouvelle-France: Identité française et identité coloniale aux dix-septième et dix-huitième siècles." *French Historical Studies* 27, no. 3 (Summer 2004): 507–40.

Benton, Lauren. *A Search for Sovereignty: Law and Geography in European Empires, 1400–1900*. Cambridge: Cambridge University Press, 2010.

– "Spatial Histories of Empire." *Itinerario* 30, no. 3 (2006): 19–34.

Berenger, Jean. "Les États de Bretagne et la colonisation nord-américaine." *Études canadiennes/Canadian Studies* 17 (December 1984): 7–17.

Bergin, Joseph. *Cardinal Richelieu: Power and the Pursuit of Wealth*. New Haven, CT: Yale University Press, 1985.

– "Crown and Episcopate in the Age of Henri IV and Louis XIII." *Proceedings of the Annual Meeting of the Western Society for French History* 20 (1993): 63–74.

– *The Politics of Religion in Early Modern France*. New Haven, CT: Yale University Press, 2015.

Bien, David D. "Offices, Corps, and a System of State Credit: The Uses of Privilege under the Ancien Régime." In *The French Revolution and the*

Creation of Modern Political Culture. Vol. 1, *Political Culture of the Old Regime*, edited by Keith Michael Baker, 89–115. Oxford: Pergamon Press, 1987.

– *The Early Trading Companies of New France, 1534–1632*. St Clair Shores, MI: Scholarly Press, (1901) 1977.

Binot, Guy. *Pierre Dugua de Mons, Gentilhomme royannais, premier colonisateur de Canada*. Vaux-sur-Mer, FR: Bonne anse, 2004.

Bitsch, Caroline. *Vie et carrière d'Henri II de Bourbon, prince de Condé (1588–1646): Exemple de comportement et d'idées politiques au début du XVIIe siècle*. Paris: Honoré Champion, 2008.

Bohaker, Heidi. "*Nindoodemag*: The Significance of Algonquian Kinship Networks in the Eastern Great Lakes Region, 1600–1701." *William and Mary Quarterly* 63, no. 1 (January 2006): 23–52.

Boiteux, L.-A. "Un économiste méconnu: Du Noyer de Saint-Martin et ses projets, 1608–1639." *Revue d'histoire des colonies* 44 (1957): 5–68.

– *Richelieu, grand maître de la navigation et du commerce de France*. Paris: Ozanne, 1955.

Bonnassieux, Pierre. *Les grandes compagnies de commerce*. New York: Burt Franklin, (1892) 1969.

Bonney, Richard. *The King's Debts: Finance and Politics in France, 1598–1661*. Oxford: Clarendon Press, 1981.

– *Political Change in France under Richelieu and Mazarin, 1624–1661*. Oxford: Oxford University Press, 1978.

Bosbach, Franz. "The European Debate on Universal Monarchy." In *Theories of Empire, 1450–1800*, edited by David Armitage, 83–90. Aldershot, UK: Ashgate, 1998.

Bosher, John F. "The Counter-Reformation in France." In *Business and Religion in the Age of New France, 1600–1760: Twenty-Two Studies*, 17–55. Toronto: Canadian Scholars' Press, 1994.

– "The Political and Religious Origins of La Rochelle's Primacy in Trade with New France, 1627–1685." *French History* 7, no. 3 (1993): 286–312.

Bossenga, Gail. "Estates, Orders, Corps." In *The Oxford Handbook of the Ancien Régime*, edited by William Doyle, 141–66. Oxford: Oxford University Press, 2012.

– *The Politics of Privilege: Old Regime and Revolution in Lille*. Cambridge: Cambridge University Press, 1991.

Boucher, Philip. "Comment se forme un ministre colonial: L'initiation de Colbert, 1651–1664." *Revue d'histoire de l'Amérique française* 37, no. 3 (1983): 431–52.

– *France and the American Tropics to 1700: Tropics of Discontent?* Baltimore: Johns Hopkins University Press, 2008.

– "French Proprietary Colonies in the Greater Caribbean, 1620s–1670s." In *Constructing Early Modern Empires: Proprietary Ventures in the Atlantic World, 1500–1750*, edited by L.H. Roper and Bertrand Van Ruymbeke, 163–88. Leiden: Brill, 2007.

Boulle, Pierre H. "French Mercantilism, Commercial Companies and Colonial Profitability." In *Companies and Trade*, edited by L. Blussé and F. Gaastra, 97–117. Leiden: Martinus Nijhoff, 1981.

Bourguet, Marie-Noelle. "Le sauvage, le colon, le paysan." In *Les figures de l'Indien*, edited by Gilles Thérien, 233–57. Montreal: Typo, 1995.

Braddick, Michael J. "State Formation and Social Change in Early Modern England: A Problem Stated and Approaches Suggested." *Social History* 16, no. 1 (January 1991): 1–17.

– *State Formation in Early Modern England: c. 1550–1700*. Cambridge: Cambridge University Press, 2000.

Brandon, Pepijn. *War, Capital and the Dutch State (1588–1795)*. Leiden: Brill, 2015.

Brazeau, Brian. *Writing a New France, 1604–1632: Empire and Early Modern French Identity*. Farnham, UK: Ashgate, 2009.

Bréard, Charles. *Le vieux Honfleur et ses marins: Biographies et récits maritimes*. Rouen: Impr. Cagniard, 1897.

Breen, Michael P. *Law, City and King: Legal Culture, Municipal Politics, and State Formation in Early Modern Dijon*. Rochester, NY: University of Rochester Press, 2007.

– "Law, Society, and the State in Early Modern France." *Journal of Modern History* 83, no. 2 (June 2011): 346–86.

– "Patronage, Politics and the 'Rule of Law' in Early Modern France." *Proceedings of the Western Society for French History* 33 (2005): 95–113.

Bremer, Francis J. *John Winthrop: America's Forgotten Founding Father*. New York: Oxford University Press, 2003.

Brewer, John. *The Sinews of Power: War, Money, and the English State, 1688–1783*. Boston: Unwin Hyman, 1989.

Briggs, Robin. "Richelieu and Reform: Rhetoric and Political Reality." In *Richelieu and His Age*, edited by Joseph Bergin and Laurence Brockliss, 71–97. Oxford: Clarendon Press, 1992.

Brunelle, Gayle. "Narrowing Horizons: Commerce and Derogation in Normandy." In *Society and Institutions in Early Modern France*, edited by Mack P. Holt, 63–79. Athens: University of Georgia Press, 1991.

– *New World Merchants of Rouen, 1559–1630*. Ann Arbor, MI: Edward's Brothers, 1991.

Burbank, Jane, and Frederick Cooper. *Empires in World History: Power and the Politics of Difference*. Princeton, NJ: Princeton University Press, 2010.

Burnard, Trevor G., and John D. Garrigus. *The Plantation Machine: Atlantic Capitalism in French Saint-Domingue and British Jamaica*. Philadelphia: University of Pennsylvania Press, 2016.

Campbell, Gordon. "Sully, Maximilien de Béthune, Baron de Rosny, Duke of." In *The Oxford Dictionary of the Renaissance*. Oxford: Oxford University Press, 2005. https://www.oxfordreference.com/view/10.1093/acref/9780198601753.001.0001/acref-9780198601753-e-3405.

Campeau, Lucien. "Biard, Pierre." In *Dictionary of Canadian Biography*, vol. 1, edited by Frances G. Halpenny and Jean Hamelin. Toronto: University of Toronto Press, 1966. http://www.biographi.ca/en/bio/biard_pierre_1E.html.

– *Les Cent-Associés et le peuplement de la Nouvelle France, 1633–1663*. Montreal: Les Éditions Bellarmin, 1974.

– *Les finances publiques de la Nouvelle France sous les Cent-Associés, 1632–1665*. Montreal: Les Éditions Bellarmin, 1975.

Canadian Dictionary of the English Language: An Encyclopedic Reference. Toronto: ITP Nelson, 1997.

Carlos, Ann M., and Stephen Nicholas. "Giants of an Earlier Capitalism: The Chartered Trading Companies as Modern Multinationals." *Business History Review* 62, no. 3 (Autumn 1988): 398–419.

Carmona, Michel. *La France de Richelieu*. Paris: Fayard, 1984.

Carpi, Olivia. "Une réconciliation ratée? Amiens au sortir de la Ligue." In *Lendemains de guerre civile: Réconciliations et restaurations en France sous Henri IV*, edited by Michel De Waele, 39–68. Paris: Hermann, 2015.

Carpin, Gervais. "Migrations to New France in Champlain's Time." In *Champlain: The Birth of French America*, edited by Raymonde Litalien and Denis Vaugeois, translated by Kathe Roth, 163–79. Montreal and Kingston: McGill-Queen's University Press, 2007.

– *Le réseau du Canada: Étude du mode migratoire de la France vers la Nouvelle-France (1628–1662)*. Paris: Presses de l'Université de Paris-Sorbonne, 2001.

Carrier, Hubert. *Le Labyrinthe de l'État: Essai sur le débat politique en France au temps de la Fronde, 1648–1653*. Paris: H. Champion, 2004.

Carrier, Isabelle. "Virtuosité procédurière: Pratiques judiciaires à Montpellier au Grand Siècle." PhD diss., McGill University, 2003.

Carter, A.T. *History of English Legal Institutions*. London: Butterworths, 1902.

Castagnos, Pierre. *Richelieu face à la mer*. Rennes: Ouest-France, 1989.

Cavanagh, Edward. "A Company with Sovereignty and Subjects of Its Own? The Case of the Hudson's Bay Company, 1670–1763." *Canadian Journal of Law and Society* 26, no. 1 (2011): 25–50.

Chailley-Bert, Joseph. *Les compagnies de colonisation sous l'Ancien Régime*. Paris: Armand Colin, 1898.

Chalumeau, G. "Saint Vincent de Paul et les missions en France au XVIIe siècle." *XVIIe siècle* 41 (1958): 317–27.

Church, William F. *Constitutional Thought in Sixteenth-Century France*. New York: Octagon Books, (1940) 1969.

Codignola, Luca. "Competing Networks: Roman Catholic Ecclesiastics in French North America, 1610–58." *Canadian Historical Review* 80, no. 4 (December 1999): 539–71.

– "The Issue of Tridentine Marriage in a Composite North Atlantic World: Doctrinal Strictures vs. Loose Practices, 1607–1738." *Journal of Early American History* 5 (2015): 201–70.

Collins, James B. *Classes, Estates and Order in Early Modern Brittany*. Cambridge: Cambridge University Press, 1994.

– *The State in Early Modern France*. 2nd ed. Cambridge: Cambridge University Press, 2009.

Cook, Peter. "Onontio Gives Birth: How the French in Canada Became Fathers to Their Indigenous Allies, 1645–73." *Canadian Historical Review* 96, no. 2 (2015): 165–93.

– "'Vivre comme frères': Native-French Alliances in the St. Lawrence Valley, 1535–1667." PhD diss., McGill University, 2008.

Coornaert, E.L.J. "European Economic Institutions and the New World: The Chartered Companies." In *The Cambridge Economic History of Europe*. Vol. 4, *The Economies of an Expanding Europe in the Sixteenth and Seventeenth Centuries*, edited by E.E. Rich and C.H. Wilson, 221–74. Cambridge: Cambridge University Press, 1966.

Cornette, Joël. *Affirmation de l'État absolu, 1492–1652*. 9th ed. Paris: Carré Histoire, 2016.

– *Histoire de la Bretagne et des Bretons*. 2 vols. Paris: Seuil, 2005.

Couillard-Després, A. *Charles de Saint-Etienne de La Tour, gouverneur, lieutenant-général en Acadie, et son temps, 1593–1666*. Arthabaska, QC: L'imprimerie d'Arthabaska, 1930.

Cowan, Mairi. "Education, *Francisation* and Changing Colonial Priorities at the Ursuline Convent in Seventeenth-Century Québec." *Canadian Historical Review* 99, no. 1 (March 2018): 1–29.

Crowley, Terry. "The French Regime to 1760." In *A Concise History of Christianity in Canada,* edited by Terrence Murphy, 1–55. Toronto: Oxford University Press, 1996.

Darsel, Joachim. *L'Amirauté en Bretagne: Des origines à la fin du XVIIIe siècle. Présentation de la thèse de Joachim Darsel, L'Amirauté de Bretagne des origines à la Révolution*. Under the supervision of Gérard Le Bouëdec. Rennes: Presses Universitaire de Rennes, 2012.

Daveluy, Marie-Claire. "Chomedey de Maisonneuve, Paul de." In *Dictionary of Canadian Biography*, vol. 1, edited by Frances G. Halpenny and Jean Hamelin. Toronto: University of Toronto Press, 1966. http://www.biographi.ca/en/bio/chomedey_de_maisonneuve_paul_de_1E.html.

Davies, K.G. "Joint-Stock Investment in the Later Seventeenth Century." *Economic History Review* 4, no. 3 (1952): 283–301.

– *The Royal African Company*. London: Longmans, 1957.

Debordes-Lissillour, Séverine. *Les Sénéchaussées royales de Bretagne: La monarchie d'Ancien Régime et ses juridictions ordinaires (1532–1790)*. Rennes: Presses universitaires de Rennes, 2006.

Dechêne, Louise. *Power and Subsistence: The Political Economy of Grain in New France*. Translated by Peter Feldstein. Montreal and Kingston: McGill-Queen's University Press, 2018.

Delâge, Denys. "L'alliance franco-amérindienne 1660–1701." *Recherches amérindiennes au Québec* 19, no. 1 (1989): 1–15.

– *Le Pays renversé: Amérindiens et Européens en Amérique du Nord-Est 1600–1664*. Montreal: Boréal, 1991.

De Luca, Kelly. "Beyond the Sea: Extraterritorial Jurisdiction and English Law, c. 1575–c. 1640." PhD diss., Columbia University, 2008.

Dent, Julian. *Crisis in Finance: Crown, Financiers and Society in Seventeenth-Century France*. New York: St Martin Press, 1973.

Desbarats, Catherine. "La question de l'État en Nouvelle-France." In *Mémoires de la Nouvelle-France. De France en Nouvelle-France*, edited by Philippe Joutard and Thomas Wien, 187–98. Rennes: Presses universitaires de Rennes, 2005.

Desbarats, Catherine, and Allan Greer. "North America from the Top Down: Visions from New France." *Journal of Early American History* 5, no. 2 (September 2015): 109–36.

– "Où est la Nouvelle-France?" In "La Nouvelle-France et l'Atlantique," edited by Catherine Desbarats and Thomas Wien, special issue, *Revue d'histoire de l'Amérique française* 64, nos. 3–4 (Winter/Spring 2011): 31–62.

Desbarats, Catherine, and Thomas Wien, eds. "La Nouvelle-France et l'Atlantique." Special issue, *Revue d'histoire de l'Amérique française* 64, nos. 3–4 (Winter–Spring 2011).

Deschamps, Léon. "La question coloniale en France au temps de Richelieu et de Mazarin." *Revue de Geographie* 17 (November 1885): 263–73.

Descimon, Robert, and Fanny Cosandey. *L'Absolutisme en France: Histoire et historiographie*. Paris: Éditions du Seuil, 2002.

Deslandres, Dominique. "'… alors nos garçons se marieront à vos filles, & nous ne ferons plus qu'un seul peuple': Religion, genre et déploiement de la souveraineté française en Amérique aux XVIe–XVIIIe siècles – une problématique." *Revue d'histoire de l'Amérique française* 66, no. 1 (Summer 2012): 5–35.

– *Croire et faire croire: Les missions françaises au XVIIe siècle*. Paris: Fayard, 2002.

– "'Et loing de France, en l'une & l'autre mer, les Fleurs de Liz, tu as fait renommer': Quelques hypothèses touchant la religion, le genre et l'expansion de la souveraineté française en Amérique aux XVIe–XVIIIe siècles." In "La Nouvelle-France et l'Atlantique," edited by Catherine Desbarats and Thomas Wien, special issue, *Revue d'histoire de l'Amérique française* 64, nos. 3–4 (Winter–Spring 2011): 93–117.

– "'Ils ont toujours conservé un même esprit': Le cas de la collaboration missionnaire entre Récollets et Jésuites en Nouvelle-France." In *Les Récollets en Nouvelle-France: Traces et mémoire*, edited by Paul-André Dubois, 109–22. Quebec: Presses de l'Université Laval, 2018.

– "Samuel de Champlain and Religion." In *Champlain: The Birth of French America*, edited by Raymonde Litalien and Denis Vaugeois, translated by Kathe Roth, 191–204. Montreal and Kingston: McGill-Queen's University Press, 2007.

Dessert, Daniel. *Argent, pouvoir et société au Grand Siècle*. Paris: Fayard, 1984.

– *Fouquet*. Paris: Fayard, 1987.

– *Les Montmorency: Mille ans au service des rois de France*. Paris: Flammarion, 2015.

Dewar, Helen. "Agents, Institutions and French Empire/State Formation." In "Historical Perspectives: New France beyond the Atlantic Turn," ed. Tina Loo and Matthew Hayday, special issue, *Canadian Historical Review* 102, no. 1 (March 2021): 85–108.

– "Government by Trading Company?: The Corporate Legal Status of the Company of New France and Colonial Governance." *Nuevo mundo mundos nuevos* (online), "Gouverner de manière impériale: Expériences françaises et ibériques aux Amériques (XVIe–XIXe siècle), 14 June 2018. https://doi.org/10.4000/nuevomundo.72105.

– "Litigating Empire: The Role of French Courts in Establishing Colonial Sovereignties." In *Legal Pluralism and Empires, 1500–1850*, edited by Richard Ross and Lauren Benton, 49–79. New York: New York University Press, 2013.

– "Souveraineté dans les colonies, souveraineté en métropole: Le rôle de la Nouvelle-France dans la consolidation de l'autorité maritime en France, 1620–1628." In "La Nouvelle-France et l'Atlantique," edited by Catherine Desbarats and Thomas Wien, special issue, *Revue d'histoire de l'Amérique française* 64, nos. 3–4 (2011): 63–92.

Dickinson, John. "Champlain, Administrator." In *Champlain: The Birth of French America*, edited by Raymonde Litalien and Denis Vaugeois, translated by Kathe Roth, 211–17. Montreal and Kingston: McGill-Queen's University Press, 2007.

Diefendorf, Barbara B. "Henri IV, the Dévots and the Making of a French Catholic Reformation." In *Politics and Religion in Early Bourbon France*, edited by Eric Nelson and Alison Forrestal, 157–79. Basingstoke, UK: Palgrave Macmillan, 2009.

Diefendorf, Barbara B., and Virginia Reinberg. "Catholic Reform and Religious Coexistence." In *Renaissance and Reformation France*, edited by Mack P. Holt, 176–201. Oxford: Oxford University Press, 2002.

Dionne, N.-E. "Vice-rois et lieutenants généraux de la Nouvelle-France." *Mémoires et comptes rendus de la Société royale du Canada* 7, no. 1 (1901): 35–46.

Dompnier, Bernard. "Les Franciscains entre fidélité à leur héritage et défis religieux de l'âge moderne (XVIe–XVIIe siècles)." In *Les Récollets en Nouvelle-France: Traces et mémoire*, edited by Paul-André Dubois, 61–97. Quebec: Presses de l'Université Laval, 2018.

Drévisson, Hervé. *Les rois absolus, 1629–1715*. Paris: Bélin, 2011.

Dubé, Jean-Claude. *The Chevalier de Montmagny: First Governor of New France*. Ottawa: University of Ottawa Press, 2005.

Dugast-Matifeux, Charles. "*Le Commerce honorable*" *et son auteur*. Nantes: A. Guéraud, 1857.

Dumas, G.-M. "Le Baillif, Georges." In *Dictionary of Canadian Biography*, vol. 1, edited by Frances G. Halpenny and Jean Hamelin. Toronto: University of Toronto Press, 1966. http://www.biographi.ca/en/bio/le_baillif_georges_1E.html.

Dunkley, Kenneth M. "Trading Companies and Privilege in Richelieu's France: The Hundred Associates of Morbihan." *Proceedings of the Third Annual Meeting of the French Colonial Historical Society* (1978): 3–15.

DuVal, Kathleen. *The Native Ground: Indians and Colonists in the Heart of the Continent*. Philadelphia: University of Pennsylvania Press, 2006.

Eccles, W.J. *France in America*. Vancouver: Fitzhenry and Whiteside, 1973.

Ekelund, Robert B., and Robert D. Tollison. "Mercantilist Origins of the Corporation." *Bell Journal of Economics* 11, no. 2 (Autumn 1980): 715–20.

Elliott, John H. "A Europe of Composite Monarchies." *Past & Present* 137 (1992): 48–71.

– *Richelieu and Olivares*. Cambridge: Cambridge University Press, 1984.

Erikson, Emily, and Valentina A. Assenova. "Introduction: New Forms of Organization and the Coordination of Political and Commercial Actors." *Political Power and Social Theory* 29 (August 2015): 1–13.

Fischer, David Hackett. *Champlain's Dream: The Visionary Adventurer Who Made a New World in Canada*. Toronto: Alfred A. Knopf Canada, 2008.

Freedeman, Charles E. *Joint-Stock Enterprises in France, 1807–1867*. Chapel Hill: University of North Carolina Press, 1979.

Frostin, Charles. "Vogue canadienne et milieu métropolitain de soutien à la mission lointaine au XVIIe siècle: L''épopée mystique' de la Nouvelle-France." In *Évolution et éclatement du monde rural: Structures, fonctionnement et évolution différentielle des sociétés rurales françaises et québécoises, XVIIe–XXe siècles*, edited by Joseph Goy and Jean-Pierre Wallot, 415–27. Paris: Éditions de l'École des hautes études en sciences sociales, 1986.

Funck-Brentano, Théophile. "Introduction." In *Traicté de l'oeconomie politique*, edited by Théophile Funck-Brentano. Paris: E. Plon, Nourrit, (1615) 1889.

Galland, Caroline. *Pour la gloire de Dieu et du roi: Les Récollets en Nouvelle-France aux XVIIe et XVIIIe siècles*. Paris: Éditions du Cerf, 2012.

Gelderblom, Oscar, Abe de Jong, and Joost Jonker. "The Formative Years of the Modern Corporation: the Dutch East India Company VOC, 1602–1623." *Journal of Economic History* 73, no. 4 (December 2013): 1050–76.

Gilles, David. "Les acteurs de la norme coloniale face au droit métropolitain: De l'adaptation à l'appropriation (Canada XVIIe–XVIIIe s.)." *Clio@Thémis* 4 (March 2011). https://www.cliothemis.com/Les-acteurs-de-la-norme-coloniale.

Gillis, John R. "Islands and the Making of Atlantic Oceania." In *Seascapes: Maritime Histories, Littoral Cultures and Transoceanic Exchanges*, edited by Jerry H. Bentley, Renate Bridenthal, and Kären Wigen, 21–37. Honolulu: University of Hawaii Press, 2007.

Glaisyer, Natasha. *The Culture of Commerce in England, 1660–1720*. Rochester, NY: Royal Historical Society and Boydell Press, 2006.

Godfroy-Tayart de Borms, Marion. "Les premières compagnies françaises de Guyane dans le contexte de la rivalité franco-hollandaise du premier XVIIe siècle." In *Le monde des compagnies. Les premières compagnies dans l'Atlantique, 1600–1650*. Vol. 1, *Structures et modes de fonctionnement*, edited by Éric Roulet, 127–44. Aachen, DE: Shaker Verlag, 2017.

Gosselin, Édouard Hyppolite. *Nouvelles Glanes historiques normandes*. Rouen: Imprimerie de H. Boissel, 1873.

Greengrass, Mark. *France in the Age of Henri IV: The Struggle for Stability*. 2nd ed. London: Longman, 1984.

Greer, Allan. "La pêche, les communs maritimes et l'empire français en Amérique du Nord." In *La Nature en commun: Ressources, environnement et communautés (France et Empire français XVIIe–XXIe siècles)*, edited by Fabien Locher, 169–86. Paris: Champ Vallon, 2020.

– *Property and Dispossession: Natives, Empires and Land in Early Modern North America*. Cambridge: Cambridge University Press, 2017.

Greer, Allan, and Kenneth Mills. "A Catholic Atlantic." In *The Atlantic in Global History, 1500–2000*, edited by Jorge Cañizares-Esguerra and Erik R. Seeman, 3–19. Upper Saddle River, NJ: Pearson Prentice Hall, 2007.

Grenon, Jean-Yves. "Pierre Dugua de Mons: Lieutenant General of New France." In *Champlain: The Birth of French America*, edited by Raymonde Litalien and Denis Vaugeois, translated by Kathe Roth, 143–50. Montreal and Kingston: McGill-Queen's University Press, 2007.

Griffiths, Percival. *A Licence to Trade: The History of English Chartered Companies*. London: E. Benn, 1974.

Guillorel, Éva. "Gérer la 'confusion de Babel': Politiques missionnaires et langues vernaculaires dans l'Est du Canada (XVIIe–XIXe siècles)." *Revue d'histoire de l'Amérique française* 66, no. 2 (Fall 2012): 177–203.

Gutton, Jean-Pierre. *Dévots et société au XVIIe siècle: Construire le ciel sur la terre*. Paris: Belin, 2004.

Hanley, Sarah. "Social Sites of Political Practice in France: Lawsuits, Civil Rights, and the Separation of Powers in Domestic and State Government, 1500–1800." *American Historical Review* 102, no. 1 (February 1997): 27–52.

Haran, Alain. *Le lys et le globe: Messianisme dynastique et le rêve impérial, XVIe–XVIIe siècles*. Seyssel, FR: Champ Vallon, 2000.

Hardwick, Julie. *Family Business: Litigation and the Political Economics of Daily Life in Early Modern France*. Oxford: Oxford University Press, 2009.

Harris, Ron. *Going the Distance: Eurasian Trade and the Rise of the Business Corporation, 1400–1700*. Princeton, NJ: Princeton University Press, 2020.

– "The Institutional Dynamics of Early Modern Eurasian Trade: The *Commenda* and the Corporation." *Journal of Economic Behavior and Organization* 71, no. 3 (September 2009): 606–22.

– "Trading with Strangers: The Corporate Form in the Move from Municipal Governance to Overseas Trade." In *Research Handbook on the History of Corporate and Company Law*, edited by Harwell Wells, 88–118. Northampton, MA: Edward Elgar, 2018.

Harvey, D.C. "Alexander, Sir William." In *Dictionary of Canadian Biography*, vol. 1, edited by Frances G. Halpenny and Jean Hamelin. Toronto: University of Toronto Press, 1966. http://www.biographi.ca/en/bio/alexander_william_1602_1638_1E.html.

– "Alexander, William, Earl of Stirling." In *Dictionary of Canadian Biography*, vol. 1, edited by Frances G. Halpenny and Jean Hamelin. Toronto: University of Toronto Press, 1966. http://www.biographi.ca/en/bio/alexander_william_1577_1640_1E.html.

Haudrère, Philippe. *La Compagnie française des Indes au XVIIIe siècle*. Vol. 1. Paris: Indes savantes, 2005.

Hauser, Henri. *La pensée et l'action économiques du Cardinal de Richelieu*. Paris: Presses Universitaires de France, 1944.

Havard, Gilles. *Empire et Métissages. Indiens et Français dans le Pays d'en Haut, 1660–1715*. Quebec: Septentrion, 2003.

– "'Les forcer à devenir Cytoyens': État, Sauvages et citoyenneté en Nouvelle-France (XVIIe–XVIIIe siècle)." *Annales: Histoire, Sciences Sociales* 64, no. 5 (2009–10): 983–1018.

– "'Nous ne ferons plus qu'un peuple.' Le métissage en Nouvelle-France à l'époque de Champlain." In *Le Nouveau-Monde et Champlain*, edited by G. Martinière and D. Poton, 89–110. Paris: Indes savantes, 2008.

Hayden, Michael J. *France and the Estates General of 1614*. Cambridge: Cambridge University Press, 1974.

Heijmans, Elisabeth. *The Agency of Empire: Connections and Strategies in French Overseas Expansion (1686–1746)*. Leiden: Brill, 2019.

Heijmans, Elisabeth, Cátia Antunes, and Julie Svalastog. "Essai de comparaison des compagnies néerlandaise, anglaise et française traitant sur la côte occidentale de l'Afrique au XVIIe siècle." In *Le monde des compagnies. Les premières compagnies dans l'Atlantique, 1600–1650*. Vol. 1, *Structures et modes de fonctionnement*, edited by Éric Roulet, 161–87. Aachen, DE: Shaker Verlag, 2017.

Henneton, Lauric. "Spiritual Geopolitics: Reconsidering Religious and Political Boundaries in Seventeenth-Century Northeastern America." *Journal of Early American History* 4, no. 3 (November 2014): 212–38.

Herzog, Tamar. *Defining Nations: Immigrants and Citizens in Early Modern Spain and Spanish America*. New Haven, CT: Yale University Press, 2003.

Hilaire, Jean. *Introduction historique au droit commercial*. Paris: Presses universitaires de France, 1996.

Hildesheimer, Françoise. *Richelieu*. Paris: Flammarion, 2004.

– *Du siècle d'or au grand siècle. L'État en France et en Espagne, XVIe–XVIIe siècle*. Paris: Flammarion, 2000.

Hindle, Steve. *The State and Social Change in Early Modern England, 1550–1640*. London: Palgrave Macmillan, 2002.

Hirsch, J.-P., and Philippe Minard. "'Laissez-nous faire et protégez-nous beaucoup': Pour une histoire des pratiques institutionnelles dans l'industrie française (XVIIIe–XIXe siècle)." In *La France n'est-elle pas douée pour l'industrie?*, edited by Louis Bergeron and Patrice Bourdelais, 135–58. Paris: Belin, 1998.

Hodson, Christopher, and Brett Rushforth. "Absolutely Atlantic: Colonialism and the Early Modern French State in Recent Historiography." *History Compass* 8, no. 1 (January 2010): 101–17.

Hoffman, Philip T. "Early Modern France, 1450–1700." In *Fiscal Crises, Liberty and Representative Government, 1450–1789*, edited by Philip T. Hoffman and Kathryn Norberg, 226–52. Stanford, CA: Stanford University Press, 1994.

– "Rural, Urban, and Global Economies." In *Renaissance and Reformation France, 1500–1648*, edited by Mack P. Holt, 62–98. Oxford: Oxford University Press, 2009.

Holt, Mack P. *The French Wars of Religion, 1562–1629*. 2nd ed. Cambridge: Cambridge University Press, 2005.

– "Henri IV et les privilèges municipaux à Dijon: La politique de la réconciliation." In *Lendemains de guerre civile: Réconciliations et restaurations en France sous Henri IV*, edited by Michel De Waele, 17–38. Paris: Hermann, 2015.

– "Redrawing the Lines of Authority." In *Renaissance and Reformation France, 1500–1648*, edited by Mack P. Holt, 202–28. Oxford: Oxford University Press, 2009.

Horguelin, Christophe. *La Prétendue République: Pouvoir et société au Canada, 1645–1675*. Sillery, QC: Les éditions du Septentrion, 1997.

Horn, Jeff. *Economic Development in Early Modern France: The Privilege of Liberty, 1650–1820*. New York: Cambridge University Press, 2017.

Hurt, John J. *Louis XIV and the Parlements: The Assertion of Royal Authority*. Manchester: Manchester University Press, 2004.

Innis, Harold A. *The Cod Fisheries: The History of an International Economy*. Rev. ed. Toronto: University of Toronto Press, 1954.

Jacobs, Jaap. "Dutch Proprietary Manors in America: The Patroonships in New Netherland." In *Constructing Early Modern Empires: Proprietary Ventures in the Atlantic World, 1500–1750*, edited by L.H. Roper and Bertrand Van Ruymbeke, 301–26. Leiden: Brill, 2007.

Jacquet, M. "Cramoisy (Famille)." In *Dictionnaire de biographie française*, vol. 9, edited by J. Barteau, M. Barroux, and M. Prévost, 1161–3. Paris: Letouzey et Ané, 1933.

Jaenen, Cornelius J. "The Frenchification and Evangelization of the Amerindians in Seventeenth-Century New France." CCHA *Study Sessions* 35 (1968): 57–71.

– "French Sovereignty and Native Nationhood During the French Régime." In *Sweet Promises: A Reader on Indian-White Relations in Canada*, edited by J.R. Miller, 19 42. Toronto: University of Toronto Press, 1992.

– "The Persistence of the Protestant Presence in New France, 1541–1760." *Proceedings of the Western Society for French History* 2 (January 1974): 29–40.

James, Alan. *The Navy and Government in Early Modern France, 1572–1661*. Rochester, NY: Royal Historical Society and Boydell Press, 2004.

– *The Origins of French Absolutism, 1598–1661*. Harlow, UK: Pearson Longman, 2006.

Jones, S.R.H., and Simon P. Ville. "Efficient Transactors or Rent-Seeking Monopolists? The Rationale for Early Chartered Trading Companies." *Journal of Economic History* 56, no. 4 (December 1996): 898–915.

– "Voyage et inspection maritime de M. D'Infreville sur les côtes françaises de l'océan, 1631." *French History* 15, no. 4: 448–90.

Kagan, Richard L. *Lawsuits and Litigants in Castile, 1500–1700*. Chapel Hill: University of North Carolina Press, 1981.

Kennedy, Gregory. "À la recherche de sa propre voie: Charles de Menou, sa famille et sa carrière en Acadie." *Revue d'histoire de l'Amérique française* 66, no. 2 (Fall 2012): 147–76.

– "Protecting their Investment: The Petit-Poitou Company and the Management of Drained Marshland Farms in the Poitevin Marsh, 1650–1720." *Cahiers de géographie du Québec* 59, no. 167 (September 2015): 275–91.

– *Something of a Peasant Paradise? Comparing Rural Societies in Acadie and the Loudunais, 1604–1755*. Montreal and Kingston: McGill-Queen's University Press, 2014.

Kessler, Amalia D. "Limited Liability in Context: Lessons from the French Origins of the American Limited Partnership." *Journal of Legal Studies* 32, no. 2 (June 2003): 511–48.

– *A Revolution in Commerce: The Parisian Merchant Court and the Rise of Commercial Society in Eighteenth-Century France*. New Haven, CT: Yale University Press, 2007.

Kettering, Sharon. *Patrons, Brokers, and Clients in Seventeenth-Century France*. New York: Oxford University Press, 1986.

Kupp, Thomas J. "Quelques aspects de la dissolution de la compagnie de Monsieur de Monts, 1607." *Revue d'histoire de l'Amérique française* 24, no. 3 (December 1970): 357–74.

Kwass, Michael. *Privilege and the Politics of Taxation in Eighteenth-Century France*. Cambridge: Cambridge University Press, 2006.

Lachenicht, Susanne, Lauric Henneton, and Yann Lignereux. "Spiritual Geopolitics in the Early Modern Imperial Age. An Introduction." *Itinerario* 40, no. 2 (2016): 181–7.

Lanctôt, Gustave. *L'administration de la Nouvelle-France*. Montreal: Éditions du jour, 1971.

– *A History of Canada*. Translated by Josephine Hambleton. Cambridge, MA: Harvard University Press, 1963–4.

Lanza, Janine M. *From Wives to Widows in Early Modern Paris: Gender, Economy, and Law*. Aldershot, UK: Ashgate, 2007.

Larin, Robert. *Brève histoire des protestants en Nouvelle-France et au Québec (XVIe–XIXe siècles)*. Saint-Alphonse-de-Granby, QC: Éditions de la Paix, 1998.

Lavallée, Louis. *La Prairie en Nouvelle-France, 1647–1760: Étude d'histoire sociale*. Montreal: McGill-Queen's University Press, 1992.

Le Blant, Robert. "Les Arrêts du Parlement de Rouen du 25 juin 1633 et les premières compagnies du Canada." *Revue des Sociétés Savantes de Haute-Normandie – Lettres* 3 (1956): 41–55.

– "La Compagnie de la Nouvelle-France et la restitution de l'Acadie (1627–1636)." *Revue d'histoire des colonies* 42, no. 146 (1955): 69–93.

– "Les compagnies du Cap-Breton (1629–1647)." *Revue d'histoire de l'Amérique française* 16, no. 1 (1962): 81–94.

– "Henri IV et le Canada." *Revue de Pau et du Béarn* 12 (1984–85): 43–57.

– "Les prémices de la fondation de Québec, 1607–1608." *Revue d'histoire de l'Amérique française* 20, no. 1 (1966): 44–55.

– "La première bataille pour Québec en 1608." *Bulletin philologique et historique* 2 (1971): 113–25.

– "La première Compagnie de Miscou, 1635–45." *Revue d'histoire de l'Amérique française* 17, no. 3 (1963): 363–70.

Le Blant, Robert, and Marcel Delafosse. "Les Rochelais dans la Vallée du Saint-Laurent (1599–1618)." *Revue d'histoire de l'Amérique française* 10, no. 3 (1956): 333–63.

Le Glaunec, Jean-Pierre, Carolyn Fick, and François Furstenberg, eds. "L'Atlantique français et ses frontières: Résistances, circulations, savoirs." Special issue, *Revue d'histoire de l'Amérique française* 71, nos. 1–2 (Summer–Fall 2017).

Lennox, Jeffers. *Homelands and Empires: Indigenous Spaces, Imperial Fictions, and Competition for Territory in Northeastern North America, 1690–1763*. Toronto: University of Toronto Press, 2017.

Lespagnol, André. "État mercantiliste et littoral dans la France des XVIIe–XVIIIe siècles. Une première forme d'aménagement de l'espace littoral." In *Pouvoirs et littoraux du XVe au XXe siècle*, edited by Gérard Le Bouëdec, François Chappé, and Christophe Cérino, 349–58. Rennes: Presses Universitaires de Rennes, 2000.

– *Messieurs de Saint-Malo: Une élite négociante au temps de Louis XIV*. Vol. 1. Rennes: Presses Universitaires de Rennes, 1997.

– "Saint-Malo, port mondial, XVIe–XVIIIe siècles." In *Histoire de Saint-Malo et du pays malouin*, edited by André Lespagnol, 89–137. Toulouse: Privat, 1984.

Levot, M.P. "La Marine française et le Port de Brest sous Richelieu et Mazarin." *Bulletin de la société académique de Brest* 1 (1858): 5–26.

Lévy-Bruhl, Henri. *Histoire juridique des sociétés de commerce en France aux XVIIe et XVIIIe siècles*. Paris: Domat-Montchrestien, 1938.

Liebel, Jean. *Pierre Dugua, Sieur de Mons, fondateur de Québec*. Paris: Le Croît vif, 1999.

Loades, David. *England's Maritime Empire: Seapower, Commerce and Policy, 1490–1690*. London: Longman, 2000.

Lozier, Jean-François. *Flesh Reborn: The Saint Lawrence Valley Mission Settlements through the Seventeenth Century*. Montreal and Kingston: McGill-Queen's University Press, 2018.

MacBeath, George. "Saint-Étienne de la Tour, Charles de." In *Dictionary of Canadian Biography*, vol. 1, edited by Frances G. Halpenny and Jean Hamelin. Toronto: University of Toronto Press, 1966. http://www.biographi.ca/en/bio/saint_etienne_de_la_tour_charles_de_1593_1666_1E.html.

– "Saint-Étienne de la Tour, Claude." In *Dictionary of Canadian Biography*, vol. 1, edited by Frances G. Halpenny and Jean Hamelin. Toronto: University of Toronto Press, 1966. http://www.biographi.ca/en/bio/saint_etienne_de_la_tour_claude_de_1E.html.

MacDonald, M.A. *Fortune and La Tour: The Civil War in Acadia*. Halifax: Nimbus, 2000.

MacMillan, Ken. *The Atlantic Imperial Constitution: Center and Periphery in the English Atlantic World*. London: Palgrave Macmillan, 2011.

– *Sovereignty and Possession in the English New World: The Legal Foundations of Empire, 1576–1640*. Cambridge: Cambridge University Press, 2006.

Mahaffie, Charles D. *A Land of Discord Always: Acadia from its Beginnings to the Expulsion of its People, 1604–1755*. Halifax: Nimbus, 1995.

Major, J. Russell. "Henry IV and Guyenne: A Study Concerning Origins of Royal Absolutism." In *State and Society in Seventeenth-Century France*, edited by Raymond F. Kierstead, 2–24. New York: New Viewpoints, 1975.

Mancke, Elizabeth. "Early Modern Expansion and the Politicization of Oceanic Space." *Geographical Review* 89, no. 2 (1999): 225–36.

– "Empire and State." In *The British Atlantic World, 1500–1800*, 2nd ed., edited by David Armitage and Michael J. Braddick, 193–213. New York: Palgrave Macmillan, 2009.

– "Spaces of Power in the Early Modern Northeast." In *New England and the Maritime Provinces: Connections and Comparisons*, edited by Stephen J. Hornsby and John G. Reid, 32–49. Montreal and Kingston: McGill-Queen's University Press, 2005.

Mancke, Elizabeth, and John G. Reid. "Elites, States, and the Imperial Contest for Acadia." In *The "Conquest" of Acadia, 1710: Imperial, Colonial and Aboriginal Constructions*, edited by John G. Reid, 25–47. Toronto: University of Toronto Press, 2004.

Marion, Marcel. *Dictionnaire des institutions de la France aux XVIIe et XVIIIe siècles*. Paris: A. et J. Picard, (1923) 1976.

Massé, Claude. "Jean Tuffet et ses activités en faveur de la Nouvelle-France (1626–1634)." *Les Cahiers de la Société historique acadienne* 18, no. 1 (1987): 5–24.

McCusker, John J. *Money and Exchange in Europe and America, 1600–1775: A Handbook*. Chapel Hill: University of North Carolina Press, 1978.

McManners, John. *Church and Society in Eighteenth Century France*. Vol. 1. Oxford: Clarendon Press, 1998.

McShea, Bronwen. *Apostles of Empire: The Jesuits and New France*. Lincoln: University of Nebraska Press, 2019.

Mims, Stewart L. *Colbert's West India Policy*. New York: Octagon Books, 1977.

Miquelon, Dale. "Le commerce huguenot entre la France et la Nouvelle-France: Histoire, réseaux, pratiques." In *Les Huguenots et l'Atlantique*, edited by Mickaël Augeron, Didier Poton, and Bertrand Van Ruymbeke, 447–51. Paris: Les Indes savantes, 2009–10.

Mishra, Rupali. *The Business of State: Commerce, Politics and the Birth of the East India Company*. Cambridge, MA: Harvard University Press, 2018.

Moir, John S. "Kirke, Sir David." In *Dictionary of Canadian Biography*, vol. 1, edited by Frances G. Halpenny and Jean Hamelin. Toronto: University of Toronto Press, 1966. http://www.biographi.ca/en/bio/kirke_david_1E.html.

Mollat du Jourdin, Michel. *Europe and the Sea*. Oxford: Blackwell, 1993.

Monet, J. "Noyrot, Philibert." In *Dictionary of Canadian Biography*, vol. 1, edited by Frances G. Halpenny and Jean Hamelin. Toronto: University of Toronto Press, 1966. http://www.biographi.ca/en/bio/noyrot_philibert_1E.html.

Moote, A. Lloyd. "The French Crown versus its Judicial and Financial Officials." *Journal of Modern History* 34, no. 2 (June 1962): 146–60.

Morin, Michel. "La dimension juridique des relations entre Champlain et les Autochtones de la Nouvelle-France." *Revue Juridique Thémis* 38, no. 2 (2004): 389–426.

– "Des nations libres sans territoire? Les Autochtones et la colonisation de l'Amérique française du XVIe au XVIIIe siècle." *Journal of the History of International Law* 12, no. 1 (2010): 1–70.

– "Propriétés et territoires autochtones en Nouvelle-France, partie 2: La gestion des districts de la chasse." *Recherches amérindiennes au Québec* 44, no. 1 (2014): 129–36.

Morrissey, Robert Michael. *Empire by Collaboration: Indians, Colonists and Governments in Colonial Illinois Country*. Philadelphia: University of Pennsylvania Press, 2015.

Mousnier, Roland. *Les institutions de la France sous la monarchie absolue, 1598–1789*. 2 vols. Paris: Presses universitaires de France, 1980.

Muldoon, James. *Empire and Order: The Concept of Empire, 800–1800*. New York: St Martin's Press, 1999.

Norberg, Kathryn. *Rich and Poor in Grenoble, 1600–1814*. San Francisco: University of California Press, 1985.

North, Douglass C. "Institutions, Transaction Costs and the Rise of Merchant Empires." In *The Political Economy of Merchant Empires, State Power and World Trade, 1350–1750*, edited by James D. Tracy, 22–40. Cambridge: Cambridge University Press, 1991.

Ogborn, Miles. "Wherein Lay the Late Seventeenth-Century State? Charles Davenant Meets Streynsham Master." *Journal of Historical Sociology* 15, no. 1 (March 2002): 96–101.

Olivier-Martin, François. *Histoire du droit français des origines à la Révolution*. 2nd ed. Paris: CNRS Editions, (1948) 1995.

– *L'organisation corporative de la France d'Ancien Régime*. Paris: Librairie du Recueil Sirey, 1938.

Pagden, Anthony. *Lords of All the World: Ideologies of Empire in Spain, Britain and France, c. 1500–c. 1800*. New Haven, CT: Yale University Press, 1995.

Paris-Jallobert, Paul. *Anciens Registres Paroissiaux de Bretagne*. Vols. 13–14. Rennes: Plihon et Hervé, 1891.

Parker, David. *Class and State in Ancien Régime France: The Road to Modernity?* New York: Routledge, 1996.

– *La Rochelle and the French Monarchy: Conflict and Order in Seventeenth-Century France*. London: Royal Historical Society, 1980.

– "Sovereignty, Absolutism and the Function of Law in Seventeenth-Century France." *Past & Present* 122 (1989): 36–74.

Parrott, David. *Richelieu's Army: War, Government and Society in France, 1624–1642*. Cambridge: Cambridge University Press, 2001.

Peterson, Mark. *The City-State of Boston. The Rise and Fall of an Atlantic Power, 1630–1865*. Princeton, NJ: Princeton University Press, 2019.

Petit, Jeanne. *L'Assemblée des Notables de 1626–1627*. Paris: A. Margraff, 1937.

Pettigrew, William. *Freedom's Debt: The Royal African Company and the Politics of the Atlantic Slave Trade, 1672–1752*. Chapel Hill, NC: Omohundro Institute for Early American History and Culture and University of North Carolina Press, 2013.

Phillips, Andrew, and J.C. Sharman. *Outsourcing Empire: How Company-States Made the Modern World*. Princeton, NJ: Princeton University Press, 2020.

Piant, Hervé. "Encadrement judiciaire des populations locales et concurrence des juges sous l'Ancien Régime: L'exemple du Valcolorois." In *Les justices locales et les justiciables: La proximité judiciaire en France, du Moyen Âge à l'époque moderne*, edited by Marie Houllemare and Diane Roussel, 125–39. Rennes: Presses Universitaires de Rennes, 2015.

Pritchard, James. *In Search of Empire: The French in the Americas, 1670–1730*. Cambridge: Cambridge University Press, 2004.

Rambeaud, Pascal. "L'Amiral à La Rochelle, l'union du ciel et de la mer." In *Coligny, les protestants et la mer*, edited by Martine Acerra and Guy Martinière, 131–43. Paris: Presses de l'Université de Paris-Sorbonne, 1997.

Rapley, Elizabeth. *The Dévotes: Women and Church in Seventeenth-Century France*. Montreal and Kingston: McGill-Queen's University Press, 1990.

Reid, John G. "Champlain: Longevity and Commemoration." In *Essays on Northeastern North America: Seventeenth and Eighteenth Centuries*, 205–20. Toronto: University of Toronto Press, 2008.

– "Sir William Alexander and North American Colonization." In *Essays on Northeastern North America: Seventeenth and Eighteenth Centuries*, 23–39. Toronto: University of Toronto Press, 2008.

Revel, Jacques. "Les corps et communautés." In *The French Revolution and the Creation of Modern Political Culture*. Vol. 1, *Political Culture of the Old Regime*, edited by Keith Michael Baker, 225–42. Oxford: Pergamon Press, 1987.

Ritch, Janet. "Discovery of the Baptismal Certificate of Samuel de Champlain." Champlain Society. Accessed 12 June 2021. https://champlainsociety.

utpjournals.press/findings-trouvailles/discovery-of-the-baptismal-certificate-of-samuel-de-champlain.

Robbins, Kevin C. "Families and Politics of La Rochelle, 1550–1650." PhD diss., John Hopkins University, 1991.

Robichaud, Léon. "Les origines d'une élite créole: Les 'principaux' habitants de Montréal au XVIIe siècle." In *Les figures du pouvoir à travers le temps: Formes, pratiques et intérêts des groupes élitaires au Québec, XVIIe–XXe siècles*, edited by Thierry Nootens and Jean-René Thuot, 13–25. Quebec: Presses de l'Université Laval, 2012.

Røge, Pernille, and Sophus A. Reinert. "Introduction: The Political Economy of Empire." In *The Political Economy of Empire in the Early Modern World*, edited by Pernille Røge and Sophus A. Reinert, 1–7. London: Palgrave Macmillan, 2013.

Root, Hilton L. *The Fountain of Privilege: Political Foundations of Markets in Old Regime France and England*. Berkeley: University of California Press, 2018.

Roper, L.H. *Advancing Empire: English Interests and Overseas Expansion, 1613–1688*. Cambridge: Cambridge University Press, 2017.

Roper, L.H., and Bertrand Van Ruymbeke. "Introduction." In *Constructing Early Modern Empires: Proprietary Ventures in the Atlantic World, 1500–1750*, edited by L.H. Roper and Bertrand Van Ruymbeke, 1–10. Leiden: Brill, 2007.

Roulet, Éric. *La Compagnie des îles de l'Amérique, 1635–1651: Une entreprise coloniale au XVIIe siècle*. Rennes: Presse universitaires de Rennes, 2017.

– "L'évolution des statuts de la Compagnie des îles de l'Amérique de 1626 à 1642." In *Le monde des compagnies. Les premières compagnies dans l'Atlantique, 1600–1650*. Vol. 1, *Structures et modes de fonctionnement*, edited by Éric Roulet, 109–25. Aachen, DE: Shaker Verlag, 2017.

– "Introduction." In *Le monde des compagnies. Les premières compagnies dans l'Atlantique, 1600–1650*. Vol. 1, *Structures et modes de fonctionnement*, edited by Éric Roulet, 5–11. Aachen, DE: Shaker Verlag, 2017.

Rowlands, Guy. *The Dynastic State and the Army under Louis XIV: Royal Service and Private Interest, 1661–1701*. Cambridge: Cambridge University Press, 2002.

Royle, Stephen. *The Company's Island: St Helena, Company Colonies and the Colonial Endeavour*. London: Palgrave Macmillan, 2007.

Ruggiu, François-Joseph. "Colonies, Monarchy, Empire and the French *Ancien Regime*." In *Crowns and Colonies: European Monarchies and Overseas Empires*, edited by Robert Aldrich and Cindy McCreery, 194–210. Manchester: Manchester University Press, 2016.

Ryder, Huia. "Biencourt de Poutrincourt et de Saint-Just, Jean de." In *Dictionary of Canadian Biography*, vol. 1, edited by Frances G. Halpenny and Jean Hamelin. Toronto: University of Toronto Press, 1966. http://

www.biographi.ca/en/bio/biencourt_de_poutrincourt_et_de_saint_just_jean_de_1E.html.

Sahlins, Peter. *Unnaturally French: Foreign Citizens in the Old Regime and After*. Ithaca, NY: Cornell University Press, 2004.

Sanborn, Frederic R. *Origins of Early English Maritime Law*. New York: Century, 1930.

Sawyer, Jeffrey K. *Printed Poison: Pamphlet Propaganda, Faction Politics, and the Public Sphere in Early Seventeenth-Century France*. Berkeley: University of California Press, 1990.

Scammell, G.V. "English Chartered Trading Companies and the Sea." In *Seafaring, Sailors and Trade, 1450–1750: Studies in British and European Maritime and Imperial History*, 1–26. Burlington, VT: Ashgate, 2003.

– *The World Encompassed: The First European Maritime Empires, c. 800–1650*. Berkeley: University of California Press, 1981.

Schaeper, Thomas J. "Colonial Trade Policies Late in the Reign of Louis XIV." *Revue française d'Histoire d'Outre-Mer* 67, nos. 248–9 (1980): 203–15.

Schneider, Robert A. *Public Life in Toulouse, 1463–1789: From Municipal Republic to Cosmopolitan City*. Ithaca, NY: Cornell University Press, 1989.

Schneider, Zoë A. *The King's Bench: Bailiwick Magistrates and Local Governance in Normandy, 1670–1740*. Rochester, NY: University of Rochester Press, 2008.

Scott, William Robert. *The Constitution and Finance of English, Scottish and Irish Joint-Stock Companies to 1720*. 3 vols. Gloucester, MA: P. Smith, (1912) 1968.

Secret, B. "Saint François de Sales et les missions à l'intérieur." *XVIIe siècle* 41 (1958): 304–15.

Seed, Patricia. *Ceremonies of Possession in Europe's Conquest of the New World, 1492–1640*. Cambridge: Cambridge University Press, 1995.

Servant, Georges. *Les Compagnies de Saint-Christophe et des Iles de l'Amérique (1626–1653)*. Paris: Éditions Champion, 1914.

Sheehan, James J. "The Problem of Sovereignty in European History." *American Historical Review* 111, no. 1 (February 2006): 1–15.

Slattery, Brian. "French Claims in North America, 1500–59." *Canadian Historical Review* 59, no. 2 (June 1978): 139–69.

– "Paper Empires: The Legal Dimensions of French and English Ventures in North America." In *Despotic Dominion: Property Rights in British Settler Societies*, edited by John McLaren, A.R. Buck, and Nancy E. Wright, 50–78. Vancouver: UBC Press, 2005.

Sleeper-Smith, Susan. "Women, Kin, and Catholicism: New Perspectives on the Fur Trade." *Ethnohistory* 47, no. 2 (2000): 423–52.

Steinberg, Philip E. "Lines of Division, Lines of Connection: Stewardship in the World Ocean." *Geographical Review* 89, no. 2 (1999): 256–60.

– *The Social Construction of the Ocean*. Cambridge: Cambridge University Press, 2001.

Steiner, Benjamin. "La première Compagnie du Sénégal (1633) et la question de l'institutionnalisation du commerce privilégié vers l'Afrique par Richelieu." In *Le monde des compagnies. Les premières compagnies dans l'Atlantique, 1600–1650*. Vol. 1, *Structures et modes de fonctionnement*, edited by Éric Roulet, 145–59. Aachen, DE: Shaker Verlag, 2017.

Stéphan, Raoul. *Histoire du protestantisme français*. Paris: Fayard, 1961.

Stern, Philip J. "'Bundles of Hyphens': Corporations as Legal Communities in the Early Modern British Empire." In *Legal Pluralism and Empire, 1500–1850*, edited by Lauren Benton and Richard Ross, 21–48. New York: New York University Press, 2013.

– *The Company-State: Corporate Sovereignty and the Early Modern Foundations of the British Empire in India*. New York: Oxford University Press, 2011.

– "History and Historiography of the English East India Company: Past, Present, and Future!" *History Compass* 7, no. 4 (July 2009): 1146–80.

Stern, Philip J., and Carl Wennerlind. "Introduction." In *Mercantilism Reimagined: Political Economy in Early Modern Britain and its Empire*, edited by Philip J. Stern and Carl Wennerlind, 3–22. New York: Oxford University Press, 2013.

Stoler, Ann Laura. "On Degrees of Imperial Sovereignty." *Public Culture* 18, no. 1 (2006): 125–46.

Streichenberger, Jean. *Sociétés anonymes de France et d'Angleterre: Les traits essentiels de la législation et de la jurisprudence des sociétés anonymes et des "compagnies limited by shares."* Paris: M. Giard, 1933.

Swingen, Abigail L. *Competing Visions of Empire: Labor, Slavery, and the Origins of the British Atlantic Empire*. New Haven, CT: Yale University Press, 2015.

Szramkiewicz, Romuald. *Histoire du droit des affaires*. Paris: Montchrestien, 1989.

Tallon, Alain. *La Compagnie du Saint-Sacrement (1629–1667): Spiritualité et société*. Paris: Éditions du Cerf, 1990.

Tapié, Victor-L. *France in the Age of Louis XIII and Richelieu*. Translated by D. McN. Lockie. 2nd ed. Cambridge: Cambridge University Press, 1984.

Thierry, Éric. "Champlain and Lescarbot: An Impossible Friendship." In *Champlain: The Birth of French America*, edited by Raymonde Litalien and Denis Vaugeois, translated by Kathe Roth, 121–34. Montreal and Kingston: McGill-Queen's University Press, 2007.

– *La France de Henri IV en Amérique du Nord: De la création de l'Acadie à la fondation de Québec*. Paris: Honoré Champion, 2008.

– "Introduction." In *Les Œuvres complètes de Champlain*, vol. 1, edited by Éric Thierry, 5–65. Quebec: Septentrion, 2019.

– *Marc Lescarbot, vers 1570–1641: Un homme de plume au service de la Nouvelle-France*. Paris: Honoré Champion, 2001.

Thomson, Erik. "Commerce, Law and Erudite Culture: The Mechanics of Théodore Godefroy's Service to Cardinal Richelieu." *Journal of the History of Ideas* 68, no. 3 (July 2007): 407–27.

– "France's Grotian Moment? Hugo Grotius and Cardinal Richelieu's Commercial Statecraft." *French History* 21, no. 4 (2007): 377–94.

Tomlins, Christopher. *Freedom Bound: Law, Labor, and Civic Identity in Colonizing English America, 1580–1865*. Cambridge: Cambridge University Press, 2010.

– "Law's Empire: Chartering English Colonies on the American Mainland in the Seventeenth Century." In *Law, History, Colonialism: The Reach of Empire*, edited by Diane Kirkby and Catharine Coleborne, 26–45. Manchester: Manchester University Press, 2001.

Trigger, Bruce. *Natives and Newcomers: Canada's "Heroic Age" Reconsidered*. Montreal and Kingston: McGill-Queen's University Press, 1985.

Trocmé, Étienne. "La Rochelle protestante." In *Histoire de La Rochelle*, edited by Marcel Delafosse, 85–154. Toulouse: Privat, 1985.

Trocmé, Étienne, and Marcel Delafosse. *Le commerce rochelais de la fin du XVe siècle au début du XVIIe siècle*. Paris: Armand Colin, 1952.

Trudel, Marcel. *Beginnings of New France, 1524–1663*. Toronto: McClelland and Stewart, 1973.

– "Caën, Émery de." In *Dictionary of Canadian Biography*, vol. 1, edited by Frances G. Halpenny and Jean Hamelin. Toronto: University of Toronto Press, 1966. http://www.biographi.ca/en/bio/caen_emery_de_1E.html.

– *Histoire de la Nouvelle-France*. Vols. 1–3. Montreal: Fides, 1963–83.

Turgeon, Laurier. *Une histoire de la Nouvelle-France: Français et Amérindiens au XVIe siècle*. Paris: Belin, 2019.

– "Pêches basques du Labourd en Atlantique Nord (XVIe–XVIIIe siècle): Ports, routes et trafics." *Itsas Memoria. Revista de Estudios Maritimos del Pais Vascos* 3 (2001): 163–78.

Vachon, André. "The Administration of New France." In *Dictionary of Canadian Biography*, vol. 2, edited by David M. Hayne and André Vachon. Toronto: University of Toronto Press, 1969. http://www.biographi.ca/en/theme_essays.html?p=16.

– "Fléché, Jessé." In *Dictionary of Canadian Biography*, vol. 1, edited by Frances G. Halpenny and Jean Hamelin. Toronto: University of Toronto Press, 1966. http://www.biographi.ca/en/results.php/?ft=Fl%C3%A9ch%C3%A9%2C%20Jess%C3%A9.

Vergé-Franceschi, Michel. "L'amirauté de France dans la deuxième moitié du XVIe siècle: Un enjeu entre catholiques et protestants." In *Coligny, les protestants face à la mer*, edited by Martine Acerra and Guy Martinière, 35–43. Paris: Presses de l'Université Paris-Sorbonne, 1997.

– *Chronique maritime de la France d'Ancien Régime*. Paris: Éditions SEDES, 1998.

– *Colbert: La politique du bon sens*. Paris: Éditions Payot et Rivages, 2003.

Verlinden, Charles. *The Beginnings of Modern Colonization*. Ithaca, NY: Cornell University Press, 1970.

Vidal, Cécile, ed. "L'Atlantique français." Special issue, *Outre-mers* 96, nos. 362–3 (2009).

Vincent, Catherine. *Les confréries médiévales dans le royaume de France, XIIIe–XVe siècle*. Paris: Albin Michel, 1994.

Waele, Michel De. "Conflict Resolution under the First Bourbons." In *Politics and Religion in Early Bourbon France*, edited by Alison Forrestal and Eric Nelson, 132–53. Basingstoke, UK: Palgrave Macmillan, 2009.

– *Les relations entre le Parlement de Paris et Henri IV*. Paris: Éditions Publisud, 2000.

Wagner, Michael. *The English Chartered Trading Companies, 1688–1763: Guns, Money and Lawyers*. London: Routledge, 2018.

Wells, Charlotte C. *Law and Citizenship in Early Modern France*. Baltimore: Johns Hopkins University Press, 1995.

Wenzel, Éric. "'Afin que ceux qui aspirent aux charges de judicature puissent estre instruits.' Le procureur-général Verrier et la formation des officiers de justice en Nouvelle-France: Une adaptation juridique?" In *Adapter le droit et rendre la justice aux colonies: Thémis outre-mer (XVIe–XIXe siècle)*, edited by Éric Wenzel and Éric de Mari, 67–78. Dijon: Éditions universitaires de Dijon, 2015.

White, Richard. *The Middle Ground: Indians, Empires, and Republics in the Great Lakes Region, 1650–1815*. New York: Cambridge University Press, 2011.

Wolfe, Michael. *The Conversion of Henri IV: Politics, Power, and Religious Beliefs in Early Modern France*. Cambridge, MA: Harvard University Press, 1993.

Wolff, Philippe. *Histoire des protestants en France: De la Réforme à la Révolution*. Toulouse: Privat, 2001.

Yates, Frances. *Astraea: The Imperial Theme in the Sixteenth Century*. London and Boston: Routledge and Kegan Paul, 1975.

Index

Acadia, 33, 39, 40, 52, 53, 56, 65, 87, 127, 132; English claims to, 138–9, 228–9; French settlement of, 27, 166, 194; governance of, compared to Saint Lawrence Valley, 202, 232, 233; grants of privileges, land, and authority in, 21, 96, 99, 202–4, 205–6, 208, 209, 215, 221, 235, 243; illegal trading in, 40–1, 44, 58; missionaries in, 270n20, 274n88; open trading zone in, 97, 103, 156
Adams, Julia, 9
Admiralty (France), 100, 106, 165, 180, 185, 284n87; compared to English Admiralty, 264n14; competing claims against authority of, 36, 37, 168; courts, 15, 37, 95, 169, 178; granting of licences by, 43, 113, 118; jurisdiction of, 40, 94, 95, 171, 255n85, 257n118, 263n10, 264n16; and viceroyalty of New France, 100, 181. *See also* Montmorency, Charles de; Montmorency, Henri II de
Admiralty of Dieppe, 140, 273n77
Admiralty of Guyenne, 96
Admiralty of La Rochelle, 56, 58, 84, 85, 88, 89, 219, 226
Admiralty of Rouen, 15, 38, 42, 56, 88, 102, 115
Africa, 166, 167, 183, 244
Aiguillon, Duchesse d', 190, 192
Ailleboust de Coulonge, Louis d', 223
Alexander, Sir William, 138, 228, 272n58
Algonquians, 11, 148, 150
Algonquins, 77, 148, 153; as objects of evangelization, 131, 144; regulation of access to homelands and resources of, 119–20, 243–4; as a sovereign nation, 146
alliance: and evangelization, 131; French approaches to, 153, 244; Indigenous approaches to, 150, 244
Anadabijou, 119, 120
Annapolis Basin, 226
Anne of Austria, 211, 233; approach to New France, 219–20, 222, 223, 232, 242; and conflict between Charles de La Tour and Charles Menou d'Aulnay, 227, 228, 233, 234; as *grand maître*, 293n62
Antilles, French. *See* West Indies, French
Ardier, Paul, 280n36
Armenonville, Charles Fleuriau d', 287n132
Armitage, David, 18
Assembly of Clergy, 127, 189, 269n13

Assembly of Notables, 165–6, 167, 169, 188
Atlantic, 98, 107; coast in France, 40, 94, 95, 169, 176; companies, 193, 194, 198, 199, 200, 289n20; European expansion into, 12, 91, 163; as explanatory framework, 18–19, 159, 229, 239; as geographical space, 6, 13, 20, 21, 61–3, 66, 84, 89, 92, 96, 100, 101, 158, 197, 217, 236, 242; ports in France, 26, 29, 64, 67, 68, 91, 177, 185; supervision of trade routes of, 7, 103, 107, 109, 239; travel across, 4, 5, 97, 99, 102
Aubert, Pierre, 287n132
Aulnay, Charles Menou d', 224, 230, 232, 292n57; conflict with Charles Saint-Étienne de La Tour, 225–7, 228, 229, 297n117; as lieutenant general of Acadia, 225, 226; strategies of, 229, 232, 240; terms of commission of, 227
Aunis, 94, 176
authority, 10, 11, 203, 235, 244; challenges to, in the French Atlantic, 68, 116, 220, 232, 233; claims to, 4, 6, 231; colonial or viceregal, relationship to state formation, 14, 90, 100, 103, 109; construction of, in New France, 3, 6, 11, 20, 93, 115, 118, 121, 134, 224, 241; contests over, in France, 6, 29, 36–7, 94, 171, 173; contests over, in the French Atlantic, 68, 80, 84, 113, 115, 116, 220, 232, 233; delegation of, in New France, 21, 66, 77, 202, 203, 212, 223, 242; fragmented nature of, in France, 8, 25, 34, 39, 82, 94, 95, 168, 176, 177, 179, 186; layers of, 21, 68, 110–12, 201, 204, 218, 221, 230; maritime, 4, 13, 95, 96, 99, 110, 122, 159, 160, 168–71, 181, 182, 196; nature of, in the French Atlantic, 199, 239, 240, 243; nature of lieutenant general's/viceroy's, 19, 44, 45, 52, 65, 101, 102; transatlantic contests over, 19, 29, 63, 84, 89. *See also* imperial power or authority; jurisdiction; sovereignty

Baie de Chaleur, 27, 205, 208
ban on trade, travel to New France, 67, 102, 250n16; contravention of, 57, 85, 240, 261n62; enforcement of, 42, 43; exceptions to, 52; opposition to, 69, 75; as temporary measure, 44
baptism, 146, 147, 150, 152, 274n88
Béarn, 125, 138, 269n9
Beaupré, 213, 293n66
Belleteste, Jean, 207, 209
Bellois, Corneille de, 30, 31, 137, 256n111
Benton, Lauren, 8, 18
Berchereau, François Chavigny de, 296n105
Berruyer de Manselmont, Jacques, 208, 209, 213, 292n48
Biard, Pierre, 274n88
Biencourt de Poutrincourt, Jean, 46, 127, 132, 202, 203, 257n121
Biencourt de Saint-Just, Charles de, 84, 87, 203; relationship with Samuel Georges and Jean Macain, 84, 87, 261n68
Bonneau, Thomas, 192
bons Français, 189
Boston, 225, 226, 229
Boulain, Richard, 259n34
Boullé, Hélène, 64, 132
Boyer, Daniel, 75–7, 85, 137

Braddick, Michael, 18
Brancas, Georges de, Marquis de Villars, 43, 175
Brazil, 94, 166
Breen, Michael, 81
Brest, 106, 176
Brézé, Jean Armand de Maillé, Marquis de, 293n62
British Empire, 12, 14, 240, 243, 248n39. *See also* English
Brittany, 22, 24, 38, 93, 170, 175; admiral of France's jurisdiction in, 264n16; and chartered companies, 177, 178, 184; incorporation of, into French kingdom, 33, 145, 273n81; opposition to privileges in New France, 34, 36, 70, 71; Richelieu as governor of, 179, 243; and royal consolidation of maritime authority, 36, 94–5, 171, 177–9, 196, 242. *See also* Estates of Brittany; Parlement of Brittany
Buffé, François, 38–9, 253n55

Caën, Émery de, 111, 156, 272n62
Caën, Ézéchiel de, 106, 107, 109, 111, 140, 272n62
Caën, Guillaume de, 107, 109, 111, 112, 117, 139, 181, 241, 284n87; assertion of commercial power, 113–16, 118, 121, 136, 138, 141; conflict with missionaries, 141, 143, 272n63, 273n75, 273n77; disputes with predecessor or successor companies, 205, 238, 267n71, 291n34; Protestantism of, 137, 140, 155–6; relationship with Indigenous Peoples, 144–5; role in government in New France, 111–12. *See also* Compagnie de Montmorency
Canso, 57, 208
Cap de Sable, 202, 204, 225, 226, 229, 290n24, 298n132
Cape Breton, 206, 207, 209, 213, 221, 227
Capuchins, 225
Cartier, Jacques, 4, 23, 24, 69, 137
Castillon, François, 284n88
Catholic Church, 92, 189, 191; conversion of Indigenous people, 145, 146, 154, 157; and French monarchy, 20, 132, 146, 157, 224; revitalization of, 126; universalism of, 146–7
Catholicism, 123, 124, 127, 128, 155; conversion to, 132, 151; as criterion of French subjecthood, 140, 142, 146; and French monarchy, 61, 125, 126, 188, 189; versus Christianity, 270n19. *See also* Christianity
Catholic League, 22, 29, 55, 127, 177, 192
Catholic Reformation, 127; characteristics of, 126; impact in New France, 127, 128, 133, 135, 145, 154, 220; role in French expansion, 12. *See also* Council of Trent
Catholics, 138, 142; as French subjects, 137, 141, 146; relations with Protestants, 155, 157
Caulier, Pierre, 52, 55–7, 59, 137, 258n14
ceremony of possession, 3, 5, 101
Chalais conspiracy, 175, 178
Chamber of Commerce (Paris), 78, 80, 112, 260n44, 260n48
Champlain, Samuel de, 3, 5, 6, 54, 69, 82–4, 123, 127, 129, 157, 158, 180, 183, 214; 1618 proposal, 78–80, 112, 260n44, 260n51; approach to conversion and assimilation of Indigenous people, 120, 130–2,

151, 275n104; commissions of, 3, 66, 73, 100, 101, 200, 258n11, 259n31, 289n15; creation of support networks in France, 64, 78–81, 132, 194, 233; as defender of privileges, 71, 75; explorations of, 119, 243; and Henri IV, 45, 61–2, 132, 257n2; judicial and governmental authority/power of, 14, 111–13, 115, 117, 118, 121, 134, 248n41; limits to effective power/authority, 118, 121; missionary advisers of, 140–1, 155, 272n63; and Récollets, 130, 133, 134; relationship with company associates, 67–8, 72, 77, 79–82, 89, 107, 110–16, 132–3, 135–6, 144, 219, 259n34, 260n55; relations with Indigenous Peoples, 77, 119–21, 131, 144, 243, 268n92; writings of, 14, 131, 132, 258n19, 261n59

Chanut, Pierre, 195, 287n133

chartered companies, 165, 166, 168; as centralizing instruments, 13, 109, 170, 171, 183, 187, 196, 242; characteristics of, 104–5, 289n20; French, in historiography, 121–3; and French standing, 7, 187; as governmental institutions, 9–10; historiography of, 9–10, 247n22; as instruments of power, 20, 164–5; and public good, 104, 106, 109, 197; and the state, 9, 248n39; as tool of European expansion, 12, 103. *See also* companies; corporations

Chaste, Aymar de, 251n19

Chastelets, Noël Juchereau, Sieur des, 295n89

Chastellain, Claude de, 287n132

Châtelet de Paris, 38, 87

Chauvin, Pierre, 26, 29, 240, 251n19; terms of commission of, 23, 24, 27

Cheffault, Antoine, 208, 209, 213, 292n48

Christianity, 50, 149; conversion of Indigenous inhabitants to, 26, 127, 131, 145, 220, 244; versus Catholicism, 270n19. *See also* Catholicism

Cinq-Mars, Henri Coiffier de Ruzé, Marquis de, 229

Cinq-Mars rebellion, 229

cis-Atlantic history, 18, 249n47

civiliser. *See* francization

Code Savary, 266n55

Colbert, Jean-Baptiste, 145, 151, 266n55; consolidation of maritime authority, 237, 244, 278n14; as rival of Nicolas Fouquet, 236, 237; as saviour of New France, 238

Coligny, Gaspard de, 93, 95

Coligny, Henri de Châtillon, Comte de, 95

colonization, 6, 130, 158, 161, 166, 239; and chartered companies, 198, 208, 295n87; and commerce, 137, 204, 215, 219; delegation of, in New France, 212, 213, 215, 221; as domestic issue, 4; and evangelization, 129, 132; importance of French-Indigenous alliance to, 11, 144, 145; and law, 5, 9; plans for, 78, 80, 133, 260n55; and state formation, 14; and trading privileges, 27, 28, 50

commerce, 5, 172, 188, 196, 198; and derogation, 108, 161, 164, 184, 251n25; and evangelization, 135, 271n46; French attitudes toward, 135, 163–4, 278n17. *See also* maritime commerce

commercial liberty, 50, 51, 58, 70, 187; approaches to, 71–2; calls for, 46–7,

49, 69, 71, 74–6; definition of, 255n95. *See also* privileges
commissions, 3, 9, 101, 152, 181, 182, 186, 218; characteristics of, 26, 53, 96, 127, 153, 193, 202; competing, 6, 81, 229; to corporations in France, 197, 216; execution or enforcement of, 25, 34, 35, 39, 43, 59; granted by French rivals, 138, 228; opposition to, 24, 25, 36, 37, 75; revocation of, 46, 73, 102; title-holders' use of, 6, 232, 240, 241; from viceroys or companies, 172, 184, 202, 203
communauté d'habitants, 11, 243, 294n76; attitude toward overseas companies, 13; definition of, 250n9; responsibilities of, 215–16
Communauté des Habitants, 206, 237, 244, 292n54; relationship with the Compagnie de la Nouvelle-France, 214–15, 217–19; relations of, with other corporations in New France, 221–2; responsibilities and structure of, 215–16, 218, 242, 294n74, 295n82
communauté d'habitants of Saint-Malo, 16, 25, 52, 53, 59; approach to privilege, 49–50, 71–2, 216; mobilization of provincial bodies, 34–5, 70–1, 74; protests of, against privileges, 24, 47, 69, 70, 75, 76; relationship to monarchy, 51
Compagnie pour la côte d'Acadie, 209, 225, 226, 230, 292n51; terms of, 208, 210, 292n57
Compagnie des îles de l'Amérique: and the Compagnie de Saint-Christophe, 287n134; comparison to the Compagnie de la Nouvelle-France, 195, 239, 293n71; relationship of, to island governors, 229–31, 232; terms of, 195, 286n116, 288n6
Compagnie des Indes occidentales, 244
Compagnie des Indes orientales, 107, 109, 266n57; characteristics of, 106, 108
Compagnie de Miscou, 208–9, 226, 227
Compagnie de Mons, 50, 56, 83, 105, 136, 193, 242; composition and reconfiguration of, 30–2, 55, 252n36, 256n111, 258n14; conflict with metropolitan corporations, 38–40, 48, 253n55; contracts with other merchants, 53–4; creation of, 30–2; and prosecution of interlopers, 40, 42–3. *See also* Dugua de Mons, Pierre
Compagnie de Montmorency, 122, 137, 155, 180, 193, 242; creation of, 107, 108; disputes with predecessor or successor companies, 112–13, 115, 117, 123, 133, 140, 205, 238, 241, 262n75, 267n59, 267n71, 267n76, 284n83; and evangelization, 140, 143; reconfiguration of, 155, 276n123, 284n87; relationship with Champlain, 110–12, 136; similarities to chartered companies, 108–9, 162. *See also* Caën, Guillaume de
Compagnie de Morbihan, 159, 195, 282n70, 286n112; and the Compagnie de la Nouvelle-France, 277n4; and consolidation of maritime authority, 170–3, 175, 177–9, 186, 187; and Dutch/English models, 182, 183, 185–6; jurisdiction of, in New France, 180, 183; terms of, 184, 185, 188–9. *See also* universal companies

Compagnie de la Nacelle de Saint-Pierre fleurdelisée, 159, 195, 282n70, 286n112; and consolidation of maritime authority, 170–3, 175, 177–9, 186; and Dutch/English models, 182, 183, 185–6; jurisdiction of, in New France, 180, 185; terms of, 170–1, 184, 185, 187, 285n101. *See also* universal companies

Compagnie de la Nouvelle-France, 4, 13, 15, 186, 196, 280n30; and the Compagnie de Morbihan, 277n4; compared to other corporations, 197–8; compared to other French companies, 188–9, 192–5, 229, 232–3, 239, 286n112; compared to rival European companies, 198–9, 200, 204–5, 289n20; and competing title-holders, 205, 217–19, 222–4, 226–7, 232, 241, 291n34, 295n82, 297n117; composition of, 181–2, 192, 255n90, 284n88, 284n89; and conflict with Huguenots, 172–3; and consolidation of maritime authority, 159, 251n23; delegation of powers, obligations, and privileges by, 202–15, 220–1, 225, 235, 243, 289n15, 290n26, 290n29; and Dutch/English models, 161–2, 182; end to, 236, 238, 244; historiography of, 158–9; relationship with Richelieu, 180, 199–201, 211, 220, 232; as religious, political, and commercial, 159, 160, 189–90, 192, 243; sources of support for, 190–1; and state and empire formation, 7; terms of, 160–2, 188–9, 267n59, 267n62, 286n111; as a tool of governance, 21; traditional and innovative nature of, 20–1

Compagnie parisienne du Cap-Breton, 207–10, 292n55

Compagnie de Rouen et Saint-Malo, 82, 100, 105, 242; comparison to the Compagnie de Montmorency, 107–9; composition of, 53, 82–3, 256n105, 258n14; creation of, 67, 82–3; dispute over contract, 102–3, 112–13, 115–18, 123, 133, 137, 139, 140, 143, 262n75, 267n59, 267n76; and evangelizing mission, 129, 130, 142–3; legal disputes with Rochelais traders, 16, 82, 84–90, 261n62, 262n73, 263n89; opposition to privileges of, 74–6, 259n34, 259n39; relationship with Champlain, 67, 72, 77–82, 89, 115, 132–3, 135, 219, 260n44, 260n55; and viceregal dispute, 73–4, 259n31, 259n33

Compagnie royale des voyages de long cours: and Dutch/English models, 185–6; terms of, 183–4, 284n94

Compagnie de Saint-Christophe, 175, 182; and the Compagnie des îles de l'Amérique, 287n134; comparison to other French companies, 159, 193–5, 239; terms of, 193–4, 287n136

Compagnie du Saint Sacrement, 154, 190, 192, 220, 222, 223

compagnies particulières, 209, 211, 214, 215, 291n36, 293n60; terms of, 205–6, 291n38

companies, 15, 142, 190, 194, 199; codification of, 266n55; English and Dutch, as models, 105, 106, 160, 167–8; evolution of, in New France, 108, 191, 201, 215; experimentations with, 159–60, 173, 182, 195–7, 210, 239, 242–3, 277n5; French, as compared to English/

Dutch, 13, 159, 295n87; and state/empire formation, 10, 160. *See also* chartered companies; corporations
company-state, 10, 199
Concini, Concino, 72, 73, 76
Condé, Henri de Bourbon, Prince de, 64, 70, 84, 88, 91, 96, 102, 112, 132, 180, 258n11, 261n59; approach to viceroyalty, 66–8, 202, 207; as both lieutenant general and viceroy, 258n8; dispute over viceroyalty, 73–4, 89; revolt and imprisonment of, 72–3, 76, 77, 231; sale of viceroyalty, 91, 254n74; terms of commission of, 65, 96–8, 193, 227, 264n28
Condonnier, Jean, 208, 210, 291n44
congé. *See* licence
Conseil d'État du roi, 15. *See also* royal council
Conseil de la Traite, 234
Conseil de Québec, 224, 234; jurisdiction of, 222
Conseil privé, 15, 226. *See also* royal council
conversion: and francization, 129; of Indigenous people, 131, 144, 146, 191, 220, 270n27; of Protestants, 146
corporations, 63, 200, 204, 214, 224; characteristics of, 33, 197–8; competition among, 39–40; French, relationship to Crown, 62, 241; and public good, 104, 109, 197, 199. *See also* chartered companies; companies
corps de ville, 173, 294n76
Coste, Mathieu de, 254n77
Coujugon, 24, 250n8
Council of Trent, 126–8, 130, 132, 148, 269n13. *See also* Catholic Reformation
courts of justice (France), 11, 69, 178; and construction of authority in North America, 6, 14, 19, 241; and jockeying over powers and privileges in New France, 58, 59, 74, 82, 87–8, 90, 101, 115, 123, 140, 142; and patronage networks, 8; rivalries among, 6, 88, 89, 263n91; role of, in French society, 62–3. *See also* lawsuits
courts of justice (New France), 220, 234, 299n149
Cramoisy, Sébastien, 181, 192, 284n89
Crown (English), 138; and chartered companies, 104
Crown (French), 15, 161, 169, 185, 229, 236, 238; approach to privileges, 44, 53, 59; as arbitrator of competing interests, 81; and Catholic Church, 132, 146, 157, 224; Catholic ideology of, 12, 189; and chartered companies, 13, 161, 165, 198, 204; and conflict with Huguenots, 6, 95, 125, 170, 172, 224; consolidation of maritime authority, 37, 94, 95, 168, 171, 173, 177, 179, 182; and corporations, 33, 51, 62, 75, 178, 179, 216, 223, 241; francization of Indigenous people, 145–7, 157; intervention overseas, 3–4, 77, 79, 243, 244, 260n51; religious policies of, 127, 128, 189; sources of financial and organizational support, 190–1, 243. *See also* monarchy (French)
customary rights, 9, 170, 178, 185; of fishermen and traders, 4, 25, 59, 239; Malouin defence of, 70, 71, 76

Dablon, Simon, 284n88
Damville, François-Christophe de Lévis-Ventadour, Duc de, 220, 227

Daniel, Charles, 207
Dareche, Martin, 56
Dauversière, Jérôme Le Royer, Sieur de La, 220, 221
Day of the Dupes, 179, 283n76
Dechêne, Louise, 10
Denys, Nicolas, 212, 227, 233, 290n26, 297n118
Des Sauvages, 258n19
Desbarats, Catherine, 10
Desportes, Pierre, 206–10, 213, 227
dévots, 128, 132, 153, 154, 192, 270n15; activities in New France, 190, 220, 223, 224; characteristics of, 126
Dieppe, 158, 251n19, 251n23
Dolu, Jean-Jacques, 100, 107, 109, 137, 140, 142, 144, 181; as an associate of the Compagnie de Montmorency, 265n32
Du May, 100, 101, 117
Du Noyer de Saint-Martin, François, 183–4, 285n96
Duchesne, David, 284n88
Dugua de Mons, Pierre, 19, 25, 35, 50, 64, 99, 137, 233, 248n41, 258n14; approach to lieutenant generalship, 52, 54, 65–6, 202, 207, 235; approach to privileges, 53–5, 241, 267n60; commission of, from admiral of France, 99, 264n28; confessional nature of enterprise of, 127; cost of privileges, 44–5, 254n74; and Dutch/English competition in North America, 46, 254n77; opposition to commission of, 37, 46, 49; privileges of, as compared to those in France, 51–2; relationship of, with associates, 29–30, 56–9, 83, 256n111, 257n123; relationship to Henri IV, 39, 61–2, 251n19; revocation of commission of, 45–8; terms of commission of, 26–8, 45, 59, 152–3, 193, 240, 250nn15–16. *See also* Compagnie de Mons
Duisterlo, Mathieu, 49, 87, 137
Duplessis-Kerbodot, Guillaume Guillemot, 201, 289n17
Dutch, 92, 94, 138, 164, 230, 279n20; companies, as compared to French, 13, 159, 199, 200; companies as models, 105, 106, 160, 182, 185, 239, 279n21; competition with French in colonization and commerce, 45–6, 48, 50, 79, 94, 138, 237; French diplomatic relations with, 125; maritime commercial and naval power of, 103, 106, 162, 166, 175, 236; similarity of imperial instruments of, to English and French, 12; and war with Spain, 92, 93, 138, 168–9, 172, 263n4
Dutch Empire, 12, 240, 243
Duval, Jean, 248n41

East India Company (Dutch), 92, 164, 182, 184, 186, 187, 199, 293n59; dominance of, in historiography, 12; principal characteristics of, 103–5, 265n48
East India Company (English), 10, 162, 182, 186, 187, 199, 211; dominance of, in historiography, 12; principal characteristics of, 103–5, 266n49
East India Company (French). *See* Compagnie des Indes orientales
Edict of Nantes, 22, 124–6, 141; revocation of, 142
Effiat, Antoine Coiffier de Ruzé, Marquis d’, 194, 284n89
empire, 7, 8, 10, 182, 228; agents of, 5, 121; conception of, 21, 239–40; as

process, 3. *See also* British Empire; Dutch Empire; French Empire; Spanish Empire
empire formation, 12, 14; characteristics of, in New France, 239, 243; role of companies in, 10, 13, 160, 242; and sea, 6–7; and state formation, 4, 238–9, 242
English, 106, 201, 225, 230; Admiralty jurisdiction, compared to French, 264n14; colonization, 48, 164, 217; companies, as compared to French, 13, 159, 199, 200, 289n20, 295n87; companies as models, 105, 106, 160, 182, 185, 239; competition with French in colonization and commerce, 50, 79, 94, 225, 228–9, 233, 237; French diplomatic relations with, 125, 173, 228; maritime commercial and naval power of, 103, 106, 162, 163, 166, 168–9, 175, 236; similarity of imperial instruments to Dutch and French, 12; as supporters of French Protestants, 138, 170; war with France, 203, 205, 228, 290n24, 291n34, 298n132
English Empire. *See* British Empire
Eon, Jean, 163, 183, 278n16
Esnambuc, Pierre Belain d', 193
estates, 20, 243, 250n9
Estates of Brittany, 4, 16, 25, 63, 70, 71; and French monarchy, 33–4, 51, 75–6; opposition to consolidation of maritime authority, 36–7, 95, 158, 177–8, 282n68; protest against commissions, 50, 59, 74, 75
Estates General, 71
Etchemins, 131
European expansion, 6, 7; instruments of, 12
evangelization, 150–1, 159, 166, 198; and alliance, 131; and commerce, 135, 137, 142–4; and definitions of subjecthood, 139; evolving role of, in New France enterprise, 128, 131, 133, 155; program, 133–4, 157; and sovereignty construction, 154; targets of, 128, 129, 244

Fancamp, Pierre Chevrier, Baron de, 220
Ferté, Jean Juchereau, Sieur de La, 295n89
financiers, 190–1, 192, 195
fishery, 52, 55, 69, 170, 172, 185; as customary right, 4; and policing of privileged trading zone, 40–1; rights to, 92, 202; tradition of open, 97, 161
Fléché, Jesse, 274n88
Florida, 42, 161
Fort Lomeron, 202
Fort Saint-Louis (in Acadia), 203, 225, 226, 290n25
Fort Saint-Louis (at Quebec), 213
Fort Sainte-Anne, 207
Fort Sainte-Marie, 203, 225, 226
Fouquet, François, 195, 208, 237, 287n133, 292n48
Fouquet, Nicolas, 236, 237
France, 71, 81, 82, 130, 131, 135, 137; in Atlantic framework, 7, 239; competition with European rivals, 92, 94, 103, 139, 162, 164, 169, 171–2, 175, 187, 225, 233; diplomatic relations with fellow European countries, 173, 189, 220, 228, 280n40; incorporation of new territories, 33, 147; maritime commercial and naval power of, 162–4, 166, 167, 170;

overseas interests of, 22, 78, 188; politico-religious situation in, 22, 51, 61, 124, 125, 127, 142, 143, 189; privileges in, as compared to North America, 44, 51–2; relationship with New France, 14, 18, 19, 21, 74, 239; role of legal institutions, 16, 19, 62, 87; subjecthood in, 141, 146.
Franciscans, 126, 128
francization, 144, 148, 150–1, 157, 244, 275n105; concept of, 147; relationship to conversion, 129, 130
François I, 23, 36, 50
French Empire: characterization of, 239–40; compared to European rivals, 12, 240, 243. *See also* empire
Fronde, 212, 229, 230, 236
furriers, competition with the Compagnie de Mons, 38–40, 46, 48–50, 59
fur trade, 29, 30, 55, 207, 229, 237; and colonization, 3, 137, 204, 214, 215, 219; competition over, with European rivals, 45; competition over, among French, 6, 27, 59, 64, 83, 86, 90, 241, 251n23; delegation of privileges to, 3, 26, 54, 57, 79, 161, 198, 205, 208, 214, 215, 240, 241; eligibility for participation in, 157, 222; and evangelization, 142, 143–4, 224; management of, 216, 218, 220–2, 234, 235, 242; and Protestantism, 136; regulation of, 25, 38; and relations with Indigenous Peoples, 77, 152; role of, in governance of New France, 216–18

Gaspé, 57, 118, 156, 208
Gaston d'Orléans, 175
Georges, Pierre, 56
Georges, Samuel, 33, 84, 137; as associate of the Compagnie de Mons, 31–2; conflict with privilege-holders, 54–9, 82–3, 85–9, 241, 258n14, 261n62, 262n73, 263n89; mercantile activities of, 30, 87; relationship with Charles de Biencourt, 84, 87, 261n68
Giffard, Robert, 222, 296n105
Godefroy, Jean-Paul, 214, 295n89, 296n105
Godefroy, Robert, 210
Goret, Étienne, 31, 57
grand maître, chef, et surintendant de la navigation et du commerce, 160, 165, 179, 182, 196, 200, 201, 242; terms of commission of, 173–5, 178, 180–1
Gravé Du Pont, François: as agent of the Compagnie de Mons, 42, 44, 54, 55, 56, 248n41; as agent of the Compagnie de Rouen et Saint-Malo, 69–70, 113–16, 118, 121, 131, 138, 141, 258n14
Greer, Allan, 10
Grotius, Hugo, 92, 156, 263n4
Guadeloupe, 230, 231
Guers, Baptiste, 100, 101, 107, 118, 123
Guise, Charles de Lorraine, Duc de, 177, 280n40
Gulf of Saint Lawrence, 226, 227, 232
Guyenne, 94, 95

Haudenosaunee, 119, 131, 149, 153, 213, 237
Havard, Gilles, 11
Henneton, Lauric, 128
Henri III, 24, 249n4, 250n12
Henri IV, 65, 94, 99, 273n81; approach to companies, 265n41; arbitration of competing interests in New France, 24, 27, 47, 59; assassination of, 19, 61, 125, 211;

conversion of, 142; and Dutch/English competition in North America, 46, 48; overseas ambitions of, 22–3, 26, 45, 48; relationship to Champlain, 45, 61–2, 130, 132, 257n2, 261n59; relations with provincial or municipal corporations, 34–7, 50, 51; religious policies of, 124
Hochelaga, 22, 249n1
Honfleur, 102, 115, 116, 251n19
Hospitallers, 191
Houel, Charles, 230, 232
Houel, Louis, Sieur du Petit-Pré, 128, 181, 284n88
Huguenots, 61, 142, 146, 228, 286n111; civil and religious rights of, 22, 124, 126, 141–2; conflict of, with the Crown, 6, 20, 96, 125, 126, 166, 169–70, 172, 177, 182, 189, 224, 279n20; practices of worship in New France, 155, 156; relations with Catholics, 155, 157; threat of, to evangelizing mission in New France, 129–30, 135–7, 139–41, 144–5, 155, 157

Île d'Orléans (New France), 213
Île de Ré, 172, 176
Illinois, 152
imperial power or authority, 115–21, 201. *See also* authority; jurisdiction; sovereignty
Indian Ocean, 12, 18, 91, 106
Indigenous Peoples, 65, 78, 91, 101, 118, 120, 121, 268n92; francization and conversion of, 127, 144–7, 244; reception of, to Christian beliefs and French practices, 148–50, 244, 274n98; relations with French, 146, 153, 161, 244
Indigenous sovereignty, 10–11, 153, 243
Infreville, Louis Le Roux, Sieur d', 176
Innu, 84, 148; as objects of evangelization, 129, 131, 144; regulation of access to homelands and resources of, 119–20; as a sovereign nation, 146; trade relations with French, 118–20
interlopers: capture by privilege-holders, 85; defiance of, 43, 56, 84, 118, 240; and policing of privileged trading zone, 40, 41, 52, 108, 113, 198; in Saint Lawrence River, 58, 118
Iroquet, 119

Jamet, Denis, 123, 129, 133
Jeannin, Pierre, 51, 64
Jesuit Relations, 192, 284n89
Jesuits, 15, 20, 127, 150, 158, 190, 208, 213, 221, 224; and evangelizing mission, 149, 154, 270n27, 274n103; missions in Acadia, 270n20, 274n88; relationship with Crown, 125, 157, 194; relations with other corporations in New France, 214, 220, 222; role in government of New France, 154–5, 223–4; as seigneurs in New France, 191, 213. *See also* missionaries
joint-stock company, 104, 160, 162, 194, 205, 210, 242; history of term in France, 266n53. *See also* chartered companies; companies
Joyeuse, Anne de, 36–7
jurisdiction, 121, 182, 185, 186, 196, 230; of chartered companies, 10, 138, 170, 180, 184, 185, 208, 212, 244; commercial, 117, 200, 204, 242; disputes over, in France, 34, 37, 40, 70, 84, 88, 90, 177, 178; disputes over, in New France,

74, 79, 81, 114, 116, 118, 136, 232; lieutenant general's/viceroy's, 27, 48, 96, 101, 227; maritime, in France, 94, 179, 187; maritime nature of, in New France, 20, 92, 93, 96–9, 108, 121, 139; overlapping nature of, in New France, 180, 196, 199, 203, 219, 224, 240, 241, 244; relationship between commercial and governmental, 68, 110, 118, 136, 216, 219, 235; relationship between maritime and territorial, 19–20, 93, 110, 121; seigneurial, 198, 204. *See also* authority; imperial power or authority; sovereignty

Kennebec River, 225
Kichesipirinis, 119, 120
Kirke brothers, 228, 229, 272n58, 290n24
Knights of Malta, 162, 230, 233, 291n44

La Hève, 204, 208, 212, 225; River, 42
La Jannaye, Étienne Chaton de, 24, 53
La Meilleraye, Armand-Charles de La Porte de, 278n16
La Ralde, Raymond de, 155, 156
La Roche de Mesgouez, Troilus de, 270n19; terms of commission of, 22–3, 27, 249n4
La Rochelle, 16, 33, 212, 226, 237; competition with other French ports in fur trade, 83, 90; and consolidation of maritime authority, 94, 95, 169, 173, 176, 242; and Huguenot conflict with Crown, 73, 95, 138, 166, 170, 177, 189; and opposition to privilege-holders in New France, 42, 82, 84, 85, 158; participation of, in privileged companies in New France, 29, 30–2, 67; protection of interests and privileges of, 29, 83, 173; Protestantism of merchants of, 29, 136–7; relative importance of, in New France enterprise, 30, 251n23, 281n52; siege of, 154, 172, 191, 236. *See also* Admiralty of La Rochelle; Georges, Samuel; Macain, Jean
La Rocque de Roberval, Jean-François de, 22, 23, 27, 249n4
Lalemant, Charles, 221, 222
Lalemant, Jérôme, 222–4
Lattaignant, Gabriel, 181, 284n88
Lauson, Jean de, 180, 181, 192, 200, 201, 213, 234, 292n48
law, 69, 199; and colonization, 5, 9; and colony-metropole relations, 14; mobilization of, by subjects, 5–6, 8, 113, 116, 240; natural, 92, 156; and relations between subjects and sovereign, 8–9, 62–3; Roman, 92, 97; and state formation, 8
lawsuits: between title-holders and interlopers, 42–3, 56–8; costs of, 257n124; description of, 15–16, 63, 257n4; impact on state and empire formation, 14; over powers and privileges in New France, 74, 85–8, 112, 143, 205, 214, 226, 241; reasons for, 6; as sources, 14–16; strategies of parties to, 78, 82, 86–90, 241, 262n82. *See also* courts of justice (France)
Le Baillif, Georges, 118, 123; as deputy of the 1621 assembly, 139–40; role in government of New France, 140–1, 155, 224
Le Borgne, Emmanuel, 226, 297n118
Le Breton, Guillaume, 259n34

Le Caron, Joseph, 129, 133, 157; *Au roy sur la Nouvelle France*, 123, 126; complaints against companies and Protestants, 135–7, 142
Le Cler, Jean, 163, 278n15
Le Havre, 43, 175, 176
Le Sueur, 42–3
Legardeur de Repentigny, Pierre, 214, 217–19, 295n89
Legendre, Lucas, 52, 55–9, 137, 258n14
Legrand, Jean, 208, 292n51
Les Cent Associés, 158, 277n4. *See also* Compagnie de la Nouvelle-France
Lescarbot, Marc, 127, 135
Letardif, Olivier, 218–19
letters patent. *See* commissions
lettre de jussion, 34–6
Libert, Nicolas, 207, 209
licence, 121, 169, 176, 214; from admiral, 4, 37, 40, 42–3, 92, 95, 113, 118, 170; from *grand maître*, 178; from viceroy/lieutenant general, 54, 67, 84, 91, 102, 200
lieutenant general. *See* viceroys
lit de justice, 35
litigation. *See* lawsuits
Louis XIII, 61, 75, 166, 175, 197, 204, 211, 220, 222, 225, 256n98, 261n59, 279n20, 283n76; and conflict with Huguenots, 125, 138, 154; and consolidation of maritime authority, 16, 170, 171, 173, 183; religious policies of, 125, 269n9
Louis XIV, 8, 142, 150, 211, 228; and the Compagnie de la Nouvelle-France, 236; as saviour of New France, 238
Lozier, Jean-François, 11, 148, 150

Macain, Jean, 84, 137; as associate of the Compagnie de Mons, 31–2; conflict with privilege-holders, 55–9, 82–3, 258n14, 261n62; mercantile activities of, 30, 87; relationship with Charles de Biencourt, 84, 87, 261n68
Macmillan, Ken, 9
Maisonneuve, Paul de Chomedey de, 221–3
maîtres des requêtes, 57, 85, 180, 192
Mancke, Elizabeth, 8
Marillac, Michel de, 167
maritime commerce, 177, 186; and chartered companies, 105, 159; claims to, 101, 103; jurisdiction over, 96, 175; memoranda on, 16, 162–5; revitalization of, 4, 158, 162–7, 174–5, 182, 183, 187. *See also* commerce
Martin, François, 31, 57
Martinique, 230, 231
Massachusetts Bay, 229; comparison with New France, 13
Massachusetts Bay Company, 199
Massé, Énemond, 274n88
Matane, 70, 96
Mauvoy, Martin de, 176, 194, 282n61, 284n89
Mazarin, Jules, 232, 236
Médicis, Marie de, 61, 74, 94, 127, 179; relationship to Condé, 65, 72–3, 89; religious policies of, 125; revolt and exile of, 76, 283n76
Mediterranean, 163, 177, 185
Mercoeur, Philippe-Emmanuel de Lorraine, Duc de, 36–7
métissage, 11
Mi'kmaq, 41, 274n88
Miristou, 120, 144, 149
Miscou, 205, 208, 215
missionaries, 5, 6, 14, 16, 18, 20, 119, 141, 158, 277n2; as agents of

empire, 121, 139, 154; approaches to, by Indigenous people, 149–51; and Catholic Reformation, 126–8; conflicts with other French actors in New France, 237; differing views of conversion among, 274n88; and evangelizing program, 130, 131; and obligations of privileged companies, 130, 195, 222; role in government of New France, 133, 224. *See also* Jesuits; Récollets
Mohawk, 119
monarchy (French): and Catholic Church, 20; Catholicism of, 125, 137, 188; francization of Indigenous people, 145, 154; and justice, 5. *See also* Crown (French)
monopoly, 49, 250n16. *See also* privileges
Montchrestien, Antoine de, 164, 279n20
Montmagny, Charles Huault de, 201, 213, 218, 221–3, 289n19
Montmorency, Anne de, 93
Montmorency, Charles de, 26, 30, 31, 94, 95, 266n57
Montmorency, Henri I de, 94
Montmorency, Henri II de, 3, 91, 101, 116, 137, 139, 153, 175–6, 180, 220; admiral, jurisdiction of, 84, 94, 95, 264n15; approach to viceroyalty, 100–3, 107, 108, 155, 156, 181, 232, 242, 265n32; challenge of, to Crown, 169, 171; dispute with the Compagnie de Rouen et Saint-Malo, 140, 142, 143; efforts to consolidate maritime authority, 7, 19, 93, 95, 96, 99–100, 107, 109, 122, 159, 173, 177–80, 182, 195, 236–7; and international experimentations with chartered companies, 103, 106, 160, 182, 265n41; purchase of viceroyalty, 91, 254n74; terms of commission of, 96, 98, 193; vision for maritime affairs, 94, 95, 175
Montreal, 148, 154, 201, 202, 213, 221–3, 234, 249n1. *See also* Ville-Marie
Morbihan, 177, 178, 184
Motin, Louis, 208, 292n51

Nantes, 176
Navarre, 145, 269n9, 273n81
navigation, 175, 177, 186; and chartered companies, 105; memoranda on, 16, 162; revitalization of, 4, 162, 166–7, 174, 187; rights or claims to, 92, 101, 103
Negabamat, 150
Nenaskoumat, 150
Netherlands. *See* Dutch
Neutrals, 120
Newfoundland, 22, 30, 40, 161; Banks of, 4, 25, 93, 108
New France, 11, 14, 15, 24, 28, 34, 44, 69, 83, 84, 86, 101, 181, 182, 186, 236; and Catholic Reformation, 127, 128, 130, 133, 135; comparison with English colonies, 13; comparison with the French West Indies, 193–5, 229, 237–8, 239; construction of sovereignty in, 115, 116, 121; evolution of companies in, 13, 108, 161, 215, 239, 242; foreign threats to, 79, 137, 139; lawsuits over powers and privileges in, 62, 86, 89, 241; links between trade and religion in, 136, 137; as maritime space, 7, 20, 91, 93, 96–99, 103, 107, 179–80; Protestant presence in, 135, 137, 140–2, 155, 157, 286n111; as province, 28, 244; regulation

of trade in, 43, 50, 53, 57, 60, 102, 243; resources in, 78; role of *dévots* in, 126, 190, 223; settlement of, 145, 183–5, 191, 197, 202; and state formation, 6, 16, 18, 19, 59, 74, 89, 90, 96, 122, 182, 239; struggles over governance of, 21, 68, 73, 89, 133, 136, 141, 200, 217, 224, 237, 241, 242; subjecthood in, 141, 146–8, 155, 157; visions of, 5, 78–80, 132
Noel, Jacques, 24, 53
Normandy, 94, 176, 251n19, 281n52; and disputes in New France, 34, 38, 40, 88, 89
Norumbega, 22, 249n1
Notre-Dame-des-Anges, 213
Noue, Anne de, 157
Noyrot, Philibert, 154, 191

Ochasteguin, 119
Ottawa River, 119

Palais de Justice, 34, 85, 180
Paris, 52, 57, 64, 75, 136, 178, 197, 225, 231; Chamber of Commerce, 78, 80; fur industry in, 38–40, 49; as headquarters of companies, 13, 106, 109, 210, 218, 251n23; participation of, in privileged companies in New France, 162
Parlement of Bordeaux, 34, 283n71
Parlement of Brittany, 278n16; and French monarchy, 51; opposition to consolidation of maritime authority, 36–7, 95, 158, 177–8; protest against commissions, 34–5, 59, 70
Parlement of Paris, 4, 51, 64, 234, 292n48; and disputes over privileges and powers in New France, 74, 77, 226; and registration of commissions, 34, 283n71
Parlement of Rouen, 34, 36, 70, 86, 283n71
parlements, 15, 16, 63, 69, 243, 282n70; resistance to overseas commissions, 34–6, 40, 59, 172
parti dévot, 125, 189
Paul, Vincent de, 126, 223
Pavillon, Etienne, 287n132
pays d'en haut, 11, 149, 151, 152
pays d'états, 33, 34, 250n9
pays des Illinois, 152
Penobscot River, 225
Pentagouet, 225
Phillips, Andrew, 10, 199
Plymouth Company, 217, 218
Poincy, Philippe de Longvilliers, Sieur de, 181, 291n44; as lieutenant general/governor in the West Indies, 230–1, 233, 284n89; strategies of, 231, 232
Pontherie, Julius de Loynes, Sieur de la, 176
Porée, Thomas, 75, 76, 259n34
Port-Royal, 97, 202, 203, 229, 257n121, 264n24; English occupation of, 205, 228, 272n58; seigneurial concession of, 208, 225
Porte, Amador de La, 176
Portuguese, overseas claims of, 23, 91
privileges, 14, 113, 146, 191, 240; to chartered companies, 104, 106, 161, 184, 185, 195, 197, 198, 212, 242; definition of, 23–4, 44, 255n95; delegation of, by viceroy, 66, 107; elasticity of, 25, 50, 52, 55, 58–60, 108, 187–8, 204, 205, 208, 241; enforcement of, 40; to fur trade, 3, 202, 206–7, 212, 215, 219, 250n16; protection of, 5, 67, 72; protest

against, 5, 46, 47, 57, 64, 84, 158, 216; value of, 44–5, 50, 51. *See also* commercial liberty
proprietorships: and empire formation, 9, 12
Protestantism, 154; calls for ban of, in New France, 134, 154; and subjecthood, 137–8, 142; threat posed by, 135, 140, 142; and trade, 136
Protestant Reformation, 126
Protestants. *See* Huguenots

Quebec, 3, 16, 64, 66, 69, 102, 118, 123, 150, 206, 226, 231; 1621 assembly at, 123, 269n1; commander of, 100, 111, 201; English occupation of, 203, 205, 228; fort at, 101, 113, 116, 121; foundation of, 52, 58; as governmental centre in New France, 201–2, 220–2, 299n149; Indigenous settlements near, 120, 144, 148–9; missionaries at, 127, 128, 154, 224; settlement of or around, 80, 180, 194, 213, 264n24; trading privileges at, above or below, 53, 96, 97
queen regent. *See* Médicis, Marie de; Anne of Austria

Ralluau, Jean, 38–9, 54
Ravaillac, François, 61
Razilly, Claude Launay de, 165, 181, 225, 226, 232, 291n44; activities in Acadia, 208–10
Razilly, Isaac de, 165, 181, 227, 232, 289n13, 290n29, 291n44; as lieutenant general of New France, 203–4, 208, 212, 224, 240; memorandum by, 166–8, 280n30, 286n121
Récollets, 3, 20, 101, 123, 126, 127, 141, 157, 158; 1616 program for conversion, 129–30, 133, 134; approach to conversion, 147; calls for ban on Protestants in New France, 142–5; and Champlain, 133, 134; history of, 128; memorandum of 1621, 133–6, 138–9; and redefinition of French subjecthood, 139, 140, 142, 145, 155; role in government of New France, 140, 143, 154–5, 224. *See also* Le Baillif, Georges; Le Caron, Joseph; missionaries
regency, 19, 21, 68, 74, 236; as moment of negotiation, 62, 64, 72, 211
rent-seeking, 44, 254n71
Ribertière, Pierre, 31, 54–5, 57
Richebourg, Quentin de, 287n132
Richelieu, 145, 158, 165, 184, 186, 187, 189, 197, 220, 261n59, 278n16, 283n76, 285n96; approach to the *grande maîtrise*, 165, 167, 175–6, 193, 242; as company associate, 175, 208, 210; and composition of companies, 190–2, 194, 208, 211, 232, 284nn88–9, 292n48; and conflict with Huguenots, 125, 172; and consolidation of maritime authority, 16, 159, 160, 166, 170, 173, 177–82, 196, 237, 243, 253n59, 282n70; death of, 211–13, 222, 239; as de facto viceroy, 180–1, 200, 202, 220, 284n83, 289n13, 290n22; and governance of New France, 202–4, 297n117; as Henri II de Montmorency's rival, 169, 171, 180, 283n80; and international experimentations with the company form, 160, 167–8, 182–3; relationship with the Compagnie de la Nouvelle-France, 161, 180–2, 196,

199, 211, 220, 232; and revitalization of French maritime commerce and navigation, 162, 166, 280n35
Richelieu River, 213
Robineau de Bécancour, Pierre, 201, 209, 210, 289n17
Rohan, Benjamin de, Duc de Soubise, 169
Rohan, Henri II, Duc de, 138
Roissey, Urbain de, 193
Rome, 138, 189
Roper, L.H., 9
Roquemont de Brison, Claude, 158, 160, 284n88
Rossignol, Jean, 42, 43
Rouen, 16, 55, 61, 112, 176; competition with other French ports in fur trade, 83, 90; participation of, in privileged companies in New France, 24, 30–2, 67, 75, 83; protection of interests and privileges of, 36, 83; Protestantism of merchants of, 136–7; relative importance of, in New France enterprise, 30, 251n23, 281n52. *See also* Admiralty of Rouen; Compagnie de Rouen et Saint-Malo, Parlement of Rouen
Royal African Company, 236
royal council, 15, 20, 112, 222, 238; arbitration of disputes in New France, 47, 57, 58, 74, 75, 80–2, 85–6, 89, 102, 112–13, 140, 214, 234, 235, 255n84, 259n39, 267n76; arbitration of disputes in the West Indies, 230–1; and enforcement of trading privileges, 38, 42–3, 50, 88; regulation of corporations in New France, 211, 221; support of colonization, 51, 79
Rozée, Jean, 195, 208, 209, 213, 217, 292n48
Sagard, Gabriel, 14
Saint-Christophe, 193, 230–3
Sainte-Croix, 65, 79, 203, 204, 228
Saint-Étienne de La Tour, Charles de, 298n132; as an associate of the Compagnie de la Nouvelle-France, 202, 290n22; comparison to Philippe de Longvilliers de Poincy, 231; conflict with Charles Menou d'Aulnay, 225–9, 297n117; evolving relations with king/queen regent, 228, 231–2, 234; as lieutenant general of Acadia, 202–4, 208, 224, 225, 234, 240; as seigneur in Acadia, 202–4, 290n25
Saint-Étienne de La Tour, Claude de, 203, 225, 229, 298n132
Saint-Jean-de-Luz, 41, 52; participation of, in Compagnie de Mons, 30–2, 252n36; request for confirmation of privileges to New France, 50, 241, 256n98
Saint John River, 203, 204; and feud between Charles Saint-Étienne de La Tour and Charles Menou d'Aulnay, 225, 226, 229; trade dispute between Rochelais traders and the Compagnie de Rouen et Saint-Malo in, 87–8
Saint Lawrence River, 3, 4, 11, 56, 68, 128, 201, 227, 243; as Catholic space, 156, 157; competition over, 48, 84, 113, 118; English claims to, 138–9, 228; exploration of, 69, 78; illegal trading in, 42, 85, 87, 88; privileged trading zone of, 53, 58, 67, 97, 98, 102, 110, 156
Saint Lawrence Valley, 11, 127, 148, 154, 194, 204, 215, 218; governance of, compared to Acadia or other regions, 202, 206, 232, 233; grants of privileges, land, and authority

in, 21, 96, 205–6, 209, 213, 214, 235, 243; role of religion in colonization of, 20
Saint-Malo, 16, 52, 55, 112, 137, 158; Catholicism of, 29, 51, 137; establishment of Admiralty at, 255n85; participation of, in privileged companies in New France, 29–32, 67, 267n60; protection of interests and privileges of, 36, 69, 71, 83, 178; relative importance of, in New France enterprise, 30, 251n23. *See also* communauté d'habitants of Saint-Malo; Compagnie de Rouen et Saint-Malo
Saintonge, 94, 128, 130
Saint-Sauveur, 79
Sales, François de, 126
Sarcel, Jehan, 31, 57
sea: and state/empire formation, 7, 168, 239; strategic importance of, 6–7, 236
sedentarization. *See* francization
Séguier, Pierre, 192, 228, 232
seigneuries, and colonization of New France, 212, 221; dues, 203, 215, 217, 219, 234, 293n63; and exercise of justice, 199, 220, 234; and fragmented Admiralty authority in France, 94, 171, 176; granting of, 160, 191, 194, 198, 201–3, 206–8, 211, 213, 215, 220, 236, 243, 244; held by lay congregations, 126
Sere, Luc, 31, 57
Sharman, J.C., 10, 199
Sillery, 150, 274n103
Six-Corps des marchands de Paris, 40, 48
société anonyme, 266n53
société de capitaux, 105, 162, 252n34, 266nn53–4
société en commandite, 105, 108, 193, 242, 266n51
société générale, 32, 105, 252n34
Société de Notre-Dame de Montréal, 154, 190, 201, 222; relations of, with other corporations in New France, 220, 221; relations of, with queen regent, 223, 232; terms of seigneurial concession granted to, 220–1, 299n149
société de personnes, 105
Soissons, Charles de Bourbon, Comte de, 64, 65, 258n11
Somers Island Company, 217, 218, 290n32
sovereignty, 3, 12, 16, 18, 21, 200; companies as a vehicle for, 10, 198, 199, 242; construction of, 11, 20, 62, 93, 115, 117, 118, 121, 200, 241; delegation of, 104, 199, 242; and evangelization, 154; extension of, through Indigenous spaces and bodies, 11, 120, 145, 153, 244; and law, 5, 9, 241; maritime, 91, 169; overseas and state formation, 4, 11, 96; and subjects' actions, 121, 139, 228; target of, 20, 157; threat to, 20, 79, 123, 141, 228; versus suzerainty, 289n8. *See also* authority; imperial power or authority; jurisdiction
spaces of power, 97, 112, 119; concept of, 93
Spanish, 118, 164; competition with French in colonization and commerce, 23, 48–50, 94, 169, 237; French diplomatic relations with, 125, 126, 189, 220, 280n40; imperial aspirations, as compared to

French, 12; maritime commercial and naval power of, 162, 163, 166, 169, 175; overseas claims of, 23, 91; and war with Dutch Republic, 92, 93, 138, 168–9, 172, 263n4
Spanish Empire, 12, 240, 243
spiritual geopolitics, 128, 157, 229
state, 8, 18, 63, 148; involvement overseas, 11, 14, 16, 243; relationship to chartered companies, 9–10, 13, 104, 199; and the sea, 7, 91
state formation, 12; characteristics of, 7, 243; and empire formation, 4, 5, 7, 11, 14, 16, 18, 19, 238–9, 242; historiography of, 7–8; role of companies in, 13, 160, 242; role of New France in, 122, 239; and the sea, 6–7, 239; subjects' role in, 8, 62
States General (Dutch), 46, 199; and chartered companies, 104
Stern, Philip, 9–10
subjecthood: criteria for, in France, 141–2; Indigenous, 146, 148; redefinition of, in New France, 139, 141, 144, 145, 147, 153, 157
subsidiaries, 215, 219, 226, 243; characteristics of, 204–6, 290n31; experimentations with, 209, 211; structure of, 210
Sully, Maximilien de Béthune, Duc de, 49, 145
Sulpicians, 191
suzerainty: versus sovereignty, 289n8

Tadoussac, 53, 84, 115, 116, 118, 119, 134
Talon, Jean, 151
Tessouat, 120
Thémines, Pons de Lauzière, Marquis de, 73–5, 77, 84, 283n73
Thirty Years' War, 229, 286n116
Thoisy, Patrocles de, 230–1
Tomlins, Christopher, 9
traders, 68, 158, 169, 177, 191; mobilization of metropolitan corporations, 63, 69; role in lawsuits, 14–15; threat posed by, to evangelizing mission, 135, 137, 139, 144–5, 155
Treaty of Montpellier, 138
Trois-Rivières, 118, 128, 201, 213, 222, 234, 299n149
Tuffet, Jean, 207

United Provinces. *See* Dutch
universal companies, 186–9, 194, 286n112. *See also* Compagnie de Morbihan; Compagnie de la Nacelle de Saint-Pierre fleurdelisée
universal monarchy, 11
Ursulines, 191, 213, 274n103

Van Ruymbeke, Bertrand, 9
Vendôme, César, Duc de, 175, 178, 283n73
Ventadour, Henri de Lévis, Duc de, 155, 180, 191, 200, 213, 220, 284n83; approach to viceroyalty, 154, 156, 283n80; and Catholic Reformation, 153–4, 190, 220, 276n120
Vermeullen, Louis, 137
viceroys, 186, 200, 201, 219, 226, 227, 242; conflict among competing, 73–4, 77, 259n31; legal powers of, 14; venality of position, 44, 254n74, 264n20
Ville-Marie, 154, 190. *See also* Montreal
Villegaignon, Nicholas Durand de, 94
Villemenon, Sieur de, 74, 96, 100, 109, 140, 176

Virginia, 227; comparison with New France, 13
Virginia Company, 199, 205, 210–11, 290n32
Voyages, 131, 132, 261n59

Wars of Religion, 27, 29–30, 38, 44, 49, 51, 61, 94, 124, 126, 130, 137, 141, 163, 251n19
Wendake, 120
Wendats, 77, 151, 153; as objects of evangelization, 129, 131, 144, 270n27; regulation of access to homelands and resources of, 119–20, 243–4; as a sovereign nation, 146
West India Company (Danish), 236
West India Company (Dutch), 104, 138, 172, 187, 199, 236, 289n20
West India Company (English), 279n21
West Indies, French, 18, 185, 186, 193, 229, 233; comparison with New France, 229, 237–8
Wolastoqiyik, 131